RICHARD S. LAZARUS

University of California, Berkeley

ALAN MONAT

California State University, Hayward

Personality

3rd edition

PRENTICE-HALL, INC., Englewood Cliffs, New Jersey 07632

BF
689
L376
1979

Library of Congress Cataloging in Publication Data

Lazarus, Richard S
   Personality.

   (Prentice-Hall foundations of modern psychology series)
   Bibliography: p.
   Includes index.
   1. Personality. I.   Monat, Alan,   joint author.
   II.   Title. [DNLM: 1. Personality. BF698 L431pa]
   BF698.L376 1979   155.2   78-27480
   ISBN 0-13-657916-7
   ISBN 0-13-657908-6 pbk.

Foundations of Modern Psychology Series

Richard S. Lazarus, Editor

Printed in the United States of America

10   9   8   7   6   5   4   3   2   1

Editorial/production supervision by
Cathie Mick Mahar
Interior design and cover design by
Virginia M. Soulé
Manufacturing buyer:
Phil Galea

Prentice-Hall International, Inc., London
Prentice-Hall of Australia Pty. Limited, Sydney
Prentice-Hall of Canada, Ltd., Toronto
Prentice-Hall of India Private Limited, New Delhi
Prentice-Hall of Japan, Inc., Tokyo
Prentice-Hall of Southeast Asia Pte. Ltd., Singapore
Whitehall Books Limited, Wellington, New Zealand

To Bunny, Dave, Mary and Jessica, Nancy and Rick, Murline, Harold and Tillie, Ron and Helene, and the rest of our families.

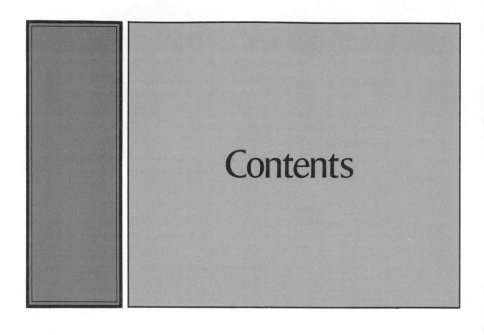

Contents

Foreword

The Foundations of Modern Psychology Series was the first and most successful in what became a trend in psychology toward groups of short texts dealing with various basic subjects, each written by an active authority. It was conceived with the idea of providing greater flexibility for instructors teaching general courses than was ordinarily available in the large, encyclopedic textbooks, and greater depth of presentation for individual topics not typically given much space in introductory textbooks.

The earliest volumes appeared in 1963, the latest in 1979 with the continuing expansion of the series into new areas of psychology. They are in widespread use as supplementary texts, or as the text, in various undergraduate courses in psychology, education, public health, sociology, and social work; and clusters of volumes have served as textbooks for undergraduate courses in general psychology. Groups of volumes have been translated into many languages including Danish, Dutch, Finnish, French, German, Hebrew, Italian, Japanese, Malaysian, Norwegian, Polish, Portuguese, Spanish, and Swedish.

With wide variation in publication date and type of content, some of the volumes have needed revision, while others have not. We have left this decision to the individual author. Some have remained unchanged, some have been modestly changed and updated, and still others completely rewritten. We have also opted for variation in length and style to reflect the different ways in which they have been used as texts.

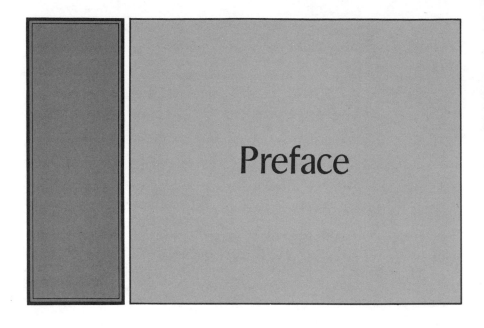

Preface

Significant changes in the focus of interest in personality since 1971, when the last edition of *Personality* was published, have helped shape the organization and content of this edition and, moreover, have mandated a genuine attempt to provide the reader with an integrated picture of this ever-expanding field. As before, the book seeks to provide an introduction and overview, yet in a modest number of pages so that it could be used in an academic quarter, or as a supplement.

We have retained the earlier organization of the "four D's" of personality (description, dynamics, development, and determinants) as it allows an orderly presentation of the major issues which continue to interest and challenge personologists. The book remains theory and issue centered. We have changed the order of things, however, so that biological and social determinants, which are somewhat independent of and yet basic to more central features of the major personality theories or orientations, come before description, dynamics, and development. And because in the last edition treatment of theories was segmented within the major rubrics of the four D's, we felt that the reader also needed to have selected theories summarized at some point, all in one place, and illustrated as concretely as possible. So, in this edition we have added a chapter which pulls together an exemplar of each of three major theoretical approaches to personality, namely, the psychodynamic, humanistic-existential, and behavioral approaches. In addition, the exemplary theories are compared in the way they might handle a particular clinical case. Finally, current topics underemphasized or not represented in the earlier editions, for example, the debate about situational versus person variables as causes of human behavior and the impact of this debate on personality assessment, the extension of developmental interests to the entire life course including adulthood, aging and death, and the women's movement with its implications for sex roles and personality, gain considerable attention in this edition.

In short, friends of earlier editions of *Personality* will find the third edition familiar and comparable in structure. They will, however, also encounter significant additions and changes that we believe add to the book's utility as an undergraduate personality text.

We want to thank our many colleagues and friends who provided refreshing and valuable comments throughout this revision. We acknowledge the following reviewers of *Personality, third edition:* Nicholas S. DiCaprio, John Carroll University; William T. Moss, Appalachian State University; Lawrence Pervin, Rutgers University; Stephen Reisman, University of Massachusetts. Several members of the Prentice-Hall staff, including John Isley (Psychology Editor) and Cathie Mahar (Production Editor), were most helpful and indispensable to the final product.

Richard S. Lazarus

Alan Monat

The Nature
of Personality

What is personality? Why, indeed, should there be any question? After all, we know what personality is—or do we? Ask the *layperson* to define the term, and we are likely to hear that personality is the impression one makes on others or the characteristics (like charm or attractiveness) which allow us to "win friends" or "be successful." This view of personality, emphasizing our public sides, is consistent with meanings often attributed to the Latin word *persona* (mask), from which "personality" was derived. In ancient times, the actors wore masks to denote their roles and consequently, personality came to refer to our public images, our exterior masks. Although *psychologists* certainly differ among themselves as to the nature of personality—these differences being the subject of this book—most view personality not as the impression or mask we present to others, but rather as what lies beneath the mask. In other words, personologists (psychologists who study personality) think of personality as the *underlying, relatively stable, psychological structures and processes that organize human experience and shape a person's actions and reactions to the environment.*

Although the interests of personologists and those studying other aspects of psychology often overlap, there are at least three important differences: 1. the personologist, more than other psychologists, is interested in variations rather than in commonalities among people; 2. the personologist is more likely to view the person as an integrated "whole" than as a series of part-functions; and 3. the

1

personologist gives more attention to stable attributes inside the person (like traits or dispositions) than to external stimuli as determinants of immediate behavior.

The first difference (an interest in variations) is more a matter of emphasis than exclusion, for the personologist is certainly interested also in those aspects or rules of personality that apply to all people. For example, for all persons there is an increase in the complexity of psychological processes from birth to maturity, and these developmental changes are of great interest to those studying personality. The psychology of personality is distinguished from other psychological disciplines by its greater concern with individual differences. For example, rather than emphasizing the fact that two people have similar fundamentalist religious views, the personologist more likely is concerned with understanding why the first person embarks upon a campaign of bigotry and hatred and the other upon a course of compassion and sympathy for the ills and frailties of human nature.

Second, by viewing the person as an integrated whole, the personologist tries to understand the distinctive manner in which the individual's part-functions (the things we do psychologically such as perceiving, learning, thinking, and feeling) are organized and combined to produce a "personality," and to determine the person's adjustments to internal and external stimuli. Although the typical psychology text usually treats each of our part-functions in a separate chapter or subchapter, reflecting an elementalistic approach common to psychology, it is a major task of personologists to integrate these various parts and to understand the person as a functioning unit or whole.

Third, no one challenges the idea that we react to stimuli in the environment. Whether physical (e.g., an oncoming speeding car) or social (e.g., our friends' expectations), these events represent powerful determinants of our thoughts, feelings, and actions. However, reference to environmental influences is usually insufficient to explain fully our behavior. Even newborn children show major variations in reaction before there has been much opportunity for different kinds of experience. In other words, each of us comes into the world with different attributes that influence our actions and reactions, and with experience we develop unique psychological foundations (such as intelligence, beliefs, motivations, etc.) which lead us to react differently from others in the same situations. Along with the environmental stimuli to which we are exposed, we must recognize another class of behavioral determinants, one which resides within us. The personologist attempts to uncover and study the nature of these internal attributes so that, with a knowledge of the external stimuli, we can increase our ability to understand and predict a particular individual's behavior.

THE STRUCTURES AND PROCESSES OF PERSONALITY

Our definition of personality introduced two important concepts which deserve further elaboration, namely, the concepts of structure and process. Generally, *structures* refer to the more or less stable arrangement or patterning of parts in a system, whereas *processes* are the functions carried out by the parts, that is, what they do and how they interact and change. Before applying these concepts to personality, let us see their application in a familiar, everyday context.

The mechanically minded reader might think of an internal combustion engine as an example of structures and processes and their interplay. The automobile engine has many parts, all connected into a system in particular ways that determine how energy is transformed from its latent form as gasoline to the synchronous turning of the wheels. The pistons, valves, driveshaft, differential, and thousands of other elements or parts comprise the structures; the explosion of the gas and air mixture, the intake and expulsion of gases, and the movement of the pistons and wheels, are all processes. Note that the movement of the pistons depends on the shape and alignment of the cylinders, and in turn, the pistons and cylinder walls eventually change their structure (wear out) as a function of that movement. Structures and processes are in continual interplay, influencing each other and sometimes even changing their function in the course of the system's operation.

Any system can be described in terms of structures and processes. We speak of geological structures (e.g., hills, river beds, foliage) and geological processes (e.g., flow of water, wind, upheavals of the earth's surface); social structures (e.g., cultural institutions) and social processes (e.g., the interaction among individuals in a group or between groups); or biological structures (e.g., tissue or organ systems) and biological processes (e.g., metabolism or cell death and replacement). Psychological systems, too, may be described in terms of structures and processes; we can speak of personality structures, as when a person is said to be intelligent or have a strong ego, and personality processes, as when a person is said to be solving a problem or engaging in self-deception.

A major difficulty with some structures and processes in science, however, is that they are not directly observable and therefore, must be constructed theoretically. For example, the oxidation of foods or metals is unlike the geological processes that we can observe fairly routinely. We cannot actually see this process take place, yet we know about it from observing the regular changes that occur when these substances are exposed to oxygen under given heat conditions.

Psychological structures and processes cannot be observed directly either, though we can learn about them by inference from their causal conditions and effects. Mental abilities are but one example of psychological structures which are not observable, although their effects are subject to inspection. Other things being equal, the person who has good mental ability will solve problems "better" or display more information than someone with rather poor ability. We cannot observe this ability directly but must infer it from its effects as assessed by tests of information and problem solving. Similarly, motives, like achievement or the desire to be liked by others, cannot be observed directly but may be inferred from observing the person in social contexts that usually bring about motive-related behaviors. The reasoning is very much like that used to speak of hunger and thirst. What are hunger and thirst? We cannot see them, yet we "know" they exist. This knowledge is based in part on our experience with the arousing conditions for these "drives" and their typical effects on behavior. For example, deprive someone of food for fifteen hours and you would not be surprised to find that person eating "like a glutton" once a plate of appetizing food made its presence.

Applied to personality the same argument holds. We do not see a personality as we see an action or a physical object. Personality refers to a theoretical inference which is made by observing psychologically relevant reactions and then conceiving logically what might be the underlying system of structures and processes (sometimes in personality called characteristics and dynamics) which would explain the behaviors. But since the personality is a complex system comprising many structures (e.g., traits and the self-concept) and processes (e.g., conflicts and defenses), an extensive set of inferences is needed, rather than a single one for hunger, thirst, or ability. Our inferences must deal with those properties of the person that are stable or consistent over time and from situation to situation, remembering too that a large percentage of our actions, thoughts, and feelings also are shaped by the context as well as by personality.

Inferring Personality

If, as we have suggested, psychological structures and processes must be inferred, what observable events do personologists use in their attempts to uncover personality? There are three categories of behavior from which inferences about personality are made: movements or actions, verbal reports, and physiological changes which accompany psychological activity, as in emotion. For reasons to be made clear later, personologists prefer to base their inferences about personality on behaviors from more than one of these categories, but because of practical limitations such as time and money, they often are forced to rely on only one category for any particular study.

ACTIONS. Actions, of course, refer to what people or infrahuman animals do. Actions have several qualities, two of which might be called "goal-oriented" and "style." The former quality, also known as the "instrumental" aspect of the action, refers to the person's intended result or goal. The action is instrumental in achieving the result. The latter quality, style, reflects mainly the characteristic manner in which the act is carried out and may have little or perhaps even nothing to do with the intended results of the action. Remember, though, that the same act can and usually does have both goal-oriented and stylistic aspects. Sometimes one or the other is more evident and hence is emphasized by the observer making inferences about its meaning for the person. Let us elaborate upon these two aspects of actions and see what they may offer for understanding personality.

The goal-oriented aspect of actions often communicates something about a person's motives, intentions, and interests even without the observer asking the person about these things. For example, consider two students: One studies most of the time and the other indulges mainly in social activities. Their choices among behavioral alternatives can lead us to infer that the first student is motivated or directed principally toward academic achievement and that the second has strong needs for affiliation (the wish to be liked and accepted by others).

The thoughtful reader might see some difficulties with the above inferences from the goal-directed aspect of an action. They are much too simple. For example, the first student might really prefer to associate with others but might be very shy and socially awkward. The possibility of affiliation with others is minimized and so this student studies constantly. Correspondingly, the second student might prefer academic achievement to socializing but feels incapable

5

and therefore avoids studying. Thus we see that motivation can be expressed directly in a person's actions, or also—whether because of internal conflict or external constraints—in the blocking of such behavioral expression and the consequent selection of substitute activities which may conceal the fundamental motive or goal. These complicated instances are especially interesting to the personologist and provide a great challenge to understanding the person.

If the substitute-activity argument is correct, then we can never really be very confident about the validity of inferences derived from a single source of information, such as the goal-oriented aspect of action. Although this latter source may provide very important information about motivation, inferences from it frequently will be incomplete and therefore should be supplemented by other behavioral evidence, such as the stylistic aspect of the action or verbal reports from the person. This additional information may force us to revise our original, sometimes over-simple inference, and to introduce complicating concepts such as inhibitions or defense mechanisms.

Turning now to the *stylistic* aspect of an action, every intentional act can be performed in a variety of ways without altering its efficiency in achieving the intended goal. For example, we can walk with a rapid or slow pace, make gestures which are expansive or inhibited, take up extensive or little space on a page, write with weak or strong pressure, use simple or elaborate sentence structure, and so on. This stylistic variation can be consistent in a given individual, although specific acts will vary in their goals and the stimulus demands. These styles often are easily recognized as marking a particular person, a fact capitalized on by leading impressionists. The person being imitated is recognized instantly from the manner of speech, as well as from certain characteristic gestures, body movements, and facial expressions (so-called "nonverbal" cues).

The importance of these stylistic qualities to personality, of course, lies not in the fact that mimics can entertain us with them, or that they sometimes can be used by police detectives in tracking down a thief by his or her *modus operandi* (style of working) from one crime to another. Much more significant is that styles may communicate certain things about the person over and above that which is learned from goal-oriented action. For example, in certain circumstances at least, facial expressions may communicate an emotional state that the individual does not wish to make public. Other styles of action, such as expansiveness or constrictedness in drawing (which we will see shortly), writing, or gesturing, may communicate unrecognized attitudes toward oneself and others. In this usage, styles are treated as expressive of some inner motivational state.

There are two issues underlying the use of stylistic aspects of action in making inferences about personality. One is whether these styles are consistent in the same individual in different situations. Years ago, Allport and Vernon (1933) did some classic research on this issue, discovering some consistency in characteristics such as tempo and expansiveness, characteristics which they referred to as "expressive movements." The consistency was greater when the two acts were performed close together in time or in comparatively similar situations, but in any case a small degree of consistency in these styles was demonstrated. Allport and Vernon were able to demonstrate then that stylistic factors may be fairly stable characteristics of people and potentially useful sources of information about the person.

The second issue is more complicated. It is whether styles of action are really *expressive* of personality characteristics or inner psychological states (and if so, which ones), or mainly reflective of the goals or intended results of an action (i.e., are *instrumental* as opposed to expressive). If facial expressions, for example, reveal emotions (disgust or anger) which the individual may not wish to communicate, this is an expressive function. Ekman and Friesen (1967) have referred to this as the "leakage" of information. It is likely that facial and bodily movements do both, that is, reveal emotional states whose communication was not intended and also serve as instrumental acts, revealing in part what the person wishes to communicate.

A good example of research which adopts an expressive interpretation of a style of action is a study by Wallach, Green, Lipsitt, and Minehart (1962). These researchers assumed that among individuals who were socially outgoing in behavior, some really preferred social isolation, while others genuinely desired social interaction. On the other hand, among those who were socially withdrawn, some actually wished for social contact, and others genuinely desired minimum social interaction. (Some readers might note the influence here of Jung's beliefs about introversion and extraversion, which we will discuss in chapter 4.) In the cases of contradictory "overt" and "covert" tendencies, the individual's social motivation certainly could not be accurately inferred from overt social action alone. Some other tendency would have to be revealed in order to make an accurate inference about motivation.

To assess social motivation more accurately, Wallach et al. added a stylistic variable that might express the underlying disposition. This was a measure of graphic constriction as opposed to graphic expansiveness, which presumably tapped the subject's "covert" wishes about establishing social ties. They requested drawings from the subjects and then noted the extent to which the drawings were either expansive (e.g., using up most of the page) or constrictive (e.g., using up very little space). They assumed that constricted drawings would be made by those who, regardless of actual extensive social interaction, preferred social withdrawal and that expansive drawings would be made by those who desired extensive social contact, even though the usual behavioral evidence of this desire may have been absent.

In addition, by using a questionnaire, Wallach et al. measured defensiveness, the tendency to conceal one's wishes, especially conflicting ones. The questionnaire assessed the willingness or unwillingness of the subjects to admit to occasional disagreeable but common feelings and experiences. For example, a subject who denied "occasionally feeling unhappy or scared" might be considered defensive (1962, p. 5).

Wallach et al. found an interesting relationship between the degree of match between actual social activity and drawings and their questionnaire measuring defensiveness. Specifically, defensive subjects who were "overtly" active socially tended to show highly constricted drawings, implying to the authors that these subjects had a "covert" wish to be socially withdrawn. Similarly, defensive subjects who were "overtly" withdrawn socially made highly expansive drawings. This sort of contradictory pattern was not found, however, in the case of the nondefensive subjects. Examples of each of the patterns observed by Wallach et al. may be found in Figure 1.

The study by Wallach et al., though not without certain questionable methods and assumptions, demonstrates the theoretical treatment of styles of action as forms of expression, that is, as communicators of personality dispositions. The empirical case for the measurement of covert social tendencies in this study depends on the uncertain assumption that graphic constriction indeed is related to the wish to withdraw and graphic expansiveness to the wish to have social ties. These wishes are assumed, with some logical consistency, to be "covert" when they occur in a person who has been shown to be defensive, that is, unwilling to admit to disagreeable traits. But the existence of the covert impulse itself has not been demonstrated directly—although the assumption relating graphic styles to covert impulses allows the authors ingeniously to interpret certain contradictory tendencies in a logically consistent way. Despite these limitations, the study does suggest that action styles often express psychological structures and processes and thus are significant to the person's psychological functioning.

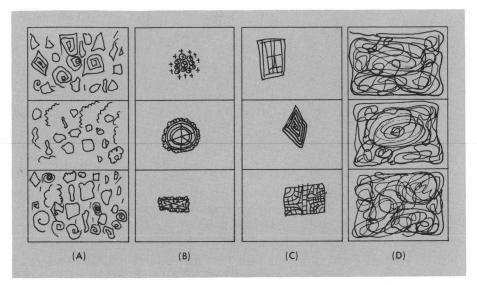

FIGURE 1. Illustrative drawings by a (A) nondefensive subject with extensive social ties; (B) defensive subject with extensive social ties; (C) nondefensive subject who is socially isolated; and (D) defensive subject who is socially isolated. (First to third drawings are arranged from top to bottom, respectively.) *(From Wallach, Green, Lipsitt, and Minehart 1962, pp. 15-17). Copyright 1962 by the American Psychological Association. Reprinted by permission.)*

Some styles of action also have instrumental value, that is, besides their expressive value, action styles often are used to achieve an intended result. For example, Rosenfeld (1966) instructed female students to seek the other person's approval in a social interchange and compared their gestures with those of female students instructed to avoid approval. The approval-seekers were observed to use more smiling and gesticulation (noticeable movements of the arm, hand, or finger) than the approval-avoiders did. This finding suggests that action styles may sometimes have goal-oriented or instrumental significance and, hence, may be used to produce a particular result. Actors are skillful at simulating action styles in order to convince the audience that the character being portrayed is feeling a certain emotion or is a certain type of person. Whether the actor necessarily feels that emotion as a result of the "role playing" is not at all clear. One must conclude that styles of action are, indeed, a source of information about the personality but that the conditions under which they unintentionally "express" an inner state or are instrumental or goal-oriented are not well established.

Styles of action (and thinking) offer fascinating possibilities for the study of personality traits and are the subject of much research in the field. However, like the goal-oriented aspect of actions, their simplistic use without confirming evidence from other sources calls into question the validity and usefulness of the inferences drawn from them.

VERBAL REPORTS. Inferences about personality structures and processes also can be derived from verbally reported introspections. People can describe and label their inner experiences and report them to an observer. In contrast to other animals, humans, through verbalization, provide valuable clues to psychological events.

There are really two kinds of introspection. In one, a subject experiencing some event is watched and the observer, by a kind of psychological sharing of the experience, judges empathically what is happening to the subject. The success of this kind of inference process depends on similarities among people; to the extent that there are individual differences in reactions to comparable stimuli, it is vulnerable to error. One person may experience primarily grief in the same situation in which another experiences gratification and a third, relative indifference. For this reason, empathic introspection is not very confidently accepted as a source of inference about personality among scientifically oriented psychologists. Yet it commonly is employed informally in our social living and by writers, and it does have considerable value as a source of hypotheses which might be tested in other ways.

The second, more usual kind of introspection, is employed widely in personality research. It uses the subject's own analysis of his or her reactions rather than an analysis by an observer. Subjects may report what they are thinking, feeling, and wishing, and what has characterized their attitudes in other situations in the past and present. Psychotherapy is a good example of this sort of data collection in which the therapist learns about the person mainly from what he or she reports in the therapy sessions. Because the therapist cannot hover over and constantly observe the patient outside the therapy context, the patient's verbalized introspections are essential to the helping process.

Special problems arise in using verbal reports to make inferences about personality structures and processes. The main one is that words can be used to disguise as well as to communicate openly. People may express what they wish other people to believe rather than what is actually true. Furthermore, what is said may arise in large measure from ignorance about oneself and one's reactions, without any intent to disguise. Thus, if we take introspection at face value, it is easy to interpret the person quite inaccurately. As was noted earlier, precisely the same problem exists in using styles of action as the basis of inference about personality. Although facial expressions, gestures, and other movements are sometimes expressive of inner processes, they also may be deliberately manipulated to produce intended effects. This problem of the accuracy of the source has been emphasized much more with self-report than with any other source of information about personality. At the same time, introspection is one of the richest sources of data in personality research.

Two solutions have been proposed for dealing with the problem of falsification in verbal report. One, advocated by writers such as Carl Rogers (1942; Rogers and Roethlisberger, 1952) and Sidney Jourard (1968), reduces the person's motivation to disguise by creating an atmosphere of permissiveness and acceptance and even mutual self-disclosure by experimenter and subject. If the main reason for falsification is the desire to create a favorable impression or to present information in a manner congruent with one's self-evaluation, then a permissive and nonevaluative attitude by the investigator should go a long way toward minimizing the distortion in the subject's self-reports. Permissiveness removes some of the motivation to distort the truth because the person is accepted no matter what is said. This approach is particularly appropriate to a therapeutic context in which the therapist-investigator, over a considerable period of time, can adequately assure the person that it is perfectly safe to speak openly and candidly. The process of self-revelation is the core of "insight therapy." The aim is to discover hidden aspects of the self which presumably lie at the root of the patient's psychological troubles (cf. chapter 7).

The difficulty with this solution is twofold: first, personality investigation cannot always adopt the time-consuming processes familiar to psychotherapy, nor is such investigation limited to a context in which, as in therapy, the person necessarily accepts an arrangement designed to reveal or disclose the truth beneath the mask. Second, in all probability, only some of the inaccuracy of verbal report stems from willful or even unconscious deception. Some of it may be based on defects in the language used to communicate inner life or on a lack of self-comprehension or insight. Thus, the above solution of acceptance and permissiveness (or mutual self-disclosure) is a partial one at best.

The second solution for dealing with the problem of falsification is to treat what the person says as behavior to be observed rather than as a fact of inner life. At the turn of the century, introspection was employed by the structuralist school of psychology under Titchener, a student of Wundt (see Boring, 1950), as the basic method of investigation of psychological experience. Titchener used trained introspectionists in attempting to study the structure of psychological experience, thus treating the person being studied as a collaborator-observer-scientist. In psychology today, the person being studied is treated differently, even when providing introspective self-reports. What the person says is regarded and observed as behavior to be understood rather than as necessarily factual. In this way, the investigator can disregard some of the things that are reported and accept others in making inferences about personality. Even in therapy, the observer can continually check the inferences derived from self-report against other behavioral or physiological evidence. As the therapist listens to what is said, careful observance is made of such motor acts as gestures, facial expressions, and physiological evidence of distress such as that communicated by facial pallor, flushing, and tremulousness. For example, if a person reporting no distress gives other behavioral evidence of disturbance, the contents of the verbal report can be qualified by this evidence. The rules for making these decisions remain fragmentary, and the problem of what to regard as a valid inference is still fundamental to personality research.

An interesting research example concerned with discrepancies between verbal reports and other behavioral or physiological signs was reported by Weinstein, Averill, Opton, and Lazarus (1968). They reviewed six experiments, all performed in their laboratory, in which two types of response measures of stress reaction were obtained while subjects were watching a disturbing movie. In each experiment, subjects were asked to report on the amount of distress they were experiencing, and physiological measures known to be affected in emotional states also were recorded. Often these two response measures disagreed, that is, some subjects reported being much more distressed than appeared from the physiological measure; other subjects reported being much less distressed than was evident from the physiological measure. Data from personality questionnaires like those employed by Wallach et al. (1962), previously described, to measure defensiveness showed the subjects to vary in the tendency to deny unfavorable and unpleasant things about themselves; some showed this tendency very strongly, others very little or not at all. It was found that those who had the tendency to deny (i.e., to be defensive) also showed comparatively higher physiological indicators of stress reactions than they had reported in the experiment.

In short, by identifying one of the correlates of inaccurate self-reports, in this case the tendency to deny distressing things about oneself, Weinstein et al. were able to improve somewhat the accuracy of the inference about inner states from self-reports. To do this it was necessary to assume that the physiological reaction was a sound indicator of emotional distress, an assumption which itself is open to some argument. In any case, if most or all of the sources of inaccuracy in self-reports could be discovered and assessed, this information, theoretically speaking, could be used to increase greatly the validity of such reports as a basis of inference about personality structures and processes.

PHYSIOLOGICAL MEASUREMENTS. As just suggested, physiological changes, particularly those associated with emotion, can be used as a source of information about internal events and hence, personality. The existence of physiological concomitants of emotion has been known for a long time and in fact, many of these reactions can be observed without technically advanced instrumentation—e.g., flushing and paling of the face, breaking out in perspiration, and trembling. Such reactions are the result of the autonomic nervous system and its influence over hormonal secretions which, in turn, affect visceral organs whose activity can be easily detected. Nowadays there are electronic instruments readily available that are capable of measuring fairly minute changes of this sort. An example of this measurement as used in experimental research in stress and emotion is shown in Figure 2.

This figure summarizes physiological activity (palmar sweating) of volunteer subjects who separately watched a film portraying three bloody accidents in a woodworking shop. While watching the film, a slight and undetectable current was passed between two electrodes attached to the subject. Because sweat contains an electrolyte (salt), the electrical conductivity of the subject's skin was easily measured by a psychogalvanometer which would indicate peaks when the person sweated (and thus "passed" current) and troughs when sweating did not occur (and resistance to current was present). Three different experimental treatments were provided. One group of subjects was told before the film started that the accidents were all staged very cleverly to look as though injuries and bleeding occurred, but that they really did not happen (a "denial" orientation). Another group was given a statement focusing, in a detached, intellectual fashion, on the social relationships among the various characters in the story (an "intellectualization" or detachment orientation). A third group was given only a very brief introductory statement that they were to watch some accidents (a "control" condition).

Two things may be noted in Figure 2. First, the high peaks of the skin conductance (representing lowered electrical resistance as a result of increased sweating) clearly occurred during the accident scenes, and the troughs (indicating lowered sweating and presum-

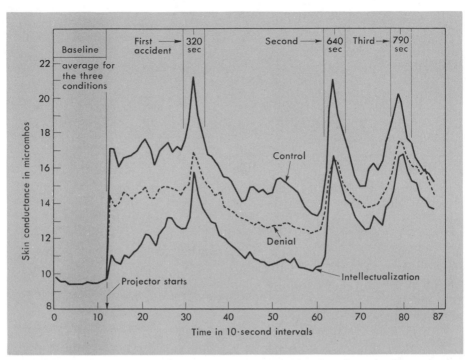

FIGURE 2. Effects of the experimental treatment (denial and intellectualization statements) on skin conductance measured while subjects watched a film showing stressful accidents. *(From Lazarus, Opton, Nomikos, and Rankin 1965, p. 628. Copyright 1965 by Duke University Press.)*

ably relaxation) appeared in benign or harmless periods between the emotional events. Second, both forms of orientation (denial and intellectualization) given to the subjects before watching the film lowered the level of skin conductance below that produced under the control condition. In effect, the emotional disturbance normally produced by the film was reduced by the "treatments." This study illustrates how stress or emotional reactions can be measured by recordings of certain physiological changes, and how these changes may be compared in different conditions.

One virtue of physiological measures is that they sometimes can be used as in the Weinstein et al. (1968) study, cited earlier, to check other response indicators of emotional processes, such as self-reports. The reader should not assume from this, however, that physiological measures or any other behavioral responses are necessarily more scientific or accurate than self-report. Physiological arousal also can be produced by conditions irrelevant to emotional states, such as temperature changes or physical movements and exer-

14

tion. Once again we must remind the reader that all response measures from which personality inferences are made, especially when used alone and without reference to other sources of information, are vulnerable to many kinds of error. The point is that inferences about personality structures and processes usually are sounder when based on multiple evidence. Each type of response evidence supplements the other in providing grist for an interpretation about the personality.

The Concept of "Depth" in Personality

Several times we have referred implicitly and explicitly to the concept of "depth" in personality, and it now should be clarified. The idea of depth has two meanings. Freudian theory, upon which we will elaborate later, uses the concept of depth to refer to forces or mechanisms inaccessible to the person, that is, unconscious. In an era (often called the Age of Reason) when humans were thought to make decisions on conscious, rational bases, Freud's idea that unconscious, irrational forces controlled most of our actions was indeed a very disturbing one. According to Freud's concept of defense mechanisms, for example, the person does not recognize certain features of his or her inner mental life. Unacceptable and hence threatening impulses and feelings are particularly salient examples. Freud regarded these as being "repressed" and unconscious, although presumably they continue actively to influence the person, guiding behavior in all major life contexts—see Table 7 in chapter 5.

In suggesting that unconscious forces dominated our life adjustments, Freud invented a colorful metaphor about the mind, likening it to an iceberg (see Figure 3). An iceberg reveals on the surface of the water only a small portion of its total mass, with the rest beneath the sea and ordinarily invisible. What a vivid way this is of dramatizing the idea that most of the mental life is figuratively deep below the surface and inaccessible! Thus, the first meaning of depth, the one emphasized by Freud and a few other theorists, is that *people are unconscious of the dominant aspects of their mental lives.*

The second meaning of depth, one we also have addressed frequently in this chapter, refers to the *inaccessibility* of personality structures and processes *to the observer,* who must conceive of personality by inference since it cannot be observed directly. This meaning of depth says simply that personality is a *theoretically based inference,* and it implies nothing about the person's awareness of his or her own mental life.

Although the former meaning of depth is more controversial

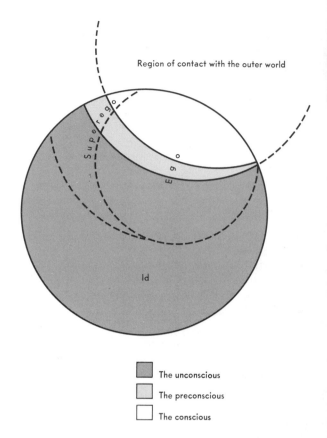

Region of contact with the outer world

Super-ego

Ego

Id

The unconscious

The preconscious

The conscious

FIGURE 3. Sketch suggesting the topographical relationship between levels of consciousness and the elements of personality structure, as elaborated from Freud. *(Adapted from Healy, Bronner, and Bowers 1930, p. 656, The Structure and Meaning of Psychoanalysis. Used with the permission of Alfred A. Knopf, Inc.)*

among psychologists than the latter, the "iceberg" analogy has continued to influence thought in personality and clinical psychology and in recent years in the lay world as well. One reason for the controversy among professionals is that foolproof methods for assessing "awareness" cannot be found, since they all depend on what the individual reports, and these reports are always in some measure suspect. Some writers argue that the concept of awareness should be expunged from psychology as a useless and untestable idea. But so pervasive and important is the concept that the reader cannot proceed effectively through the study of personality without confronting it repeatedly.

TWO STRATEGIES OF RESEARCH
ON PERSONALITY

Throughout the modern history of psychology, opinions on how to expose personality to study have differed and have taken the form of two styles or strategies: the *nomothetic* and *idiographic* approaches. Major distinctions characterizing these approaches are whether it is better to study personality: 1. in groups of persons or intensively in a few select individuals and; 2. by emphasizing one or at best a few properties of people or by trying to gain a sense of the "whole" person. Let us examine these distinctions a little more closely.

The nomothetic approach to personality says in effect that emphasis should be on a particular personality trait (or occasionally on several traits) studied in many persons so that we may make generalizations about how such traits determine the behavior of people. It is important, this approach says, to establish that some given trait or traits guide behavior in a particular way and that this influence, observed in a given sample of persons, is repeatable with other samples. The nomothetic search clearly is directed toward the establishment of general principles or norms (standards) of personality functioning.

On the other hand, the idiographic approach typically makes a detailed examination of a single individual in a variety of respects, situations, or times of life in order to capture the "essence" of the person. Generalizations about the particular person studied are the goal here, but extension of these principles to others is hazardous and usually not acceptable because of the unrepresentative nature of the "sample."

Examples of Nomothetic
and Idiographic Research

NOMOTHETIC RESEARCH. In nomothetic research, a certain trait, say aggressiveness, is varied by selecting subjects who differ with respect to it (or by using a correlational analysis to relate the variation in aggressiveness to other variables), thus producing two or more populations for study, one very aggressive and one lacking or lower in that quality (a middle group also may be used). It does not matter (for the purposes of that study) that the subjects within each group differ greatly from one another in other respects, if they at least share that one trait, i.e., aggressiveness.

17

A study by Hetherington and Wray (1964) illustrates a relatively complex type of nomothetic study using two personality variables and two situational contexts. Two personality traits were assessed by different questionnaires. One of these questionnaires required subjects to state their feelings and actions in certain types of situations which often elicit *aggression*. Some subjects reported strong feelings of aggression and others did not. In another questionnaire, the *desire for approval* or social acceptance was similarly measured. On the basis of the questionnaire data, the authors selected four types of subjects: one type was high in aggression and high in desire for social approval; a second was high in aggression but low in desire for social approval; a third was low in aggression but high in desire for social approval; and the fourth group was low in aggression and low in desire for social approval.

Next, each subject was given a series of photographed cartoons to evaluate on a scale from extremely funny to extremely unfunny. The cartoons expressed aggression. It was assumed that if they were thought to be funny, the subject accepted the aggressive implication comfortably, while if they were judged as unfunny, aggression was disapproved or perhaps a touchy subject. These ratings were made under two conditions: half the subjects were given an *alcoholic drink*, and the other half was tested *without having drunk anything alcoholic*. The purpose of this was to study the disinhibiting effects of alcohol on the acceptance and expression of aggression through the ratings of the humorousness of the aggressive cartoons.

The results of Hetherington's and Wray's study are complex but most interesting. Under nonalcoholic conditions, highly aggressive subjects who also had a high need for social approval were more disturbed by the cartoons and rated them as much less funny than did both subjects who were low in aggression and those who were high in aggression but low in desire for social approval. However, the alcohol resulted in the increase in ratings of funniness by the subjects who were high in aggression and had a strong desire for social approval. In effect, the alcohol disinhibited those with strong desires for social approval, thus allowing them to enjoy the aggressive humor which otherwise would have been disturbing. The subjects high in aggression but low in the desire for social approval showed no change between drinking and nondrinking conditions.

Hetherington and Wray suggested that subjects with low aggressive needs apparently do not have much impulse to express aggression either when drinking or not. However, those high in aggression and also high in desire for social approval have strong aggressive impulses, but they inhibit these because of the strong desire for social approval. It is not clear whether the effect of alcohol results from its tendency to reduce the fear of social censure for an aggressive impulse, or because social approval ceases to be as important under the influence of alcohol.

We need not dwell on the details or defects in the study by Hetherington and Wray to make clear the nature of the nomothetic strategy of personality research. The most striking nomothetic feature is the isolation and examination of two traits or dispositions of personality, in this case, aggressiveness and desire for social approval. The study sought to generalize about persons regarding the role of these personality traits in determining behavioral reactions. The emphasis was not placed on a single person observed in a variety of contexts, but on persons in general (as reflected in a particular sample) who happened to have high or low amounts of the traits in question. Although these two traits were isolated from all of the other possibly relevant qualities of personality, this study is an advance over the simplest version of nomothetic research in which the behavioral effects of only a single trait are examined, and in only one situation. For Hetherington and Wray, it was possible to study the interplay of both traits by examining how each influenced the other in determining aggressive behavior. In this way nomothetic research attempts to get a little closer to the ideal of studying the whole personality including, as it does, multitudes of traits, each of which presumably influences the behavioral outcome in given situational contexts.

IDIOGRAPHIC RESEARCH. Idiographic research, with its emphasis on intensive studies of individuals, tries to preserve the sense of wholeness and uniqueness of the personality system and its functioning in a variety of life conditions. The idiographic strategy is perhaps best illustrated by the case study. Here a single individual is examined from the point of view of past and present functioning in a variety of life contexts. There are numerous examples of case studies in the literature of psychology and other related disciplines, such as psychiatry and social work. There have been several books which attempt to teach abnormal psychology through outstanding literary examples (e.g., Gogol's *Diary of a Madman* and Nabokov's *Pnin*, see Stone and Stone, 1966).

Some idiographic case studies have had a considerable impact on the study of personality, particularly those published by Freud and Allport. Freud published six major case studies which continue to influence the thinking of clinical and personality psychologists. For example, in the Schreber case, Freud (1933c) studied an autobiographical account of a paranoid patient and set forth the principle that paranoia was based on unconscious homosexual urges which had been transformed into hate and then projected onto another person. Although this view has not been supported empirically, Freud's formulation of the role of projection in paranoia is still accepted by many clinicians (Kleinmuntz, 1974; Nathan and Harris, 1975).

In 1965, Gordon Allport published a set of 301 letters written over a period of more than eleven years by a woman ("Jenny") concerning her relationship with her son. Allport compiled the letters and from them constructed a portrait of Jenny's personality from the point of view of several different theoretical systems. The following excerpt, from Jenny's first letter to her correspondents, concerns rage over her son's actions (Allport, 1965, pp. 8–9).* Try to get a sense of this fascinating woman but do not come to any hasty judgments for there are still three hundred letters to be read!

It was in Brooklyn that he met the old maid with money who bought and married him. He never even mentioned money to me again. Never once offered to help me in any way.

I am a strongly intuitive person, am subject to impressions—beliefs—prejudices etc. not founded on any basis of reason.

It was my "feeling" for a long time that Ross was lying to me—when he said he could not come to see me because he was so very busy, I felt that he lied. When he spoke of his low salary I felt that he lied. Yet I was ashamed: I never tried to prove, or disprove, anything. I thought "the boy is all right—every word he says is probably true—it is I who am mean, suspicious, and hateful—forget it," and so the time went by.

The day he was married he said he could not keep his appointment with me to put up a shelf I needed because he had to stay at the store and help take inventory. I knew he lied that day, and was angry—I asked why should an efficiency man in a Dept. Store take inventory. He said it was mean of me to doubt him, and that all I had to do was telephone the 7th floor of the store and ask for him. He knew I would not do that. He ran his bluff—he just lied.

The last day I spent in New York before coming here [Chicago], last September, I went to Jersey and saw the General Mgr. of the place where Ross had such splendid prospects. I wanted to know why Ross left, and what salary he had received. He left because they asked him to leave, his work was not satisfactory. He received $75 a week for 6 mos. $75. Think of it! I was starving on 14. Sick, so sick—in a room without heat—a bed without a blanket—no winter coat—weight 97 lbs. Think of it! Ross was too "hard pressed" for money to spare $25 a month, and gave only 20 and even that for only 2 months. And he received over *three hundred dollars a month for six months.*

When at the store only a very short time he borrowed from the Co. $150.00 said he was married and his wife had to undergo an operation. He finally repaid the loan. He actually had the nerve to take to the office a sporting woman and her illegitimate child who he introduced as his wife. The men laughed behind Ross's back for the woman was stamped, as they all are, and they knew he lied.

Ross brought this same woman and her brat to my house one Sunday evening and I was angry and told him that if he ever brought any more prostitutes to my house I would have them both arrested. Anyone, short of a fool, would know what she was at one glance.

This is my first letter (I am all trembling). My next will be No. 2— New York.

> Au revoir,
> Lady Masterson

EVALUATING THE TWO RESEARCH STRATEGIES. Clearly there are advantages to and limitations of both strategies. The nomothetic approach to personality has the advantage of making possible generalizations about people who share the trait(s) in question. Because of the scientific requirements of repeatability, control, and careful measurement, what one says about a given sample of subjects then can be applied to others, enabling the establishment of global principles of personality structures and processes for people in general. A major limitation, of course, is that no individual is studied as a "whole" person. Thus, in nomothetic research we never see characterized an actual personality. Concepts of such a personality must be reconstructed or synthesized, so to speak, from a more or less piecemeal manipulation of isolated traits whose role in influencing behavior has been the focus of nomothetic study. As nomothetic research becomes more ambitious by considering more and more individual traits and their interaction, and by studying these traits in a variety of situations, it also becomes more cumbersome and less practical.

The major advantage of the idiographic approach to personality is that the person is viewed as an integrated unit (rather than as a collection of separate traits), reacting as a total entity or system to whatever situations it may face and with a continuity between the past, present, and future. This sense of integration and continuity is undoubtedly a great advantage; however it is bought at a high price, that of not readily being able to generalize about other persons. This could be overcome, of course, by studying many individuals, but such extension would be extremely costly and typically is not pursued systematically.

Although it is always hazardous to make generalizations about persons from a single or even a few cases, there are occasions when generalization can be successful. As Dukes (1965) has shown so well, single cases have been used in the history of psychology to establish important principles. This happens when little important variation in some process is found among different cases and when the investigator has identified correctly the regularizing principle. One example is the classic study by Morton Prince (1920) of a case of multiple personality, modern versions of which are Thigpen and Cleckley's (1957), *The Three Faces of Eve*, and Schreiber's (1973), *Sybil*. Prince identified the major characteristics of this fascinating disorder so well, and the pattern observed in such cases appears to be so typical that, although published several decades apart, these reports all have much in common. Nevertheless, a single case cannot establish broad generalizations about a phenomenon unless there are other cases with which to compare it, and the successful use of such a case to establish a valid principle is certainly the exception rather than the rule.

We should note that although it need not be so, case studies tend to be somewhat global and impressionistic rather than precise and carefully oriented to measurement. Furthermore, it is difficult to establish with idiographic study the variables important or not important to a person's functioning. In practice, most idiographic study is highly intuitive and descriptive and does not usually satisfy the criteria set forth by the more "science-centered" personality researcher.

Historically, there has been considerable dispute over the comparative virtues of the two research strategies, and the arguments typically have placed them in opposition to one another (e.g., see the classic debates between Gordon Allport, 1962, favoring the use of the idiographic approach and Robert Holt, 1962, arguing for the nomothetic position). It seems to us, however, that neither strategy of research is fully sufficient in itself. One provides a crucial supplement to the other. For example, as typically used, the idiographic approach is too global and fails critically in the esteemed values of science, that is, controlled observation, precision of measurement, and repeatability. This is not a necessary feature of idiographic research, since it too could be and has been done at least with careful measurement. Still, control and repeatability are difficult to achieve in the study of the single case, making the creation of valid general principles exceedingly unlikely. On the other hand, the nomothetic approach to research fails because of the distortions of nature resulting from analysis, its study of parts in isolation, and its failure to examine the full range of reactions to a variety of life contexts. Without our being able to draw on the holistic and naturalistic perspective of the idiographic strategy, the errors of analysis cannot be readily overcome. The idiographic and nomothetic strategies tend to be pursued by different investigators, because different interests and skills are involved in each approach. Nevertheless, their mutually supplementary use is required in the creation of a viable science of personality.

It is rather disturbing to note, therefore, that despite some heroic exceptions (e.g., Allport, 1965; White, 1966; White, Riggs, & Gilbert, 1976), personologists have been pursuing in recent decades the nomothetic strategy almost to the total exclusion of the idiographic approach (see reviews by Adelson, 1969; Argyris, 1968; Carlson, 1971; and Schultz, 1969). As one might expect, this has led to a rather shallow understanding of personality and has prompted one personologist (Carlson, 1971) to ask legitimately, "Where is the person in personality research?" It seems as if the study of the whole person has been abandoned: a statement supported by the finding that of over two hundred personality studies from two major personality research journals surveyed in 1968, *"not a single published study attempted even minimal inquiry into the organization of personality variables within the individual"* (Carlson, 1971, p. 209, italics in original). We agree wholeheartedly with Allport (1962) and others that the idiographic study of the whole individual remains a relatively underdeveloped territory in personology and deserves considerably more attention.

PERSONALITY THEORY

Before examining the nature of personality theory and the kinds of conceptual issues of concern to personologists, let us learn a little bit about Jay, who is described briefly in the following sketch:

> Jay Smith is thirty years old, single, and shows plenty of promise as a young physician. Acquaintances describe Jay in glowing terms, e.g., as being highly motivated, intelligent, effective, creative, attractive, and charming. "If they only knew," thinks Jay frequently. For Jay, unbeknownst to others, is terribly insecure and anxious. When asked once by a psychologist to pick out some self-descriptive adjectives, Jay selected introverted, shy, overweight, inadequate, dull, unhappy, and afraid of people—not an enviable self-image!
>
> Jay was the first-born in a family of two boys and one girl. Their father, a successful medical researcher, loved all the children but favored Jay—there was something special, he thought, about his eldest child. And what dreams he had for Jay! Dr. Smith wanted to instill a

strong desire for achievement so that someday Jay would strive to become successful, wealthy, and most of all, independent. He wanted very much to be proud of his little "bundle of joy," as he affectionately referred to Jay. Their relationship remains as close today as it was during Jay's childhood.

Jay's mother has always been career-oriented but she has frequently experienced considerable conflict and frustration over her roles as full-time mother, housekeeper, and financial provider. Much of this conflict, unfortunately, was communicated subtly to the children, especially when they were quite young. For some reason, these anxieties particularly affected Jay—as reflected perhaps in intense and frequent childhood fears of animals, darkness, and separation. Mrs. Smith was amicable toward all her children but tended to argue and fight more with Jay than with the others, at least until Jay was about six or seven years of age (when the bickering subsided). Today their relationship is cordial but it lacks the dynamics, vitality, and closeness apparent between Jay and Dr. Smith.

Throughout elementary and high school, Jay was popular and did well academically. Athletics, student government, newspaper reporting, performing in school plays, and dating were all regular parts of Jay's social calender. When asked once by a favorite teacher about future goals, Jay replied definitively, "I plan on going into medicine because I enjoy helping people, particularly when they are sick and must be taken care of." The teacher, familiar with Jay's talents, abilities, and physical handicap (a slight congenital hearing impairment), never doubted Jay's sincerity or determination. Yet, despite Jay's lofty goals and ambitions, off and on between eight to seventeen years of age, there were strong feelings of loneliness, depression, insecurity, and confusion—feelings perhaps common to all during this age period but, nevertheless, stronger than in most youngsters and all too real and distressing.

Away from home for the first time, Jay's college days proved exciting and challenging—a period of great personal growth and pain. New friends and responsibilities gave Jay increased self-confidence and zeal for pursuing a medical career. Several unsuccessful romantic involvements proved disheartening, though, and led to increased study efforts—interpersonal relationships would always be threatening and disastrous for Jay. This aspect of life, the failure to achieve a stable and long-lasting relationship with that "special someone," bitterly gnawed at Jay's inner being. "After all," Jay would muse, "aren't people supposed to fall in love and marry?" "What is wrong, why can't I ever maintain a serious relationship for any length of time?"

Thanks to the excellent work during college, Jay was easily admitted to medical school. After the initial excitement, however, the hard realities took hold. More years of difficult work, intense competition, and, naturally, possible failure. The severe pressures and work load forced Jay to ignore potential romantic involvements, though there were many casual friends always to be contacted for brief diversions.

While Jay tried not to dwell on personal feelings and conflicts during this period of life, they crept through periodically: "I don't deserve to be a doctor"; "I won't pass my exams"; "Who am I and what do I want from life?"; "Why can't I meet that special person?"; "Will I ever be truly happy?"

At the medical school graduation ceremonies, Dr. and Mrs. Smith were as proud as they could possibly be. After all, their daughter was now officially, Dr. Jaylene Elizabeth Smith, and she had graduated at the top of her class!

Now that you know Jay somewhat, what can you infer about her personality? For example, how much stability do you find in Jay's actions, thoughts, and feelings across situations or over time? Is achievement one of her prominent and consistent characteristics and if so, why? Are there any clues as to why Jay has had repeated difficulties with heterosexual relationships? Why does she have such a poor self-image and an apparent fear of failure (or perhaps of success) when the "facts" do not seem to warrant such beliefs? What role, if any, has her physical impairment played in determining or shaping her personality? Could her experiences as a woman in a male-oriented society have been responsible for many of her behaviors and beliefs and if so, in what ways? And finally, could being a first-born child or a female with two male siblings have contributed significantly to Jay's personality development? These are just a sample of the kinds of questions personality theorists might ask about Jay in order to gain an understanding of her personality structures and processes.

Of course, before seriously beginning to answer any of the above questions, the personality theorist would need considerably more information about Jay, preferably from as many kinds of resources as possible, e.g., personality tests, behavioral observations, interviews, and so on. But even armed with this additional information, the theorist's task would be a most difficult one. There are simply too many possible answers to any one of the above questions to state categorically that Event A (or Events A1, A2, and A3) led to or caused Behavior B. Moreover, because theorists have their own personal and professional biases, some are likely to stress certain kinds of answers (and approaches) to the above questions while ignoring or rejecting others.

For example, some theorists (cf. Coan, 1977) would prefer to approach Jay from a biological perspective, emphasizing anatomical, physiological, and biochemical influences on her personality—e.g., inherited traits, body build, or hormonal secretions. Others might prefer a social perspective, viewing Jay from the vantage point of her relationships and roles with others (e.g., siblings, parents, peers) or with social institutions (e.g., marriage, education, career). Other perspectives are possible, of course, like psychological and spiritual ones (emphasizing Jay's thoughts, feelings, or relationships with nature). The reader should not get the impression that these varied approaches to personality are necessarily mutually exclusive—they are not! The point is that there are many ways to study and conceptualize personality, and each may yield vital and equally valid information about the person (cf. Wiggins, Renner, Clore, & Rose, 1976).

It is often distressing to the beginning student to discover how many different ways there are of conceptualizing personality. The myriad of theoretical systems is confusing, and it frustrates the desire for simple authoritative statements about structures and processes. The multiplicity of theories reflects two realities—first, the great richness and complexity of the subject matter of personality and second, the early stage of knowledge at which the science of personality remains at present.

With respect to the early stage of our knowledge, the science of personality, like psychology as a whole, is very new, having had its modern beginnings shortly before the turn of the century. Of course, learned people had speculated about such matters for thousands of years, and their ideas make up part of the philosophical background for the modern theoretical systems. Among the speculators were the Greek philosophers, Aristotle and Plato, and the Greek physician, Hippocrates, who introduced a personality typology based on the idea that temperament depends on the distribution in the body of certain fluids. Although the details of this idea were discarded long ago, the general point bears a striking resemblance to the current concept that temperamental characteristics are greatly influenced by the distribution of body hormones.

In any case, scientific, empirically oriented approaches to personality are relatively recent developments, and knowledge has not yet advanced far enough to consolidate the diverse theoretical systems into a single, generally accepted system of thought. If we knew enough and had a sufficiently comprehensive and detailed framework of thought, theories which could be shown to be inadequate would be discarded and whatever was valuable in them incorporated into one single, widely accepted system of thought. But the presence of so many systems claiming our serious consideration suggests inadequacies in each of their formulations and in the available evidence with which to evaluate them. In spite of many similarities among them, each of the theories remains influential because it contributes some valuable element which the others do not, and because it cannot yet be discarded or incorporated satisfactorily into another.

Neither the student nor the expert can "know" the field of personality without a familiarity with the most important of the theoretical systems designed to conceptualize it. Reviewing these theories is itself a large task and is impossible to do thoroughly in this book. Books that do so, such as that of Hall and Lindzey (1978), can be confusing to students because they provide summaries of each system of thought, without analyses of how they are similar and on what points they differ. The latter has been attempted by Maddi (1976) but is written at too high a level for the relative beginner. Yet some review of personality theory must be attempted because the very substance of personality, including its definition, depends on the theoretical system for viewing it.

Each personality theory belongs to a larger class of theories of which there are a number of specific variants, too many to cover here. The main classes of theory differ from each other in their fundamental tenets or assumptions about human nature. Whatever their terminology, the important thing is to understand these assumptions, which are central to the conceptualization of personality. We have selected one or two instances to represent each of the main classes of theory and to illustrate the viewpoint(s) by pointing to central issues on which the classes of theory differ. These issues fall within four main rubrics of personality: determinants (the biological and social forces that shape personality), description, dynamics (how personality works), and development. The subsequent chapters of this book are devoted to each of these rubrics (sometimes called the "four D's" of personality), contrasting the selected systems of thought in their response to the issues and providing examples of research on them. In chapter 7, we shall integrate materials from these issue-oriented chapters and apply several theoretical approaches to our illustrative case study, Jay, in order to demonstrate concretely the importance of personality theory to understanding individual people. Chapter 8 will be devoted to the principles and techniques of personality assessment, the crucial enterprise of measuring personality constructs.

Personality Determinants— Biological Factors

There are two broad kinds of personality determinants, biological and social. These seldom affect our personalities in isolation of one another but tend instead to interact in complex and often unknown ways. For clarity's sake, however, we will discuss them separately, devoting this chapter primarily to biological determinants of personality and chapter 3 to social determinants. The information presented here about biological and social determinants is pertinent to all personality theories. This is not to say that all theorists agree in their respective emphases on biological and social factors (for they most certainly do not), but only that our present discussion will be general in nature and will deal with materials likely to be of concern to most personologists.

Many students often lose interest when personality is examined from a biological perspective, perhaps because they think of personality largely in terms of anxieties, frustrations, conflicts, or defense mechanisms and assume that "learning" and "environmental" factors are involved exclusively. It seems inconceivable, though, that our long evolutionary history as a species or our individual genetic backgrounds and physiologies would have no bearing on our thoughts, feelings, and actions (and, thus, personality). Consider momentarily one of Jay's prominent characteristics, her intelligence (see chapter 1). While it is tempting and certainly valid to explain her many "intelligent" and well-adapted behaviors largely in terms of social-environmental factors, we should not minimize the fact that her parents also seem to be bright and probably have passed on genetically to Jay considerable intellectual potential. To ignore these biological influences would surely lead to a distorted or at best, an incomplete picture of Jay's personality. In the following pages, we shall illustrate some of the basic findings, methodologies, and issues important to the study of personality from a biological perspective by referring to current research on varied topics, including mental disorders, aggressiveness, and intelligence.

BIOLOGICAL AND CULTURAL EVOLUTION

To understand personality from a biological standpoint requires first that humans be placed in a phylogenetic context, since our anatomy and physiology are products of evolution from earlier and simpler organisms. About human evolution, Lerner and Libby have written that:

> . . . almost all biologists agree that organic evolution is a reality, and that humans (the currently dominant species on this planet), and all other existing kinds of life, were not always the way they are now, but descended with modification from preexisting forms. The concept of evolution stresses the idea that Earth was not always as it is, but has a historical past. One of the features of the process of evolution is that it embraces a historical continuum, in which there are no sharp borders. Thus, it is possible to distinguish nonliving material from living organisms in a general way, although the exact point at which one turned into another is a matter of somewhat arbitrary opinion. Similarly, the precise point in history at which creatures that can be described as human beings first appeared on Earth is a matter of definition (1976, p. 2).

Darwin's (1859) contribution to the ancient idea of *biological evolution* was to propose a workable mechanism for it and to demonstrate by painstaking observations of animal and plant morphology that there was, indeed, structural continuity among the diverse species. The mechanism Darwin proposed was that biological characteristics evolved because of their adaptiveness to the environment through the process of "natural selection." Through this process, characteristics antithetical to the survival of the species were dropped or suppressed, and those promoting species survival were retained and passed on to subsequent generations through genetic mechanisms. As a result of continuing natural selection and by means of feedback from the environment which determined whether a trait was adaptive or maladaptive, humans eventually arrived on the scene. Some properties were shared with lower forms of life and others were uniquely human. Early humans evidently appeared in the Pleistocene geological epoch about 500,000 years ago,* and evolved into their current form perhaps about 10,000 years ago. As for the psychological and behavioral qualities of human beings that distinguish them from other forms of mammalian life, Lerner and Libby (1976) suggest: the capacity for a high degree of educability, the ability to communicate with contemporaries and with their descendants, an extended time sense, a consciousness of self, the capacity to plan and direct their own evolution, and the ability to control the physical environment (pp. 23-24).

The physiological continuity which humans show with lower forms of life was documented effectively by Darwin. His evidence included the finding that structurally similar organisms could be found widely distributed over the earth, and hence they must have the same ancestors. A second type of evidence came from comparative anatomy and embryology, in which it was demonstrated that widely different species showed striking anatomical resemblance, both in their skeletal arrangement and in embryological development. An illustration of anatomical-skeletal continuity may be seen in Figure 4, and the striking similarity between the embryo stages of various vertebrate forms is diagrammed in Figure 5.

Biological evolution is a continuing process and is, presumably, still taking place today. This continuing evolution depends on two factors: first, that there be genetic variation among the different organisms within the species, so that some traits may be selected and passed on to subsequent generations and others suppressed; and second, that these genetic traits be related to the fitness of the species for adapting to changes in the available environments. Geneticist Dobzhansky (1967a) suggests that both conditions are probably met today, making the inference that evolution must be continuing a reasonable one. Many genetically influenced human traits, for example, intellectual capacity, vary from person to person, and it is likely that they affect the chances of survival and therefore the chance to reproduce before premature death. The elements of evolution are present today as they were in the past.

There is one other requirement for biological evolutionary change to take place. Human environments must also change so that new adaptive demands can be made. Only if the environment changes will there be natural selection as a result of adaptive success and failure under these conditions, thus permitting new traits systematically to emerge that are better suited to the new conditions, and old traits no longer viable in the environment to be dropped out.

---

* More recent evidence has suggested that their appearance might have been much earlier than this, far earlier in fact that anyone hitherto had suspected.

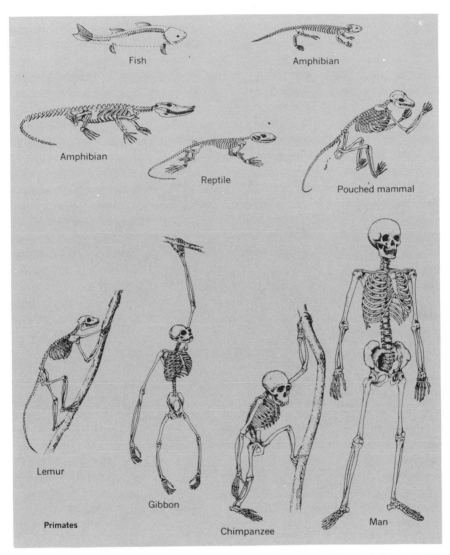

FIGURE 4. Comparative Features of Skeletons on different rungs of the evolutionary ladder. Both fossil and living forms are represented. Notice the similarities in anatomical structures for all these diverse creatures. *(From Heredity, Evolution, and Society, Second Edition, by I. Michael Lerner and William J. Libby. W.H. Freeman and Company. Copyright © 1976.)*

It is evident that biological evolution is a very slow process, and it is difficult to document any important biological changes since "modern" humans evolved approximately 10,000 years ago. However, *cultural evolution* has been extremely dramatic, and the rate of change in patterns of society during the past 5,000 years surely has accelerated. Consider, for example, the changes in the

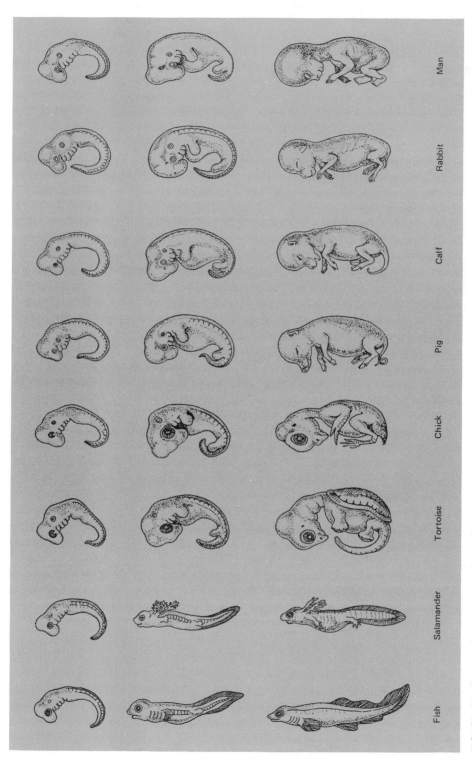

FIGURE 5. Comparative stages in the embryology of vertebrate forms. Here too the similarities are striking. *(From Biology: Its Human Implications, First Edition, by Garrett*

Fish   Salamander   Tortoise   Chick   Pig   Calf   Rabbit   Man

past 200 years or so. There is no doubt that the present human environment is markedly different from that hundreds of years ago, or perhaps even 50, particularly in the case of the world's industrialized societies. Not only are there striking social changes, but there are physical changes too, many of which pose serious adaptive problems, for example, the increase in population, air pollution, and the presence of harmful chemical agents in our water and food. As for population, Petersen and Matza (1963, p. 14) have observed that the world's human population was about 500 million in 1650. In three centuries, it expanded to five times that amount, reaching 2.5 billion in 1950. It is expected to be between 6 and 7 billion by the end of the century.

The implications of this rapid cultural change have been expressed dramatically and in a rather foreboding fashion by Toffler (1970) in *Future Shock* and more positively by Aldous Huxley in the following provocative passage:

> Anatomically and physiologically, man has changed very little during the last twenty or thirty thousand years. The nature of genetic capacities of today's bright child are essentially the same as those of a child born into a family of Upper Palaeolithic cave-dwellers. But whereas the contemporary bright baby may grow up to become almost anything—a Presbyterian engineer, for example, a piano-playing Marxist, a professor of biochemistry who is a mystical agnostic and likes to paint in water-colours—the palaeolithic baby could not possibly have grown into anything except a hunter or food-gatherer, using the crudest of stone tools and thinking about his narrow world of trees and swamps in terms of some hazy system of magic. Ancient and modern, the two babies are indistinguishable. Each of them contains all the potentialities of the particular breed of human being to which he or she happens to belong. But the adults into whom the babies will grow are profoundly dissimilar; and they are dissimilar because in one of them very few, and in the other a good many, of the baby's inborn potentialities have been actualized (1965, p. 32).

GENETIC INFLUENCES

Charles Darwin believed that mental as well as physical characteristics were inherited and evolved from the struggle for survival. Without a hereditary mechanism through which biological traits could be passed on to the next generation, there could be no evolution. One of the foremost early behavior geneticists was Francis Galton, Darwin's half-cousin. Galton made many contributions to psychology, including the innovation of statistical methods and the development of mental testing. One of his most important contributions was the study of the inheritance of intelligence (1869). He showed that there is a much greater number of extremely able persons than might be expected by chance among the relatives of intellectually bright people, and he tried to refute the criticism that this might be the result of economic, social, and educational advantages by showing that the correlation was higher when the family relationship was genetically closer. The use of twins and other forms of consanguinity (blood relationships) in assessing hereditary influences was introduced thus by Galton.

Darwin's work in evolution had created a climate clearly favorable to a hereditary point of view, and Galton's writings were further influential in advancing the cause of behavior genetics. However, a workable theory about the actual mechanisms of heredity was sorely needed. Johann Gregor Mendel helped supply such a theory with his research on the garden pea, although it took the world of science thirty-four years after it was published, in 1865, to discover it. There were other major contributors around this period, for example, a Dutch biologist, Hugo de Vries, a German botanist, Carl Correns, and an Austrian, Erich Tschermak, each of whom performed independent experiments that led to the recognition that Mendel had indeed discovered the formal basis of genetic transmission. Shortly after, several other researchers demonstrated that animals as well as plants follow Mendel's laws of genetics, and a British biologist, William Bateson, coined the term "genetics" to refer to this emerging area of biological science. Shortly after the turn of the century, many key hereditary notions, such as the gene, dominance and recessiveness, hybrid, genotype, and phenotype were already well known. Over the next several decades, advances were made in knowledge about the anatomy of genes and chromosomes, the process of mutation, and the interplay of genetic structures.

Most of the early knowledge of genetic mechanisms concerned molar units of analysis (dealing with larger structures like chromosomes). In more recent years, progress in the understanding of the genetic mechanism has tended to be at the molecular level, that is, with the biochemical molecules of which the genes are constructed and the manner in which they influence the cytoplasm of the cell and its metabolic activity. The biochemical substances which have gained the most attention in recent years and which have even become known to the layperson through the popular media, are the *nucleic acids*. One of these, ribonucleic acid (RNA), has been of particular interest to psychologists because of hypotheses about its role in the chemical transmission of memory. However, it is deoxyribonucleic acid (DNA) which seems to be of critical importance to genetics, because it contains the genetic information passed on to the developing cells of the embryo, and it directs the embryo's development into the full-grown baby through its chemical action. Whatever aspects of the person's physiological structure are inherited are evidently carried by the DNA molecule, of which the gene is a portion or segment.

The DNA molecule resides in every cell nucleus and serves as the template for the construction of RNA, which evidently migrates out of the nucleus into the cytoplasm of the cell where it plays a key role in the synthesis of the cellular proteins. These proteins, some of which are enzymes serving as catalysts for biochemical activities, determine the functions of the cells. In effect, the DNA "tells" the cells of the body how to make the proteins which comprise the cell substance, which in turn controls how the cells should act. It contains the "genetic code" for protein synthesis, which is communicated to each cell of the body through its messenger, the RNA molecule.

The answer to the question of how nucleic acids influence cell development thus appears to be in the process of protein synthesis. Proteins are large biochemical substances made up of smaller substances called "amino acids." There may be several hundred amino acids (of twenty different types) linked together in a chain, and this chain comprises the structure of the protein. The links of the chain are arranged in a given order, and it is the order or pattern that defines the particular protein. Many combinations and permutations are possible in the protein molecule, and these combinations determine how the cells and the tissues (muscle, gland, bone, nerve) grow and function. As stated, the DNA influences this growth and function by instructing the cells how to make the proteins, that is, how to order the chain of linkages among the twenty types of amino acids comprising the cellular proteins. In this way, DNA carries the genetic information about the sort of creature that is to be produced, and through RNA, carries that information to every cell in the body of the developing organism.

Variability and Heritability

To understand the role of heredity in the production of any trait requires a grasp of two key concepts, "variability" and "heritability." Confusion, particularly over the latter, has contributed greatly to misunderstandings on the part of laypeople and scientists alike about the application of genetics to social problems and to the relations between heredity and environment in human development.

Interest in the issue of genetics itself arises because within a species such as Homo sapiens, there is much *variation* in physical and psychological traits. Since many of the traits of offspring seem similar to those in parents and grandparents, it is reasonable to assume that they must be passed on from generation to generation. One reason for the variation in traits among people is that the varying properties found in different people are transmitted to their own offspring but are not possessed by all.

It is also evident that each of us lives different lives and is exposed to different environmental experiences, and this too could be important in producing the variability among us. Every trait, however, is the result of the *interplay of both factors,* genetic and environmental. The question is thus raised as to how much of the given variation found in a particular trait, say physical height or intelligence, is the result of hereditary influences, and how much is the result of environment.

The concept of *heritability* is the quantitative estimate of the amount of such variability that is attributable to genetic factors. It is a precise and technical concept, which requires first that the degree of variation in a trait be assessed in some given species and in a given environmental context. Heritability is a ratio or proportion, technically the square of the amount of variation that is due to genetic factors divided by the square of the amount of total variation observed for the trait in question. In other words, it is essentially the proportion of total variance of the trait that can be shown to be attributable to inheritance.

The concept of heritability can be understood more clearly if we imagine some extreme hypothetical situations which, of course, never occur in reality. Suppose, for example, we had a large group of individuals with identical genes, the sort of thing that occurs on a small scale when we have identical twins. And suppose this population with identical hereditary properties is placed in highly diversified environments, each individual going into a different environmental setting to live. In this case, any variations we found among the traits manifested by the respective individuals would be entirely the result of environmental factors. Heritability would be zero—none of the variation could be attributed to genetic factors, these being the same in every case. On the other hand, suppose we had another large group of individuals who were heterogeneous in genetic background, as would be the case for unrelated individuals or for that matter, for any two individuals who were not identical twins. Now we place this group in homogeneous environments, recognizing in our hypothetical example that this would be technically impossible, since in reality there would probably never be two environments exactly alike. In this instance, any variations among traits that might be observed could not be the result of environmental variation since there was none and thus, heritability would be unity—genetic factors would account for all of the variation. Between these two extremes lies the bulk of instances in which heritability varies in the degree of trait variance it can account for, lying somewhere between zero and one.

Hereditary and environmental contributions to trait variation depend on a number of factors, for example, the trait in question, the specific environmental context of that trait, the species involved, and the context of other hereditary traits. Each of the above factors determines heritability. For example, given a comparable environment, some traits are more influenced by genetic factors than others—the role of heredity is greater in purely physical traits, such as stature, than it is in psychological traits. Some traits are influenced by a single gene inherited directly from the parent, as in the case of hair and eye color, and others, such as height, are produced by many genetic factors which combine to produce the effect. There is no single gene for the shape of the nose, although that shape is undoubtedly influenced by many genes. This is important because any given genetic factor may have different (sometimes opposite) end effects depending on the other genetic components with which it interacts. As stated, the environmental context in which heritability is evaluated is important too. For example, in a culture in which everyone has an adequate diet, the heritability of weight will be high because the total variation would not be influenced very much by nutritional variations. On the other hand, when diet varies markedly, the index of heritability will be correspondingly lower, since dietary variations will influence greatly the weight variations found in that population.

What this means is that heritability can never be judged in the abstract but only in a particular context, that is, in some given environment, in a particular species, in respect to a particular trait, and in a given genetic matrix. The index of heritability will change as any of these factors is changed. Thus, it is totally misleading, for example, to speak in general of the role of inheritance in intelligence, since technically such a role will vary greatly wherever and whenever the assessment is made, depending on all of the above considerations. This point is stubbornly missed and confused by laypeople and scientists alike who, often with perfectly honorable intent, use genetic principles to explain social problems and have intense emotional problems with the heredity-environment (or "nature-nurture") issue.

A good example of the hazards of speaking about hereditary

determinants in the abstract is the controversy stirred up among social scientists by Arthur Jensen (1969) and William Shockley (1972). These prominent researchers suggested that hereditary bases existed for intellectual differences observed on standard IQ tests between black and white Americans and also that so-called "compensatory" education programs for minorities were essentially useless because intelligence, being largely genetically determined, could not be raised significantly by education. Unfortunately, it is impossible to resolve such a controversial stance in the abstract, without specification of the relevant population, the exact trait considered, and knowledge of its environmental context. The following historical and somewhat personal account by social psychologist Philip Zimbardo (Zimbardo & Ruch, 1975) documents nicely many of the biases and fallacies pervading the IQ controversy:*

> Let us briefly put the Jensen-Shockley position into its appropriate historical context before outlining its fallacies. This context includes the anti-immigrant hysteria that led Pearson and Moul to "prove" that Jews were "somewhat inferior physiologically and mentally to the native population" of Britain (1925, p. 126). In turn-of-the-century America the attempt to keep the American people "pure" also called on the mental test movement to provide the intellectual foundation for both eugenics programs and immigration quotas. Little distinction was made between various types of "degenerates"—the criminal, the insane, the poor, and the "feeble-minded." They were housed in "charitable and correctional public institutions," many of which demanded their sterilization before release.
>
> An influential book by Carl Bingham, *A Study of American Intelligence*, provided the necessary justification for Congress to pass in 1924 the first immigration law restricting immigration from various countries according to a "quota system." Bingham concluded, on the basis of a highly inappropriate set of correlations, that the Nordic and Alpine countries of Europe sent their better racial stock, while those who emigrated from the Mediterranean countries were of biologically inferior racial stock. This generalization was based on the evidence that immigrants who had been in the U.S. more than 16 years scored higher on IQ tests than more recent immigrants. The more recent immigrants tended to be from southern Europe, while the established immigrants were from northern Europe. Thus time and place are confounded in this correlation. It is interesting to note that the highest intelligence test scores were found for white, Anglo-Saxon, male immigrants—the group that has traditionally held the positions of political, economic, and social power in the United States (and the general category into which most of the contemporary nativists fall).

* From Psychology and Life, Ninth edition, by Philip G. Zimbardo and Floyd L. Ruch. Copyright © 1975, 1971, 1967 by Scott Foresman and Company. (Reprinted by permission).

Higher IQ is a predictor of a better quality of life in an environment that rewards verbal skills and intellectual performance with formal education, better jobs, and positions of eminence. Overall IQ predicts scholastic achievement well, but not many other skills important for coping and adapting to the nonscholastic environment that most people face every day. There is no available evidence for Shockley's "80 percent heredity" assertion in any group other than Caucasians. It is false logically and empirically to further assert that because of the heritability of IQ, environmental interventions—such as compensatory education—will have negligible effects on intelligence. Height, which is obviously an inherited characteristic, has been shown to be modifiable from one generation to the next by environmental changes (Cavalli-Sforza & Bodner, 1971). Heritability coefficients tell us nothing about the potential effectivenes of environmental changes. If Head Start programs are ineffective, it may not be because the children have failed, but because the programs were poorly designed. We will see throughout this text that whenever there are "social problems," the political reaction is to blame people rather than social situations. Nativist arguments have been quite influential in the search-and-destroy operations designed to eliminate "problem people."

I might well be stomping grapes in Sicily today instead of teaching at the university where Terman and Shockley did their work if all those "inferior" Mediterranean types had been restricted from entering this land of opportunity in my grandparents' day. I'm glad the nativists didn't win (p. 202).

We will have more to say about race differences a little later, but the reader interested in a fuller account of the emotional complications of this problem may want to refer to the discussion presented in *Patterns of Adjustment* (Lazarus, 1976). Only if the concepts of heritability and variability are understood clearly, can the reader avoid the same pitfalls into which the uninformed and often even the learned, seem to fall.

The Study of Hereditary Influences— Methods, Findings, and Issues

Although it is important to guard against the careless and overgeneral attempt to identify the hereditary component in psychological traits, this component can and has been studied systematically by a variety of methods. Seldom has the quantitative variable of heritability been evaluated in these studies, but some insight into the role of genetics in many human traits is usually provided. The most commonly studied psychological trait is intelligence, possibly because of its great importance to human adaptation and the fact that it can be measured with reasonable reliability.

FAMILY BIOGRAPHY. The earliest work which attempted to show that certain characteristics run in families and are, by inference, inherited, used the *family biography,* or the pedigree method. Galton's own research, which surveyed a number of different families for evidence of a hereditary basis for genius, belongs to this type. There are others (e.g., Dugdale, 1877; Goddard, 1912) also which received considerable attention. But the problem with the family biography approach is that it cannot separate hereditary and environmental influences. The approach fails because genetically undesirable parents bring up their children under unsatisfactory conditions. Therefore, even if their genetic legacy is tainted, the situation in which the descendants are reared also is likely to be grossly inadequate. It is simply impossible to identify the respective roles heredity and environment have played using this approach by itself.

However, the family biography can be supplemented by more sophisticated statistical analyses and controls, as in the highly respected research on a biochemical defect known as phenylketonuria (PKU), sometimes called "Folling's disease" after its discoverer. Folling had shown in 1934 that some instances of mental retardation were associated with the abnormal excretion of large amounts of phenylpyruvic acid in the urine. Later, Jervis (1937) demonstrated clearly that the defect was inherited. By studying the family biographical patterns of the victims, Jervis came to the conclusion that the disease followed the classical Mendelian pattern of recessive genes, and that it was probably caused by a single gene pair. Because of this careful detective work revealing that the disease followed Mendelian ratios, and partly because of the straightforward diagnosis of the disease through urinalysis, most of the deficiencies of the family biography method were avoided in this case, as they had not been in Dugdale's and Goddard's works. All doubt about the hereditary nature of PKU was dispelled when the mental defect was later traced to reduced ability of the body to convert phenylalanine, an essential amino acid, into tyrosine (Jervis, 1959; Grossman, 1973). The resulting mental retardation is now thought to be caused by the toxic neural effects of the accumulated phenylalanine. If the child is given a diet free of this substance and high in tyrosine before six months of age, the disorder can be materially improved (Heber, 1970).

The case of PKU has been given great attention in psychological circles, despite the fact that it accounts for a very tiny proportion of the cases of mental retardation, because it shows the manner in which some defects can be directly inherited. It is sometimes considered to be a prototypical example of the genetic-constitutional determination of inadequate mental functioning. The argument goes something like this: As with other forms of mental retardation, PKU was once unknown, as was its cause. Hence it is possible that these other forms of mental retardation whose cause is now unknown will also be shown to result from inherited defects. This argument, however, has been challenged. One might point out, for example, that severe mental retardation is very rare, and most cases of retardation are of the mild variety. Severe forms of retardation are probably in a class by themselves and are not representative of the more usual, mild instances. Moreover, as Zigler (1967) has noted, most cases of mental retardation should not be viewed in terms of the inheritance of a single gene carrying the defect (as in the case of PKU) but rather as the product of the combination of many genes. Varying levels of intellectual ability are normally distributed among the population so that some individuals, unluckily, fall at the lower end of the distribution. Zigler's argument makes the distribution of intellectual ability analogous to a game of chance, such as poker, in which four of a kind or a straight flush is unusual statistically; however, such hands will appear from time to time, just as exceptionally poor hands do. Many cases will occur in which intellectual level is weak but not really because a disorder has been inherited. PKU is clearly a specific *defect* and low intelligence, although it is undesirable, need not be so at all.

Twins. Researchers attempting to isolate heredity from environment also have turned to studies of *twins*, in particular to the theoretically ideal "co-twin control" method invented by Galton. This technique requires studying identical twins who have been reared apart under different environmental conditions. Ideally, the *co-twin control* method properly administered holds genetic factors constant (identical twins have identical heredity) and permits the isolation of the effects of environmental variation. One difficulty is that instances of identical twins reared apart are few in number. A second difficulty is that it is harder than most people realize to determine whether twins are really identical. Third and most important of all, most of these twins are separated very late in childhood or placed in similar environments. The converse of this approach, holding environmental factors constant and varying heredity, is technically impossible to produce.

Despite the relative rarity of opportunity, a number of researchers have undertaken studies of identical twins—investigating behavioral characteristics such as intelligence, as well as physical factors such as height, weight, and incidence of disease—after the twins have been separated and placed in foster homes by public welfare agencies. They all have tended to unearth great similarities among the separated identical twins in the incidence and pattern of diseases and even in the results of intelligence tests. For children who have been tested on intelligence before adoption and then studied after some time in a foster home, intellectual functioning remained similar between twins in spite of the environmental variation. Yet there were also changes, especially when environmental variations were extreme. These changes were least evident in physical characteristics and most evident in behavioral characteristics such as intelligence-test performance.

In extreme instances of environmental variation, the higher-scoring twin invariably had received considerable educational and cultural advantages as a result of the foster placement. One study reports a woman who had an IQ of 116 and was a college graduate, although her identical twin had an IQ of 92 and had no schooling beyond the second grade. Here is a case in which, despite identical inheritance, twins differed strikingly in intellect, presumably as a result of altered and markedly unequal environmental circumstances.

Another example of the use of twins to assess the hereditary component of psychological traits is research by Irving Gottesman (1966). If it can be shown that identical twins are more alike in a certain trait than fraternal twins are (who do not have identical inheritance), a strong case can be made for a hereditary contribution to that trait. Gottesman used personality tests such as the California Psychological Inventory (see chapter 8) and others to compare the identical or monozygotic (single-egg) male and female twins with fraternal or dizygotic (two-egg) twins. The sample of subjects consisted of seventy-nine pairs of identical twins and sixty-eight pairs of fraternal twins. The variances for both types of male twins on four of the CPI scales are shown in Table 1 (the lower the variances, the more alike are the twin pairs), along with the heritability indexes which Gottesman calculated. The higher the heritability index, the higher is the proportion of the total variance contributed by heredity. Considerably greater similarity was found between identical twins than between fraternal twins.

One variation on the twin approach has been employed extensively by Franz Kallmann (1953) in his research on the hereditary contribution to schizophrenia and other psychoses, which generally are characterized by "loss of contact with or difficulty recognizing reality, notable alterations in mood, and severe distortions of thought and perceptual processes, frequently characterized by hallucinations or delusions" (McMahon, 1976). Kallmann's variation on the twin approach is called the "method of concordance," because it deals with the likelihood that one member of a sibling pair will have a

Table 1

	Some of Gottesman's Data on Personality Test Variances for Identical and Fraternal Twins		
CPI TEST SCALE	IDENTICAL	FRATERNAL	HERITABILITY INDEX
Dominance	41.342	80.706	0.49
Sociability	46.082	90.838	0.49
Achievement via conformance	76.297	66.625	0.00
Self-acceptance	53.848	99.787	0.46

(Reprinted with permission from Journal of Child Psychology and Psychiatry, 7, I. I. Gottesman, "Genetic variance in adaptive personality traits," 1966, p. 203, Pergamon Press, Ltd.)

specified condition (for instance, schizophrenia) when it is known that the other member has it. Comparing the *index of concordance* among identical twins, fraternal twins, full siblings, and half siblings, it is possible to gauge roughly the hereditary contribution. Although the index of concordance is not as precise a measure of this as the index of heritability, the reasoning is quite the same.

Essentially, Kallmann's method is this: He digs through hospital records of patients with schizophrenia, manic-depressive psychosis, or involutional melancholia to identify those who have an identical twin, fraternal twin, full sibling, or half sibling. He then seeks to determine the adjustive status of that twin or sibling. The index of concordance is simply the percentage of times that the second member of the pair has the same pathology as the hospitalized first member of the pair. Kallmann reported that the index of concordance for identical twins is dramatically higher than that for fraternal twins, which in turn is higher than for half sibs and unrelated pairs of individuals. Figure 6 presents Kallmann's indexes of concordance for three types of psychosis and for the several types of genetic relationship.

Kallmann does not believe that the various disorders studied are directly inherited but rather that genetic factors dispose a person to develop the disorder. To support his position, he cites the reasoning in the case of tuberculosis. A person cannot become tubercular unless he or she comes in contact with the disease-producing bacteria. Thus, the disease cannot be directly inherited, only the disposition or lack of resistance to the illness. The same argument is offered for schizophrenia and other psychoses. If a person has a strong genetic disposition to respond to life stress with schizophrenia and is exposed to the appropriate environmental conditions, the illness will occur. Kallmann does not suggest the nature of this disposition physiologically, which of course would have to be

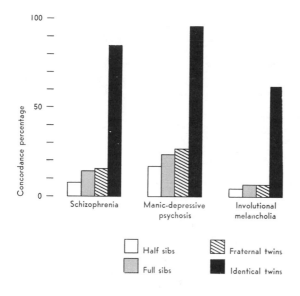

FIGURE 6. Indexes of concordance established by Kallmann for various mental disorders. *(Reprinted from Heredity in Health and Mental Disorder, Franz J. Kallmann, M.D., with the permission of W.W. Norton & Company, Inc. Copyright 1953 by W.W. Norton & Company, Inc.)*

known to establish fully the logical case, but he thinks his data offer good evidence that we should look for the genetic and physiological determinants of psychosis.

Kallmann's research remains highly controversial, and it is difficult to assess the degree of genetic component of the various psychopathologies from it because of methodological problems. Indeed, his research has been severely criticized by psychologists interested in the etiology of mental illness. Some object—and the probability that this may have happened is strong—that Kallmann severely exaggerated the concordance rates for identical twins, although to what extent cannot be known at present. The same person who obtained the records of mental illness, Kallmann, also determined whether the second member of the pair showed evidence of the disorder. This would pose a sticky problem when the second person was not actually hospitalized, and the extent or nature of his or her psychopathology had to be judged. Since Kallmann knew the original genetic classification and had strong convictions about the role of genetics, he may have unwittingly exaggerated the incidence of concordance. The method of concordance also has some fundamental weaknesses. For example, the living environments of identical twins are probably more alike than those of fraternal twins, since parents are acutely conscious of identicalness, and since twins too tend to regard themselves as alike and therefore dress alike and react alike (this was particularly true when Kallmann began his research many years ago). The high incidence of concordance for identical twins could be due as much to like environment as to genetic uniformities.

44

Moreover, the twins studied by Kallmann had lived together most of their lives; hence the crucial environmental influences which might have contributed to illness in one were probably present also in the other.

Other investigators have attempted to repeat Kallmann's research with essentially comparable results (Thompson, 1965), though the concordance ratios for both identical and fraternal twins have tended to be much lower than those reported by Kallmann. For example, in recent studies, concordance rates for schizophrenia have tended to average about fifty percent for identical twins and nine percent for fraternal ones—the expected incidence in the general population is approximately one percent (see Kleinmuntz, 1974; Page, 1975; Rimm & Somerville, 1977). Even these most recent studies, however, suffer from methodological difficulties and are perhaps no more definitive than Kallmann's. The imperfect data are much more likely to be accepted as proving a hereditary determination of severe mental disorders, such as schizophrenia, by those psychologists who tend to favor a biological approach and to be rejected by those with a social psychological viewpoint. The issue of the role of heredity in mental disorders remains a controversial one.

Selective breeding. Another method for studying the effects of heredity on behavioral traits is experimental and uses *selective breeding* for the trait in question. An example is the research of behavior geneticist, Theodosius Dobzhansky (1967b) with Drosophila, a species of fruitfly. Behavioral tendencies of these flies to move upwards or downwards when released from a tube or to be attracted or repelled by light, have been selectively bred over many generations to produce distinctively different types of Drosophila. Even earlier research by Robert Tryon (1940) is another example. Tryon bred generations of rats for brightness and dullness in going through a laboratory maze. Starting with 142 unselected white rats, he assessed their effectiveness in learning the maze, then bred the bright rats with other bright rats and the dull ones with other dull rats. He did this for twenty-one generations. After only eight generations, even the dullest of the bright rats did better on the maze than the brightest of the dull. These data clearly demonstrate a hereditary component in rat intelligence. It is, of course, not without hazard to generalize from rat or fruitfly to human, or from the process of learning mazes to other intellectual functions. Still, these findings provide impressive evidence of the genetic component in adaptive intelligence.

Karyotyping. A relatively new and sophisticated technique, called karyotyping, is used also by some to study relationships between heredity and behavior. Although karyotyping has been used successfully to identify the genetic bases of such disorders as Down's (Mongolism), Turner's, and Klinefelter's syndromes (see McKusick, 1964), our discussion will emphasize the *proposed* and highly controversial relationship between the 47,XYY karyotype and human aggressiveness.

Chromosomes, which contain the units of heredity (the genes), may be identified and examined by the process of karyotyping. Typically, the white blood cells are stained when the chromosomes are dividing and then are photographed; the chromosomes then may be identified and arranged in a standard sequence called the karyotype (Wiggins et al., 1976). In humans, the karyotypes for the normal female and male are similar but are *not* identical. Specifically, there are typically twenty-two identical pairs of chromosomes in males and females (called autosomes), with one member of each pair being contributed by each parent. A final (twenty-third) pair of chromosomes, however, is different in females and males and determines sexual characteristics, like body hair and physical size. The female has a matching pair of these sexual chromosomes (yielding a karyotype of 46,XX) while the male has one sexual chromosome like that of the female and one that is different (yielding a karyotype of 46,XY).

As suggested earlier, cell division sometimes goes awry, leading to unusual karyotypes and often to related behavioral problems (like mental retardation). One chromosomal abnormality recently attracting attention is the male XYY pattern (the karyotype is 47,XYY), with its proposed link to aggressiveness and even criminality (see Johnson, 1972). Spurred by sensational and often erroneous reports (such as those claiming incorrectly that mass murderer Richard Speck had the XYY chromosomal pattern—see Shah, 1970a, 1970b), many researchers have attempted to uncover possible relationships between the extra male Y chromosome and acts of violence. For example, the XYY defect seems to occur in roughly two of every one thousand births in the general male population (Coleman, 1976; Johnson, 1972). Yet the chances of finding the chromosomal abnormality among males institutionalized for criminal offenses are much greater, with about twenty to forty of every one thousand inmates having the XYY pattern (Court-Brown, 1967; Jacobs and coworkers, 1965; Jarvik, Klodin, & Matsuyama, 1973). The XYY male has been described as being unusually tall with borderline intelligence and a tendency toward highly aggressive episodes (Coleman, 1976). Interestingly, though, XYY inmates usually have not been convicted for violent crimes against people but instead for crimes involving property offenses—a finding casting some doubt on a presumed relationship between XYY and aggressiveness toward others (cf. Witkin and coworkers, 1976).

If methodological weaknesses in the above studies are overlooked for the moment (see Witkin et al., 1976, for an excellent discussion of these problems) and a relationship between the XYY pattern and aggressiveness is acknowledged, we still must determine the nature of the relationship. That is, are the two factors related in a direct or indirect manner? Establishing a direct relationship between the XYY pattern and aggressiveness would require evidence that, for example, the production of "masculine" hormones (e.g., testosterone) or the presence of neurological defects (e.g., brain-wave abnormalities) differed between XYY and control subjects—and such evidence is negligible (see Wiggins et al., 1976). Furthermore, keep in mind that not all XYY males are aggressive and that most of those incarcerated for crimes of violence are not XYY males.

For these and other reasons, many now are suggesting that if a relationship between XYY and aggressiveness does exist, it must be an indirect one. For example, the XYY pattern may influence directly certain attributes, such as large physical size or low intelligence, which in turn may provoke fear in others and consequently (and indirectly) may lead to aggressiveness in the XYY male. Witkins et al. (1976) even have suggested that the XYY criminal may not actually commit crimes at a higher rate than others, as suggested by some studies, but is simply less adept at escaping detection (because of lower intelligence).

Although karyotyping has provided a means for identifying different genetic patterns, in many cases (like the XYY karyotype), the relative contribution of hereditary and environmental factors remains a difficult issue. Regarding the role of the extra Y chromosome in the production of aggressive behavior, the consensus currently is that genetic factors probably are important here but so are environmental ones. As Goldstein (1975) has stated: "If the XYY Syndrome is a cause of violence, it is only a contributory one which requires other conditions for aggression to occur and, in any event, is capable of accounting for only a small proportion of total violence" (p. 8). One might note too that the emphasis on the XYY karyotype has done little to increase our understanding of aggressive acts in females and therefore, the overall utility of karyotyping for the investigation of human aggression (and perhaps many other behaviors) may be quite limited. Nevertheless, the technique has shown some promise, primarily in identifying the genetic bases of gross abnormalities such as Mongolism, and any judgment of its potential usefulness for understanding personality may be premature.

The Race Issue

During World War I it was discovered that white army induct-ees obtained higher scores on tests of intellectual functioning than Negro inductees. The data also showed, however, that blacks grow-ing up in certain Northern states, such as Pennsylvania, Ohio, New York, and Illinois, were superior even to white recruits from the South. The most impressive subsequent study was done by a social psychologist, Otto Klineberg (1935), who showed that Southern Negro children improved in intelligence test scores after having moved to New York City and that the improvement was related to the length of time they had been there. Thus the differences could not be due to selective migration, and clearly showed that environment had had a marked effect on intelligence test scores. There are few researchers in this field today who are not aware of the validity of this point.

Most behavior geneticists doubt that there are any important differences among the races in broad adaptive traits such as intelli-gence. For one thing, the concept of race itself is vague and ill-defined and as is pointed out in the 1952 UNESCO statement on race, there is no evidence for the existence of so-called pure races. Gottesman, a well-known psychologist interested in genetic factors, writes that: "My evaluation of the literature on race differences has led me to conclude that the differences observed between the mean IQs of Negro Americans and other Americans can be accounted for almost wholly by environmental disadvantages which start in the prenatal period and continue throughout a lifetime" (1968, p. 63). This does not mean that there are no genetically determined differ-ences in constitution among human groups; there obviously are, or else race would be an entirely meaningless concept, which it is not. But it means that such differences are relative (there are no pure races) and are not of major importance to the adaptive functioning of human racial groups.

In his handling of this matter, anthropologist S. L. Washburn in a presidential address to the American Anthropological Association goes even further, saying, "I am sometimes surprised to hear it stated that if Negroes were given an equal opportunity, their IQ would be the same as the whites. If one looks at the degree of social discrimi-nation against Negroes and their lack of education, and also takes into account the tremendous amount of overlapping between the observed IQ's of both, one can make an equally good case that, given a comparable chance to that of the whites, their IQ's would test out ahead. Of course, it would be absolutely unimportant in a demo-cratic society if this were to be true, because the vast majority of individuals of both groups would be of comparable intelligence, whatever the mean of these intelligence tests would show" (1963, pp. 529-30).

The final sentence of the above quotation illustrates the defects of a form of thought which has been discarded by knowledgeable behavior geneticists in recent years, one that has been referred to as *typological thinking*. There is a strong tendency to pigeonhole individual people into categories or types. It is a useful way of simplifying things but in behavior genetics, typological thinking is a very misleading habit. It encourages, for example, the image of a single gene responsible, say, for intelligence, or for any other complex psychological trait in which one might be interested. If the person has the gene, then he or she ought to have the trait. This image conforms to the Mendelian laws of heredity which are so useful in analyzing certain simple traits such as those Mendel studied in the pea plant. It occasionally works well with rare disorders, such as PKU. But in most instances of human psychological traits, this thinking is inadequate and no longer provides an accurate picture of genetic processes, or of the way geneticists think about the problem. Combinations of genes are necessary to produce particular physiological and behavior effects, each trait usually being the product of interaction among large numbers of genes. This is known as *population* or *statistical thinking* in contrast to typological thinking.

Geneticists today speak of the *gene pool* to refer to the hypothetical total number of genetic influences which may be found within a species or in a group of individuals. Even when there is selective breeding, this original gene pool is evidently not lost. For example, the many genes related to "brightness" and "dullness" in the rats which Tryon had bred over many generations were not lost over these generations, but remained latent within both populations even after they had been bred into two distinct behavioral types. When they were no longer being selectively bred for brightness or dullness, the original distribution of maze learning ability rapidly returned to each group. As pointed out by Dobzhansky (1967b), this is a very useful property for organisms since, even though there has been selective breeding in the past, when new changes occur in the environment, the process still can reverse itself. That is, the basis of natural selection can be changed readily without the species becoming terribly vulnerable and unable to draw upon its full range of adaptive mechanisms. The gene pool remains slow to change irreversibly, and it is not known how much time might be needed for this to happen. The bridges are not burned by selective mating and retreat to earlier types of traits is possible.

Such a situation implies that races or types in which the gene pools are distinctively different are not likely to develop easily. It also means that the types or categories into which people are placed in classification by traits are less important than are the individual differences, which cannot be readily explained by membership in a type. Dobzhansky effectively states the case against typological thought:

> Man in the street is a spontaneous typologist. To him, all things which have the same nature are therefore alike. All men have the human nature, and an alleged wisdom has it that the human nature does not change. All Negroes are alike because of their negritude, and all Jews are alike because of their jewishness. Populationists affirm that there is no single human nature but as many human natures as there are individuals. Human nature does change. Race differences are compounded of the same ingredients as differences among individuals which compose a race. In fact, races differ in relative frequencies of genes more often than they differ qualitatively. . . .
>
> To say that we do not know to what extent group differences in psychological traits are genetic is not the same as saying that the genetic component does not exist. It is a challenge to find out. If individuals within populations vary in some character, be that blood grouping, or stature, or intelligence, it is quite unlikely that the population means (averages) will be exactly the same. What matters is how great is the intrapopulational variance compared to the interpopulational variance. Skin pigmentation is individually variable in probably all races, but the interracial variance is evidently larger. Although precise data are not available, it is at least as probable that the relation is reversed for psychological traits. In simplest terms, the brightest individuals in every class, caste, and race are undoubtedly brighter than the average in any class, caste, or race. And vice-versa the dullest individuals in any of these groups are duller than the average of any group. There are sound biological reasons why this should be so. Very briefly, in the evolution of mankind the natural selection has worked, nearly always and everywhere, to increase and maintain the behavioral plasticity and diversity, which are essential in all human cultures, primitive as well as advanced (1967b, pp. 47-48).

Environmental Influences

By no means has all of the research on the determinants of adaptive intelligence or other personality traits been designed to extract the influence of genetic factors—much of it has been oriented toward the influence of environmental variations. Some of it should be discussed here to balance the discussion of hereditary influences.

Since this turns our attention away from biological influences and toward the subject of the next chapter, it seems best to mention it only very briefly. We shall limit ourselves to a short discussion of a striking piece of research by Skeels (1940, 1942, 1966) on the impact of an impoverished verus enriched environment on intellectual development. One reason that Skeels's research is unusual is that it involves a follow-up of the same children twenty-one years after the original observations were made.

Two groups of children first were observed, thirteen in the experimental group, twelve in a contrast or control group. All were mentally retarded and had been placed in an orphanage. The experimental group had been moved out of the orphanage to an institution with much stimulation and warm relationships with mother substitutes. The contrast group stayed behind in the unstimulating, impoverished environment. Marked differences later were observed in the intellectual level and functioning of the two groups, although they had started at about the same level, with the experimental group having been actually slightly inferior. In two years, the experimental group had gained 25.8 IQ points, while the controls had lost 26.2 IQ points. Eleven of the former children were adopted later and continued to show improvement in intellectual level, but the two not adopted had declined somewhat.

Twenty-one years later all the cases were found and again the comparison between groups was made. None of the thirteen children who had been moved to the superior environment had become a ward of any institution, public or private. Their median education was completion of the twelfth grade; four had one year or more of college, of these one had graduated from college, and another was doing some graduate work. All were self-supporting. In the contrast group, one had died in adolescence in a state institution for the mentally retarded; four still were wards of institutions, one in a mental hospital, the other three in institutions for the mentally retarded. Their median education was less than the third grade. The enriched and deprived environments had made themselves felt very substantially in the overall level of functioning of the two groups.

General Conclusion Concerning Genetic Influences

What can be concluded from the above review of some of the research and research methods on genetic factors in the development of psychological traits? The fundamental conclusion is in a sense banal, that psychological characteristics are influenced *both* by hereditary and environmental factors. The conclusion is banal largely because it is so general and so self-evident.

There can be little doubt that hereditary influences do exist. What is mainly lacking in our knowledge now are the details of the relationship, those facts necessary to specify in more technical fashion the heritability of a given trait under particular conditions, and some knowledge of the physiological structures that mediate the genetically influenced trait. For example, if one assumed with Kallmann that schizophrenia has a hereditary basis, at least in part, evidence is still lacking for the physiological differences between the schizophrenic and nonschizophrenic in order to account for the susceptibility to the disorder. Let us recognize that what is inherited, after all, is an anatomy of some sort, a physiological structure which functions in certain ways and grows out of the hereditary influence on cell differentiation. Variations in this structure must underlie, in part, many of the psychological differences that we observe. How anatomical and physiological differences might lead to variations in personality must be considered next.

PHYSIOLOGICAL INFLUENCES

The general argument that an animal's physiology contributes to its behavior is grossly supported by taking a phylogenetic perspective, that is, by comparing the physiological structures of animals at different phylogenetic levels and observing that their characteristic patterns of behavior vary. For example, when neurological structures are relatively similar, as they are within phyla or species, characteristic behavior is also similar; when the neurological makeup differs markedly, as it does particularly across phyla, striking behavioral differences also appear. But the statement of such a relationship and nothing more is too general and obvious. What is needed is that the details of this influence be clarified and documented. The problem of relating physiology to psychological functioning becomes more difficult, complex, and subtle within a species such as humans. There are two reasons for this: first, because when we are working within a species the variations in physiological structure are not so obvious, although they clearly do exist; and second, humans are the most complex of animals, physiologically and psychologically, and their behavior is governed by many more variables which can easily escape our notice or understanding.

The subject of personality tends to emphasize humans rather than infrahuman animals, but much of the evidence for the relationship between physiology and stable patterns of behavior (from which personality is inferred) comes from studies of animals. This is partly because of the greater complexity and difficulty of studying humans and partly because of restrictions on the kinds of research that can be performed. There are also marked individual differences among infrahuman animals within the same species, and it is quite reasonable to conceive of animals as possessing personalities too, although the jump to humans is always suspect. Our objective in this section is to illustrate physiological influences on adaptive behavior and to analyze the ways in which these relationships can be applied to personality.

While the socially oriented psychologist attempts to understand psychological functioning and malfunctioning in terms of disturbances in social relations, the physiologically oriented psychologist prefers to explain these disorders at the level of physiological structure and function. In general, the influence of physiological factors on behavior can be studied in two ways. One is by experimental methods to create temporary physiological states and to observe their behavioral effects (as is done in drug studies). The other way is to examine stable, naturally occurring differences among humans or infrahuman animals in glandular, neurological, or other organ structures as possible correlates of variations in behavior (as is done in studies of body build and temperament).

Physiological factors (and as already noted, genetic ones too) can affect behavior either directly or indirectly. In *direct influence*, normal behavior is altered by damage to tissues or by structural or functional conditions in the nervous system. For example, metabolic disturbances that result from inadequate functioning of the endocrine gland system may produce behavioral effects, such as hyperactivity, sluggishness, and reported anxiety. Damage to the brain from physical injuries or diseases such as syphilis can produce impairment in adaptive behavior and changes in a person's relationship with other people. There is no doubt that these disturbances are definitely produced by damage to the brain tissue, although the mechanism by which the damage is reflected in behavior is not entirely clear and will not be understood fully until the precise relationship between the brain and psychological functioning is known.*

Indirect influences occur when physiological states have social

* See the work of Gazzaniga (1967), Ornstein (1973), and Sperry (1964) for an introduction to some of the current research relating brain structures and processes to psychological functioning. For example, "split-brain" studies, where the tissue connecting the two hemispheres of the brain has been cut, have suggested that each hemisphere partly specializes in particular functions (e.g., verbal tasks or spatial and perceptual abilities)—a finding implying, in a sense, that two separate "brains" cohabit the same skull.

consequences which in turn affect the individual's behavior. Physical handicaps, like Jay's hearing impairment, are examples of indirect influence, because they may produce negative or disturbed reactions in other people that make the handicapped person feel inadequate, attempt to compensate for the defect, perhaps withdraw from social contacts, or resort to another form of adjustment. A girl who is physically unattractive may develop an insecure or compensating personality, strongly influenced by this physical fact. Similarly, a young boy endowed with considerable physical strength and large stature probably will discover in playing with other children that he is stronger than they are, and thus develop a personality different from that of a lad who is sickly and puny.

The range of examples of physiological influences on adaptive behavior is large, and one must be highly selective in a brief treatment. Two examples will be given here. The first is of the relationship between body build and temperament. The second illustrates the effects of hormones on adaptive behavior. Although the illustrations are selective, essentially the same general points could be made about other physiological factors that have been omitted because of lack of space.

Body Build and Temperament

An early prototype of the relationship of physiology and personality is Hippocrates' classical theory that temperament depends on the relative proportions of four main body humors—black bile, yellow bile, blood, and phlegm—each corresponding to four types of person, the melancholic, choleric, sanguine, and phlegmatic. The major modern representative of this theme is the "constitutional psychology" of William H. Sheldon (1940, 1942). Its immediate ancestor was the work of Kretschmer (1925), who had divided people into four physical types, (1) the frail, linear *asthenic,* (2) the vigorous, muscular *athletic,* (3) the plump *pyknic,* and (4) the inconsistent *dysplastic* for whom portions of the body could be asthenic and other portions simultaneously pyknic or athletic. Kretschmer maintained that temperament and even the type of mental disorder an individual might develop depended on the body type with which one was endowed. For example, schizophrenics were apt to be asthenic in body build, and manic-depressives were likely to be pyknics.

Besides pursuing this line of research much further than Kretschmer, Sheldon developed a system of scale measurements for the varieties and dimensions of body build as well as for the varieties and dimensions of temperament. He also suggested an embryonically oriented theory of the relationship between body build (or "somatotype") and temperament, in which it was assumed that each of the various portions of the body's tissues, say the digestive organs (endomorphy), the muscle and bone (mesomorphy), or the nervous system (ectomorphy), has been differently emphasized in the development of the individual, resulting in different patterns of psychological response.

Sheldon assumed a direct influence of the dimensions of body build on temperament, although he also acknowledged that cultural attitudes toward and stereotypes about body builds also may influence the growing person as well. For example, there is a widespread tendency to assume that fat people (called "endomorphs") are jolly, and thin people (called "ectomorphs") are anxious, serious, and intellectual. Shakespeare expresses this idea in Julius Caesar's remark, "Yond Cassius has a lean and hungry look; he thinks too much: such men are dangerous" (*Julius Caesar*, i, 2, 192). With such a cultural stereotype, it would not be surprising for fat people to grow up with a personality different from that of thin people, the expectations of others being an important influence on one's self-image.

Sheldon has reported extensive research demonstrating a moderate link between body type and temperament. However, there is considerable doubt about the mechanisms underlying this relationship, since correlational evidence cannot answer the question of whether the influence is direct or indirect, or even whether there is any cause-and-effect relationship at all. Few advances on the problem have been made since Sheldon's pioneering efforts. The basic ideas behind it remain highly controversial among psychologists interested in personality, and the problem has never entered the mainstream of personality psychology.

The Biochemical Control of Behavior

Nowhere is the impact of physiology on adaptive behavior more clearly expressed than in the influence of hormones. Everyone is aware of the existence of the *endocrine glands*, the network of hormone factories which secrete biochemical substances of great potency directly into the bloodstream to be carried to internal organs throughout the body. One usually speaks of the endocrine glands as a system, because one gland influences the other rather than working in isolation. Within this system, the *pituitary* appears to be the most important; it secretes many hormonal substances which regulate other glands in the system. Figure 7 lists the endocrine glands and portrays their approximate locations in the body.

The potency of endocrine hormones for influencing behavior

and adaptive functioning becomes most evident when there is a disease or defect of one of the secreting glands. Examples include the effects of too little or too much *thyroid* hormone. Behaviorally, too much results in agitation and sleeplessness among other things, and too little is apt to produce lethargy and fatigue. These effects are likely to be known by the layperson because so many people take pills to overcome thyroid deficiency. Another equally striking example involves the pancreas, sections of which (the islet cells) secrete a powerful hormone known as *insulin*. Insulin regulates the amount of sugar in the blood stream; its action is to withdraw sugar from the blood and to store it in the liver. This is important because the functioning of the muscles of the body and, indeed, of the cells of the brain depends on the oxidation of sugar. If there is too little sugar available, adaptive thought and action cannot take place; if there is too much, the person suffers from the disease of diabetes. The amount of insulin released from the pancreas must be enough to keep the blood sugar level from becoming excessive and yet provide enough to permit the brain and muscles to function successfully.

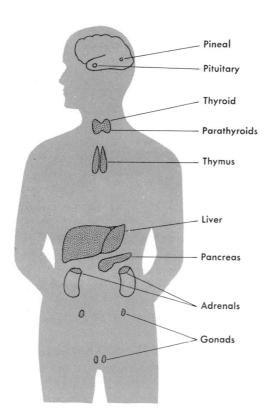

FIGURE 7. The endocrine glands and their approximate locations.

Occasionally an individual suffers from an insulin disorder, and the symptoms communicate dramatically the vital role of hormones in psychological functioning. One such disorder, for example, is an insulin-secreting tumor of the pancreas. Under these conditions, insulin continues to be secreted into the blood stream regardless of the blood sugar level. In such a case, excessive withdrawal of sugar from the blood and cells of the brain produces severe symptoms such as physical weakness, mental confusion, double vision, and even coma or convulsions. An individual chronically beset by this disorder may not realize the nature of the difficulty but feels unable to deal adequately with the ordinary requirements of living. In severe cases paranoid symptoms may even be displayed, or one may periodically experience psychotic-like attacks. All of these profound mental effects are produced by a hormone-secreting tumor that may be no larger than a small match head.

In recent years the *adrenal glands* have received much attention from psychologists because they are so important to stress and emotion. There are two main portions of the adrenals, both producing specialized hormones which have different functions. The outer portion of the gland is known as the "cortex" and produces several hormones called "corticosteroids." These regulate metabolic activities such as protein, fat, and carbohydrate breakdown, and in this way are very important to sustaining adaptive activities over long periods of time during which the person or animal is exposed to stressful circumstances. The functions of these adrenal cortical hormones have been particularly emphasized by physiologist Hans Selye (1956, 1976), whose writings and research on the body's adrenal-based, physiological defenses against stress have been very influential. In consequence of this work, stress reactions often are studied by measuring the secretion of adrenal hormones in the blood or urine.

The other main portion of the adrenal gland is the inner part, called the "medulla." Here there are secreted at least two (and probably more) hormonal substances, "adrenaline" and "nor-adrenaline." There is some evidence that *adrenaline* is emphasized in emotional reactions such as fear, and *nor-adrenaline* is the major hormonal component in reactions such as anger, although this generalization is probably overly simple, and the empirical case made for it is rather weak (Frankenhaeuser, 1975). There are two lines of evidence. First is the observation that herbivorous (plant-eating) animals seem to have higher secretion ratios of adrenaline to nor-adrenaline than carnivorous (flesh-eating) animals have. This would make sense if anger and attack were associated mainly with nor-adrenaline, fear and withdrawal with adrenaline. The evidence thus suggests that glandular makeup is consistent with the characteristic life adjustment of the species.

A second line of evidence is that adrenaline and nor-adrenaline produce measurably different, though overlapping, end-organ effects when injected into the person. There are also common-sense observations which seem to be consistent with the idea that the biochemical correlates of anger and fear are different. For example, anger is thought to produce a reddening or flushing of the face, and we use the expression "red-faced" anger. On the other hand, fear seems to be associated with blanching or paling of the face and a drying-up of the mucous membranes. Who has not found his or her mouth almost too dry to speak clearly on facing an audience for the first time? Some classic studies by Wolff (1950) also have confirmed the above common-sense impressions. A patient with a disorder which required keeping his stomach open for a time was observed. A window was installed in the opening so that the gastric activity could be examined. When the patient seemed angry, the stomach lining was engorged with blood, appeared red, and became moist; when he seemed afraid, the lining was pale and dry. It is quite likely that such effects are produced in part by activity of the endocrine glands, in particular, the adrenal medulla.

Let us consider one more illustration of the role of biochemical substances in adaptive behavior, before we attempt to examine the manner in which personality itself may be shaped by physiology. The illustration is of hormonal influences on *aggressiveness*. Animal species vary greatly in aggressiveness. For example, the wild Norway rat must be handled with great care to avoid its fierce attacks. However, after many years of breeding this animal for purposes of experimentation, researchers have produced a very tame animal which can be handled easily and roughly without the risk of attack. The wild Norway rat has adrenal glands that are far larger than those of the domesticated version.

It has been assumed for a long time that aggressiveness also is related to sex hormones, since male animals typically are more aggressive than females—see our earlier discussion of genetics and aggressiveness. A remarkable piece of evidence about this comes from a study by Clark and Birch (1945, 1946), who experimented with chimpanzees. Most animal species, including chimpanzees, maintain social dominance hierarchies (sometimes referred to as "pecking orders"). Some animals behave consistently in a dominant fashion over all the others; others are dominant over some but submissive with others; still others fall to the very bottom of the dominance scale. Dominance usually means considerable control over the food supply, with the dominant animal usually satisfying himself first. Clark and Birch observed that when two chimpanzees were allowed to fight over a peanut which was presented a number of times in a cup between them, one tended to emerge as the dominant animal—he always took the peanut first each time until no longer hungry. However, when the experimenters injected the subordinate chimp with a dose of male sex hormone, he overturned the dominance relationship created earlier and tended to establish dominance over the other chimp.

This is a very clear and interesting example of the influence of the male sex hormone on adaptive behavior. However, since human behavior seems to be far less controlled by such hormones than the behavior of infrahuman animals, it is not altogether clear to what extent the findings of Clark and Birch apply to the human context, although it is not implausible that some such mechanisms also could be at work in human individual differences in aggressiveness (e.g., see the work of Scaramela and Brown, 1978, demonstrating a relationship between aggressiveness in hockey players and the male sex hormone, testosterone).

How Hormones and Other Physiological Factors Might Influence Personality

The above account illustrates the biochemical control of adaptive behavior. It shows that immediately circulating hormones momentarily affect the actions and reactions of animals, particularly infrahuman animal species. Remember, however, that the subject of personality depends on two themes, first, the existence of more or less stable or enduring patterns of psychological functioning and second, manifest individual differences in these patterns—see chapter 1. To progress from the above examples of how hormones influence behavior to the manner in which they might affect personality, we must make three logical, inferential leaps.

The first is to assume that stable individual differences in some behavioral traits could be a result of different amounts of hormone coursing through the system. For example, we might expect different degrees of aggressiveness in people to be associated with different amounts of, say, male sex hormone. This does not necessarily imply a one-to-one or exclusive relationship. The person's social experience probably plays an important role, too, in increasing or toning down the biologically shaped aggressiveness. The resulting behavior pattern is undoubtedly a product of the interaction of both hormonal and social factors, and it is unlikely that any complex personality or temperamental quality could be the result of only a single physiological influence. The male sex hormone might provide some of the impetus for aggressiveness. However, there are probably a host of other biochemical and neurological elements which operate together in some complex and unknown geometry to determine the behavioral outcome, not to speak of the unquestioned role of social experience or of the immediate situation as well.

The influence of hormones on personality is not a new idea. About thirty or forty years ago when medical research and practice began to recognize the powerful impact of hormones on behavior, overly simple assumptions about individual differences in personality and glandular makeup began to burgeon and to reach the lay public. It was assumed, for example, that what had been learned about thyroid deficiency and its treatment also could be applied to the individual who functioned within normal limits, for example, to increase energy or help the person to relax. In time it was discovered that successful treatment for cases of endocrine defect would not work in normal cases. Moreover, the endocrine glands functioned as part of an organized system, so that injections with a hormone usually had repercussions, often serious ones, throughout the entire system. With the discovery of the complexity of the problem, initial enthusiasm about hormones cooled. Today, although the potential implications of the hormonal control of personality still have the same force, we recognize how far we are from the degree of understanding of the problem that would be necessary for the practical control of adaptive behavior.

The second inferential leap is somewhat more complicated and even more fascinating to consider. It is that hormones have a marked effect on the development of the person from conception on and could influence personality by influencing the formation of the physiological structure and function which is established early in life. Furthermore, the very hormones which determine how the physiological structure will develop are in turn influenced by early life experiences (in infancy and perhaps even *in utero*). In sum, individual differences in hormonal activity (produced both through genetic influences and early life experience) could create physiological structures quite different from person to person, or animal to animal, resulting in varying patterns of behavior throughout the remainder of life.

Evidence for the above principle comes from the work of Seymour Levine (1966; also Levine and Mullins, 1966) in which the effects of male and female sex hormones at critical periods of development of the rat were studied. There appear to be distinct differences between the male and female brain that determine sexual activity. Levine argues that in mammals the brain is essentially female at birth until a certain stage of development when the male's brain undergoes sex-related changes. In the rat this stage occurs a very short time after birth. If testosterone is absent at this stage, the brain will remain female; if it is present, then the brain will develop male characteristics. Females injected with testosterone at this early period fail to develop normal female sex behavior in adulthood. They also fail to acquire normal female physiological patterns—their ovaries are dwarfed, and their ovulation cycle is absent. Similarly, males who are castrated during the first few days after birth and hence are deprived of testosterone at this critical period, show signs of female physiology and female behavioral receptivity in adulthood. Similar findings have been reported in the guinea pig. Moreover, if a newborn rat is administered thyroid hormone, its thyroid functioning is permanently suppressed for the rest of its life. This suggests to Levine that there is a portion of the brain which might be called the thyroid "thermostat" or regulator, and that in effect it has been permanently adjusted too low by the early administration of thyroid hormone. There is evidence therefore to support the inferential leap of the second type, that hormonal levels early in life produce changes in the central nervous system, so that regulatory activity of circulating hormones later in life is permanently altered too. Although the nature of these changes in the brain is not known, Levine argues that they must have occurred if we are to understand the permanence of the hormonal effects over the animal's lifetime as a result of the experimental treatments in infancy.

There are two ways in which hormonal influences on the developing physiological structure could be produced. First, there is the possibility that genetic influences will create varying levels of glandular production of a given hormone. In this event, some animals will start out with more of the hormone than others. A second possibility is that the experiences to which animals are exposed will produce different circulating amounts of a given hormone at critical early periods in life. It is known that the handling of animals by humans, interactions with other animals, stressful situations, and so on, all influence the circulating levels of hormones such as hydrocortisone, adrenalin and testosterone. For example, when an animal ecological system becomes too heavily populated for the given food resources of the environment, a survival struggle that generates severe stress is created. Under such stress conditions, the adrenal glands secrete far more hydrocortisone than usual. As a result, the animals become less resistant to disease and less capable of mating and reproducing. Christian and Davis (1964) have suggested this as one of the biological mechanisms through which animal population levels are kept relatively constant. When the population grows too large, survival and breeding are impaired and population size is reduced; when it falls below a given point, survival and breeding again improve, with a subsequent increase in the population size. The overall level of population in the long run fluctuates around some normal, constant level (except in modern human populations, which appear to be a special case). In any event, early life experiences affect hormone levels, which in turn permanently influence the nervous system on which later regulation of adaptive behavior by circulating hormones and environmental forces depends.

We have saved the largest inferential leap of all for last, that is, the possible connections between principles derived from infrahuman animal forms, even such low ones as the rat, and those appropriate to humans. Does the work of Levine have anything to do with the relationship of physiology to human personality? To suggest it does require that we overlook provisionally the differences among the physiological structures (for example, the brain) of humans and infrahumans; although as we go from the macrostructure of tissue systems to the microstructure of individual cells and subcellular structures, the differences in structure and function become less impressive. A human gene will act biochemically in essentially the same way as a rodent gene. The same hormones are found in rats and humans. Yet human behavior is infinitely more complex than that of lower forms of animal life, just as a human's overall physiology is also more complex. Human behavior is also far more flexible and more sensitively keyed to environmental forces and learning than is that of lower animals.

It is hazardous and probably unwarranted to argue that Levine's findings, and others like them, have direct and specific applicability to humans, although they might well have a general relevance. One of the things which makes this work on lower animals potentially fascinating is precisely the possibility that the principles derived from it will be applicable to people. Few of us really have much interest in rats as such, but we do have a great deal of interest in those things that we as humans share with them. The inferential leap, however, must be highly disciplined, and we must be continuously on guard against overgeneralization in the absence of comparative data in each species.

Although the socially oriented personality researcher has little direct interest in documenting the inferential leaps considered above, the search for rules about how physiological structure affects adaptive behavior and personality should be taken seriously by all personologists. People obviously are living creatures like other animals and as such, an understanding of human behavior will require biological as well as social rules.

Having considered some of the significant issues and findings concerning biology and personality, let us turn now to a discussion of the social determinants of personality.

Personality Determinants– Social Factors

3

Social factors influence personality in immediate or transient interactions as well as throughout life. These social factors, often called "contemporaneous" and "developmental" influences, are the themes of this chapter. These two basic ideas are: 1) For all humans, every behaving situation is really a social one, whether the person is alone or in the company of others. The presence of other people is usually a powerful influence on how one acts and reacts; but even when alone, we remember or imagine how others react to what we do or think and this too has a great influence on us. 2) Over the course of development, from the very earliest moments of postnatal (and possibly even prenatal) life, every person has a host of experiences with other people which influence the developing personality structure. Our discussion of these social factors will deal first with the effects of the immediate social situation on our reactions (i.e., *contemporaneous* influences) and then with the effects of past social events which contribute to reactions in the present (i.e., *developmental* influences). In each case, we shall present briefly some research illustrations of the social influences in question and then offer some possibilities for why and how these social variables have such a powerful impact on personality.

CONTEMPORANEOUS SOCIAL INFLUENCE

Social situations can influence virtually every human psychological function. They can affect what and how we learn, how we perceive and judge the environment and the events in it, the language with which we describe and think of events, our motives, the manner in which we cope with life demands, the feelings we have for others, and the manner in which we experience and express emotional reactions. Below are a few concrete research examples of contemporaneous social influences, primarily ones dealing with conformity or "yielding" to the pressures of others.

Examples of Contemporaneous Social Influence

Representative instances of contemporaneous social influence have been revealed and analyzed by social psychologists in many ways and settings. A favorite approach has been to place subjects in contrasting social settings and make observations about how they act.

In a well-known study dealing with *perception* and group influence, Sherif (1935) had subjects judge the apparent movements of a stationary pinpoint of light. When a pinpoint of light is viewed in a completely dark room without any reference points, it seems to move, a phenomenon called by Sherif, "the autokinetic effect." The extent and pattern of this movement vary from person to person and are determined by purely internal psychological factors. When subjects work alone over a number of trials, each develops a stable, characteristic *autokinetic effect*. One subject may report relatively little movement (a few inches, for example) in a particular direction, but another subject may report a large movement in a different direction. This becomes an individual norm or standard which is repeated consistently from trial to trial.

When subjects work in groups of two or three, each announcing his or her own judgment, the influence of one subject on the other then is found. Gradually group rather than individual norms are established. The group norm tends to represent a compromise among individual norms, with extreme cases pulled in by the group in both the degree and patterning of the estimated movement. Sherif's subjects, who had had previous experience with the autokinetic phenomenon and who had established their own norms, gradually gave up these individual norms in response to the behavior of the group.

64

These group norms persisted even after the subjects were allowed later to work alone again. Subjects who had had no prior individual experience rapidly achieved group norms which persisted when these subjects later worked alone. In other words, individual norms always gave way to the social interaction, with the group norm finally being adopted by the individual and persisting in the solitary situation. Sherif's experiments dramatically illustrated the powerful effects of a group situation.

However, what would happen to subject yielding in a situation in which the stimulus to be judged was *not* as ambiguous or unstructured as a pinpoint of light in a dark room? Asch's research (1952, 1956), with socially based influences on *perception*, looked specifically at this kind of situation. In the best-known study, subjects compared a series of standard lines with several alternatives and announced to the experimenter in each case the alternative line that was the same length as the standard. When the subject did it alone, there were virtually no errors, suggesting that this perceptual task was not particularly difficult. The same task also was performed in a group of persons, each of whom had been instructed secretly by the experimenter on exactly how to respond. In one of the groups consisting of seven confederates and one "real" subject, Asch had all the confederates give the same incorrect answer before it was the "real" subject's turn. He found that about one-third of the time, the "real" subject made "errors" in the direction of the group norm or standard. Table 2 shows the comparison of the frequency of subject errors in the solitary situation with that in the group situation. As can be seen, the number of errors increased dramatically, all of them being the result of "yielding" to the pressure of the social group.

As a final example of contemporaneous influence from a somewhat different perspective, let us look briefly at the controversial yet important work of Stanley Milgram (1963, 1965, 1974). Milgram wanted to find out whether subjects would yield to or *obey* the persistent orders of an authority figure (a Caucasian male experimenter in a white laboratory coat from a prestigious eastern university) and carry out a presumably distasteful act: Would he or she repeatedly administer an electric shock to a fellow subject who complained frequently of discomfort and pain, and of suffering from a "heart condition"?

In a typical Milgram experiment, a paid volunteer subject would enter the laboratory and meet the experimenter and another subject (who was really a confederate). The two subjects were told that they would be participating in a study designed to assess the effects of punishment on learning. Though selection appeared to be

Table 2

Distribution of Errors in Experimental and Control Groups of Asch Study on Group Pressures

NUMBER OF CRITICAL ERRORS	FREQUENCY OF ERRORS IN EXPERIMENTAL GROUP* (n = 50)	FREQUENCY OF ERRORS IN CONTROL GROUP (n = 37)
0	13	35
1	4	1
2	5	1
3	6	
4	3	
5	4	
6	1	
7	2	
8	5	
9	3	
10	3	
11	1	
12	0	
Mean	3.84	0.08

*All errors in the experimental group were in the direction of majority estimates. *Adapted from Asch, 1952.*

by chance, the "real" subject was chosen in all cases to be the "teacher" and the confederate the "learner." The teacher was instructed to shock the learner every time a mistake was made on a list of word pairs and to increase the shock one step on the intensity scale for each mistake. This intensity scale, labeled clearly on the shock generator, ranged from 15 volts (marked as "slight shock") to 450 volts (marked as "Danger: Severe Shock"). It is important to realize that the teacher and learner were put in separate rooms when the experiment began and that no electric shock was actually delivered to the learner (a fact unknown to the teacher). The learner was trained to give a standard sequence of correct and incorrect responses to the word-pair task as well as specific reactions to the supposed shock (like discomfort and pain cues and insisting that the experiment be stopped). In fact, if the teacher ever reached 300 volts (a planned certainty unless the teacher decided to quit), the learner was instructed to become extremely upset and finally to refuse to respond any longer. This made it appear that he might have fainted, or worse, have suffered a heart attack. Despite this extreme situation, the experimenter's task was to insist repeatedly that the teacher continue to read the word pairs and to consider a failure to respond by the learner as an incorrect response. Thus, as the experiment progressed, the teacher was pressured into giving increasing amounts of shock to a suffering individual unwilling or unable to participate any longer.

Milgram was interested primarily in the reactions of the teacher rather than in the effects of punishment on learning. Would this person continue, at the insistence of the experimenter, to administer increasing amounts of shock to another apparently distressed and possibly endangered human being, or would the teacher refuse to continue the experiment? What would you do? Most people, including college students and psychiatrists, say they would expect very few subjects actually to administer the most severe levels of shock, particularly after the learner no longer responded. In fact, Milgram found that sixty-five percent of his sample delivered the maximum intensity of shock! Most of the subjects (teachers) did show signs of severe distress and conflict about continuing, but they did finish the experiment—in other words, they yielded to the experimenter's commands despite their inner turmoil about doing so.

Mechanisms of Contemporaneous Social Influence

In Sherif's, Asch's, and Milgram's research, there is noticeable evidence of contemporaneous social influence. There still is the problem, however, of understanding what made the subjects vulnerable to that influence. A considerable proportion of the research on social influence has been aimed not merely at demonstrating such effects but at comprehending their mechanisms, that is, at answering the theoretical question of why.

There have been two main methodological approaches to studying the mechanisms of contemporaneous social influence. One was initiated by Asch himself and consists of attempting to obtain from the subjects through interviews a picture of the psychological processes occurring during social pressure. The other consists of experimental attempts to evaluate the hypothetical conditions under which such pressure will or will not change behavior.

Asch interviewed each subject after the experiment described earlier and sought an explanation for the frequent yielding to the group. When confronted with their mistaken judgments, some subjects admitted that they had realized the seven other "subjects" had been wrong; however, the unanimity of the "other subjects" made them experience severe distress about being deviant and led them to yield to the sensed pressure. Other subjects reported experiencing equal distress but with such an array of evidence against them, decided that they somehow must have misunderstood the task or had a failure in eyesight (e.g., like not seeing an illusion that others are experiencing). Finally, a small proportion of subjects expressed utter surprise at discovering their errors and reported not remembering any conflict or even being influenced by the other subjects.

These interview responses suggest that there may be three quite different processes involved in this situation of social influence: (1) the threat of disapproval of or rejection for being deviant, with which a subject can attempt to cope, either by adamantly "sticking to one's guns" in spite of the distress or by volitionally knuckling under to the group; (2) the threat posed by doubts that one has correctly appraised the requirements of the task, leading to a search for confirmation or disconfirmation of one's judgment and to yielding or nonyielding depending on the conclusion of the search; and (3) the resolution of threat by a kind of denial or repression in which the person has accommodated perhaps without even being aware that he or she has done so.

It might be noted too that Milgram's approach to understanding the mechanisms of contemporaneous social influence also has included subject interviews to determine why they went along with the demands of the experimenter, even though they were experiencing great conflict about doing so. Many of the interviews strongly suggest mechanisms like those found by Asch. For example, some subjects continued the experiment because they felt they were overreacting to what really must be an innocuous situation—after all, no one would be permitted to undergo extreme risk in a controlled laboratory study, especially at a well-known university! In other words, some of Milgram's subjects continued despite their distress, because they told themselves that they must be exaggerating or misperceiving the learner's discomfort and vulnerability.

The second type of approach to understanding the mechanisms of contemporaneous social influence can be illustrated by Stanley Schachter's (1951) ingenious study showing how groups exercise their power over individuals. His research attempts to validate experimentally the first process mentioned above by Asch, that is, that deviating from social standards is apt to be punished by the group. Schachter created an experimental situation to test what might happen to the deviating individual. Through advertising, Schachter was able to create a number of "natural" groups made up of college students who wished to engage in discussions about current social issues. At the first meeting of the groups we are interested in, he asked the members to discuss and give judgments about a court case involving a delinquent who was shortly to be sentenced for a criminal act for which he had been found guilty. The group had to decide whether to recommend clemency or strong discipline to the presiding judge. The case was presented so that a position in favor of clemency would be the predominant reaction.

Into this setting, and following in the tradition of Asch's use of confederates to create different social structures, Schachter introduced three types of accomplices, each trained to behave in a particular fashion. One, the "middleman," always adopted the dominant position of the group and stuck to it throughout the discussion. A second, the "slider," always began by taking a deviant position from the group but later was won over by the group's arguments. A third, the "deviant," took a position at odds with the group members and maintained it regardless of the social pressure to do otherwise. Many such groups were created in this research study.

In the early stages of the discussions, Schachter found that the group usually directed intensive conversation toward the deviant, presumably in an effort toward conversion. But as time passed without a change in the deviant's stance, the members of the group ceased to communicate with the person, thus isolating the deviant from social contact. When asked to evaluate the members to determine who would continue to participate in later discussions, the group also rated the deviant as less acceptable than the other types of confederates. Perhaps most revealing of all, the consistently deviant individual was less often elected to important committees and when elected or nominated to an administrative function, it was more often to an unimportant committee which entailed labor without power or influence. These latter findings are schematized in Figure 8, which shows the frequency above or below chance expectancy with which the deviant was nominated either to the unimpor-

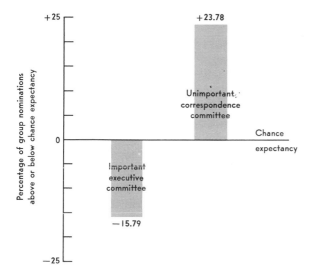

FIGURE 8.   Percentages above and below chance of assignments of "deviate" members to important and unimportant committees. *(Adapted from Schachter, 1951, p. 199. Copyright 1951 by the American Psychological Association. Reprinted by permission.)*

tant correspondence committee or to the important executive committee. Schachter's research highlights one of the major ways in which the social group influences the individual, by controlling rewards and punishments and acceptance or rejection.

Before leaving this topic, the reader should remember that we spoke earlier of two main types of social factors, contemporaneous and developmental influences. It would be a mistake to view the two as separate and totally independent, for in life both are always operating simultaneously, one affecting the other. We have separated them here for convenience and clarity. Let us turn then to developmental social influence which, parenthetically, has been of greater interest to personologists.

DEVELOPMENTAL SOCIAL INFLUENCE

How is the personality itself fashioned over a lifetime by the social system into which the child is born? To answer this, some variables of social structure need to be identified, since they impinge on us as we develop and, along with the biological givens with which we are born, help shape our individual personalities. The task of analyzing the social structure of any society—that is, the ways in which people and their daily and life roles are organized—belongs mainly to sociology and cultural anthropology and as one might expect, there have been many divergent proposals about how this is best accomplished. We cannot enter here into the debates about the best way of analyzing the social structure. In the discussion that follows, two broad types of social variables will be used to illustrate how society influences personality: the variable of culture and the variable of social class. As in our discussion of contemporaneous social influence, our first task will be to give some examples of the influence of cultural and social class variations on personality. Following this, we shall turn to theoretical analyses of how such influence is accomplished, that is, to the mechanisms by which personality is fashioned by variables of social structure. We shall discuss sex typing in some detail also, as a topic important to developmental social influence and socialization processes. More specifically, our treatment of developmental social influence will lead us to the important problem of how children learn about maleness and femaleness and the appropriate behaviors and roles for each sex. In chapter 1 we talked about Jay and asked several questions about her personality, e.g., could her experiences as a woman in a male-oriented society have been responsible for many of her behaviors and beliefs and if so, in what ways? The sexual stereotypes and expectations of a society do seem to play a major role in determining gender identities and the consequent behaviors of males and females (cf. Mischel, 1970; Money, 1974); we must see therefore how these social factors affect psychological sex differences.

Cultural Influences on Personality

The interplay of personality and culture is a vast topic, and its interest to social scientists has grown greatly in recent years. This is seen in the increasing number of books and journals that have been published reviewing the findings and methodological problems of cross-cultural research on personality.

Among the most interesting instances of this relationship are studies which have examined the patterns of psychopathology in different cultures and subcultures. Cultures vary greatly, for example, in their expressed attitudes toward alcohol and drugs; in the manner in which illness, death, and bereavement are viewed; in orientation toward emotional expression; in the role patterns of various members of the family, and so on. These variations in turn influence greatly such disturbances as alcoholism and drug addiction, and physical and mental illness.

Let us begin with *alcohol* and *alcoholism*. Considerable differences in rates of alcoholism exist among various national and ethnic groups. In New York City, certain groups like the Chinese, Italian, and Jewish populations have an unusually low incidence of problem drinking. The Irish, in contrast, have a great deal of difficulty with drinking and in this group, personality disorder is very likely to be accompanied by alcoholism (Kleinmuntz, 1974; Opler, 1959).

Heavy drinking also is common among the Japanese. But their national attitudes toward drinking seem to permit drinking patterns that seldom lead to serious occupational and social problems, or to the personality deterioration associated in our society with alcoholism of the "skid row" type. William Caudill, an anthropologist with long experience in the Japanese culture, has written provocatively about this:

> It is striking that there is much drinking by men in Japan, and a great deal of male dependency and passivity, but there is little alcoholism as this would be defined in the United States. Some aspects of this question may be illustrated by a simple thing like a whisky advertisement in *Bungeishunju* (a popular monthly magazine) which says a great deal about attitudes in Japanese culture when it shows a pleasant old gentleman smilingly anticipating the pleasure of drinking the six

bottles of whisky he has saved up, while his gray-haired elderly wife kneels on the floor and counts her money. The caption reads, "To each his own happiness." Further understanding is provided by the fact that the wife in the Japanese family manages the money and, circumstances permitting, gives her husband an allowance on which to go out and do his drinking. It is not likely that such an ad, nor the cultural circumstances represented in it, would occur in the United States, and from this example it is possible to gain some appreciation of the influence of the cultural context on the patterning of instinctual gratification.

One might say reasonably enough of the above example that it is merely an ad in a popular magazine, although the ad gains a certain validity from the fact that it would not be likely to appear unless it were acceptable in the culture and useful in selling whisky. That such an ad, however, had its counterpart in behavior was brought home to me in the experience of several of my friends in Japan. I had one friend with whom I spent many evenings drinking and talking. He had a habit on one night each week of taking the allowance provided for the purpose by his wife in the family budget and going out to drink with his cronies. When he arrived home late in the evening his wife would meet him at the door, help him off with his shoes, prepare a snack for him in the kitchen, and then assist him to bed. Equally, I had another friend whose job entailed great responsibility and power. He liked to drink American whisky, and I would occasionally bring him a bottle as a gift. He saved these bottles and others, until his store amounted to several dozen. His plan was to wait until a suitable vacation period permitted him the leisure to drink them up. This vacation became a reality in the interim between one important job and another, and he was able to put his plan into effect.

These examples would seem to indicate that the Japanese man does not anticipate rejection from others because of his drinking and is less likely, at least through stimulation from this outside source, to feel guilty about his drinking (1959, pp. 215-16).*

It is notable that in Japan the drinking pattern is evidently a highly disciplined one, in which drunkenness occurs during periods of leisure rather than as a companion to the ordinary responsibilities of life. The Japanese man demands of himself a high degree of tension-producing discipline and responsibility, and he releases these tensions by explosive episodes of drinking at times and in circumstances that do not impair his functioning. In order to understand the varying patterns of drinking and alcoholism among different peoples, it is evidently necessary also to understand the diverse cultural values associated with them.

Reaction to *pain* and *illness* also varies greatly among different

---

* Reprinted with permission of Macmillan Publishing Co., Inc. from *Culture and mental health* edited by M. K. Opler. © Macmillan Publishing Co., Inc. 1959.

cultural groups. For example, interviews with Jewish-American and Italian-American mothers by Zborowski (1958, 1969) have shown that mothers of both ethnic groups who had recently immigrated were overprotective and overconcerned about their children's health, compared with mothers from families who had lived in the United States for many generations and had become fully assimilated. The more recently immigrated also tended to exaggerate pain and respond to it emotionally, but the "Old Americans" were more stoical about pain and adopted an "objective" stance in reacting to it. Also consistent with the above are findings of Mechanic (1963), who noted that American Jews visited doctors and took medication much more often than either American Protestants or Catholics, even when their educational and economic levels were held constant. And in a study comparing Irish- and Italian-Americans, Zola (1966) observed marked differences between the two groups in their presentation of medical complaints, even when the actual diagnosed disorders were the same. The chief complaint of the Irish-American group more commonly revolved around the eye, ear, nose, and throat, compared with other parts of the body in the case of Italian-Americans. Zola suggested that the symptoms of illness reflect the particular preoccupations and values of that culture. To support this point, he noted that when the Irish and Italians in his sample were asked to identify the most important part of their body, more Irish than Italians emphasized the eye, ear, nose, and throat, thus making understandable their penchant for medical complaints about these areas. Theoretically, the relationship could go the other way, with bodily values being determined by the nature of medical complaints, but this is not the way Zola interpreted the direction of causality here. In any case, there seems to be a strong relationship between a culture's values and its characteristic ways of dealing with matters of health and illness.

One of the most interesting examples of the link between culture and illness patterns may be found in studies by Singer and Opler (1956; also described in Opler, 1959) of the personality characteristics and symptomatology observed in Irish-American and Italian-American schizophrenic patients. Schizophrenia is the most serious and widespread of the psychotic disturbances, and Singer and Opler carefully examined through observation, case history data, and personality tests, sixty male schizophrenic patients in a mental hospital in New York City, ranging in age from eighteen to forty-five. Half of the patients were Irish-American, half Italian-American, all of them varying from first to third generation Americans. Both groups were Catholic, comparable in education and socioeconomic status, and had been hospitalized at about the same time. The only important way in which they differed was in their Irish or Italian ethnic background.

The choice of Irish and Italian ethnic groups was based on knowledge of certain differences between them in family structure and personal values, differences which might be reflected in the specific manner in which the symptoms of serious mental disorders might be expressed. For example, in the Irish family the mother plays a dominant and controlling role, whereas in the Italian family the father dominates and the mother defers to him. Moreover, for the Irish, sexual activity is subordinated to procreation; sexual courtship is mild and extended in time, with marriage delayed and celibacy encouraged; sexual feelings are typically regarded as sinful and are a source of guilt. In contrast, for the Italian, sexuality is an accepted part of life and tends to be cultivated as part of the assertion of healthy maleness. In short, inhibition and delay of gratification and a maternally dominated family are emphasized in Irish culture, but in the Italian an expressive acting out of feelings and a male-dominated family are stressed. On the basis of these cultural differences, Singer and Opler anticipated differences in the emotional pattern expressed by Irish and Italian schizophrenic patients.

Marked differences in symptomatology conforming to the cultural differences indeed were found. The Irish patient was more inhibited and beset by fear and guilt, and the Italian patient was more emotionally expressive. Moreover, the Irish schizophrenics felt hostility toward female family figures but largely controlled it; the Italian patient tended to be more overtly hostile, aiming this hostility mainly at male parental figures. Alcoholism was a frequently observed symptom among the Irish and extremely rare among the Italians.

In these examples and many more that space prevents citing, personality (as evidenced by patterns of psychopathology) is closely intertwined with the cultural context in which the person is reared.

Social Class Influences on Personality

Human societies, like those of many infrahuman animals, tend to be organized into strata or hierarchical layers. Social classes form one of the most common of stratification principles. Since the research of sociologist W. Lloyd Warner (e.g., Warner and Lunt, 1941), it has been evident to social scientists that Americans arrange themselves in social classes and usually recognize their position in this hierarchy when asked. Although the details of this early research need not concern us here, its most important message was twofold: (1) The manner of life and the values on which life is predicated vary as functions of social class. (2) Social class variations create rather strong barriers to social interaction among the members of each class. These social barriers are of great sociological and psychological interest and suggest a tremendous disparity between the American ideal of social equality and the American reality of social stratification. Not only does social class influence who interacts socially with whom, but it also has a strong impact on personality-relevant characteristics such as motives, values, life styles, the ways in which people view themselves via the life experience it produces, and the manner in which parents rear their children. Social psychologist Roger Brown illustrates the matter pleasantly in the following passage:

> The life style differences arborealize into the flimsiest trivia. Upper-class Americans like martinis before dinner, wine with dinner, and brandy after dinner; beer is a working-class beverage. The upper class likes a leafy green salad with oil and vinegar, while the lower class likes a chopped salad or head of lettuce with bottled dressing. If you are middle-class you say *tuxedo*, where the upper-class says *dinner jacket*; in England you say *mirror* where the aristocracy says *looking-glass*. If you, like me, give your trousers a little hitch when you sit down so that they will not bag at the knee, then you are quite irredeemably middle class (1965, pp. 132-33).*

Naturally, the importance of social class differences lies not in the trivia of a few preferences, expressive styles, or the manner in which one handles his trousers when sitting, but in the major life values and patterns of behavior the person adopts. Each social class tends to live in given residential areas inhabited by people who share common socioeconomic, educational, and occupational characteristics, and common attitudinal and value patterns, even to the extent of their voting behavior. For example, Robert Tryon (1955a, 1955b, 1959, cited in Krech, Crutchfield, and Ballachey, 1962) was able to predict with considerable accuracy (a correlation of $+.90$) the voting behavior of people of varying social class memberships in San Francisco in the election of 1954 which concerned a number of local and state political propositions. Through his surveys he found that given community areas were quite stable as places where people of given social strata would live. Some living areas were "high quality" or exclusive, others comprised mainly less educated, skilled and semiskilled workers, and still others were made up of ethnic and racial minorities living in crowded and segregated neighborhoods. *De facto* segregation of ethnic and racial groups in residential areas

---

* (From *Social Psychology* by Roger Brown, Copyright © 1965 by The Free Press.)

and in school communities is all too well known today to dispute. To name some of the personality-relevant differences that have been found between the social classes, people who grow up in different sections will probably be exposed to and develop personalities built from different values and attitudes toward sex typing, education, psychiatry, premarital and extramarital sex, masturbation, religion, and liberal versus conservative political thought, and have different degrees of access to medical and psychiatric attention and hence different life expectancies.

What about barriers to social interaction produced by social stratification? Studies have shown that voluntary social relationships such as friendship and marriage have tended to follow social class lines. For example, the social activities of 199 men in Cambridge, Massachusetts were studied by Kahl and Davis (1955). Each participant was asked to name his three best friends. The social class (based on occupational levels) of all those named was then examined and compared with that of each informant. Those who were named as friends were generally in the same social class as the person naming them. In similar research, Hollingshead (1949) studied high-school students who were linked together in social cliques and found that they were usually of the same social class. For example, among the students who dated, sixty-one percent belonged to the same social class and thirty-five percent to immediately adjacent classes. Only four percent were two classes apart. Hollingshead also showed that in New Haven, Connecticut, where his surveys were conducted, marriages generally were within the same or adjacent classes. Although these studies are fairly old, there is no reason to assume that the relationship between social class and social interaction is different today.

Of all the life-style variations associated with social class membership, perhaps the most interesting and important concerns the manner in which children are reared, since to be preserved, class variations must be passed on to subsequent generations through *childrearing* patterns. Noticeable class-based differences in childrearing have been found. These first came to the forefront following publication of a study by Davis and Havighurst (1946) which was based on data obtained in 1940. They found that middle-class parents were considerably stricter with their children than lower-class parents were. The specific childrearing practices surveyed by these researchers reflected great interest in weaning and toilet training as a result of the impact of the Freudian theory of psychosexual development (see chapter 6). Among other things, Davis and Havighurst observed that middle-class parents weaned their children and began toilet training earlier than lower-class parents did.

The findings reported from Davis and Havighurst's research and those of others were believed for a time to reflect stable social class differences in childrearing. Then, over fifteen years later, Sears, Maccoby, and Levin (1957) reported the opposite, that middle-class mothers in Boston were actually more permissive toward their children than lower-class mothers were. What appeared to be a contradiction in findings was reconciled subsequently by Bronfenbrenner (1958) who suggested that the childrearing practices originally noted by Davis and Havighurst actually had changed over the ensuing years. He cited, for example, the content analysis by Wolfenstein (1953) of a bulletin on childrearing practices entitled *Infant Care,* published by the U. S. Children's Bureau from 1929 through 1938. In the 1930s, there had been great emphasis on regularity and the tendency to feed and arrange sleep times for the child by the clock. The dominant attitude was that one should never yield to the baby's resistance or demands, and that the parent must win out over the child in the struggle for domination. But in the next decade, middle-class attitudes toward the child had totally changed. The child was now viewed as engaging in a valuable and harmless effort to explore the world and was regarded as needing mainly benevolent attention and care. Parents were advised to give in to the child's demands in order to make him or her less demanding later. The attitude had shifted from one of severity and rigidity to one of permissiveness and flexibility.

Why had the social class differences originally observed by Davis and Havighurst also changed? The answer is not clear. The inference made by Bronfenbrenner is that the literate and educated middle-class mothers and fathers of the 1930s and early 1940s had been strongly influenced by the mass media and the books written by professionals in mental health and child care. It was largely the educated middle-class parents who read these publications, an example of which is the tremendously popular book by Benjamin Spock, *Baby and Child Care,* which epitomized the relaxed attitude toward raising children. This does not explain, however, why professional workers changed their view of childrearing or whether they were even responsible for the change among laypeople. Perhaps the middle-class professional members of society merely went along with the dominant and changing social view. In any event, there had been a shift in the middle-class value system, a shift perhaps reflected today in the fact that deviant youth groups, such as hippies and political activists, seem to come mainly from the relatively affluent middle-class rather than from lower-class society. The influence of the "Protestant ethnic," which emphasizes discipline, self-control, and the postponement of gratification, had greatly weakened among the middle-class, post-Depression, post-World War II children. As for the lower classes, it is possible that they have not yet caught up with the middle class. That is, the lower classes have absorbed the original middle-class standards of yesteryear (of the 1920s) and have not yet cast them off as the middle-class has done. And they still are trying to gain the economic and social advantages taken for granted by the ensuing generations of the middle class.

In the modern era when communication of standards has tended to shift from magazines and books, which require high literacy and education, to television, which brings essentially similar messages about childrearing to middle-class and lower-class parents alike, the social class differences just noted may disappear altogether. It also is possible that the same leveling process could occur across cultures as they become less isolated from each other (e.g., television via satellite and McDonald's in France), thus reducing the bond between culture and personality, too.

It is tempting here to ask the question about the relative superiority of permissiveness or authoritative approaches to childrearing, but the answer would require an analysis of the valued qualities of personality, as well as more information about the effects of these approaches on personality. There is no scarcity of opinion. For example, it has been alleged that the types of mild psychopathology seen in clinics have shifted from mainly neuroses in Freud's day to mainly character disorders today; the implication being that the shift from strong authority to permissiveness in childrearing has been responsible. But these statements are based on rather casual impressions rather than on hard data.

Nevertheless, the question is of great interest to the layperson and to researchers in child development. For example, Diana Baumrind and A. E. Black (1967) at the Institute of Human Development of the University of California have reported results from an eight-year study of three groups of nursery school children. They found that the most warm and permissive parents produced children who were the least self-reliant, exploratory, and self-controlled. On the other hand, the children of authoritarian parents were discontented, withdrawn, and distrustful. Children from a middle group, whose parents were controlling and demanding (Baumrind called this authoritative), yet also warm, rational, and receptive to the child, proved to be the most self-reliant, exploratory, self-controlled, and content with themselves and in their relationships with others. It would appear that neither extreme of authoritarianism or permissiveness results in the actualization of many of our positively valued traits of personality. Studies along these lines offer some promise of establishing through empirical data the childrearing practices that promote those personality traits we most highly value, regardless of their association with a given social class. In any event, it begins to be clear that childrearing patterns within social class groups are not at all rigidly fixed.

Consideration of childrearing practices as a function of social-class variables illustrates another point, of great importance to the social scientist, concerning the levels of analysis dealt with by different disciplines in theory and research. Social class is essentially a sociological variable, that is, it deals with the manner in which societies of people are organized rather than with individuals per se. The point becomes clearer if we consider for a moment how social-class membership might affect personality development. Social class is an aspect of the social system, and it is only at the points at which membership confronts and affects the individual person that we can understand its psychological impact. If the behaviors of parents do not differ as a function of social class, or if the individual's experience does not differ if he or she belongs to one or another social class, then social system variables such as social class have no psychological implications. Childrearing practices are an important dimension of developmental social influences because the social experiences of individual children are the social basis of personality formation. Social classes are of interest to psychologists because persons growing up within them are likely to be influenced in predictable ways, although not all parents are affected in the same way by these variables. It is the individual parent's behavior toward the child that in the final analysis is one of the critical social variables of developmental social influence. This problem of levels of analysis has been explicated most effectively by Smelser and Smelser (1963). The core of the problem of developmental social influences is to be able to identify past experiences of the individual person, whatever they may be and however they may be related to the social structure, that help to produce a given personality which in turn reacts in the present to a social event.

Mechanisms of Developmental Social Influence

The key idea is very simple—the person acquires through social experience the norms or standards of the society in which he or she lives. For example, the child growing up in a middle-class family in the 1920s and 1930s is likely to have had very different experiences with discipline than a child growing up in the same era in a lower-class family had. Or, a black child will have a very different set of experiences leading to the development of a self-concept than a white child will. Not only does each of us grow up in a particular culture and subculture (including social classes, ethnic groups, regions, and urban or rural settings), but each person has a particular set of parents; every child's family will have its own distinctive characteristics as a social unit. To complicate things, even the parental family unit is a combination of two distinct people, the father and the mother, each with a unique personality and value system. It is no wonder that each person becomes a distinctive individual like no one else, even while ignoring individual differences in biological makeup. We need to know the rules by which such variations produce distinctive individuals, and the idea that we acquire the standards of the setting in which we live is too general to allow us to understand the process of social influence on personality development.

There are two main psychological mechanisms proposed by theorists which concern the socialization of the child. In both cases, the child's parents are the primary agents since they are usually the main adults in contact with the child at the early critical stages of personality development. However, the mechanisms apply equally well to any social figures with whom the child has a close functional relationship. One mechanism emphasizes the learning principle of reinforcement; the second assumes some form of identification in which the person takes over the attitudes and behavior patterns of someone else. We shall discuss each separately. (For a detailed review of these mechanisms, see Mischel, 1970).

Socialization through reinforcement-learning. In its more general form, *socialization through reinforcement learning* is a principle stating that we learn whatever directly results in the reduction of tension or pain or the production of satisfaction. The values and behavior patterns of parents and other significant adults are said to be acquired by the child because these adults systematically use rewards and punishments to shape the behavior and attitudes of their children. Earlier we saw a social analogy of this sort of reinforcing power relationship in the experiment by Schachter (1951) on the manner in which a social group punishes an individual for being deviant.

The theoretical principle of reinforcement has been more important to and probably has had more support among psychologists over the past half-century or so than has any other method of explaining learning and development. When an animal is rewarded for making certain responses, there is an increasing tendency for it to continue to make that response again in the same context. Likewise, when a person is rewarded for behavior by things he or she wants, such as money, praise, or good grades, the tendency to do whatever it was that led to the reward in the first place is increased. Conversely, punishment for undesired behavior, such as speeding in one's car, making too much noise in a library, stealing, fighting, and so on, car, making too much noise in a library, stealing, fighting, and so on, tends to result in the inhibition of such behavior in the future. As a very general rule of thumb, our behavior is indeed controlled by whether or not we anticipate that it will be followed by a positive condition of tension-reduction or a negative condition of pain or harm. One of the clearest formulations of this principle was offered *Learning and Imitation*. A modern version may be found in Aronfreed (1968). Reinforcement in the shaping of behavior also is emphasized today by psychologists interested in behavior modification, a point of view exemplified in well-known texts of abnormal behavior and personality by Ullmann and Krasner (1969) and Krasner and Ullmann (1973)—cf. chapter 7.

The effects of punishment in "stamping out" responses, however, are far from simple or clear, even in simpler organisms such as the rat and the pigeon, and reinforcement adherents who have dealt with complex situations by no means adopt a single-minded conception of its role in the development of personality. Its effects are clearly dependent on the conditions under which reinforcement has taken place and the complex mix of variables to which the person is exposed in any new situation. Although reinforcement is of great importance in guiding human behavior and in the development of personality, it has become increasingly evident that, because it was the only major principle for so long, it has been considerably overextended as the basis of learning (cf. chapter 5).

A particularly good example of the insufficiency of a simple reinforcement principle may be observed in efforts to train persons to control aggression. The outcomes of these efforts are sometimes contrary to expectation. For example, reinforcement-learning principles imply that the parent who severely and consistently punishes a child for aggressive acts will eventually stamp out the undesirable behavior. Nevertheless, it has been observed that delinquents and criminals are likely to have physically cruel, rejecting parents and to have been subjected to much punishment in their childhoods. Punishment alone has not stamped out their aggressiveness and deviancy—quite the contrary. Sheldon and Eleanor Glueck (1950) earlier suggested that delinquents were unimpressed with punishment because they had had so much experience with it from their rejecting parents. And more recent detailed studies of the family backgrounds of delinquents, by William and Joan McCord (1956, 1958), provide further evidence that violently aggressive delinquents have typically been severely rejected by their parents and often brutally beaten. This retention of the pattern of aggressive disobedience in these boys, despite frequent and severe punishment, is embarrassing to a strict and exclusive application of the reinforcement-learning point of view and suggests that other forms of learning (e.g., by imitation) must be involved.

Brown makes this point in the following passage:

> Parents who beat their children for aggression intend to "stamp out" the aggression. The fact that the treatment does not work as intended suggests that the implicit learning theory is wrong. A beating may be rewarded as an instance of the behavior it is supposed to stamp out. If children are more disposed to learn by imitation or example than by "stamping out" they ought to learn from a beating to beat. This seems to be roughly what happens (1965, pp. 394-95).*

The effects of punishment probably depend greatly on a host of other factors as well, such as its consistency, the joint use of reward when appropriate behavior occurs, the attitude (e.g., love or hate) with which it is given, the belief by the child that his or her actions can or cannot control the occurrence of the rewards or punishments (e.g., nothing the child does seems to make any difference), the values of peers toward the infraction, whether the object of the punishment is a boy or girl, and so on. The complexity of the problem of childhood discipline and of its effects is apt to be unrecognized by the layperson but is emphasized by many writers in the field of child development who have reviewed the research evidence (e.g., Becker, 1964).

Socialization through identification. The basic idea in *socialization through identification* is that we acquire behavior patterns and values after seeing them in others and imitating or modeling them. Various terms have been used to refer to this type of process, such as identification, internalization, introjection, modeling, socialization, and observational learning (of chapter 7).

It is important to recognize that copying someone else's behavior or values can be done with varying degrees of attitudinal involvement. Social psychologist Herbert Kelman (1961) has suggested several degrees of involvement with "compliance" representing the weakest and "internalization" representing the strongest. For example, we can act in *compliance* with the values of the other person without actually adopting these values as our own. This may be done only to obtain a favorable reaction from the other, as when

* (From *Social Psychology* by Roger Brown, Copyright © 1965 by The Free Press.)

the attitude being expressed is privately disputed or when we laugh at a joke without thinking it funny. In *internalization,* another's influence is accepted and made one's own because it is intrinsically rewarding to do so.

When Freud spoke about identification, he meant an unconscious acceptance of the parent's values, with these becoming a deeply ingrained part of the person's own system of values. The term identification or internalization usually implies more than a "skin-deep" acquisition or show of behavior. Rather, it is an acceptance of the behavior as one's own, sometimes without the recognition that it is being done.

There are four variations of the identification principle referring to different theoretical bases on which the process rests:

1. The identification is said to take place according to the *similarity* of the person to the object of identification. Thus, in the Freudian system, the boy normally takes on the values of the father (and conversely the girl takes on those of her mother) partly because of the boy's perceived similarity to the father—he is marked by everyone as a boy who will ultimately take over the father's role—and he perceives his sexual similarity to the father as being masculine (e.g., having a penis) rather than feminine. Freud attempted in this way to explain not only the mechanism underlying the adoption of the moral values of the parents but also to explain sex typing, that is, the tendency of the boy to adopt a masculine role and the girl to adopt a feminine role. (cf. Kohlberg's, 1966, views on cognitive developmental principles mentioned later in this chapter.)

2. Identification is considered to be based on *envy* of the possession of the good things of life. In effect, the child is more apt to identify with those adults who are thought to possess or consume the important things of life.

3. Identification is thought to be based on the *power to control* the disposition of the good things of life.

4. Identification is based on the need to *neutralize threat* from some powerful person. This is the form of identification which was emphasized most in Freudian theory and has been referred to by such psychoanalytically oriented writers as Bruno Bettelheim (1960) as "identification with the aggressor." As we shall see in chapter 6, according to Freud's psychosexual theory the boy represses his sexual (Oedipal) urges toward the mother and his hostility toward the competitor-father in order to avoid the danger of castration. In doing so, he internalizes the father's values, becoming like him. This process of *identification with the aggressor* in Freudian theory is the basis for the formation of the superego or conscience. Bettelheim gives some remarkable examples of identification with the aggressor in the behavior of concentration camp inmates during World War II, and Elkins (1961) suggests the same sort of mechanism for the American Negro slave. This identification forms one of the meanings underlying the expression, "Uncle Tom." It implies the adoption (perhaps unconscious) of the white man's values by the black in an effort to curry favor or feel secure in the white man's world. This variation of identification stems from the powerlessness of the person (the child, the concentration- or prison-camp inmate exposed to "brainwashing,"

and the Negro slave) that makes him or her feel too threatened to express any individuality. Crucial to this sort of mechanism is absolute control by the powerful parent figure over rewards and punishments.

In recent years a growing number of studies have been designed to compare some of the alternative mechanisms of socialization which have been mentioned above. One of the most exhaustive experiments was performed by Bandura, Ross, and Ross (1963), who created four kinds of models for identification, each representing a slightly different basis of identification. One adult model controlled a wonderful collection of toys, another adult was the fortunate recipient of them, a third model was a child who watched without getting anything, and a fourth model was a child who received the toys just as in the case of the second adult. Each of the models was made to perform actions which could be easily imitated, and the experimenters observed which model was copied by the child. It was found that the subjects (all children) imitated mainly the adult who controlled the toys, rather than the other models. Thus, it would seem that control over resources rather than possession or consumption of them served as the basis of imitation or modeling in this experiment. Although imitation and identification may not be equivalent concepts, perhaps some of the same conditions underlie both.

Other research has attempted to compare the relative potency of reward and punishment compared with identification in the control of behavior. The data are as yet too limited to permit very definite conclusions and in all probability, both identification and reinforcement mechanisms are involved in most life situations. The complex character of the mechanisms underlying socialization is summarized well in a statement by social psychologist Roger Brown:

> Parents can affect the behavior, the conduct of children in at least two ways: by direct reward or punishment and by providing a model for imitation. It now looks as if power were the prime factor making a model attractive for imitation though such factors as nurturance and vicarious rewards may also be important. With two parents to manifest power and administer direct reward and punishment there are many possible kinds of family pattern, many kinds of learning problems presented to children. For some kinds of behavior, for example speaking the local language, all forces work in the same direction. Both parents model English and both reward for it. For some kinds of behavior the pattern will be complex, for example assertiveness. Perhaps father manifests considerable assertiveness and has more power in the family than his non-assertive wife. Perhaps both parents reward assertiveness in their son and not in their daughter. Both children might be expected to try out being assertive on the model of their

impressive father and the son's performance would be confirmed by approval but the daughter's would not be. Does the daughter perhaps retain a desire to behave assertively, a latent identification with her male parent, that leads her to try out assertiveness in new groups where the reinforcement program may be different? Learning by identification is certainly a complex geometry and it is likely that what we now know is not more than the rudiments (1965, p. 401).*

SPECIAL APPLICATION: SOCIALIZATION AND SEX TYPING

Our discussion of developmental social influence so far has largely neglected an extremely important issue: Do personality differences exist between males and females in our society and if so, to what extent are social influences responsible for such differences? Because personologists recently have devoted considerable attention to investigations of psychological sex differences, and because male-female roles may be changing and are the subject of much attention, it would be useful to survey some of the major findings and relate them to the problems discussed in this chapter. The development of "sex-appropriate" behaviors will be discussed in later chapters, too (e.g., see chapter 6).

Although personologists and others have been interested in the psychology of sex differences for some time, the field has been plagued by myths and stereotypes, as well as by inadequate research and theories (see Williams, 1977). For example, personality researchers, often viewing potential differences between the sexes as a nuisance, traditionally have conducted their studies with subjects from only one sex (usually males)—thus leaving us with very little useful knowledge of psychological sex differences, of women, or of personality in general (Babladelis, 1977; Carlson, 1971). Moreover, theorists, particularly those favoring the influential Freudian viewpoint, have long attempted to explain personality from a masculine perspective, thus seeming to equate "male behaviors" with "normality." This often has led theorists and therapists alike to view women, a priori, as inadequate or abnormal if they show "male-oriented" qualities (Broverman and coworkers, 1970; Chesler, 1972).

Perhaps because of the feminist movement, personologists seem more concerned today in exploring psychological differences between men and women, with the hope of developing a more effec-

* (From *Social Psychology* by Roger Brown, Copyright © 1965 by The Free Press.)

tive understanding of human personality and potential. A thirst for more empirical information about women has emerged as seen in the recent appeal for women's courses on campus and the influx of relevant books (e.g., Bardwick, 1971; O'Leary, 1977; Sherman, 1971; Williams, 1977) and journals (e.g., *Psychology of Women Quarterly, Sex-Roles,* and *Signs*). One only can hope that this current interest in the "psychology of women" will lead to a better comprehension of personality in *both* men and women.

PERSONALITY DIFFERENCES BETWEEN THE SEXES. It seems that all cultures have certain assumptions about appropriate and inappropriate sex-role behaviors for males and females, though particular cultures may have beliefs which are quite divergent from those in other cultures (Kagan, in Janis, Mahl, Kagan, & Holt, 1969; Mead, 1935). These sex-role standards greatly influence the psychological development of each sex. Kagan notes that:

> Most of the psychological differences between adult men and women are the result of these different standards for the sexes. In our culture, men are supposed to be aggressive and women dependent when attacked or frustrated. Men are expected to inhibit signs of strong fear, emotion, and weakness; women are expected to cry if stress is intense and to display their emotions overtly. Men should be interested in athletics, mechanics, science, and mathematics; women in the arts, cooking, gardening and literature (in Janis et al., 1969, p. 475).

Of course, people do not have to accept their culture's sex-role expectations, but evidence does suggest that most, if not all, individuals in our society evaluate themselves against culturally defined maleness and femaleness (Donelson, 1973). Even the most liberated among us has incorporated on some level society's sex-typing standards, largely because this kind of ideology and social influence is taught throughout our lives in a most subtle and profound way (Bem & Bem, 1970).

Over the years, a handful of researchers has tried to study various psychological processes among the sexes to determine whether differences, in fact, do exist (see Maccoby & Jacklin, 1974, for a review of these findings). Some of the processes studied have included cognitive styles, intellectual ability (including mathematical and verbal skills), sensation and perception, and self-esteem. A comprehensive discussion of the relevant (and often unexpected) findings is beyond the scope of this chapter; we would like, however, to present briefly the findings pertaining to aggression and dependency, as these personality characteristics generally are considered to be clearly sex-linked and hence have received extensive attention by personologists.

Aggression. Studies on sex-related aggression have consistently reported greater aggression (particularly of overt forms such as physical attack) in males than in females; this is true throughout the life span (beginning at about age three) and across cultures. Moreover, there is a great deal of developmental stability in aggression for males but not for females. That is, an aggressive boy is likely to become an aggressive adult while the same is not very likely of an aggressive young girl. As Kagan and Moss (1962) have noted:

> The pattern of social rewards and traditional sex-role standards act in concert to discourage the direct expression of aggression in girls and women. It might be anticipated, therefore, that aspects of aggression would be more stable for males than for females. This is precisely what occurred, for overt aggression to mother and frequent tantrums during childhood predicted adult aggressivity for men but not for women (p. 85).

There is substantial evidence, however, that females too are frequently aggressive, if we do not adhere to a narrow, and some would say "masculine," concept of aggression. That is, once we are willing to view acts of hostility, such as insults or withdrawing support, as aggressive in nature then females most certainly must be seen as aggressive beings (Bardwick, 1971; O'Leary, 1977). For example, Feshback (1970) reports that female first-graders are more likely than their male counterparts to reject or exclude a newcomer from their group, regardless of the newcomer's sex.

In general, then, although males are more likely to display aggressive behaviors than females, females are not the totally nonaggressive people often portrayed by some researchers and popular stereotypes. It seems that although females learn overt forms of aggression, they rapidly develop strong inhibitions (often associated with guilt and anxiety) against the display of direct aggression; they learn that such aggression would not be appropriate to their traditional sex-role pattern (Bandura, 1973). But females are aggressive in many ways, and future research must attempt to measure different kinds of aggression. As Bardwick (1971) notes:

> To measure the true levels of aggression in males and females one must include verbal aggression, interpersonal rejection, academic competitiveness, gossip (especially against other girls), deviation from sexual standards, passive aggression, the manipulation of adults with power, withdrawal, tears, and somatic complaints—as well as fighting, hitting, and biting (p. 134).

Dependency. Young children are dependent on others to fulfill basic needs such as hunger, thirst, safety, and warmth. As they mature, however, dependency generally is discouraged and independence is encouraged. The common stereotype is that females in our society are permitted, if not actually urged, to remain much more dependent than males, who must eschew dependency at all cost. To what extent then are there significant differences in dependency behaviors between males and females?

Dependent behaviors such as touching, clinging, attempting to get close to others, and social responsiveness imply a strong reliance of one individual on another for attention, affiliation, and nurturance (cf. Bowlby, 1969; Maccoby & Jacklin, 1974). Viewing dependency in this light, studies on sex differences have reported generally inconsistent findings, though the overall trend is that females are sometimes, but not always, more dependent than males (Mischel, 1976). An often-cited study supporting the notion that females are more dependent than males is the longitudinal research of Kagan and Moss (1962). They found considerable stability in dependency behaviors from childhood to adulthood for females but not males. In other words, dependent girls typically became dependent women and dependent boys often became independent men. Kagan and Moss suggested that society gives more freedom to females than to males regarding dependent and independent behaviors, and so it is reasonable to expect a pattern of dependent (or independent) behaviors in young girls to remain relatively constant over time. Males, on the other hand, are often punished socially for dependent behaviors once they begin school, and hence there is a potential for conflict in males over dependency. It is not surprising that many boys eventually give up their dependent behaviors for independent ones.

Despite findings like those of Kagan and Moss, many other investigators have been unable to find sex differences in selected dependent behaviors. For example, males and females generally do not seem to differ significantly in suggestibility, conformity to social pressures, clinging when young to their mothers, forming close ties with others, or seeking attention from nursery school teachers (Hollander & Marcia, 1970; Maccoby & Jacklin, 1974; Serbin, O'Leary, Kent, & Tonick, 1973).

In short, sex differences in dependent behaviors are much more difficult to substantiate than, say, sex differences in aggressive behaviors. If the stereotype about females being more dependent than males has any basis in reality, it is tenuous indeed. But, as O'Leary (1977) suggests, when females do act in a dependent fashion, they are less likely to be punished than similarly acting males.

Mechanisms.   Sex typing, and the resultant differences in behavior which often occur, may be explained in large part by the principles of socialization discussed earlier, namely, reinforcement-learning and identification. But a third principle, one we feel is highly akin to the similarity version of the principle of identification, also has been proposed to account for the emergence of sex-typed behaviors, i.e., socialization through *cognitive-developmental* processes (Kohlberg, 1966). This principle says in effect that once children are able to categorize themselves as boys or girls, they will begin to act accordingly. In other words, at some point along the path of cognitive development (roughly between ages three and seven), children learn their sexual gender as well as the rules governing gender-appropriate behaviors; they then attempt, in order to achieve a sense of consistency, to match their behaviors to the sex-role standard. Children will consequently identify with their same-sexed parents because of a perceived gender similarity.

Most likely, all three principles of socialization operate in the development of sex-typed behaviors, though any one process may assume greater importance than the others at times, depending on the circumstances and the developmental progress of the child. Williams (1977) illustrates the interrelationship of the three principles (reinforcement, identification, cognitive development) as follows:

> Consider, for example, the four-year-old girl who gets "dressed up" for a brief appearance at her parents' party. She is willing to do this because of a history of reinforcement with praise, approval, and warm compliments from adults when she "looks pretty," a harbinger of things to come. She wears a long skirt like her mother's and helps to pass the hors d'oeuvres, modeling from her mother the appropriate ways that a female behaves as a hostess. At the same time, she can see that all the other women are dressed similarly, and she can observe their tone of voice, their gestures, and the kinds of things they talk about. From this experience and numerous others like it she forms generalizations about the state of being female in her world. All three kinds of learning are occurring, each facilitating the other, to organize the child's sex-role concepts and sex-typed behavior (pp. 164-65).

Two additional points should be mentioned. First, our emphasis on the role of social factors in the development of sex-typed behaviors should not obscure the importance of biological forces. For example, as noted in chapter 2, sex hormones (like testosterone) do contribute in significant ways to aggression in infrahumans and probably in humans too. Nevertheless, bear in mind that human behavior is highly malleable and influenced by learning to a great extent. Whether a particular behavior occurs depends greatly on many social factors (including past experiences, the present situation, and the culture) as well as on biological ones.

Second, some of the current research on personality differences between the sexes has taken the position that men and women who have *both* masculine and feminine psychological characteristics may have more flexibility (psychologically and behaviorally) than individuals who are rigidly sex-typed (Bem, 1975). For example, it is possible that so-called "androgynous" individuals (those possessing both masculine and feminine traits) may meet situational demands effectively without feeling compelled to employ traditional sex-typed behaviors—i.e., they act according to the needs of the problem rather than according to stereotyped expectations. On the other hand, individuals who feel they must act in a consistently sex-typed manner regardless of the situation, probably have to suppress rigidly those aspects of their personalities not congruent with the sex-typed standard. Whether androgyny becomes eventually a gauge of mental health, as Bem speculates, or another remains still-to-be adequately researched proposal for maximizing human potentialities, it is nevertheless a fascinating and provocative concept.

REFLECTIONS: SOCIALIZATION AS PASSIVE OSMOSIS VERSUS ACTIVE DIGESTION

In recognizing how much we acquire from the social environment in which we grow up, we must not forget that only certain things are taken from any adult figure to be part of our personality, while other things are rejected or ignored. Remember that we do not emerge as identical or perhaps even similar to either of our parents. As we mature we pick up some of the values of each parent and reject others. When we say that a girl is like her mother, we are correct but we have ignored the many ways in which she is also different, and when we say a girl is different from her mother, we are also correct but we have ignored the many ways in which she is similar.

There is a very important implication in the above qualification, that is, a person is an evaluating organism, sifting through and selecting those models and attributes with which to identify. As Brown (1965) has observed, the best concept for understanding socialization may be that of active digestion, not of passive osmosis. In osmosis, one tissue passively soaks up the substance on the other side of a semipermeable membrane, as a sponge soaks up fluid. There is no judgment and little selectivity involved in the process, only an automatic absorption of that which can pass through the membrane filter when the pressure is greater on one side than the other. In digestion, some things are accepted and transformed or altered by the system through catabolic processes; other things are rejected, depending on whether they fit the requirements imposed by the biochemistry of the substance and are capable of the metabolic transformations produced by the enzyme action. In the socialization of the person, the parental or societal values are not automatically absorbed but are selectively dealt with, and very little about how this actually works is known.

The latter model of socialization, implying evaluation and selection, was mentioned briefly in our discussion of sex typing and is rather clearly implied in the work of Piaget (1948) and his followers (e.g., Kohlberg, 1963) on the acquisition of morality. In the young child, moral concepts are at first rigidly and quite passively drawn from parents and other adult authorities. This rigidity corresponds to the relatively primitive, sensori-motor stage in the development of adaptive intelligence (see chapter 6). Piaget has shown how pre-adolescent children follow strictly the "rules of the game" as laid down by adults even when it would make more sense to do otherwise. Wrongdoing is seen literally as the violation of rules rather than in terms of intentions, abstract justice, or the objectives of the game.

Beyond about eight or so years of age, the child's conception of morality becomes increasingly psychological rather than objective, relative rather than absolute, and capable of being modified on the basis of group decision. This change in the process of socialization corresponds to the growing emphasis on conceptual rather than concrete, stimulus-centered forms of thought. The person becomes increasingly a thinking, judging individual, actively searching for useful principles, rather than a passive receiver of what the culture imposes. Increasingly, the individual becomes capable of picking and choosing those things with which to identify and those things to reject.

One wonders to what extent the values a person has acquired more or less passively in the early stages of development remain as permanent, unconscious "gut reactions" and are merely overlaid with the more rational and flexible qualities that Freud called secondary process thinking, and Piaget referred to as conceptual modes of thought. Psychologists commonly make the distinction between the primitive, or developmentally early layers of mental activity, and the more advanced and later ones. Whether basic identifications formed early in life are ever lost, or ever cease to influence our adaptive life, is not very clear. The idea that they are not lost is one of the cornerstones of the psychoanalytic approach to psychopathology. The current vogue of seeking contact with the more primitive and inaccessible aspects of one's experience through drugs or Dionysian forms of therapy or group activity, as in Esalon and Synanon, stems from this assumption of two levels of psychological functioning—the impulsive, primitive, and unconscious, and the controlled, rational, and surface mental life. It is argued that the search for understanding oneself requires contact with this primitive portion of one's mental life. The process of identification may involve both of these levels of mental activity, each operating in accordance with somewhat different rules.

In this chapter we have seen how social influence works in two areas of psychological functioning, contemporaneously and over the developmental life history of the person. These are not separate and independent problems, since the mechanisms of immediate social influence not only operate at each moment but also help us account for the formative processes that shape the personality over the long run. For example, the processes of identification and of reinforcement are undoubtedly occurring in the person in each social situation. These same processes, taking place over the person's life span, comprise a cumulative story of social experience that has produced the individual's particular personality. Once the personality begins to be established, then along with contemporaneous social influences, it too affects the person's social action and reaction. The latter two sets of influence, the social situation and the personality structure, are crucial determinants of the person's behavior from the very first moment that the personality begins to form. The study of one is incomplete without consideration of the other.

BIOLOGICAL VERSUS SOCIAL DETERMINANTS: THE PRINCIPLE OF INTERACTION

As noted earlier, it is misleading to think of biological and social factors as independent determinants of personality. They have been treated as separate entities in chapters 2 and 3 for the sake of convenience but in reality these determinants interact in complex ways, as we have suggested frequently (cf. discussions of intelligence or sex typing). Yet, interestingly enough, personality theorists clearly differ in the relative emphasis they give to biological or social (cultural) factors, and thus their theories can be compared along a biology-social continuum. Some points of view, in other words, grant heavy weighting to the biological givens and their role in shaping personality and adjustment, while others, at the other end of the continuum, virtually ignore biological forces and stress the role of experience and the structure of the society (e.g., see chapters 5 and 7).

Freud, for example, took a position very close to the biology pole of the biology-social continuum. Psychosexual stages of development (see chapter 6) were seen clearly as biologically determined, universal patterns to be found regardless of the social system in which they occurred. Social systems themselves, in fact, were seen as outgrowths of these biological forces (see chapter 5). It was not the child's experience which motivated the transition through the sequence of developmental stages—such shifts were the products of biological maturation, and the developmental sequence was presumably a product of the hereditary genes of the species.

This strong biological emphasis was rejected or modified by other theorists of the "neo-Freudian" tradition (e.g., Erikson, Fromm, Horney, Adler). Although the neo-Freudians have accepted the idea of biological givens, these were expressed in social terms; for example, the need for autonomy, belonging, identity, and relatedness. In most neo-Freudian works, in fact, the list of basic human needs tends to be expressed more in interpersonal terms than in tissue-centered or biological terms. Thus, although they did not disregard biological givens, those givens were clearly oriented to social existence.

Even greater emphasis on the social origins of personality is found among those sociologists and social psychologists who stress the concept of *social role;* these theorists exhibit little interest in the native biological conditions emphasized so much by Freud and to some extent by the neo-Freudians. Very close to the social pole of the biology-social continuum, social role theorists view the fundamental units of analysis of personality as the interactions of people and the effects of these interactions on the development of the person. Such relationships are largely governed by the organized social roles of the culture. That is, institutions prescribe how a person must behave (role patterns) and should regard himself or herself.

Despite the frequent tendency to see personality determination as being either biological or social in nature, many feel the issue should not be stated so simplistically, as an either-or position. Even in lower animals, instinctual behaviors that were once thought of as invariant and fully determined by neurological and hormonal mechanisms turn out to be quite dependent on both biological processes *and* environmental controls (e.g., see Lehrman's, 1964, description of the ring dove's reproductive behavior cycle). All organisms are influenced by a constant interaction between biological and social forces, with both kinds of forces affecting behavior. At the human level, the newborn child arrives in the social world with a considerable assortment of temperamental characteristics or dispositions which influence how the social environment will react to him or her; and in turn, the social environment affects the manner in which the biological maturation will take place. For example, an excitable, irritable infant may be an exhilarating experience for an energetic parent, but a source of intense annoyance and stress for the lethargic parent. Conversely, the lethargic child might bore the former parent, but not the latter; or such a child might need the kind of stimulation which the energetic parent could give. And the irritable child might profit better from parental handling which screens and protects it from overstimulation. In all probability, such parental reactions brought into being by the child's inherent characteristics will act in turn on the child in molding his or her development.

Such *interactions* suggest the limited scope of an analysis of personality which is based on an either-or point of view concerning biological and social determinants. In the discussion of biological factors one must bear in mind that half of the story of the determination of personality is being neglected; and in the discussion of social factors, one must remember too that such determinants always operate in the context of a particular biological system. The only valid reason for separating them is for convenience and simplicity of presentation.

Having surveyed the nature of personality and some of its biological and social determinants, it is appropriate now to discuss in detail specific issues and theories of personality. In chapter 4, we shall examine several approaches to the description of personality.

Personality
Description

A fundamental task of personality theory is to *describe* the structures of the system with which it is dealing (see chapter 1). A descriptive language is required which enables the creation of a psychological portrait of people in general and of a given person in particular. Though much of our earlier discussions concerned personality description, we did not label or emphasize it as such or treat it in a systematic manner. For example, our listing of Jay's characteristics in chapter 1 (e.g., shy and intelligent, was an informal, common-sense attempt at describing her personality structures. Let us turn now to several theoretical and more formal approaches to personality description, keeping in mind that not all theorists emphasize the description of personality structures—a fact we shall discuss later in this chapter.

How the basic structures of personality might be set forth can be illustrated by reviewing Freud's (1949, 1961) thoughts on the matter. He conceived of personality as a *tripartite* arrangement, consisting of three major structures or subsystems, the "id," "ego," and "superego," each with its own special characteristics. Somewhat oversimplified, the *id* comprises the internal drive or motive forces, the *ego* operates the controlling and adaptive properties, and the *superego* is concerned with the moral values and ideals which are internalized from culture and family (in effect, conscience). Normally, these three structures operate together under the leadership of the ego (not without considerable conflict, however) to ensure the person's survival and well-being. As you might well assume, the id, ego, and superego have been regarded often as the biological, psychological, and social components of personality.

Freud's conception of the structures of personality has become perhaps the most common way of thinking about the various "parts" of the system. This is not because everyone who uses these terms adopts the Freudian view in every detail, but because in this system are all the general components of personality recognized as important, that is, drives or motives, controlling and adaptive structures, and the internalized moral values which are the product of socialization. Used in such a general way, the terms id, ego, and superego become neutralized, so to speak, from the specific ways in which Freud used them in his theory of dynamics and development. When used as originally intended by Freud, each of these subsystems is viewed as operating and developing according to the theoretical assumptions of Freudian theory. However, to most psychologists and laypeople outside the Freudian context, id, ego, and superego have become merely an eclectic, shorthand way of referring to fundamental structures and functions of personality. Since many theoretical systems employ these terms without necessarily implying all that Freud meant by them, if one hears the word id, ego, or superego, it may be necessary to ask whether it is being used in the Freudian sense or in some other way.

A good example of the confusing use of the same term to connote something different may be found in Carl Jung's personality theory, which overlaps Freud's, but also is quite different in important ways. Jung was one of the early group of innovators around Freud who later quarreled with him and went his separate theoretical way. Jung used the term "ego" to refer to processes that were entirely conscious, while Freud emphasized that the ego's activities were at times unconscious. By sometimes using the same terms having different meanings, and sometimes using different terms having the same meaning, personality theorists unintentionally have created widespread confusion among both laypeople and professionals.

Many personality theorists have discarded the tripartite concept of the structure of personality in part or altogether. Though Jung (1916) thought of personality as basically consisting of three structures (the ego, personal unconscious, and collective unconscious), he also emphasized the concept of the "self" as an emergent structure which eventually (in later life) harmonizes the other conflicting parts. The concept of *self* today is found in a number of theories as the central unit of personality; for example, those of Carl Rogers (1951, 1961), Abraham Maslow (1968, 1970), and Kurt Goldstein (1940), each of whom has presented overlapping and influential theories of personality. In these theories, the individual is described and understood by gaining access to his or her "self-concept" (ideally, a flexible, changing perception of personal identity), which is believed to play a major and determining role in the person's behavior.* Still a different picture of personality structure was offered by Otto Rank (1952) who, like Jung, was one of the original group of thinkers with Freud in the early days of psychoanalysis. Rank also left the Freudian movement to establish a system of his own. He abandoned the tripartite division of personality and substituted the elements of *will* and *counterwill* which were in perpetual conflict, mobilized by the fear of separation and the opposing fear of loss of identity. The outcome of this struggle was expressed in the emergence of a personality fitting one of three types: the "average man," "neurotic man," or "artist."

It is evident that there are many ways to describe personality structure, each arising from some particular conception of human nature. The above examples by no means exhaust those which have been tried. It takes little imagination to foresee that each version will result in quite different, concrete descriptions. Moreover, within each broad category of structure—such as id, ego, superego, self, self-concept, or will—is a variety of more specific attributes which must be considered to fill out the bare bones of the system. To do this one finds two basic kinds of language used, the language of traits and of types.

THE LANGUAGE OF TRAITS

The simplest and most traditional way of describing a person is to identify characteristic patterns of behavior and then to label them with trait names. "Traits" are dispositional concepts which refer to *tendencies* to act or react in certain ways. Psychological dispositions

---

* The concept of *self*, like that of ego, is used rather differently by many theorists. For example, some refer to the self as a person's evaluation of himself or herself (*self-as-object*), and others see it as what a person does, like thinking, remembering, and perceiving (*self-as-process*). Personologists, unfortunately, often use these self-concepts interchangeably or inconsistently and sometimes bewilder their readers (see Hall & Lindzey, 1978).

are presumably "carried around" by the person from situation to situation and imply a certain likelihood of behaving in some given way.* Traits must be distinguished from "state" concepts which refer to a reaction which is taking place *now*. For example, we usually mean by the statement "Jay is an anxious person," that Jay is likely to become anxious in certain situations (e.g., in which threats to her self-esteem are involved), though she is not necessarily anxious at this moment. "Jay is anxious" implies that she is anxious *now*. Having the trait of anxiety does not suggest that the person always will be in a state of anxiety, but only that he or she is highly disposed to react with anxiety in given kinds of situations.

An example of the trait-state distinction drawn from a non-psychological context might clarify this. The word "flammable" is often seen printed on the sides of petroleum trucks, though seldom do such vehicles explode. Nevertheless, the potential (or disposition) is ever present. Given the right conditions (e.g., a match or a collision), the fuel is likely to burst into flames, turning the potential into a reality (or "state" condition). Returning to personality, a trait (like shyness or aggression) does *not* mean that the person is always behaving in ways implied by the trait, but only that in certain conditions the trait is likely to influence behavior.

In terms of their contents, there are many possible kinds of traits. For example, there are: motive traits referring to the kinds of goals to which behavior is directed; ability traits referring to general and specific capacities and skills; temperamental traits, such as tendencies toward optimism, depression, and energy; and stylistic traits involving gestures and styles of behaving and thinking not functionally related to the goals of that behavior. Traits theorists have approached the task of defining trait categories quite differently. For example, although Cattell (1950) included motives within the category of traits, Murray (1938) and McClelland (1951) distinguished between traits and motives, traits involving characteristic means by which goals are attained.

Every language contains large numbers of words that define personality traits. People are described as shy, aggressive, submissive, lazy, melancholy, easy-going, ambitious, and so on. Traits may refer to surface manifestations such as aggressiveness, or to deeper or more inferential qualities such as beliefs, or capacities to control the expression of impulse. In any case, the descriptive aspects of person-

---

* Personologists conceptualize *traits* in different ways. For example, some view traits as merely descriptions of empirically stable behavior patterns, but others conceive of them as underlying determinants of behavioral consistencies and differences (e.g., like the dispositional point of view we have emphasized).

ality theory depend on a language of traits or dispositions, and each theory sets up its own terms with which to picture a specific person or people in general.

Some theoretical systems are more explicit than others in setting forth the various traits which make up the personality. Kurt Lewin (1935), for example, believed that it was a fruitless task to try to list all of the motives that impel people to action, or all the concepts that they might have about various recourses to action. The result has been that Lewin's system of personality theory never led to extensive clinical application, a major task of which is the diagnosis and description of patients suffering from various emotional and adjustive difficulties. By contrast, Henry Murray (1938) went to great pains to list and describe the basic human tendencies. Among the social motives, he listed need for achievement, for dominance, autonomy, aggression, affiliation, nurturance, and the like. As a result, those concerned with personality description in both clinics and research, were given a useful vocabulary with which to differentiate one person from another. Hence Murray's analysis stimulated the popularization among professionals of a list of traits which could be employed in personality description. The same thing occurred with Freud's ideas about psychosexual stages (oral, anal, and phallic) and his concepts of ego-defense mechanisms. The existence of a rich vocabulary of traits makes it easier for personality researchers and clinical psychologists to differentiate descriptively between one person and another.

The dean of personality trait psychology unquestionably has been Gordon Allport (1937a, 1961). Allport regarded the trait as the natural unit of description of personality, and he and Odbert (1936) examined an unabridged English dictionary finding 17,953 words designating personal forms of behavior out of a total of 400,000. This was too many to use effectively. Dropping all those which dealt with temporary mood states, those which were primarily evaluative rather than descriptive, and those which designated mainly physical rather than psychological qualities, Allport and Odbert narrowed down the list of trait names to 4,541. These were thought to make a good starting point for the study of personality. Allport then set about formalizing in theory what is part of the common-sense, intuitive approach to personality used by the layperson when the latter attempts to describe someone, as in a letter of recommendation.

Allport emphasized the idea that traits are integral properties of a person, not merely part of the beholder's imagination. Here traits refer to actual neuropsychic characteristics which determine the individual's behavior. They can be identified only by observing and separating the person's central and essential qualities from the peripheral and unimportant ones. Allport also emphasized the uniqueness of every person, not only in each trait but also in the organization of these traits into an integrated whole. Allport differentiated between cardinal, central, and secondary traits. A few people are dominated by a single focus of behavior and may become known for this focus, which when it exists, exemplifies the *cardinal* trait. One example might be the legendary Don Juan, whose life style was expressed in terms of heterosexual conquest. Allport believed that usually about five to ten trait terms would describe the main characteristics which distinguish one individual from another, and he called these *central* traits. He defined *secondary* traits as attributes which are either peripheral or weak and therefore relatively unimportant in characterizing the person and his or her life style.

Two other features of Allport's view of traits also should be mentioned. One has already been considered in chapter 1 and is Allport's tendency to champion an idiographic approach to the study of personality, as opposed to the nomothetic approach. This is consistent with his emphasis on the uniqueness of a person's traits and of personality in general. The other feature is Allport's view that traits are not independent entities within a person but rather are an interdependent set of attributes which combine to produce behavioral effects. Thus, a single complex act cannot be blamed on a single trait but is always the product of a set of interdependent traits, each contributing to some aspect of the behavior. For example, many traits contribute to a person's telling a story in a social gathering. Not only are motivational traits involved, say, with entertaining others, showing off, or avoiding offense, but stylistic traits in the manner in which the story is told, say, bashfully, boringly, or expansively, play a role too. The traits of a person combine to form a coherent cluster, an interrelated way of life, an organized whole. This structure is contained in the single concept of the self, or "proprium" as Allport referred to it.

The proprium (Allport, 1955) concerns all the particular characteristics belonging to the person, including one's body image, one's sense of self-identity, self-esteem, self-extension, rational thinking, knowing, and the like. These individual functions develop over the life span of the individual. The proprium or self, in Allport's analysis of personality, is used adjectivally as a concept which acknowledges the importance of qualities such as self-esteem and self-concept, without grouping these qualities into a "little man within the man" which governs behavior. This "man within the man" is often implied in personality theory, seeming to be an explanation for behavior, when it really is an example of the circular device of naming instead of explaining. Circular explanations beg the question "Who or what tells the little man within the man what to do?" The concept of self, or proprium as Allport labeled it, is not an entity governing behavior and separate from everything else but a term for a group of important intimate functions which distinguish the person from all others.

If Allport is the dean of trait theory, then Raymond Cattell must be one of its main architects and engineers, because Cattell's (1950) main effort has been directed toward systematically reducing the list of personality traits to a manageably small number through a statistical method called "factor analysis." This method analyzes the intercorrelations among personality-relevant behaviors elicited by a wide variety of observational and test methods, determines which personality measures go together and which do not, and serves as the basis of inferences about the factors which underlie the observed pattern of covariation.

Cattell illustrates the approach with a pattern of measures we can easily understand. Suppose, for example, we measure the ability of a group of college students to do four things, use calculus, understand the subject of physics, play football, and ice-skate. As we might expect, when these four abilities are correlated with each other, those who do well in calculus are found also to do well in physics, and those who do well in football also skate well; but performance in the academic subjects turns out to have little or no relationship to performance in the physical sports. Factor analysis would reveal two factors or source traits underlying this matrix of intercorrelations, one which might be called "mathematical and science ability," the other "athletic ability." Naturally, in the case cited, the existence of the two factors which sum up the intercorrelations of the four variables or trait elements is so obvious that the computation of factor analysis would hardly be necessary. However, if the correlation matrix contained many variables, comprising dozens of personality tests, then the statistical computations of factor analysis would be necessary to analyze effectively the pattern of interrelationships and reveal the various factors that could explain it.

Cattell (1965) has pointed out that if one takes a few hundred young men or women and arranges to have them rated by people who know them well on sixty different trait elements, from about twelve to twenty independent factors or "source" traits can be identified by factor analysis. Tests then can be devised to assess these factors. Cattell has developed a questionnaire for this purpose which he calls the 16 P.F. Questionnaire, because it is designed to measure the sixteen source traits which he thinks can account for the most important trait elements in personality. Table 3 illustrates the sixteen factors or source traits. They are presented here to suggest the substantive content of the most important source traits of personality as seen by one distinguished researcher in this field.

The methods in this statistical process and the issues surrounding its use need not concern us here. Suffice it to say that factor analysis as employed by Cattell and others is one method of attempting to determine the basic trait sources of personality variation. This analysis then can be used in personality description and the evolution of personality theory. Cattell's approach to personality description and his working assumptions about personality turn out to be quite different from those of Allport. Although both use the language of traits, they each conceive of and investigate personality quite differently.

Trait Research: Locus of Control

As a prototype of trait research, let us examine one of the currently most investigated personality dispositions, the *locus of control dimension* (see reviews by Lefcourt, 1966, 1976; Rotter, 1966, 1971; Rotter, Chance, & Phares, 1972). This dimension, thought to be a relatively stable personality characteristic, refers to an individual's *belief* that rewards or reinforcements result from personal actions and skills (internal locus of control) or from factors outside of oneself (external locus of control). As Rotter (1966) has stated:

> When a reinforcement is perceived by the subject as following some action of his own but not being entirely contingent upon his action, then, in our culture, it is typically perceived as the result of luck, chance, fate, as under the control of powerful others, or as unpredictable because of the great complexity of the forces surrounding him. When the event is interpreted in this way by an individual, we have labeled this a belief in *external control*. If the person perceives that the event is contingent upon his own behavior or his own relatively permanent characteristics, we have termed this a belief in *internal control*. (p. 261)

Rotter (1966) and his colleagues developed a twenty-nine-item, forced-choice questionnaire (the I-E Scale) to measure the locus of control dimension. Each item consists of a pair of alternatives, and the task requires subjects to pick the alternative (*a* or *b*) which they most believe to be true for themselves. Scores on the questionnaire

Table 3

Sixteen Factors or Source Traits and Their Descriptions

FACTOR	LOW SCORE DESCRIPTION	HIGH SCORE DESCRIPTION
A	*Reserved,* detached, critical, aloof, stiff Sizothymia	*Outgoing,* warmhearted, easygoing, participating Affectothymia
B	*Dull* Low intelligence	*Bright* High Intelligence
C	*Affected by feelings,* emotionally less stable, easily upset, changeable Lower ego strength	*Emotionally stable,* mature, faces reality, calm Higher ego strength
E	*Humble,* mild, easily led, docile, accommodating Submissiveness	*Assertive,* aggressive, competitive, stubborn Dominance
F	*Sober,* taciturn, serious Desurgency	*Happy-go-lucky,* enthusiastic Surgency
G	*Expedient,* disregards rules Weaker superego strength	*Conscientious,* persistent, moralistic, staid Stronger superego strength
H	*Shy,* timid, threat-sensitive Threctia	*Venturesome,* uninhibited, socially bold Parmia
I	*Tough-minded,* self-reliant, realistic Harria	*Tender-minded,* sensitive, clinging, overprotected Premsia
L	*Trusting,* accepting conditions Alaxia	*Suspicious,* hard to fool Protension
M	*Practical,* "down-to-earth" concerns Praxernia	*Imaginative,* bohemian, absent-minded Autia
N	*Forthright,* unpretentious, genuine but socially clumsy Artlessness	*Astute,* polished, socially aware Shrewdness
O	*Self-assured,* placid, secure, complacent, serene Untroubled adequacy	*Apprehensive,* self-reproaching, insecure, worrying, troubled Guilt proneness
Q₁	*Conservative,* respecting traditional ideas Conservatism of temperament	*Experimenting,* liberal, free-thinking Radicalism
Q₂	*Group dependent,* a "joiner" and sound follower Group adherence	*Self-sufficient,* resourceful, prefers own decisions Self-sufficiency
Q₃	*Undisciplined self-conflict,* lax, follows own urges, careless of social rules Low self-sentiment integration	*Controlled,* exacting will power, socially precise, compulsive, following self-image High strength of self-sentiment
Q₄	*Relaxed,* tranquil, torpid, unfrustrated, composed Low ergic tension	*Tense,* frustrated, driven, overwrought High ergic tension

---

Adapted from Cattell, Eber, and Tatsuoka (1970, pp. 16–17). Reproduced by permission.

may range from 0 (strong internal belief) to 23 (strong external belief); the remaining six items are "filler" items and are not scored. A sample of the kinds of alternatives provided in the questionnaire are as follows (Rotter, 1971, p. 42): a) "In my case the grades I make are the results of my own efforts; luck has little or nothing to do with it"; b) "Sometimes I feel that I have little to do with the grades I get." Selecting alternative a here would suggest a belief in internal locus of control while alternative b would suggest a belief that external factors control outcomes. Notice that, as with all trait dimensions, scores here indicate points along a continuum rather than "internal" and "external" types. That is, individuals do not represent one type or another but rather display varying degrees of internality or externality. (See our later discussion in this chapter on the language of types.)

What behavioral differences have been demonstrated between subjects falling at various points along the locus of control dimension? Because of the great number of empirical studies of this trait (at last count, well over three hundred investigations have been conducted), only a few findings can be mentioned here. Interesting comparisons have been made of coping strategies for dealing with stressful situations. For example, Seeman and Evans (1962) found that among a group of tuberculosis patients, internals knew more about their situations, questioned the medical staff more, and expressed less satisfaction with the feedback or information they were receiving from the hospital personnel than did externals.

Sims and Baumann (1972) suggested that coping with the threat of natural disasters such as tornadoes may be related to one's belief in personal control. Specifically, Sims and Baumann were struck by a rather interesting piece of data: in Illinois fewer tornado-related deaths are reported annually than in Alabama, though both states are on a major tornado pathway and have about equal numbers of storms of about equal severity. Perhaps there are proportionately more externals in Alabama than in Illinois, and so Alabamians might be more likely to react to tornado threats with fatalism and inactivity, thus decreasing their chances of surviving an actual tornado. The results of Sims and Baumann's study strongly supported this possibility, as many more people from Alabama than from Illinois endorsed sentiments like "God controls my life" and that "luck" was an important determinant of their fates. People in Illinois apparently make active efforts (like listening to television or radio broadcasts) to deal with tornado threats while those in Alabama generally do very little to prepare themselves for imminent disaster, or they fail to "watch the sky" when there are signs of tornado activity.

Other studies have shown internals to be more persuasive in

getting others to change their attitudes, to be more resistant to conscious manipulation, to be more independent, and to be less conforming than externals. Regarding the latter finding, Crowne and Liverant (1963) tested internals and externals in an Asch conformity situation (see chapter 3). When the standard instructions were given, internals and externals did not differ in their yielding behavior. But when allowed to bet money provided by the experimenters on their judgments, something interesting occurred. Externals began to yield significantly more than internals, and internals bet more on themselves when going against the majority than did externals; the latter subjects actually bet more when they yielded than when they resisted the group pressures (indicating a lack of confidence in their independence).

Little research has been conducted on how locus of control beliefs develops, but there is evidence that cultural and social factors play important roles (e.g., Battle & Rotter, 1963; Graves, 1961). Lefcourt (1966) summarized the findings relating locus of control and ethnic and socioeconomic variables:

> In all of the reported ethnic studies, groups whose social position is one of minimal power either by class or race tend to score higher in the external-control direction. Within the racial groupings, class interacts so that the double handicap of lower-class and "lower-caste" seems to produce persons with the highest expectancy of external control. Perhaps the apathy and what is often described as lower-class lack of motivation to achieve may be explained as a result of the disbelief that effort pays off. (p. 212)

In short, the locus of control dimension has proved of considerable value to personologists in their attempts to understand individual differences in relating to the world. Of course, a simple trait by itself will be of limited utility in predicting behavior, so future studies also must incorporate other traits as well as important situational determinants. (See our discussion in chapter 1 on idiographic and nomothetic research strategies.)

Having looked at the concept of trait in some detail, let us turn to another kind of descriptive language, typologies.

THE LANGUAGE OF TYPES

The type approach to personality description is an extension of the reasoning used in the trait approach. Whereas a variety of traits can be assigned to a single person, and we say he or she has this or that trait or pattern of traits, in the "type" approach a broader, more unifying scheme, that of classification or pigeonholing, is adopted. A person is classified as belonging to a *type* by the pattern of traits displayed. If the person shares a trait pattern with a large group, then with the members of that group he or she belongs to a type, thus simplifying description immensely since each shared trait need not be listed separately for each individual. For example, if naïveté is observed to go with certain other qualities, such as the tendency to great changeability of affect, blocking, amnesia, and so on, then this collection of traits might be referred to simply by the single inclusive category called "repression" as a defensive style. An opposing type also can be identified as "isolation" or "intellectualization." Having isolated these two opposing defensive categories, each made up of clusters of traits that often are found together, one now can say that because the person has one or the other set of traits, he or she is a member of one or the other type. Types, therefore, are usually made up of complex systems of opposing traits that have been simplified into a few main categories.

As in the case of traits, a vocabulary of types has existed for thousands of years. As noted in chapter 2, the best known typology in ancient Greece was that of Hippocrates in the fifth century B.C. Theorizing that the body contained four fluids or humors—yellow bile, black bile, phlegm, and blood—Hippocrates speculated that personality depended on which of these humors predominated in the person. Yellow bile went with a "choleric" or irascible temperament; black bile with "melancholy"; phlegm with the sluggish, apathetic, or "phlegmatic" person; and blood with the cheerful, active, or "sanguine" person.

Among laypeople, the best known, modern personality typology perhaps is that proposed by Carl Jung (1933) describing introverts and extroverts. Jung's typology is far more complex than most people realize and deserves some elaboration here. Introversion and extroversion refer to basic *attitudes* in the personality and describe the channeling of psychic energy ("libido"). The flow of energy in the *introvert* is toward the inner, subjective world, and energy in the *extrovert* is funneled toward the outer, objective world. Although these two attitudes are mutually exclusive (they cannot occur simultaneously), they can fluctuate from time to time in the same individual. Jung believed, nevertheless, that people tended to rely on one attitude more than the other, and that individuals could be typed primarily as introverts (when an orientation to internal affairs predominated) or as extroverts (when an orientation to other people and things predominated).

As we suggested above, Jung's typology is more complicated than first meets the eye. Besides postulating two basic personality attitudes, Jung identified four psychological *functions* (thinking, feeling, sensation, and intuition) which could be experienced either in an introverted or extroverted manner. *Thinking* and *feeling* refer to opposite (and mutually exclusive) ways of making judgments and decisions. The thinking function engages in highly intellectual pursuits such as classifying and organizing facts—processes which help us to understand the world. The feeling function, in contrast, tells us whether we like or dislike our observations—a decision based upon pleasant or unpleasant feelings. *Sensation* and *intuition* both are perceptual in nature and refer to opposite (and mutually exclusive) ways of gathering or taking in information. Sensation is the direct experiencing of the world, in an open and nonjudgmental manner—a function emphasizing what we see, hear, feel, taste, and smell. Intuition, on the other hand, emphasizes possibilities or essences rather than realities—in other words, the intuition function involves immediate experience which "goes beyond" facts. The following passage illustrates the operation of these functions in a familiar context:

> Suppose that a person is standing on the rim of the Grand Canyon of the Colorado River. If the feeling function predominates she will experience a sense of awe, grandeur, and breath-taking beauty. If she is controlled by the sensation function she will see the Canyon merely as it is or as a photograph might represent it. If the thinking function controls her ego she will try to understand the Canyon in terms of geological principles and theory. Finally, if the intuitive function prevails the spectator will tend to see the Grand Canyon as a mystery of nature possessing deep significance whose meaning is partially revealed or felt as a mystical experience. (Hall & Lindzey, 1978, p. 125)

None of the functions is preferable theoretically to the others but like the attitudes, we adopt one function most of the time, i.e., it becomes dominant. An individual may be "typed" according to his or her dominant attitude and function. This means that there are eight basic personality types, representing combinations of introversion or extroversion with thinking, feeling, sensation, or intuition. Each type is characterized by a unique combination of traits—see Table 4. For example, the thinking introvert is described by Jung as being theoretical, intellectual, and impractical, while the thinking extrovert is characterized as being objective, rigid, and cold. Space limitations prohibit a more detailed clinical description of the eight types, but the following passage presents a shorthand caricature of

Table 4

		ATTITUDES	
		Introversion	Extroversion
FUNCTIONS	Thinking	theoretical, intellectual, impractical	objective, rigid, cold
	Feeling	silent, childish, indifferent	intense, effervescent, sociable
	Sensation	passive, calm, artistic	realistic, sensual, jolly
	Intuition	mystical, dreamer, unique	visionary, changeable, creative

Jung's Personality Typology with Correspondng Traits

Adapted from *Beneath the Mask: An Introduction to Theories of Personality* by Christopher F. Monte. Copyright © 1977 by Christopher F. Monte. Reprinted by permission of Holt, Rinehart and Winston and Christopher F. Monte.

Jung's types. Perhaps the reader can find himself or herself there:

> As a mnemotechnic device Ania Teillard [1948] imagined the story of the dinner of the psychological types: The perfect hostess (feeling-extroverted) receives the guests with her husband, a quiet gentleman who is an art collector and expert in ancient paintings (sensation-introvert). The first guest to arrive is a talented lawyer (thinking-extroverted). Then comes a noted businessman (sensation-extroverted) with his wife, a taciturn, somewhat enigmatic musician (feeling-introverted). They are followed by an eminent scholar (thinking-introverted) who came without his wife, a former cook (feeling-extrovert), and a distinguished engineer (intuitive-extroverted). One vainly waits for the last guest, a poet (intuitive-introverted), but the poor fellow has forgotten the invitation. (Ellenberger, 1970, p. 702)

In short, Jung's typology attempts to pay tribute to the complexity of personality rather than to deny or minimize its uniqueness. Jung felt that pure types represented extreme cases and that within any one type there was a wide range of potential variation. No one type, moreover, was considered to be ideal or better than the others. In fact, Jung believed that one should develop all sides of the personality, which meant that underdeveloped aspects (like introversion in the extrovert) must be consciously cultivated. As one theorist has noted, Jung felt "the attainment of self to be ideal. This process involves growing out of your personality type, as it were, so that none of one's human capabilities is submerged and unconscious" (Maddi, 1976, p. 307).

In one important respect, Jung's typology, particularly the intro-

108

version-extroversion dimension, is not an ideal example of the concept of typology, because introverts and extroverts are frequently thought of as falling along a continuum rather than as representing a dichotomy. In modern typological thinking (e.g., Cattell, 1965; Eysenck, 1952), types are distinguished from each other by being qualitatively different rather than being merely different in degree. This is illustrated in Figure 9, in which Distribution A shows a normal statistical distribution (bell-shaped curve) of people who are high or low on a particular trait such as intelligence or ego-control, with most people falling in the middle range; Distribution B shows two distinct groupings, one at the low end and one at the high end. Distribution B more nearly represents what is meant by types than does A. There is little point in using type classifications for Distribution A. It would be like calling tall people different in type from short people, when in actuality there is a continuum with most people falling somewhere in the middle range. The concept of typology is used more suitably when the types are separated and display qualitatively different properties, as in breeds of dogs, types of animal species, or people who prefer to use different forms of defense mechanisms such as denial versus projection. Freud's typology of oral, anal, and phallic types, discussed below, would be an example

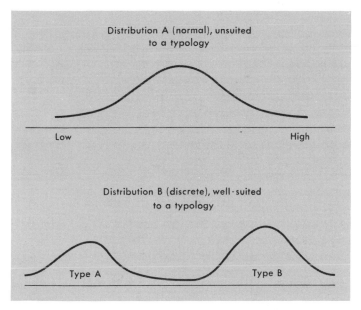

FIGURE 9. A normal distribution or continuum, and a discrete distribution on which typological thinking is founded.

of a typology that more nearly reflected such qualitative differences.

Freud's (1933b) typological categories arise from the theory of psychosexual development. As will be seen in more detail later (chapters 6 and 7), in this theory everyone is said to pass through three infantile psychosexual stages which are distinguished according to the primary means of sexual gratification characteristic to each. In the oral stage, erotic activity centers on the lips and mouth, in the anal stage on stimulation of the anus, and in the phallic stage on the genital organs. In the course of psychosexual development, some individuals fail to progress normally to the next stage. Although they reach chronological adulthood, the primitive psychosexual tendencies characteristic of the respective immature stage persist, and these govern the personality and produce the characteristic psychological traits connected with that stage.

Freud identified three types of personality based on the "fixation" of psychosexual or libidinal energy at a given immature stage of development. The *oral* type is characterized by passive, dependent attitudes toward others, in which the person continues to seek sustenance (as in feeding) from others. Depending on when fixation occurred, the oral type is either optimistic, immature, and trusting, or pessimistic, suspicious, and sarcastic about the prospects of gaining and retaining the needed sustenance. The *anal* type also has two substages, the first identified with outbursts of aggression, sloppiness, and petulance, the second with obstinacy, orderliness, and stinginess. The *phallic* type is characterized by adolescent immaturity, with heterosexual conflicts stemming from an unresolved Oedipus complex. Psychologically, the phallic period (and type) is apt to be stormy, with sharp emotional swings and preoccupation with the choice of a love object.

A Typology for Today:
Type A and Type B Personalities

Is susceptibility to coronary heart disease related to personality? Traditionally, variables such as high blood pressure, diabetes, serum lipids, and excessive cigarette smoking have been implicated as primary causes of heart disease. Some physicians now are seriously investigating the possibility that psychological factors also may contribute to diseases of the heart. Perhaps the most influential and controversial approach along these lines is the one popularized by Friedman and Rosenman (1974). These medical researchers suggest that personality factors relating to a pressured life style contribute to the onset of coronary disease, above and beyond the influence of the earlier-mentioned risk factors. Friedman and Rosenman argue that there are basically two types of personalities, Type A and Type B, which can be assessed via specially designed interviews—questionnaires also have been designed by other investigators for assessing these personality types. The Type A individual is characterized by an excessively competitive drive, striving for achievement, aggressiveness, impatience, hostility, and a strong sense of time urgency. The Type B individual lacks these qualities and is more relaxed and easy-going. In their samples of urban Americans, Friedman and Rosenman have found that about fifty percent are true Type A personalities and forty percent are Type B personalities. The remaining ten percent show mixed characteristics though the researchers believe that with refined testing procedures, they will show that "most Americans are in fact either Type A or Type B, though in varying degrees" (1974, p. 69). (Some current researchers, cf. Rowland and Sokol, 1977, are assessing these personality characteristics more as traits than as a typology, but the theoretical view still treats these personality differences as "types.")

Studies have shown that Type A individuals are almost three times more likely to develop heart disease than Type B individuals and moreover, that Type A's are five times more apt to have a second attack and twice as likely to have fatal attacks (Rosenman & Friedman, 1971a, 1971b). In addition, studies of top company-managers have shown extreme Type A individuals to be higher than others in a number of risk factors associated with heart disease. For example, the Type A managers reported more stress symptoms and had higher blood pressure, cholesterol, and triglyceride levels; they were also more likely to be cigarette smokers (Howard, Cunningham, & Rechnitzer, 1976).

Findings such as these are interesting but difficult to interpret because the cause-and-effect relationship remains unclear. For example, Friedman and Rosenman (1974) argue that a pressured life style can, and does, lead to a rise in cholesterol and hence produces a greater risk of coronary disease. However, it would be equally possible to argue that high cholesterol can make you, say, more aggressive or hostile, though no one seriously proposes such an idea. The confusion occurs because not only is the relationship between Type A behavior and heart disease tenuous, but the exact psychological and physiological mechanisms linking these variables are not known currently.

In summary, Friedman and Rosenman have postulated a simple though important personality typology, one which eventually may be able to predict successfully those individuals highly susceptible to coronary disease (and perhaps other disorders as well). Currently, however, the research is largely correlational in nature and any definitive conclusions relating personality, stress, and heart disease seem premature. If additional research gives further credence to the existing body of knowledge, we may be able to develop effective intervention strategies for altering Type A behavior patterns and concomitantly, for lowering the risk of heart disease (see Rowland & Sokol, 1977, for a concise review of the Type A research).

Reflections: Traits and Typologies

Three points should be emphasized in connection with trait systems and typologies. First, as we have said, in reasoning, typologies are closely interdependent with trait analyses. There are a number of traits which one must possess if he or she is to be assigned to a given type, say, the anal personality. If the person shows the trait combination of obstinancy, orderliness, and stinginess, then he or she closely fits the anal type. Thus, trait and type analyses represent a common, interdependent style of thinking and speaking about personality structure.

Second, trait analyses and typologies usually are based on certain theoretical propositions about personality structure and process. The author of a typology, for example, usually has some explicit or implicit principles in mind about the way personality works. Hippocrates thought of mental life as dominated by fluids or humors, and his typology was a reflection of this concept. Jung expounded the idea that some psychological functions were emphasized in the person's life style (he called them "superior functions"), while others were subordinated and unconscious ("inferior functions") although the latter were important and sometimes even demonic forces in the personality. His typology, involving always a polarity such as extroversion-introversion, or thinking-feeling, reflected this notion. Similarly, Freud was trying to articulate concepts about psychosexual development and dynamics in his typology of oral, anal, and phallic personalities.

Third, typological thinking in personality seems to be more congenial with an idiographic research approach and a more global view of the personality, while trait thinking appears more congenial with the nomothetic approach and the measurement of individual attributes. If people can be categorized into a limited number of types or pigeonholes, then an individual could be selected as an ideal example of each type, and studied intensively; the individual is studied as a representative of a whole class of persons sharing some property. And since typologies in personality tend to be built around major qualities, such as an entire "life style" rather than discrete and minor variations, the approach lends itself readily to global analysis. In contrast, trait analysis implies the existence of many individual personality attributes, each of which appears in varying amounts in different persons. These traits and the task of generalizing about their functions in people generally become the focuses of interest, rather than the individual person as an organized whole. Thus, there seems to be an ideological link between typologies and the idiographic research strategy, and between trait analysis and the nomothetic research strategy.

There are other personality traits and typologies besides those we have emphasized. Each personality theory makes use of somewhat different ways of describing the personality structure, that is, each identifies different units of description which fit the theoretical assumptions of the system. Most theories have a language of traits and types, since this enables the structure of personality in the terms of that particular theory to be made concrete. Such a language is fundamental to personality description.

THE UNIT OF ANALYSIS
IN PERSONALITY DESCRIPTION

A number of issues illustrate divergences in the way personality structure is conceived and described in different personality theories. There is one issue, however, which stands out as particularly important, not only in personality theory, but in all of psychology, and is the concern of the remainder of this chapter. This issue is the unit of analysis used in the study of the person. Two main alternatives have been emphasized, though both are dependent upon the other for a complete understanding of the person. First, the *person in the situation* can be the primary unit of analysis, with the emphasis on the *situation* or the stimulus as physical reality to which the person must respond in accordance with its *objective* qualities. Second, the *person* can be the primary unit of analysis, with the emphasis not on the situation as objective reality but on the person's perceptions of the situation, that is, as it is *subjectively* apprehended. Let us examine these two outlooks with our attention centered in each case on the role of the stimulus or situation.

The Stimulus as Objective Reality

One of the striking things about animal and human behavior is that it is highly adaptive; actions and reactions are well attuned to the stimulus world. We respond to sounds, sights, touch, and so on, in ways predictable from a knowledge of the physical characteristics of such stimuli. When we reach out to pick up an object, we do not usually overreach or underreach, but our fingers accurately extend the right distance to it. As we pass one another in the street we do not bump, because our senses seem to recognize the realities of the stimulus world and permit us to respond appropriately. We also get accurate feedback from our actions allowing us to adjust them as necessary.

Personality theories that have emphasized this adaptive sensitivity of the organism to the physical world have tended to be associated with an interest in the mechanisms of *learning*. The focus of their attention is directed at how we learn to react appropriately in one way or another to the stimuli to which we are exposed. Reactions then are seen as arising from stimuli whose basic elements are light waves, sound waves, shape, weight, size, distance, pressures on the tissues, or chemicals that reach sensory receptors. In other words, we respond to objective, physical stimulus events arising in the outer environment, as well as to those arising in the inner environments of our bodies. From this point of view, all behavioral responses are made to objective physical stimuli and through the processes of learning, they become established as habits of adjustment to them.

Although many psychologists of this persuasion were earlier concerned only with the principles of learning, some of them also came to recognize that such propositions about learning might be applied to behavior in general and to personality. Therefore, theories of learning tended to become theories about the whole of human psychological functioning. Perhaps the best-known instance of such a general behavior theory was that of Clark Hull (1943) whose views have had great influence on psychology over the past several decades. But the explicit extension of this form of thought to personality is best represented by the writings of John Dollard and Neal Miller (1950). From their point of view, personality consists of the habits of reaction a person acquires in response to physical stimuli through learning. The fundamental principle is that an association or bond is formed between these stimuli and the reactions that are elicited in their presence. The emphasis is on the objective, physical stimulus as the event which elicits the response and which can be defined without reference to the responding organism. Description of the person thus is made in terms of such learned systems of habits of response. The basic ingredient, then, of individual differences in personality consists of divergent habit patterns, whether these habits are simple skills or complex emotions, motives, beliefs, defenses, or neurotic symptoms.

The Stimulus as Apprehended by the Person

A class of personality theories identified as "phenomenological" in point of view sharply contrasts with the above view of personality. These theories are derived from an emphasis on perception and cognition rather than learning. For such a theorist, defining a stimulus physically and objectively poses a problem, namely, that our perception of objects is not necessarily identical with the objects themselves. Our senses do not directly transmit physical objects. Rather, we respond to representations of objects, that is, objects as mediated by our perceptual apparatus and by our individual interpretations. The phenomenologist argues that physical objects themselves do not determine our responses. Rather, the person's intervening structures and processes that mediate the physical stimuli do. From this point of view, the causes of action must be reconstructed through inferences about these mediators or psychological representations of external stimuli.

Instead of focusing on the objective physical stimulus, *phenomenological* theories of personality emphasize mediating cognitive processes, such as perceptions and conceptions about events; the "phenomenal" rather than the objective world of events. They argue that the cause of action is the world as a person apprehends it privately, and this private world can be quite different from objective reality. Their descriptions of the personality are descriptions of those mediating cognitive processes which distinguish one individual from another and presumably cause or greatly influence behavior. In short, the unit of analysis is the *person*, since within him or her are to be found the key constructs on which behavior is to be built. We cannot know the individual by reference to the situation, since this operates only through the subjective-cognitive processes lying inside the person.

Phenomenological theories of personality have two main forms, one that is built around the concept of the "self," and another that refers in general to cognitions about the world. The first class includes the personality systems of influential writers as Carl Rogers (1947, 1951), Abraham Maslow (1970), Kurt Goldstein (1940), and some features of Henry Murray's (1938) account of personality. The second class includes, among others, Kurt Lewin's (1935) field theory and George Kelly's (1955) theory of personal constructs. Space does not permit elaboration of each of these approaches to personality description, but the main forms are illustrated by brief discussion, first of Lewin's field theory and then of Rogers's self-concept theory.

Cognitions about the World: Lewin's Approach

For Lewin the psychological representations of the world, referred to as the "life space," consist of the person's needs and the available potentialities of action as he or she apprehends them. Every aspect of a person's physical environment that is not part of the *life space* and to which the person does not directly respond is the "foreign hull." To understand a person's behavior at any moment we must reconstruct and describe the life space at that moment, which means that we must understand the psychological forces then in operation.

These forces are usually described by Lewin graphically in topological diagrams that include: goal regions (shown as enclosed places); positive and negative valences (designated by plus or minus signs) which identify desirable or undesirable aspects of the life space; vectors (arrows) which point out the directions to which a person is pulled; and barriers (lines separating the person from positive goals) which block or slow down the approach to any goal region. Many forces may affect the life space, and the person's behavior at any time is a result of them. The Lewinian diagram of the life space presented in Figure 10 is interpreted as follows:

> ...a child passes a candy store, looks in the window, and wishes she had some candy. The sight of the candy arouses a need, and this need does three things. It releases energy and thereby arouses tension in an inner-personal region (the candy-wanting system). It confers a positive valence upon the region in which the candy is located. It creates a force that pushes the child in the direction of the candy.
>
> Let us say that the child has to enter the store and buy the candy. This situation can be represented by Figure A. Suppose, however, that the child does not have any money; then the boundary between her and the candy will be an impassable barrier. She will move as close to the candy as possible, perhaps putting her nose against the window, without being able to reach it (Figure B.).
>
> She may say to herself, "If I had some money, I could buy some candy. Maybe mother will give me some money." In other words, a new need or quasi need, the intention to get some money from her mother, is created. This intention, in turn, arouses a tension, a vector,

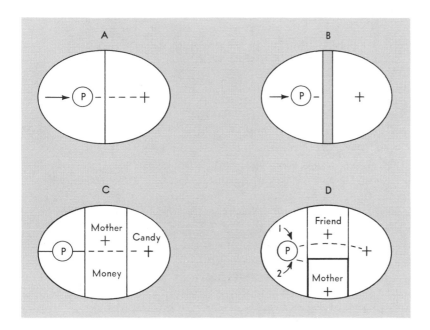

FIGURE 10. Lewinian diagram representing the changing life space of a child in a specific psychological transaction with the environment. *(From Hall and Lindzey, 1978, pp. 409-10).*

and a valence that are represented in Figure C. A thin boundary has been drawn between the child and the mother on the assumption that she has to go home, find her mother, and ask her for money. Another thin boundary has been drawn between the mother and the candy to represent the effort required to return to the store and make a purchase. The child moves to the candy by way of the mother.

If the mother refuses to give the child any money, she may think of borrowing it from a friend. In this case, the region containing the mother is surrounded by an impenetrable barrier, and a new path through the region containing the friend to the candy is transcribed (Figure D).

This topological representation could be endlessly complicated by introducing additional environmental regions and boundaries of varying degrees of firmness, and additional needs with their coordinate tension systems, valences, and vectors. (From Hall and Lindzey, 1978, pp. 409-10.)

The important elements in the Lewinian system are these: Psychological events are considered in terms of the construct of life space, which involves subjective definitions of the environment. Inferences about the life space are always derived from systematic observation of the person's behavior in the environment. Yet the terms of the analysis of behavior and setting are not static traits and stationary objects, but the person's own subjective apprehension of the environment and his or her relationship to it.

The "Self": Rogers's Approach

The self-theory of Rogers is also phenomenological, and its concepts too are couched in the language of subjective experience (for example, what we want and how we think and feel). The Rogerian concept that is analogous to Lewin's life space is the "phenomenal field," and the core (or most important aspect) of that field is the "self-concept," that is, a person's notion of who he or she is in relation to the environment. It is this *self-concept* which determines behavior. This phenomenal self is, for a person, reality. One does not respond to the objective environment but to what he or she perceives it to be, regardless of how distorted or personalized that perception may be. These subjective realities are tentative hypotheses which a person entertains about environmental situations.

One person will conceive of himself or herself as a reformer with the mission of correcting certain worldly ills and helping others to "see the light." Another person's self-concept, in contrast, may include the image of a "realist," able to accept gracefully, and even benefit from, the weaknesses of human nature and our social institutions. Self-concepts are complex and variable, and they determine how persons will react to and deal with a wide variety of situations. These conceptions of who and what one is not only comprise central values and belief systems, but also include images of oneself as physically strong or weak, attractive or unattractive, popular or unpopular, and so on, based partly on the reflected appraisals of other people with whom one has had contact. According to Rogers, this differentiated portion of the phenomenal field, the self-concept, determines or influences all behavior. Most behavior, indeed, is organized around efforts to preserve and enhance this phenomenal self. Parenthetically, Rogers writes also of an *ideal self*, which is the self a person would most like to possess, and furthermore, he believes that a positive correlation between the self and the ideal self suggests good adjustment.

Although Lewin reconstructs a person's life space with its multiplicity of psychological forces by systematically observing how that person acts in different naturalistic and experimental situations, Rogers identifies the *self-concept* largely from introspection. Rogers learns about an individual's self-system by listening to introspective verbal reports about his or her conceptions of self and the world, usually in the context of psychotherapy (see chapter 7 for a detailed examination of Rogers's theory and approach to psychotherapy).

Further Comparisons

The two viewpoints from which to regard the stimulus are not as far apart in reality as they look, and to state these positions without some qualification is a gross oversimplification. Remember that both points of view must contend with two kinds of events, 1) those in which human behavior is highly adaptive and seems responsive to the environment, and 2) those in which behavior is maladaptive and seems to be based on faulty perceptions of or judgments about the environment. Obviously, personality theories must be used to deal with both kinds of events and to the extent that they are used successfully, the points of view will not be as far apart as first appears. Moreover, although the stimulus may be defined independently of the respondent in the *person in the situation* perspective, theorists of this persuasion still acknowledge that its effect will depend on the present state of the individual, his or her previous experience, and genetic constitution. There is the danger that the differences in point of view may be overstressed.

But differences between the two main viewpoints of the stimulus extend to issues about the manner in which humans ought to be conceived and studied. Learning theorists, such as B. F. Skinner, are strongly behavioristic, tending to be suspicious of easy speculation about private inner experience and of excessive reference to constructs which cannot be directly observed; they prefer to link their ideas about humans and personality more closely to observable behavior. Their preference for a science of human beings is one that emphasizes the analysis of behavior into its basic elements. They assume that even the most complex patterns of behavior can be reduced to simpler elements and in fact, that only in this way can personality be understood. They tend, with some exception, to be nomothetic rather than idiographic in orientation. They are interested in a reductive analysis of complex events to the common properties on which the behavior of all organisms depends, even that of the rat, worm, and cockroach, all of whom are assumed to learn by means of forming associations between stimuli and responses. Humans are thought of as merely more complex instances of such a basic process.

In contrast, the phenomenologically oriented theorist assumes that the organized system that we call personality cannot be synthesized readily from a molecular analysis of its component elements. There is a positive value in such terms as system, integration, and organization; in short, the phenomenologist is "holistic" and "molar" rather than "analytic" and "molecular." The units of analysis here are apt to be complex and to include goals as well as means by which goals are achieved. Perhaps most important of all, the phenomenological theorist freely speculates about those inner, mediating, cognitive processes, such as the self-concept or the life space, taken as the real determinants of actions and feelings.

The distinction between the molar and molecular (or atomistic) approach can be found also in modern research and theory in perception. Sensory psychologists traditionally have thought of perceptions as built from numerous minute sensory impressions when physical stimuli impinge on the sense organs, such as the eyes and ears. The nervous system is thought to respond in ways parallel to the physical stimuli which strike the sense organs, collating and organizing these impressions deep within the brain. This view is molecular in emphasis. In contrast, Gibson (1966) has viewed perception in a molar fashion as the active process of seeking information about the environment. As he put it, "The eyes, ears, nose, mouth, and skin can orient, explore, and investigate. When thus active they are neither passive senses nor channels of sensory quality, but ways of paying attention to whatever is constant in changing stimulation. In exploratory looking, tasting, and touching, the sense impressions are incidental symptoms of the exploration, and what gets isolated is information about the object looked at, tasted, or touched . . . " (p. 4).

Personality also may be viewed as a passive accumulation of associations between stimuli and responses, that is, as a complex collection of simple and discrete conditioned reactions, or as an organized unit (system) actively searching the environment for relevant cues for the requirements of adapting. This difference is important in characterizing the thinking styles and assumptions of the various personality theories about human nature and how the person should be studied. It may be found in every field of psychological study but is most evident in personality, because it is a field that attempts to integrate the many psychological functions of the person into a comprehensive framework.

Where do the Freudian and neo-Freudian approaches to personality fall in this analysis? The answer is not clear and will depend somewhat on which of the various psychoanalytic viewpoints one is talking about, for example, Freud, Jung, Rank, Adler, or whomever, and which aspects of theory one is considering. It seems to us that Freudian theory is somewhat in-between in its treatments of the stimulus, although probably it emphasizes the stimulus as objective reality more than as subjectively apprehended. For example, Freud sought to understand the individual on the basis of his or her actual (objective) life experiences, and the patterns of healthy or neurotic reaction (mostly the latter) which resulted from these experiences. The sources of trauma in the life of the person were treated as real events. Misperceptions and idiosyncratic forms of adjustment were understood in terms of the acquisition of the neurotic defense mechanisms. This position could be accommodated readily within the association-learning framework of Dollard and Miller (1950). In fact, the main personality-relevant work of these authors, *Personality and Psychotherapy*, was primarily a translation of large portions of psychoanalytic theory into association-learning terms, and the translation was not very difficult to make. This suggests that Freudian theory and association-learning theory must have much in common, including their basic approach to the stimulus as an objective event.

There are phenomenological leanings in Freud too. For example, Freud was not very reductionistic, and there was much speculation about inner mediating processes which supposedly were hidden from view. He focused more on the distortions of reality (as in defense mechanisms), which were mediated by the not-so-healthy ego of the neurotic, than on effective adaptation. Neo-Freudians, such as Jung, introduced mediating, organizing concepts such as the self. All psychoanalytic writers have relied more heavily on introspection as the source of information about personality structure and process than on observing behavior, although both were used. That is, the psychoanalytic therapist always was alert to behavioral evidence which contradicted the verbal introspection of the person, and inferences about the personality from this introspection were qualified by reference to behavioral signs of conflict and defense.

To summarize and conclude, it should be clear by now that the varying descriptive units used by different theories derive from divergent assumptions about human nature and how it should be studied. Whether one adopts the Freudian framework of id, ego, and superego, the association-learning framework of learned habits of response to physical, objective stimuli, or the phenomenological framework of self-concept, certain philosophical predilections for thinking about humans are revealed by the choice. The differences in descriptive units are not merely terminological but go to the heart of the theorist's beliefs about human nature. Yet in the last analysis, whatever descriptive language is used, the facts of human behavior and of the individual differences in that behavior provide the constant reality against which to evaluate the adequacy of that language and its conceptual underpinnings. Humans are the same; only the systems for conceiving and describing them vary.

A Challenge to Personality:
The Specificity of Behavior

An important issue, implicit in much of our discussions of personality so far, is currently being debated among many personologists and concerns the stability of human behavior. Specifically, theoretical accounts of personality structure (and hence description) typically assume that behavior is relatively stable from one situation or time to another. For example, before labeling Jay as "shy," we would want to observe her in a number of different situations with a variety of people. If she consistently, though not necessarily constantly, isolated herself from others and displayed an awkwardness on those occasions when social interaction did occur, we then with some confidence could describe her as being shy and expect that this description would help us to make accurate predictions of her behavior in future situations. Naturally, to the extent that situational factors strongly influenced her behavior, our "person" variables (or descriptions) would be of limited utility, though still of importance.

A basic assumption of personality description, then, is that behavior is relatively stable. But is this assumption in line with empirical observations of behavior or does it need revision? In recent years, some behaviorally oriented personologists, known more specifically as social learning theorists, have argued that the evidence for behavioral stability is extremely poor and that personologists should shift their emphasis of study accordingly from that of the person (and his or her traits or motives) to the many situational variables which evoke and maintain behavior. One rather threatening implication of this position for personology is that a major pursuit of most personologists (identifying and describing basic personality structures) has been and is largely irrelevant to the understanding of human behavior. Let us briefly examine some of the arguments and data (see chapter 7 for further elaboration of the social learning viewpoint).

For most of us, there is little question that we and others display fairly consistent (stable) behavior. In fact, this consistency is often the basis for "knowing ourselves" and for negotiating and predicting interpersonal relationships. Nevertheless, some theorists, like Walter Mischel (1968, 1969), have maintained that: 1) in many cases, this consistency appears to be greater than it actually is because our minds act as effective "reducing valves," taking in discrepant information and then condensing it into seemingly consistent phenomena, and 2) the consistency, when it does exist, has little to do with personality dispositions (like traits) but rather with the fact that we typically see our acquaintances (and they see us) in the same or similar contexts. But if the situational forces in these familiar settings (or the settings themselves) change, e.g., by reinforcing different actions, people's behaviors probably will change too, regardless of any presumed or existing personality characteristics.

Mischel has gathered much correlational evidence to support his position that behavioral specificity (i.e., the fact that behavior is greatly influenced by situations and therefore is subject to considerable variability) is more common than most people assume it to be. In a review of studies of the stability of behavior across situations and over time, Mischel (1968) noted that the greatest stability has been found for *cognitive* and *intellectual* functions (including self-descriptions) and the least for *personality* dimensions such as attitudes to authority, moral behavior, aggression, and rigidity (intolerance for ambiguity). Mischel notes too that the inconsistency in personality-related behaviors is not a function of poorly constructed measures but rather is a reflection of nature. In short, Mischel concludes that there is very little evidence that personality-relevant behaviors are stable and in fact, they show considerable specificity across situations and over time.

Mischel's interpretations and methods are certainly open to criticism, and others have argued convincingly that the studies he reviewed in fact *do indicate* behavioral *stability* (e.g., Block, 1968; Bowers, 1973; Carlson, 1971; Pervin, 1975). Even his rather artificial separation of cognitive and intellectual behaviors from those related to personality is suspect. Cognitive factors are intimate aspects of personality and simply cannot be delimited clearly from it (see chapter 6). Moreover, the "either-or" nature of Mischel's argument overlooks several important possibilities, namely, that stability could vary for individuals, traits, or situations (cf. Pervin, 1975). In other words, some people could show more behavioral stability than others, certain traits in an individual could show more stability than others, or some situations could create more specificity than others (e.g., Bem & Allen, 1974).

Despite these and other shortcomings, Mischel's challenge is valuable for several reasons. First, it reminds us of a vital and often ignored source of behavioral influence, namely, the *environment*. As we suggested earlier, individuals must be flexible and capable of discriminating important environmental cues, if they are to "adapt" to their surroundings. Second, Mischel's views offer an optimistic balance to the often pessimistic outlook on human nature adopted by some personality theorists (e.g., Freud). By emphasizing behavioral flexibility, Mischel reminds us that behavior, including maladaptive behavior, is capable of *change*, if we become aware of its maintaining conditions and then make the appropriate environmental alterations.

There also is some danger in Mischel's criticisms, particularly in their tendency to polarize an issue badly in need of reconciliation. The issue regarding the most effective descriptive strategies for dealing with personality has a long history in psychology, as we discussed in our last section and as may be noted by Murphy's (1947) warning some time ago of the "organism error" and the "situational error." Mischel's extreme environmentalistic position seems to many to be as sterile as the one he attacks. One is reminded of Kurt Lewin's dictum that behavior is a function of the person *and* the environment. To ignore either variable just is not good business (or theory!).

But fortunately, many personologists as of late have given up the simplistic separation of the person and the environment and have begun to explore the interactions of these two intimate variables (cf. Bowers, 1973; Endler & Hunt, 1969; Magnusson & Endler, 1977; Pervin & Lewis, in press). In all fairness to Mischel, even he (1973, 1976) and other social learning theorists like Bandura (1974), seem to have "softened" their original positions considerably. For example, Mischel now is suggesting that though situations still are to be regarded as important determinants of behavior, they only influence the individual if he or she construes them in particular ways. In other words, although Mischel is not advocating the study of so-called "static" person variables (e.g., traitlike dispositions), he is arguing for an assessment of internal *cognitive* factors (e.g., competencies, encoding strategies, and expectancies)—a radical departure from traditional behavioral approaches such as the behaviorism of Skinner (1971).

In short, our concerns of polarization here may be without justification as Mischel and some of his critics seem to have reached a "meeting of the minds," perhaps marking the beginning of a more fruitful era of personality research and theory. As Pervin (1975) notes:

> In arguing against the view of man as an empty organism buffeted entirely by situational forces and for the view that we must understand behavior as it is embedded in relation to specific conditions, Mischel seeks to emphasize both organism and environment variables. The empty organism of an extreme Skinnerian is rejected as much as the encapsulated organism of the extreme Freudian. In arguing for both consistency and variability in behavior, for both internal and external determinants, for both organism and environment variables, Mischel seeks to end a controversy that pits persons against situations to see which is more important. (p. 501)

Although the issues we have discussed concerning personality description are important, they most certainly are not the sole interest of personality theorists. For example, the significant task of accounting for human motivation is an important and difficult challenge for all theorists. Accordingly, we now shall turn our attention to a discussion of personality dynamics (or processes).

Personality Dynamics

A major concern of personality theory is understanding how personality function or works. That is, the dynamics of personality must be formalized so that we may describe and predict its operation and how the dynamic processes are reflected in the way the person acts and reacts. As you might recall from chapter 1, in geology, dynamics are illustrated by the action of wind and water on rock and earth. Dynamics in an automobile engine would include the intake of fuel and its explosion in the cylinders, the escape of exhaust, and the conversion of the resulting energy into turning the drive shaft and wheels. In investigating personality dynamics, we must look to psychological processes rather than to physical ones.

As with description, the dynamics of personality are conceived differently by various personologists. Although theories diverge on many issues pertinent to dynamics, this chapter concentrates on human motivation, one of the most important. Motives are forces that energize and direct human behavior. Personality theories differ concerning the nature and organization of these forces and the manner in which they are set in motion and controlled. Our account will be concerned less with the details of motivation and more with broad lines of thought, that is, with basic assumptions. Other books are available that deal with the substance of motivation, for example, with types of motives and their arousal (e.g., Arkes & Garske, 1977).

The motivational assumptions of the most influential theories of personality fall within three main types; tension-reduction, those supplementing tension-reduction with additional principles such as effectance (wanting to have an effect on the environment), and force-for-growth. The tension-reduction point of view is best represented by Freud and some of the neo-Freudians, as well as by the association-learning approach of Dollard and Miller. The effectance model has been outlined most fully by Robert White. Although strictly speaking he does not have a full-scale personality theory, White speaks eloquently for any such theory which would base its conception of dynamics on the principle of effectance. The force-for-growth point of view includes the personality theories of Rogers and Maslow, its most influential protagonists.

THE TENSION-REDUCTION MODEL

The fundamental principle of this position is a simple and elegant one, that all behavior (in humans as well as in infrahuman animals) can be understood as an effort to reduce tension. This principle has a close connection with two other modern themes. The first is Darwin's (1859) theory of evolution, which emphasized "natural selection" as the process by which those species or biological attributes poorly adapted to their environments were weeded out while well-adapted ones survived. This Darwinian theme encouraged psychology to adopt a general biological orientation to humans, and focused interest on adaptive behavior. Not only was survival important but so was the achievement of an ideal state of balance in one's inner environment. This could be achieved by adaptive activities which prevented hunger, thirst, excessively lowered body temperature, and so on. This view also was encouraged by the work of the great physiologist Claude Bernard, a contemporary of Darwin who did the pioneering work on the concept of "homeostasis," i.e., the maintenance of balance in the internal environment. Adaptive activities could contribute to homeostasis because behavior was governed by the principle of tension-reduction. The absence of the ideal homeostatic steady-state resulted in painful tension (as when one is hungry or thirsty), and led to behavior, such as eating, which reduced the tension.

The second modern theme stems from the need for a principle by which tension-reduction could be achieved, that is, so that animals and humans could learn to engage in the behavior that preserved homeostasis. This was the principle of "association" which had its origins in the writings of certain philosophers of the eighteenth century, for example, David Hartley (1705-1737) and James Mill (1773-1836). It stated that one idea becomes connected to another through association in time or space. Complex mental life and adaptive behaviors could be viewed as accumulated from such associations. Learning to reduce tension could be achieved successfully by higher organisms by the association of adaptive behavior with the appropriate cues; we eat in the presence of hunger cues and drink when thirsty. The reader should not assume that all theories of learning adopt a tension-reduction or associative framework; there are others. However, the tension-reduction and association principles have been important ones in the history of psychology.

All theories espousing the principle of tension-reduction postulate two kinds of drive forces, those which are primary and largely innately given, and those which are secondary or social and the product of learning. Let us examine two prominent versions of this form of analysis in personality theory, that of "Freudian Psychoanalysis" and "association-learning through reinforcement."

Freud's Psychoanalysis

Although Freud (1925) acknowledged two classes of drives, those which are biologically inherent and those which evolve from life experiences, he (unlike the association-learning theorists) did not emphasize the manner in which the latter drives were learned. For Freud the primary drives or instincts were of two categories, the "life instincts" contributing to the survival of the person and of the species (e.g., sexuality), and the "death instincts," involving self-destructive forces which could be turned outward toward others and which produced aggression and war. Freud's entire theory of personality was built around the transformations in the sexual and aggressive drives, the fruits of living in a social world.

The behavior of the human infant, as seen by Freud, is organized around the *pleasure principle,* which has the flavor of a minimum tension or tension-reduction concept. Everything that the infant does reflects the tendency to seek immediate pleasure through the direct discharge of instinctual energy. For example, libidinal (sexual) drives must be instantly discharged to avoid painful tension, and this discharge could sometimes occur through various automatic motor reflex actions. The requirements for discharge also differ according to the psychosexual stage of the child. Oral forms of discharge are at first appropriate, but later the erogenous zone of the body on which the sexual drive is focused (and thus the pattern of discharge) shifts, first to the anal and then to the genital region (see discussions of Freud's psychosexual stages in chapters 6 and 7).

In certain spheres, reflex actions are not always applicable. They are sometimes proscribed or limited by the culture, as in sexual climax from masturbation or defecation. In other cases, an object is necessary to produce the discharge; one cannot, for example, eat unless there is food. In such instances, the person must find a suitable object for gratification by searching the environment. This search is facilitated by another mechanism through which discharge is made possible, that is, the *primary process*, by which a person forms an image or hallucination of the appropriate object. This image often is referred to as a "wish-fulfillment." Although it presumably does permit some discharge of tension, it is insufficient, and the main function of the primary process is to facilitate the search for the suitable object.

It is not altogether clear whether Freud assumed that the person learns through experience about suitable objects or has inherent images that are part of the species, or both. Research by Tinbergen (1951) with lower animals, such as fish and fowl, suggests that they are constructed with built-in "releaser" mechanisms which automatically result in specific adaptive responses when they are provoked by the appropriate stimulus. For example, the male stickleback fish, even without previous experience, will engage in aggressive activity merely on viewing the red underbelly of another stickleback, and a complex pattern of aggressive responses is automatically elicited when that stimulus is present. In fact, the male responds in almost the same way to even a poor cardboard drawing of a fish, as long as the bottom portion is the appropriate red. It is conceivable that even in higher organisms, suitable releasers of action could stem in part from inherited neurological mechanisms, although these releaser mechanisms would not be so rigid or automatized in operation as in lower animals. The latter possibility has never been adequately demonstrated for humans, and so we tend to emphasize learning rather than biological inheritance when considering Freud's concept of the primary process wish-fulfillment.

A research example of what might be loosely called wish-fulfillment in human adults, probably accentuated because of their extreme deprivation, comes from observing the fantasy behavior of men participating during World War II in military experiments on the effects of semistarvation (Keys and coworkers, 1950). For many weeks volunteers did full-time physical labor while being fed a diet severely reduced in caloric value. Some rather interesting personality effects of this semistarvation were noted, including tremendous preoccupation with food, placing on the walls of the barracks food "pin-ups" showing juicy steaks and other appetizing dishes, and frequently expressed determination to change vocations in favor of food-oriented occupations such as cook or restaurateur. We might regard these activities as examples of primary-process wish-fulfillment: The chronic and powerful craving for food led the men to search for images of food objects ordinarily capable of reducing hunger-induced tension. Hallucinations in mentally disturbed patients, as well as distortions of perception in normal people, can be thought of as instances of this primary-process conjuring up of images of satisfying objects.

The trouble with the primary process is that often we cannot discharge libido directly and immediately, either due to social inhibition (as in toilet discipline in the young child), or the unavailability of the actual object required to produce discharge (as in food or a sex partner). From this delay or thwarting of gratification, there emerges the "secondary process" which operates according to the "reality principle." It must do two things. First, it must protect the person against external dangers and second, it simultaneously must make possible the discharge of tension by gratification of the instincts. The environment must be evaluated to determine whether instinct-discharge is possible and safe, and the necessary objects to permit this discharge must be found. The *secondary process* is the way Freudians conceptualize the development of adaptive behavior in the child. It is another way of speaking about the emergence and growth of the "ego." Ego development is the same as that implied in the development of the secondary process; when we refer to the former we are speaking in terms of one of the major structures or subdivisions of the personality, that is, the *ego*, which operates in accordance with the rules of secondary process.

The ego must be capable of inhibiting the expression of instincts until a safe, satisfying object is found. The *reality principle* therefore requires the postponement of immediate gratification, and this is likely to produce pain in order to produce later gratification more safely. Freud regarded all complicated mental activities such as learning, perception, memory, and reasoning as functions of the ego. In fact, he considered all secondary process mental activity to be based on the adaptive requirements of the postponement or frustration of immediate drive discharge. Postponement and frustration are, to all intents and purposes, inevitable for the developing child. By following the reality principle and utilizing the secondary process, the ego inhibits direct instinctual discharge and finds substitute or transformed methods of gratification.

There are many examples of the operation of the secondary process and its inhibition of direct and immediate discharge of tension. Socialized toilet behavior which evolves from infancy to later childhood and lasts throughout life is one. Defecation must be withheld until the appropriate time and place even though the bodily impulse calls for immediate discharge. This withholding requires the capability to control the anal sphincter muscles and the cognitive processes necessary to recognize social pressures about the "proper" things to do. Similarly, anger and the impulse to attack must be inhibited and either diverted to safe objects and situations, or transformed into more socially accepted impulses. The father, for example, who cannot control rage toward his child when the child's behavior leads to frustration, may wind up beating the child so severely as to cause serious injury or even death. Such cases continually occur in our society and demonstrate the failure of secondary process activity in a disturbed adult who is unable to control impulses and perhaps even to foresee the consequences of his or her actions (reality principle). Without these constraints against immediate gratification, it is difficult to see how any society could exist, for without them people could hardly live together in reasonable harmony and safety. (For a related discussion, see our later section on self-control and Mischel's, 1976, summary of delay of gratification research.)

Freud thus subscribed to the division of motives into those that are inborn and physiological (primary drives) and those that are acquired (social motives). Sex is an example of an inborn physiological force (the id), and learning, perception, and engaging in a wide range of socialized behavior represent the Freudian versions of secondary or social motives. The latter ego motives arise only because the pleasure principle cannot always operate. A person is born into a society that interferes with the direct gratification of the instincts through social regulations aimed at channeling human instincts into socially acceptable paths. This results in the creation of new forms of drive discharge, which are in a sense similar to the secondary motives emphasized in association-learning through reinforcement theory. Let us turn now to this second version of the tension-reduction model.

Association-learning through Reinforcement

The principle of reinforcement states that an association will be established between any stimulus and response when a drive has been gratified, that is, when the response to a stimulus succeeds in reducing the tension created by an unsatisfied drive. Not all association-learning theories are based on this reinforcement principle, though it probably has been the most influential in association-learning theory, and certainly the one which has been used most in applying learning theory to personality. We cannot discuss here the alternative principles or their histories. Suffice it to say that John Dollard and Neal Miller (1950) have become the most articulate spokespersons for the "association-learning through reinforcement" view of personality.

Dollard and Miller identify four concepts as important to the learning process: "drive," "response," "reinforcement," and "cue." *Drive* is what initiates responses. This primary basis of human motivation stems from unsatisfied tissue needs. We must take nourishment, replenish water, sleep, and prevent excessive variation in body temperature, to mention some of the most important examples of tissue "deficits." Their presence creates tension or discomfort. This tension serves as a drive stimulus to behavior until responses are made which succeed in eliminating the deficit (*reinforcement*), after which the drive subsides. In effect, we learn the behavior (*responses*) that enables us to gratify tissue needs and reduce their related drive tensions. Because these biological drives arise from the way animals are constructed and survival depends on satisfying them, they often are referred to as *primary drives.*

Secondary or *social drives* do not arise directly from inherited tissue needs but are learned through the association of social experiences with the reduction of primary drive tensions. For example, the affectionate responses of the mother become associated with the elimination (or reinforcement) of hunger tensions in the young child when she feeds it. Consequently, the child comes to want such affectionate responses from the mother and from others, just as the innate satisfaction of filling the stomach is desired. In short, through the process of feeding an association between affection and the reduction of hunger is acquired and a new or secondary drive for affection is created. These associations or connections are formed between responses and certain *cues*, or stimuli, in the environment. If the reinforcing response is eating, a person must identify those stimuli to which the response is appropriate. These situations may be the presence of food or environmental circumstances in which food may be found—for instance, a refrigerator can be an appropriate cue for obtaining food. In sum, under conditions of drive and in the presence of cues or stimuli, a person makes responses that reduce the drive; those responses that reinforce are learned so that later the appropriate cues again will elicit them.

In addition to these elements of association-learning through reinforcement, Dollard and Miller specified certain other characteristics of learning. For example, the strengthening of connections between certain cues and drive-reducing responses also implies the converse, the weakening of other connections and the elimination of inappropriate responses that may have been tried before. This elimination of previously learned responses by withholding reinforcement is called "extinction" and is essential to learning, because learning could not take place unless unwanted acts were extinguished along with the establishment and strengthening of desired acts.

According to still another principle, "stimulus generalization," responses that have been learned in association with one specific cue may be transferred to other similar cues or situations. If we have learned to be afraid of speaking up in one particular social situation, the response of fear is then likely to be induced by other social situations. The greater the similarity between the situations, the greater the likelihood that a response learned to one will generalize to the other; and conversely, the less the similarity, the less the likelihood of generalization. No two cues or situations are ever precisely the same; therefore, consistency of behavior would never occur without *stimulus generalization*. Because we recognize and therefore can respond to stimuli as similar for many physical and subjective reasons, specification of the qualities that determine psychological similarity among situations remains one of the most perplexing problems in learning theory. The reason for which a person responds or fails to respond to stimuli as similar is difficult if not impossible to predict without a knowledge of internal psychological events.

Stimulus generalization is very important, but if responses learned for one stimulus generalized indiscriminately to others, learning could not occur since the same response then would be made to all stimuli. For adaptive behavior to develop, a person also must learn to distinguish among stimuli so that he or she responds to the correct one. To give a concrete example, we must learn to differentiate a refrigerator that contains food from a cabinet that contains material incapable of reducing our hunger drive. The process by which we differentiate appropriate from inappropriate cues is called "discrimination." Just as stimulus generalization is required in order for a given response to spread to all members of a class of appropriate cues, *discrimination* is required to permit us to select the proper class of cues that will produce drive reduction (see chapter 4 for a related discussion on behavioral consistency and specificity).

Finally, through "anticipation" we identify the probable consequences of a stimulus or response before it happens, and thereby can learn to perform actions that will reduce a drive in the future and to avoid those that will have painful or dangerous consequences. *Anticipation,* in other words, helps the individual react appropriately to an impending danger or benefit.

Complex social motives, such as the desire to achieve or to be liked, are assumed to be learned in the same way as simpler responses are, such as tying a shoe or hitting a typewriter key. Rewards also can be learned. We learn to accept expressions of approval as rewards, because the approval was associated in childhood with the reinforcement (by parents or other adults) of primary drives such as hunger and thirst. In other words, we learn that approval is connected with desirable consequences, even though approval itself may have had no intrinsic biological value.

According to the principles of learning briefly sketched above, we can learn any complex pattern of response in this way, including neurotic symptoms such as phobias and hysterical paralyses and the defense mechanisms connected with these disorders. The source of these maladaptive responses is the emotional drive of fear, which is said to be reduced by the neurotic symptom or the defensive activity (see our later discussion of anxiety and Table 7). From this point of view, clearly any characteristic of personality—motives, inhibitions, defense mechanisms, and so on—may be learned from the same set of laws of association-learning by reinforcement.

Dollard and Miller offer many illustrations of the application of the principles of learning they espouse to the learning of pathological symptoms such as phobias, compulsions, alcoholism, and defense mechanisms such as regression, displacement, rationalization, and projection. A case of phobia which they describe is an excellent illustration:

> The essential points are illustrated by a case of a pilot who was interviewed by one of the authors. This officer had not shown any abnormal fear of airplanes before being sent on a particularly difficult mission to bomb distant and well-defended oil refineries. His squadron was under heavy attack on the way to the target. In the confusion of flying exceedingly low over the target against strong defensive fire, a few of the preceding planes made a wrong turn and dropped their bombs on the section that had been assigned to the pilot's formation. Since not enough bombs were dropped to destroy the installations, the pilot's formation had to follow them to complete the job. As they came in above the rooftops, bombs and oil tanks were exploding. The pilot's plane was tossed violently about and damaged while nearby planes disappeared in a wall of fire. Since this pilot's damaged plane could not regain altitude, he had to fly back alone at reduced speed and was

subject to repeated violent fighter attack which killed several crew members and repeatedly threatened to destroy them all. When they finally reached the Mediterranean, they were low on gas and had to ditch the airplane in the open sea. The survivors drifted on a life raft and eventually were rescued.

Many times during this mission the pilot was exposed to intensely fear-provoking stimuli such as violent explosions and the sight of other planes going down and comrades being killed. It is known that intense fear-provoking stimuli of this kind act to reinforce fear as a response to other cues present at the same time. In this case, the other cues were those from the airplane, its sight and sound, and thoughts about flying. We would therefore expect the strong drive of intense fear to be learned as a response to all of these cues.

When a strong fear has been learned as a response to a given set of cues, it tends to generalize to other similar ones. Thus one would expect the fear of this airplane and of thoughts about flying to generalize to the similar sight and sound of other airplanes and thoughts about flying in them. This is exactly what happened; the pilot felt strongly frightened whenever he approached, looked at, or even thought about flying in any airplane.

Because he had already learned to avoid objects that he feared, he had a strong tendency to look away and walk away from all airplanes. Whenever he did this, he removed the cues eliciting the fear and hence felt much less frightened. But ... a reduction in any strong drive such as fear serves to reinforce the immediately preceding responses. Therefore, we would expect any response that produced successful avoidance to be learned as a strong habit. This is what occurred; the pilot developed a strong phobia of airplanes and everything connected with them.

Similarly, he felt anxious when thinking or talking about airplanes and less anxious when he stopped thinking or talking about them. The reduction in anxiety reinforced the stopping of thinking or of talking about airplanes; he became reluctant to think about or discuss his experience.

To summarize, under traumatic conditions of combat the intense drive of fear was learned as a response to the airplane and everything connected with it. The fear generalized from the cues of this airplane to the similar ones of other airplanes. This intense fear motivated responses of avoiding airplanes, and whenever any one of these responses was successful, it was reinforced by a reduction in the strength of the fear.

When all of the circumstances are understood, as in this case, there is no mystery about the phobia. In fact, such things as the avoidance of touching hot stoves or stepping in front of speeding cars usually are not called 'phobias' because the conditions reinforcing the avoidance are understood. Our contention is that the laws of learning are exactly the same, although the conditions are often different and much more obscure, especially when the fear is elicited by the internal cues of thoughts or drives (1950, pp. 157-59).

This sort of learning-oriented view of the acquisition of symptoms underlies the modern approach to psychotherapy of "behavior therapists," who seek to extinguish unwanted symptoms and behaviors by producing the conditions of unlearning or extinction. Their premise, like that of Dollard and Miller, is that "the laws of learning are exactly the same" for the acquisition of any habit, be it pathological (symptom) or desirable. The Freudian conception of the acquisition of a symptom is quite different. It might be asked, for example, why this particular pilot developed a "phobia" for airplanes while other pilots subjected to the same stress did not. Strong fear reactions of this sort do not usually persist long after the experience has ended, and only when they do should the symptom suggest a genuine phobia. The Freudian would assume that in such cases, and perhaps even in the case of the pilot cited by Dollard and Miller, there was some connection between this event and an unremembered one from childhood. Only such a connection would dispose this particular pilot to develop his symptoms. Perhaps the events of the bombing mission aroused forbidden or unacceptable impulses which reinstated earlier guilt or fear. Although this is not mentioned by Dollard and Miller, it is common for airmen in such situations to feel great guilt for their own survival and the death of their buddies. Although the extreme personal danger to the pilot seems to be the outstanding feature of the mission, the total event encompasses all sorts of dynamic complications stemming from the pilot's relations with the other men with whom he shared the danger. Precisely this sort of issue currently divides psychotherapists who adopt views similar to those of Dollard and Miller or other learning theorists from those who see pathological symptoms in Freudian terms as expressions of more subtle, usually hidden or unconscious forces, which may have had their origin in early childhood and may have been reactivated by some current event (see chapter 7 for further comparisons of these viewpoints).

Overview of the Freudian and Association-learning Versions of Tension-reduction

It should be clear that Freud and Dollard and Miller subscribe to a tension-reduction point of view. In both systems, drive-tensions activate behavior through which adaptive behavioral solutions to the tension are found. These views were much influenced by the British associationistic philosophers' assumptions about mental life and by Darwin's (1859) thinking about evolution and natural selection. Freud's analysis came first, and Dollard and Miller explicitly translated it into the language and format of association-learning theory which they believed was more susceptible to scientific verification. Although not all that is essential in Freud was incorporated into this translation, the fact that both share many fundamental assumptions is illustrated by the ease with which this translation was made.

In spite of the similarities between Freud's theory and association-learning reinforcement theory, there are four very significant differences in the way they view motivation. One difference is in the use of the term "discharge" in Freud's theory, as opposed to "deficit" in Dollard and Miller's. In the latter, the elimination of tissue deficit is the reinforcement or reward which stamps in the adaptive behavior. The model relies on the concept of a need which must be filled. For Freud, the model is one of mounting, undischarged energy. The analogy is that of a steam boiler in which the level of pressure rises until released by discharge through exit valves or by explosion. In short, in the deficit theory gaps or deficits need to be filled in, but in Freud's discharge theory, pressure needs to be released.

A second difference stems from the nature of the connection between the original tissue drive and the secondary or social motive which it creates. In association-learning theory, the connection between the primary drive, perhaps hunger or thirst, and the secondary or social motive is purely accidental. For example, when affiliative behavior is displayed toward the child by the mother, it tends merely by chance to become associated with the reduction of a primary drive tension such as hunger; that is, these two events are connected or associated because they occur together coincidentally in time or place, not because there is any biological link between them. In contrast, Freudian theory postulates a more biological connection between the life instincts and social motives. The latter are viewed as derivatives of the former, that is, as substitute (sublimated) versions of the former. For example, altruistic affection is viewed as a desexualized or neutralized form of libidinal energy. The sexual drive can be modified to permit discharge in some other, perhaps more acceptable, manner. The new or modified forms of discharge are not as adequate as the original, but they do allow the sexual energy to be drained off, so to speak. The closer the form of the sublimated outlet is to the original drive, the more satisfactory the discharge of tension is assumed to be.

Both systems of thought have some difficulty in dealing with the high degree of autonomy which the social motives seem to have in adult life. These motives eventually seem to depend no longer on their original connections with the primary drives. Although working for income may have its origins in the need for food and other forms of sustenance, long after the individual has more than enough income, work continues to have a strong motive power of its own. As Gordon Allport (1937b) stated, it has become "functionally autonomous" of its primary drive origins. Closer to the Freudian scheme, modern ego psychologists, such as Hartmann (1964) and Rapaport (1967), have dealt with this difficulty by introducing the concepts of "neutralization" of sexual drives and "ego autonomy." These are quite similar in scope and design to Allport's principle of *functional autonomy.*

Although the principle of functional autonomy makes intuitive sense, at least descriptively, its mechanisms or rules of operation have not been made clear. The conditions under which a social motive will or will not become an independent motive force in its own right have not been established. This remains an unresolved problem in the theoretical analysis of the relationships between primary or biological drives and secondary or social motives.

A third difference between the theories of Freud and Dollard and Miller is in the nature of the primary drives emphasized by the two systems of thought. Dollard and Miller do not specify the particular drive contents which might be central or peripheral to personality development. All the survival drives on whose gratification life tends to depend are mentioned, and hunger and thirst are treated as prototypical of all primary drives. Although Freud did not reject the idea that these drives played an important role in adaptation, he saw them as having little significance for the personality. As Freud saw it, the biologically critical drives of hunger and thirst are not surrounded by social conflicts and taboos, as are sex and aggression. Since the management of the former is not a major source of guilt and anxiety, those drives are not likely to result in psychopathological outcomes, except perhaps in rather extraordinary circumstances. In contrast, sex and aggression have great importance to Freudian thought. Because they are major sources of conflict in human life and since they are often linked to guilt and anxiety, they play a crucial role in personality development. Hunger and thirst are peremptory in that they cannot be postponed or repressed without endangering life, but sex and aggression as drives can be repressed without this danger and thus are likely to be associated with neurotic problems. Notice too that sex and aggression as drives are not compatible with the deficit model of Dollard and Miller in which some substance, such as a nutritive element, is absent and must be replaced, but they are compatible with the discharge model of Freud. Thus, in a review of the differences between the two tension-reduction theories, there is an interesting connection between points one and three.

A fourth and final difference is the way in which unconscious processes are seen. Dollard and Miller accepted the notion of unconsciousness but gave it a rather special meaning. In their view, unconsciousness arises from the failure of the person to label verbally the components of his or her experience adequately, or from the active process of extinguishing (repressing) a label. Our language fails to label adequately all our drives and reactions, their nuances, and the features of our physical and social environment. In some societies, there are many terms for colors of particular importance to that ecology; in other societies, these verbal distinctions may not exist. These gaps in language are particularly important in early childhood before the person has acquired the means to label and verbalize psychological events. Impulses (drives and motives) and events occurring at these times may never be labeled at all. According to Dollard and Miller, these impulses and events are experienced without awareness, because of this failure of labeling or because of the blocking of a *verbal label*. For Freud, it is the blocking of impulses from awareness through the defense mechanisms of the ego, that in large measure accounts for unconscious mental activity (see Table 7).

Despite these differences, both Freudian and association-learning theory (at least the reinforcement version of it popularized by Dollard and Miller) share the basic principle of tension-reduction in their conceptions of human behavior and its motivation. Whether expressed by the term "pleasure principle" or "principle of reinforcement," all behavior without exception is seen by both as a means of reducing tension, even that behavior which seems on the surface to produce more tension than it reduces. In the Freudian view of these seemingly contradictory instances, for example, as when organisms seem to choose painful rather than benign behavioral alternatives, the tension-reduction principle is not regarded as violated. Rather, the principle is believed to be suspended in the interests of learning more effective means of overcoming obstacles to tension-reduction via the reality principle. We often choose what appear to be detours or circuitous routes in order to ensure better tension-reduction in the future. Freud supplemented the pleasure principle with the notion of the death instinct which also accounted for nonpleasurable behaviors, but this notion has been rejected as circular and unnecessary by most Freudians today, and it will be ignored here. In any case, the contradictions of much behavior to the tension-reduction principle are only *apparent* contradictions; they are explained as necessary detours rather than as suspensions of the principle.

Challenges to the Tension-reduction Principle

The chief advantage of tension-reduction as an explanatory principle is its elegance—its basic simplicity. Its disadvantages are in the instances, alluded to above, when it fails to conform to our subjective experience and with certain empirical evidence. With respect to contrary subjective experience, pleasure does not always seem to be merely the reduction of pain. Wanting to go to the movies or eat a meal seems to be a positive attraction, and only at times does this sort of desire seem subjectively to be based on the need to reduce a gnawing unpleasantness produced by tissue deficits. Of course, such a difficulty is not necessarily fatal, since many correct ideas have conflicted with common sense, as did the proposal that the earth revolved around the sun rather than the other way around.

For empirical evidence which does not easily fit the tension-reduction principle, there are a great number of instances in which people, and even infrahuman animals, appear to seek stimulation rather than to reduce it. These instances often are difficult to explain away comfortably as being detours on the way to tension-reduction. For example, how does one explain thrill seekers (e.g., parachutists, auto racers, daredevils), or people who die rather than betray a trust, or those who risk their lives for a principle? Tension-reduction in such cases seems to be abrogated in favor of some other principle of motivation.

It has been shown, too, that animals who are not evidently driven by any of the usual primary drives still show curiosity or exploratory and manipulative behavior. Harlow (1953) has demonstrated, for example, that when they are not hungry or thirsty, monkeys will work even harder to obtain the reward of being able to look out of a window at people and things going on about the cage than when they are caught up in primary drive tensions. Infants, too, appear to engage in more exploration and manipulation when evidently physically sated than when suffering from primary drive tensions.

Exclusive reference to tissue needs or deficits as the basis of drive-related behavior seems particularly deficient as an explanation in certain instances in which such needs do not produce motivated behavior. McClelland, Atkinson, Clark, and Lowell (1953, pp. 7-22) have effectively marshalled evidence which dethrones tissue needs as the fundamental motivational source. Among other things, they cited experiments in which a nonnutritive substance, saccharine, was an effective motivator merely because of the sweet, pleasant taste it creates. They also referred to other instances in which tissue deficits do not lead to motivated behavior when these are not known to the person. A passage from McClelland et al. forcefully makes this point:

> ... Certain difficulties with this model [survival, tension-reduction] may be summarized briefly. In the first place, some survival needs produce a motive and some do not. For example, it is now known that vitamin B_{12} is necessary for the production of erythrocytes, and without B_{12} the organism will suffer from pernicious anemia and die. Yet a person suffering anemia or B_{12} deficiency behaves in no way like a motivated person, at least as determined by any of the usual measures of motivation. Another example would be the breathing of carbon monoxide which leads to sudden death and certainly to a tissue need, but which apparently produces no activity or behavior suggestive of a state of motivation. If anyone feels that these are merely isolated exceptions to the biological-need theory of motivation, a very brief perusal of the medical literature should convince him of the great number of pathological organic conditions that by definition constitute tissue needs, but which do not give rise to any kind of 'driving' stimulus or motive. Granted this fact, it follows that the presence of a biological need is not a reliable index of the existence of a motive (1953, p. 15).

Traditional tension-reduction explanations of the above anomalies appear forced, and other, perhaps more satisfactory solutions have become popular in psychology. One of these recognizes that the tension-reduction principle is often valid but insufficient, and attempts to supplement it with additional principles. The usual solution is to add to the original list of primary drives another category which is based not so much on what happens in the peripheral tissues but rather on the structures of the brain.

When this solution was proposed originally, it was assumed that these brain structures emerged with increasing encephalization, that is, with the evolutionary development of the brain. New drives such as curiosity, exploration, manipulation, and the like, were invoked on the assumption that these were unique to higher organisms (such as humans). They do not operate because of tissue deficits (as in hunger) which are communicated by chemical action to the central nervous system, but entirely through neural processes which are not dependent on peripheral tissues. However, in recent years the evidence has grown that these "new" drives operate in lower animals too, such as the rat and cat, as well as in the monkey and human. More and more, psychologists and animal behaviorists have come to recognize these drives as characteristic of animal life (see for example, Dember, 1960). In any event, this solution of expanding the list of drives to include nontissue-deficit types serves as a second type of motivational model, in addition to tension-reduction.

APPROACHES SUPPLEMENTING THE TENSION-REDUCTION MODEL: EFFECTANCE

The most explicit and perhaps the most useful account of this newer line of reasoning as applied to personality may be found in the writings of Robert White (1960, 1963). His analysis begins as a sharp critique of Freud's psychosexual theory and skillfully proceeds to point out that something more is needed to understand the behavior of the child. White wants to add the principle of "effectance" (wanting to have an effect on the environment), which he sees as encompassing better the important psychological events of childhood and explaining better a person's exploration and manipulation throughout life. A person develops competence not merely to discharge instinctual drives better, as Freud had argued, but because *effectance* motivation is an inherent property of the child at birth. It is, in short, as much of a primary drive as is hunger, thirst, or sex, and is much more important than these drives in helping us understand the remarkable human skills which develop in dealing with the environment.

White thinks that drives such as hunger, thirst, and sex have been given too much importance in the analysis of the personality. He concedes that the Freudian psychosexual theory explains much, particularly the sorts of pathology which can develop as a result of internal conflicts over the sexual and aggressive urges. But the aspects of behavior of interest to White, and which he feels are not encompassed by the Freudian approach, are powered by the effectance drive and are not derivatives of the sexual drives. White states:

> The theory that we learn what helps us to reduce our viscerogenic drives will not stand up if we stop to consider the whole range of what a child must learn in order to deal effectively with his surroundings. He has much to learn about visual forms, about grasping and letting go, about the coordination of hand and eye. He must work out the difficult problem of the constancy of objects. . . . He must learn many facts about his world, building up a cognitive map that will afford guidance and structure for his behavior. It is not hard to see the

biological advantage of an arrangement whereby these many learnings can get underway before they are needed as instruments for drive reduction or for safety. An animal that has thoroughly explored its environment stands a better chance of escaping from a sudden enemy or satisfying a gnawing hunger than one that merely dozes in the sun when its homeostatic crises are past. Seen in this light, the many hours that infants and children spend in play are by no means wasted or merely recuperative in nature. Play may be fun, but it is also a serious business in childhood. During these hours the child steadily builds up his competence in dealing with the environment (1960, p. 102).*

In subsequent statements, White examines each of the psycho-sexual stages posited by Freud, matching the description of the child's erotic activity at each stage against observations of other things the child does as well. For example, in the oral stage in which the child is presumed by Freud to be preoccupied mainly with stimulation of the oral cavity—sucking, feeding, taking in things through the mouth, and maintaining comfort and security— White argues that the child does many other things, ignored by the psychosexual theory, things which manipulate the environment and produce competence. This manipulation is an example, says White, of the operation of the effectance drive. His discussion of this is instructive:

> For one thing, there are clear signs that additional entertainment is desired during a meal. The utensils are investigated, the behavior of spilled food is explored, toys are played with throughout the feeding. Gesell suggests that at one year of age a toy in each hand is the only guarantee that a meal will be completed without housekeeping disaster. A similar situation prevails during the bath, when water toys are needed and when the germ of scientific interest may express itself by 'dabbling water onto the floor from the washcloth.' More important, however, is the infant's growing enthusiasm for the doctrine of 'do it yourself.' ... Around one year there is likely to occur what Levy (1955) calls 'the battle of the spoon,' the moment 'when the baby grabs the spoon from the mother's hand and tries to feed itself.' From Gesell's painstaking description of the spoon's 'hazardous journey' from dish to mouth we can be sure the child is not motivated at this point by increased oral gratification. He gets more food by letting mother do it, but by doing it himself he gets more of another kind of satisfaction—a feeling of efficacy, and perhaps already a growth of the sense of competence (1960, p. 110).*

White also contrasts what he sees in the baby's behavior with

* (Reprinted from *Nebraska Symposium On Motivation* edited by M.R. Jones by permission of University of Nebraska Press. Copyright © 1960 University of Nebraska Press.)

what the classical psychoanalytic theory of psychosexuality appears to require: "The psychoanalytic hypothesis of oral libido requires us, first, to merge nutritional satisfaction with erotic satisfaction; second, to find the motivation of all the competence sequences in oral eroticism" (1960, p. 113). Such a merger could be produced by association of oral eroticism with feeding as Freud assumed; that is, during feeding, the mucous membranes of the mouth are stimulated. It also might occur through secondary reinforcement as argued by association-learning theory, that is, oral stimulation is connected with reduction of the hunger drive. And finally, it could occur through the process of symbolism, the one activity, oral stimulation, coming to be symbolic of the other, loss of hunger and security. About this White suggests:

> Connections of this kind assuredly exist. I have no intention to dispute what Erikson, among others, has shown about symbolism in children's play and about the erotic and aggressive preoccupations that lead to play disruption. But we lose rather than gain, in my opinion, if we consider the child's undisrupted play, six hours a day, to be a continuous expression of libidinal energy, a continuous preoccupation with the family drama, as if there could be no intrinsic interest in the properties of the external world and the means of coming to terms with it. We lose rather than gain if we look only for an incorporative element in the infant's cognitive and motor behavior, remembering, for instance, that he puts the clothespin in his mouth but forgetting that he uses it to bang on the chair (1960, p. 113).*

White makes similar analyses of the other two psychosexual periods (anal and phallic). In each case, he concludes that the decisive psychological struggles of the child do not occur solely, for example, in the feeding situation or in the bathroom with toilet training but rather, in all settings in which the child is expressing its innate drive for effectance, that is, in the sandpile, on the tricycle, in learning to manipulate and comprehend the world. White does not deny that primary tissue needs from which hunger, thirst, sex, and other drives emerge are necessary to motivational development, but only that the really important human drives are to be active, to explore, to manipulate and control, and to produce and accomplish. These are contained within the general rubric of the effectance drive, that is, the wish to have an effect. It is biologically plausible that effectance, or whatever one wishes to call the drive, is expressed through the neural tissues which emerged with the phylogenetic development of higher species, such as humans, and is part of each person's inheritance.

White's position is important because in contrast to the tension-reduction stance it argues that much of our cognitive and social behavior should not be regarded as being derived from so-called primary drives, such as hunger or sex, but rather as being the product of a primary or innate drive of its own. The person explores, manipulates, and thinks, not merely because these are instrumental to gratification of some primary drive, but because it is intrinsically gratifying to do so as a result of the way people are constructed. This supplements the tension-reduction formulation. In some respects, humans now are said to be *tension-producers*, as well as tension-reducers, at times seeking the lowering of drive tensions and at other times seeking to heighten such tensions. Many writers recently have argued that some optimal level of tension (rather than no tension) is the norm or baseline toward which humans strive, a level that is neither too high nor too low. This hypothetical level is difficult to specify, because there are no satisfactory ways to assess it, but ultimately such a concept might have considerable predictive power.

The above principle, of which White's account is one of the clearest and most persuasive, has not led to any new systems of personality theory. However, it has taken many forms, has penetrated deeply into the literature, and has become a respected mode of thought in general psychology. Its precursors are seen in some of the neo-Freudian writers who have abandoned or qualified the tension-reduction principle, for example, in Jung, Rank, Adler, and Fromm. There are also many current examples in personality theory in which the point of view is opposed to a strict tension-reduction position, including Murray (1938), McClelland (1951), Kelly (1955), and Maddi (1976). Although these differ in important respects, space prevents discussion of each variation. Rejection of total dependence on the theme of tension-reduction is also a cornerstone of a newer type of psychoanalytic thought, often referred to as "ego psychology" (e.g., Hartmann, 1964; Rapaport, 1967). Two features characterize this psychoanalytic ego-psychology movement: 1) The ego is presumed to develop partly from existing inherent neurological structures, rather than entirely from the failure of discharge of the life instincts. The ego has its own energy for growth and differentiation, so to speak, rather than depending for this upon the id, as Freud had postulated. As in White's analysis, adaptive thought is an instinctual or inherent property of the developing person. This aspect of the ego—that which does not grow out of or stay embroiled in conflict and struggle over libidinal discharge—has been referred to as "the conflict-free ego sphere." 2) Psychoanalytic ego psychology turns its attention much more than Freud did to adaptive and nondefensive functions of the ego such as perception and problem-solving. A longstanding gap between psychoanalysis and the more traditional concerns of general psychology thus is bridged somewhat by the abandonment of a strictly tension-reduction view of human motivation.

THE FORCE-FOR-GROWTH MODEL

"Force-for-growth" is an expression identifying a cluster of theoretical views about human motivation with one, shared, basic idea. It is that humans have a built-in force or urge to grow and when given the opportunity to express the highest qualities of thought, creativity, altruism, and humanitarianism, they will do so. This view perhaps is best represented by two writers, Carl Rogers (1951, 1961, 1972) and Abraham Maslow (1968, 1970, 1971), although elements of the idea of inherent potentiality for growth may be found in the writings of many of the neo-Freudians, such as Jung, Adler, Fromm, and especially in Rank's works.

The central motive in humans, according to Carl Rogers, is the tendency toward *self-actualization*. Rogers assumes that under appropriate conditions people will express higher values than those embodied in the primitive instincts of self-preservation, that is, the avoidance of pain and the seeking of sensual pleasure. An example of this *force-for-growth* in operation is the adolescent who normally seeks independence and autonomy, even though it is safer and more comfortable remaining dependent on his or her parents. Another is a person's willingness to jeopardize comfort and security in order to support an unpopular principle. Despite discomfort, an inherent growth process leads a person toward individuation and higher development. Characteristic directions of movement of healthy (or "fully functioning") individuals, those people whose growth processes are unhampered, are shown in Table 5.

The concept of *self-actualization*, as defined by Maslow, is that a person always strives toward realizing his or her inner potentialities. Maslow identified a hierarchy of needs and values, ranging from the most primitive which humans share with lower forms of life, to those characteristic of only the most advanced types of organism. The hierarchy of needs in humans ranges from the lowest survival needs such as hunger and thirst, to higher needs including

Table 5

Negative and Positive Directions Characteristic of the Fully
Functioning Person
(Largely derived from statements of clients)

NEGATIVE DIRECTIONS (MOVING AWAY FROM)	POSITIVE DIRECTIONS (MOVING TOWARD)
Away from shells, facades, and fronts	Being in a continual process of change and action
Away from a self that one is not	Trusting intuitions, feelings, emotions, and motives
Away from "oughts" (being less submissive, less compliant in meeting standards set by others)	Being a participant in experience rather than being its boss or controlling it
Away from disliking and being ashamed of self	Letting experience carry one on, floating with a complex stream of experience, moving toward ill-defined goals
Away from doing what is expected, just for that reason alone	Moving toward goals behaviorally, not compulsively planning and choosing them
Away from doing things for the sake of pleasing others at the expense of self	Following paths which feel good
Away from "musts" and "shoulds" as motives for behavior	Living in the moment (existential living); letting experience carry one on
	Possessing greater openness to experience
	Being more authentic, real, genuine
	Moving closer to feelings and self (more willingness to yield to feelings and not to place a screen between feelings and self); journey to the center of self
	Accepting and appreciating the "realness" of self
	Increasing positive self-regard (a genuine liking and sympathy for self)

From DiCaprio (1974, p. 371)

belonging and love, esteem, and cognitive and esthetic needs, such as a thirst for knowledge and a desire for beauty (see Table 6). According to Maslow, higher needs will not be gratified or permitted expression unless the more urgent primitive needs are satisfied.

The force-for-growth philosophy implies that, if given the opportunity, humans will express their advanced nature. When they do not do so, it is because the social conditions of life continue to require a survival struggle to a degree that prevents the realization of higher potentials. For Freud, cognitive and esthetic needs are sublimated expressions of the primitive sexual and aggressive instincts and in fact come into being because these instincts are inhibited through social living. For Rogers and Maslow, however, these cognitive and esthetic needs are inborn qualities whose expression depends not on thwarting but on favorable life circumstances.

We noted that the origins of the force-for-growth philosophy in

Table 6

Maslow's Need Hierarchy

5. SELF-ACTUALIZATION NEEDS

    Need to fulfill one's personal capacities
    Need to develop one's potential
    Need to do what one is best suited to do
    Need to grow and expand metaneeds: discover truth
                                create beauty
                                produce order
                                promote justice

   4. ESTEEM NEEDS

      Need for respect
      Need for confidence based on good opinions of others
      Need for admiration
      Need for self-confidence
      Need for self-worth
      Need for self-acceptance

      3. LOVE AND BELONGING NEEDS

         Need for friends
         Need for companions
         Need for a family
         Need for identification with a group
         Need for intimacy with a member of the opposite sex

         2. SAFETY NEEDS

            Need for security
            Need for protection
            Need for freedom from danger
            Need for order
            Need for predictable future

            1. PHYSIOLOGICAL NEEDS

               Need for relief from thirst, hunger
               Need for sleep
               Need for sex
               Need for relief from pain, physiological imbalances

Note: The "actualization needs" imply activity whereas the lower needs imply the fulfillment of a deficit ("need to" vs. "need for"). *From DiCaprio (1974, p. 243)*

personality theory can be found among the neo-Freudians, who increasingly emphasized the social basis of personality and who questioned the primacy of the life and death instincts as propounded by Freud. For example, Jung (1953) suggested that in middle life people become less dominated by libidinal urges and turn toward more philosophical, spiritual concerns about the meaning of life and their place in the universe. Alfred Adler (see Ansbacher and Ansbacher, 1956), too, maintained that people have a natural (inborn) tendency to concern themselves with "social interest" and communion with others. Otto Rank (1952), who comes the closest to being the direct forerunner of the force-for-growth school of thought, argued that the fundamental struggle in humans is between the desire for social union and the need to become separate or individuated. The person who is most successful in synthesizing these two opposing tendencies was called by Rank "the artist," presumably because he or she can be simultaneously at one with others and a separate, distinguishable individual. Psychoanalyst Erich Fromm (1941, 1955) has gone even further, attempting to specify the kind of society that permits our individuation while sustaining our needs for security and belonging. Having reexamined history from feudal times, Fromm maintains that humans have not yet evolved a society that permits the gratification of these conflicting but inherent needs.

We might note a kind of implicit evolutionary assumption in the force-for-growth point of view (and also in White's), that as we move from primitive to higher animals, new structures of the brain evolve which introduce new needs and capacities. This assumption is most explicit in Maslow's theory. Humans are at the highest end of the phylogenetic scale. They carry with them many needs and capacities not found in lower animals. Self-actualization in humans, therefore, requires the gratification of these later evolved needs. The force-for-growth concept has been criticized as mystical and value-laden, since it flirts so continuously with the evaluation of humans in terms of normative judgments of high and low, advanced and primitive, good and bad.

REFLECTIONS:
IMPLICATIONS OF THE THREE
MOTIVATIONAL MODELS

Of the three viewpoints that have been reviewed above, White's has the fewest implicit values. His emphasis is on the drive for effectance and the consequent development of competence to master the environment. The desirability of competence is the central value of the model, but precisely what competence consists of and what people might do with this competence is not a subject of immediate interest.

The drive for effectance could lead to diverse results. It could, for example, lead to an infantile, destructive lust for power, as in the cases of Hitler or Stalin, or it could express itself in self-actualization (in the manner suggested by Maslow or Rogers), in which the highest and most humanistic virtues are revered. The effectance drive could result in artistic creativity or in a banal, sterile output. It could even produce frustrated inaction or bitterness toward those forces or persons who prevent one from doing things. There could be innumerable forms of competence, depending on life circumstances. Effectance does not have any built-in direction, since it is merely the inherent desire to have an effect.

This relative *value neutrality* in the effectance model is in sharp contrast with the tension-reduction and force-for-growth viewpoints. The divergent values about people and society implied in these latter positions display themselves most clearly in two intellectual spheres. One concerns *conceptions of human nature*, that is, the inherent drive-properties with which humans come into the world. The second concerns *conceptions of human society* and its role in shaping the human condition. Although one risks overstatement in making this contrast of values and stating its implications, the effort permits us to see a relationship between the assumptions of personality theory and some of the pressing social problems of our day. Let us begin with the fundamental conceptions of humans which are held by the tension-reduction and force-for-growth viewpoints.

Conceptions of Human Nature

One can perceive in the tension-reduction philosophy a competitive, conflict-laden, survival-oriented, and perhaps somewhat pessimistic outlook. Humans are seen as the latest version in a long line of evolutionary development based on the principle of *survival of the fittest*. Through the process of natural selection through breeding, the species and biological properties best adapted to the environment have evolved. Whenever humans fail in their adaptation, it is because of changes in the environment to which selective breeding has not yet provided modifications. For example, their natural aggressiveness once might have had value by facilitating the management of environmental dangers, but these same tendencies and the emotionality accompanying them are unsuited to the present, industrialized, social environment in which aggression has few useful outlets. Now it results in internal disturbances whose consequences are psychosomatic disorders. In any case, the principle of natural selection is still in force, and human biological, primary drives still determine how we fare in the modern world. To the extent that these drives no longer facilitate biological or social survival, they have become unwanted vestiges of an ancestral animal past, perhaps to be discarded eventually.

In the above analysis, *self-interest* is the fundamental force that energizes and directs human behavior, although this force can be modified and redirected somewhat by the social system. Humans struggle individually to survive and flourish by replenishing tissue deficits and discharging drives such as sex and aggression. However, this self-interest poses an interesting dilemma. In one sense it is the enemy of a society which thrives on order and harmony. One person's success may mean another's failure. This means that if people are to live in relative harmony with their fellow beings, the drives expressing self-interest must be controlled or transformed in such a way as to blunt their danger to others and to the social system on which humans today depend.

Freud saw the fundamental human problem as the control and transformation of the animal instincts into "healthy," socially constructive, and acceptable modes of discharge. These instincts, in one sense, are bad, because they can destroy people and their society. In both the Freudian and association-learning versions of tension-reduction, the highly valued human patterns of moral concern, altruistic love, and esthetic appreciation are not biologically inherited but grow out of thwarted instinctual drives. The motivating tensions thus produced create the sublimations of these drives into socially desirable motives (Freud), or yield new social motives when the latter forms of behavior are associated with the reduction of such tensions (Dollard and Miller). Thus, positive human traits are learned or secondary, and selfish traits are mainly products of biological inheritance.

Nowhere is the idea of the necessary opposition between society and the animal part of human nature more stressed than in Freudian theory, with its emphasis on primitive sex and aggression. A clinical example is the dramatic form of psychopathology known as multiple personality, a case of which, Miss Christine Beauchamp, first was fully described by Morton Prince (1920). More recently, other cases have been reported by Thigpen and Cleckley (1957) and Schreiber (1973). Aspects of Miss Beauchamp's personality became "dissociated" from each other, as if the various conflicting impulses within her could no longer be integrated into a harmonious whole. During the course of the illness, three distinct personalities emerged, two of them particularly contrasting. One of the personalities was a sexually promiscuous, outspoken, and ribald woman who ridiculed the side of herself which was inhibited, moralistic, and prudish. The patient seemed to alternate from one phase to the other, with little warning as to when one or the other would dominate. The inhibited personality appeared to be totally unaware of the activities of the other, uninhibited one. Most instances of multiple personality seem to manifest at least two personality extremes, one inhibited and overcontrolled (in a sense, oversocialized), the other uninhibited and undercontrolled (in a sense, animallike). What could be more in keeping with the Freudian image of people as a mixture of primitive, animal instincts and learned, internalized social constraints!

There is also a fine literary example of this dual image in Robert Louis Stevenson's famous novel, *The Strange Case of Dr. Jekyll and Mr. Hyde.* First published in 1886, its theme continues to be popular, as seen by the several movie versions made in the United States (see Figure 11). Mr. Hyde is the "evil," animal part of human nature consisting mainly of a mixture of sexual and aggressive (sadistic) impulses. Dr. Jekyll, a physician, is the "good" part which is tragically overwhelmed when he has the temerity to experiment with a chemical potion unleashing the animal part. Dr. Jekyll expresses to the other physicians of his time the shocking idea that these good and bad qualities exist together in all people.

One can see clearly in the Freudian viewpoint a presumed

FIGURE 11. Dr. Jekyll and Mr. Hyde as portrayed in the film by actor Frederick March. (Culver Pictures, Inc.)

phylogenetic continuity between humans and lower animals. It is an idea which shocked the Victorian world of Freud, as it shocked the physicians addressed by Dr. Jekyll in Stevenson's book. These men lived in a time when it was fashionable to believe that humans were distinct from, and above, infrahuman animals. In religious circles, only humans were believed to have pure souls. Church dogma attributed evil to the Devil, and to Original Sin which caused humans to fall from grace. To suggest a continuity with the animal world, as Darwin did, was to challenge humans' uniqueness and to make them little better morally than the lower forms of life. Freud said, too, that people have all the base instincts found in other, lower animals. This deeply threatened and offended the Church and the public, and led to persistent and widespread condemnation of Darwin's and Freud's concepts. Although the religious and "scientific" positions are really not irreconcilable, they seemed so and produced a long-standing, fundamentalist, ideational struggle which has not ended to this day (see Beach, 1955, for further discussion of this).

It is important to recognize that Freud's views of animal behavior and instincts were quite inaccurate and overly simple. For example, from careful observations by modern ethologists and animal ecologists, it has become evident that there are many forms or *patterns of animal aggression*, and that these may be based on quite different physiological mechanisms (Moyer, 1967; Rothballer, 1967). There are, for example, "intraspecies" and "interspecies" aggression, the stimuli, response topography, and functions of which are probably quite different from each other. *Interspecies aggression* involves attacks on animals of other species, as in the seeking of food by carnivores or the maternal protection of young against predators. *Intraspecies aggression* consists of attacks on members of the same species, as when two males are in competition over territory or mating. If indeed these forms of aggression have different biological roots and if one argues that aggression in humans is carried down phylogenetically from their animal ancestors, then the question arises as to which of these forms, if either, demonstrates the evolutionary origin of human aggression.

Humans are evidently the first primates to be carnivorous predators (interspecies aggression), the great apes being mainly vegetarians. It is thought by some that this change represents the beginnings of human aggression. These interspecies aggressive tendencies may have been useful to early humans, since they might have aided in their survival against other predators. Anthropologist Louis Leakey (1967), however, has proposed that it was their offensive smell and taste which preserved them more than anything else. In any case, most aggression in humans seems to be of the intraspecies type, since their savagery toward one another is the most striking and at the root of a large number of their social problems. This aggression could be linked to the territorial aggressions found widely in the lower animals, that is, the tendency to fight other members of the same species over a section of ground or over a mate.

There are some remarkable differences between human and infrahuman animals in this, however. For example, when lower animals fight within their species, they rarely kill. They engage in what has been called, "ritual aggression" (see, for example, Hall, 1964; Lorenz, 1966; and Matthews 1964). For example, when a male challenges another male for territory or a mate, there is much sound and fury but seldom a fatality, because the loser usually defers to the victor before he is seriously injured and if he appears smaller and weaker, he may never make the challenge at all. Upon discovering his own vulnerability, he simply turns tail, exhibits a passive posture, and withdraws. The victor is quite content to let him go; he has proved his point and taken over the territory. Only when both animals are confined in a small space so that escape is not possible will one kill another as humans do. It has been suggested, too, that humans kill because their weapons make withdrawal before fatal damage is done difficult, and that their long memory and strongly developed ego are often deadly additions to the usual animal intraspecies aggressive tendencies.

The biological bases of aggression are far from clear, and there are those who find the argument that aggression has such an origin unsupported by evidence. They emphasize the social factors in aggression rather than the biological, arguing that learned responses to frustration provide the main basis of aggression in humans (cf. chapter 3). Whatever the ultimate answers turn out to be, questions about the origins of aggression are of great interest to biological and social scientists alike, because of the great dangers of self-annihilation through modern warfare and weaponry.

Although this brief discussion of aggression may have seemed like a digression, it was designed to prevent the usual kind of oversimplified analysis that stems from a limited understanding of the complex problems of the biological origins of human drives. Freud's thinking on the subject of aggression was consistent with the knowledge of his era, and this knowledge has become outdated. Nevertheless, his general argument that humans are suffused with drives which have to be controlled is a forceful and widely respected position. Its implications for the solution of social problems are strikingly different from the implications derived from the image of humans projected by the force-for-growth theorist.

Force-for-growth theorists acknowledge that humans have the self-centered, survival-oriented drives emphasized by tension-reduction theories. Granting these, however, they argue that there are still other inherent and more important biological properties in humans. If they are nurtured, these other properties can become predominant. The variants of these arguments are many, each attempting to specify in greater or lesser detail the fundamental drive attributes or needs that reach their peak in human beings. Overall, these theorists emphasize human relationships, that is, they postulate needs which express humans' social rather than tissue-centered nature. The fundamental needs of humans are not seen as derived from more primitive tissue needs. Rather, they tend to be defined in social or interpersonal terms, although these too are regarded as biologically inherited dispositions motivating the person throughout life.

For example, recall Abraham Maslow's (1970) approach (see Table 6). Motives are conceptualized as falling within a hierarchy, ranging from the survival needs such as hunger and thirst, up the evolutionary scale toward higher needs such as safety, then belonging and love, esteem, and self-actualization. The "higher" needs will not be gratified or permitted expression unless the prepotent and more primitive needs are first satisfied. In other words, the tissue needs and those related to safety and security, are urgent and tyrannical when threatened, but the "higher" needs involving self-actualization remain latent under conditions unfavorable to their emergence. The latter will be expressed only when a person is freed from the tyranny of lower-order needs.

Another example is the analysis by Erich Fromm (1947, 1955). His list of fundamental human needs includes *relatedness* or belonging, to feel a part of the group; *transcendence,* to become a creative person rising above one's animal nature; *identity,* to be unique; and having a stable *frame of reference,* to have a consistent way of perceiving and comprehending the world.

Aside from the lists of fundamental human needs, there is not so much to say about motivational dynamics from the perspective of the force-for-growth theories. These theories have been somewhat more vague about how motives work and the conditions under which they will emerge compared with tension-reduction theories. In recent years force-for-growth theorists have had much to say about the defects in society, sharing a common view that the failure of people to develop in healthy ways and to express their potential is the result of the damaging effects of the social conditions under which they live. Concern has tended to be with questions of how the social order should be arranged in order to maximize human potentiality for growth, given the set of socially oriented needs that comprise their motivational systems.

Conceptions of Human Society

It already has been pointed out that the tension-reduction model sees the social system as providing necessary restraints on the animal instincts. These restraints are necessary for two reasons: first, so that means will be developed for overcoming inevitable obstacles to survival and comfort; and second, to make possible a secure, orderly, and stable mode of life for humankind. Again, Freud has been most explicit about how society developed and in what ways it transforms the primitive instincts.

Freud (1957) argued that the instincts of sex and aggression must be restrained by social rules and that culture is the outgrowth of these instincts and the organized ways of controlling them. With appropriate social rules, a strong ego develops which is capable of seeking safe and successful avenues for instinctual discharge. Without adequate limits and discipline permitting the development of a strong ego, personality would be warped by neurotic solutions, by character disorders in which there are insufficient moral development and inept life styles, or by psychoses in which there has been regression to infantile, pregenital forms of libidinal expression unsuitable to adult life. Freud saw an analogy between the psychological development of the individual and the evolutionary transition of humans from the unrestrained expression of the sexual and aggressive instincts through the acceptance and internalization of social rules. This analogy may be illustrated by considering the mating behavior of the herd animal.

In the case of the migratory seal, the mature bulls begin to arrive at the mating site in the spring ahead of the females. On arrival, the bull stakes out a plot of land, its size and desirability depending on his capacity to seize and hold it against all other competitors. When the females arrive, he creates a harem and continues to resist challenges by other bulls. The largest and strongest "beachmasters" are most successful, mating with many females. Throughout the mating period there is continual competition over the territory and over the females. Each year, new competition emerges in the form of young males who are maturing and becoming powerful enough to challenge the old bull for his territory and harem. Old bulls who are no longer capable of driving off the challengers retire to the outskirts of the mating beaches, removed from the females and unable to mate; young bulls too puny to succeed also remain in the periphery. This mating struggle can be viewed as a phylogenetically primitive version of the Oedipus situation (see chapter 6).

There is no incest taboo among the herd animal to cool down this perpetual struggle. Humans, however, collectively have made a "social contract" which includes a universal taboo against incest. For example, the son is prevented from accepting his mother as an erotic love object when he becomes an adult. The Oedipus complex in infancy and childhood is a repetition ontogenetically (i.e., developmentally) of the phylogenetically primitive mating process of the herd animal, deriving its power to motivate from essentially the same drive sources. We see in Freudian theory that *the role of society is clearly to inhibit humans' unrestrained and destructive primitive urges so that a stable family system can develop, and to permit the emergence of the higher mental processes.* Humans are then free to love unselfishly, to accept restraint of their impulses, and yet to discharge the libidinal energy in adequate, substitutive forms which can benefit the rest of humankind.

What has been said above about Freudian theory and the tension-reduction model suggests that this view would contribute to our understanding of transgressions against the social order, such as those transgressions associated with marginal social groups like the slum dweller, vagrant, hippie drop-out, welfare recipient, or alcoholic. Tension-reduction views also should tell us something about childrearing. It turns out, however, that one's response to problem groups and problem children depends on which features of tension-reduction are emphasized. Freud actually argued that during the crucial early years of pregenital (oral, anal, and phallic) psychosexual development, extremes of restraint or permissiveness were traumatizing, inhibiting the normal progression from one stage to the next. For example, too much oral supply (feeding, nurturance) would lead the developing child to expect it in perpetuity and make it unwilling to move toward the next stage (anality). Likewise, too little would lead to distrust of the environment and the continuing search thereafter to make up for the deficiency.

Some of the central assumptions of the tension-reduction point of view imply that humans survive by developing competence to master the environment or to adapt to it. Since the qualities of this competence are, in part, passed down genetically through the process of natural selection, deviant groups then may be seen as human failures. In some instances, these failures are attributed to biological deficiencies; in others, they can be viewed as the product of a stunted or warped ego resulting from traumatic conditions of life. Undoubtedly, both biological and social processes are involved. In any case, when the emphasis has been placed on competition and the struggle for mastery, as it is above, the solution must be in appropriate discipline and environmental limits, and when these have been lacking, in retraining. This stance has a Darwinian influence which underlies the tension-reduction position; the assumption is that the primary biological forces in humans are those of self-interest and survival. Altruism and other human ideals are seen merely as derivatives of such self-interest.

It would be oversimple to regard the tension-reduction model as lending itself exclusively to a discipline-centered orientation. Its protagonists surely would not argue that *any* social system is adequate merely because it restrains humans' animal instincts. Although a strong ego (or in association-learning terms, an adequate habit system) is essential to healthy functioning, and although such an ego cannot come into being without firm limits imposed by the social order, a repressive society is as defective as an overly permissive one. The former produces neurosis as in Freud's day; the latter, disorders of character or socialization (as portrayed in the movie *A Clockwork Orange*). Without adequate substitute forms of discharge, tension-reduction must fail. Excessive restraint makes it difficult or impossible to find creative solutions to life problems.

It must be remembered that Freud formulated his personality theory while attempting to treat neurotic patients who were, presumably, victims of a too repressive Victorian society, and it would have been out of character for Freud to argue that this repressiveness was desirable. On the other hand, when Freud's daughter, Anna, lectured in the United States after World War II, she is said to have made the interesting observation that the major maladjustments seen in clinics had changed from predominantly neurotics to character disorders, that is, to persons with inadequate socialization and competence for getting along in society. She attributed this to the shift from the excessive Victorian discipline of her father's day to the excessive permissiveness in post-World War II childrearing, with the impairment of self-discipline. In this connection it is ironic that Freud has long been presumed guilty of arguing in favor of unlimited permissiveness, and he was blamed for the breakdown of childrearing discipline, merely because he was critical of the damaging effects of the repressiveness of his own times. Although one should not overstate it, the tension-reduction principle does somehow affirm the importance of a firm, restraining hand and a stable social order as the means by which primitive people are civilized. By restraining the animal in humans, society enables the development of valued, social motivational derivatives from the primary drives, since the former are not present without the proper social experiences. Both too much discipline and too flexible limits are bad for the development of psychological health, each leading to somewhat different forms of deviance. The precise limits of this generalization have never really been spelled out and without considerable research and evidence, the general principle does not lend itself very well to a program of childrearing with concrete recommendations.

How is the same issue dealt with by the force-for-growth model? Here too there is great danger of oversimplification. The force-for-growth protagonist seems to have been somewhat more inclined to take a militant position than the tension-reductionist has, at least by emphasizing that society is the main culprit in psychological failures rather than a necessary asset in restraining the drives of self-interest. The force-for-growth theorists say that society resembles a jungle, so to speak, in which survival is always threatened. Therefore, existing and past social systems have continued to keep humans insecure, frightened, and helpless. This promotes the expression mainly of the prepotent survival needs but inhibits the expression of the more fragile, but just as basic, higher social needs unique to humans. To force-for-growth theorists, the task of society is not the restraint of humans' primitive drives, but rather the nurturance of those drives which contribute to their self-actualization. Only in a secure, supportive setting can the latter be expected to appear. Inner human nature is fundamentally good, but society thwarts its expression.

If we consider from this point of view the marginal or deviant segments of the society, the onus clearly is placed on the society for not providing such individuals or groups with sufficient security to nurture the growth tendency present in everyone. The existence of social failures only proves the inadequacy of the social system rather than implying adaptive insufficiency.

Force-for-growth theorists seem to be espousing a permissive ideal for the social system and presumably for parental behavior. The one-sidedness of this stance probably results from the wish to emphasize the evils of existing societies and to attack a more established view. In all likelihood, this sanguine view of human capacity to express its highest nature without environmental restraints would probably be qualified by force-for-growth writers, if they had to detail concretely the ideal conditions of child development. Most reasonable people recognize that discipline of some sort is essential to healthy development, and the argument tends to be over what kind of discipline and over what are its healthy forms in contrast to unhealthy and confining ones. The difference between points of view is mostly in emphasis. They are characteristically oversimplified by the public, and by those who for their own personal or ideological reasons want to argue for one or the other extreme position. The problem is a very emotional one. The more general and abstract the discussion is, that is, the less it refers to a specific context or to particular persons and behaviors, the more fruitless is the debate, and the more refractory it is to resolution by scientifically acceptable evidence. As it now stands, without the necessary specification and research, the issue can be dealt with only by speculative analysis which in the long run must give way to dependable knowledge.

Maslow (1964) has gone further than most force-for-growth theorists (except perhaps Fromm) in trying to conceptualize the essential quality of the society which might promote self-actualization. He has found the general answer in the concept of "synergy," introduced by the cultural anthropologist Ruth Benedict. Self-actualization requires that the person express his or her own personal identity without being alienated from society. To a greater or lesser extent, most cultures make this difficult or impossible, because gratification of oneself usually harms or, at least, rarely benefits the group. Synergy expresses the extent to which the institutions of a culture make possible individual productivity while providing mutual advantage for the individual and the group. Maslow expresses it as follows:

> ... the conclusion that emerges is that societies where non-aggression is conspicuous have social orders in which the individual by the same act and at the same time serves his own advantage and that of the group.... Non-aggression occurs (in these societies) not because people are unselfish and put social obligations above personal desires, but when social arrangements make these two identical... (1964, p. 155).

From the force-for-growth point of view, the solution for deviance and marginality is not further discipline, or the attempt to point the person to socially desired directions by reward and punishment, but is in making the person feel secure and free from threat. Then the person can afford to be what he or she is capable of becoming: a humane, socially conscious, artistic, creative, and altruistic individual. Punishment, especially when it is excessive, creates warped people instead of self-actualized ones. Any adaptive adequacy which may emerge from the survival struggle is apt to be devoted to selfish ends rather than to the welfare of one's fellow being.

It is probably no accident that the force-for-growth philosophy has had a great appeal to the intellectual youth of today who have rebelled against the defects of a modern, industrial, competitive society. It is interesting, too, that a common answer to the criticisms of such youth is a tension-reduction answer, that without stress or struggle for survival, the affluent societies would not have achieved their spectacular wealth and mastery over the environment. It is also worth noting that a large segment of today's rebellious youth is accused of having it too easy, economically, compared with their insecure, Depression-era parents.

Although the above implications may have been somewhat overdrawn, it is particularly important to recognize that political and social ideology can be linked to the issues of personality theory. The divergent, theoretical assumptions about the nature of human motivation are, in a sense, ideologies, dogmas, or philosophies, rather than scientifically tested propositions. At this time, so little is actually known about the conditions under which competence, altruism, love, aggression, and so on, are to be found, that one must be very wary of accepting any of these philosophies as scientifically respectable. These philosophies do serve as alternative working assumptions whose acceptance and rejection tend to be made on the basis of plausibility and esthetic value. In the proposals for social change made by social scientists and political ideologists, these philosophies often remain as unstated assumptions. Someday perhaps, we will have a broader and more adequate empirical basis for choosing between them or for adopting different ones.

OTHER ISSUES OF PERSONALITY DYNAMICS

Thus far, we have compared several theories of personality dynamics in terms of general motivational principles assumed to underlie human behavior. While our survey of necessity has been brief, there are two additional issues (or assumptions) which deserve some elaboration here, namely, the role of *anxiety* and of *self-control* as motivational forces in personality.

Anxiety

Because it seems to play such a vital role in the functioning of personality, anxiety has been studied extensively by personologists (see, for example, Spielberger, 1972). In general, personologists have regarded anxiety as an unpleasant emotional state which usually motivates individuals to engage in behaviors which either reduce or eliminate the anxiety or avoid it altogether in future situations. The exact nature of anxiety and the available ways of coping with it are viewed differently by the various theorists we have discussed in this chapter.

For example, Freud (1926) regarded anxiety as a "specific state of unpleasure" which acts as a distress signal to the ego, telling it that danger is imminent. This danger can originate from one or more sources, providing a basis for differentiating various kinds of anxiety. The most sensible kind of anxiety, called *reality anxiety*, is brought about by something in the person's external world (some might call this "fear"). There is an objective danger here, like a vicious animal or a difficult task, and the person's anxiety is proportionate to the threat. In *moral anxiety*, danger is more subjectively based, emanating from the superego. The person experiences feelings of inadequacy, guilt, and shame over expressed sexual or aggressive needs or even over thoughts about them. In moral anxiety, the person is threatened with punishment from his or her own conscience. *Neurotic anxiety*, too, has a subjective internal source, but in this case the culprit is the person's id rather than the superego. Instinctual impulses may threaten to overwhelm the ego's controls and may lead to the direct expression of socially unacceptable behaviors and to punishment from others.

Freud believed that when the ego cannot cope with anxiety in a realistic and logical fashion (e.g., by obtaining instructions on how to study for examinations or on how to protect yourself in dangerous situations) anxiety-related tensions may have to be reduced by defense mechanisms. These unconscious psychological maneuvers are commonly used and help the ego to ward off anxiety by falsifying or distorting reality. Prolonged or extensive use of defense mechanisms often can lead to serious adjustment problems (e.g., neuroses), because they seize valuable time and energy resources from more adaptive activities. At any rate, defense mechanisms protect us from realizing the source of whatever is threatening us and therefore are effective temporary methods for reducing anxiety. A listing of some common defenses is presented in Table 7.

According to Dollard and Miller, the neurological and physiological basis of fear (or anxiety, which they consider to be essentially similar states) is innate and largely elicited by our built-in tendency to avoid pain. Fears of specific stimuli (e.g., a hot stove), however, are rapidly reinforced by pain and then often generalized to other stimuli (e.g., developing a fear to associated cues like "kitchens" or

Table 7

Common Ego Defense Mechanisms

REPRESSION—excluding unacceptable impulses, ideas, or feelings from consciousness. For example, in repression, feelings of hatred or lust toward one's parents are blocked from awareness.

REGRESSION—returning to a less mature level of adaptation, especially under extreme frustration or stress. For example, regression may be seen in the fired executive who begins to act in an extremely dependent and helpless fashion, requiring relatives to attend to his or her every need.

PROJECTION—attributing unacceptable ideas or impulses to others rather than acknowledging them as one's own. For example, unconscious homosexual impulses may be projected upon others, so that now the person is troubled by the homosexual behavior of other people and not by his or her own desires.

RATIONALIZATION—justifying an act or idea that is unacceptable because it is unreasonable, illogical, or inconsistent. For example, the individual who fails to achieve a much-desired and hard-fought-for goal then decides that failure really was "for the best" or "a blessing in disguise."

REACTION FORMATION—transforming dangerous or painful urges into their opposite forms, though the original urges persist unconsciously. The transformed urges often are felt or expressed in excessive and exaggerated ways, for example, a mother's hatred of her child is transformed into maternal oversolicitousness.

DENIAL—rejecting or distorting those aspects of reality which consciously are unacceptable. For example, the person maintains that the death of a loved one "just did not happen."

SUBLIMATION—modifying unacceptable impulses into socially acceptable activities. For example, sexual impulses may be channeled into painting or sculpturing nudes, while aggressive tendencies may be discharged by choosing to become a movie critic.

DISPLACEMENT—shifting impulses and feelings about one person or object toward a safer or less dangerous person or object. For example, aggressive feelings toward the boss are totally inhibited, but expressed later toward family members, pets, or furniture.

INTELLECTUALIZATION—removing or isolating feeling from a thought so that the thought can remain conscious without the associated affective charge. Thinking about impulses to murder someone without getting upset or anxious, or talking in a detached way about a recent divorce or personal failure without feeling the disappointment and hurt are common examples.

IDENTIFICATION—incorporating the thoughts, feelings, and actions of another to increase one's sense of worth or to reduce threat from powerful others. The child acquires parental standards and values partly through identification with its parents.

The above defense mechanisms are a sample of those typically employed in everyday life. Their moderate use may help protect the individual from disturbing negative emotions like anxiety, guilt, and shame, though excessive use may impair adjustment. These mechanisms are believed to operate unconsciously. Most defense mechanisms, especially repression, are used in conjunction with other defenses and, hence, are seen only rarely in their "pure" forms.

to similar events like a match or fireplace). This makes fear a powerful *secondary drive*:

> The helpless, naked, human infant is born with primary drives such as hunger, thirst, and reactions to pain and cold. He does not have, however, many of the motives that distinguish the adult as a member of a particular tribe, nation, social class, occupation, or profession. Many extremely important drives, such as the desire for money, the ambition to become an artist or a scholar, and particular fears and guilts are learned during socialization. (Dollard & Miller, 1950, p. 62)

Dollard and Miller also emphasize the relationship between fear and conflict, the latter being a situation in which two or more strong and incompatible drives exist simultaneously. Conflict, which is often central to the learning of neurotic behavior, is elicited by, and elicits, fear. There are different kinds of conflict, depending on the presence of tendencies to approach or avoid the relevant goal(s). For example, in an approach-avoidance conflict (see Figure 12), the individual is at variance with whether or not to reach a particular goal and may have great difficulty in resolving his or her indecision. Recalling our illustrative case study, one might argue that many of Jay's problems or difficulties (see chapter 1) were outgrowths of her perhaps unrecognized approach-avoidance conflict over becoming a professional. Although wanting to become a doctor, Jay probably also experienced many doubts and uncertainties about this prospect because of society's traditional values regarding women and careers. Other typical kinds of conflict include avoidance-avoidance and double approach-avoidance situations. Dollard and Miller, in their description of fear and conflict, offer the following advice to therapists:

> According to the preceding analysis, pure approach-approach choices are easily resolved; conflict should appear only when avoidance is present. This suggests that whenever unexplained indecision and conflict appear, the therapist should look for concealed sources of avoidance. Since fear is one of the strongest sources of avoidance, he can often profitably ask: "What is feared?"
>
> The relationship also works the other way. As has been suggested, the subject who is not physically restrained will soon escape from most fear-producing situations unless he is prevented by conflict. This conflict can be produced by other sources of avoidance that keep him away from the avenues of escape or by unsatisfied drives that motivate him to approach feared goals. Therefore, when unexplained fears persist, the therapist should ask: "What conflicting tendencies prevent the patient from escaping the fear-provoking stimuli? What frightening thing does he want to do?" (1950, pp. 367-368)

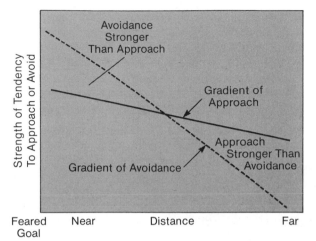

Figure 12. Simple graphic representation of an approach-avoidance conflict. The tendency to approach is the stronger of the two tendencies far from the goal, while the tendency to avoid is the stronger of the two near to the goal. Therefore, when far from the goal, the subject should tend to approach part way and then stop; when near to it, he should tend to retreat part way and then stop. In short, he should tend to remain in the region where the two gradients intersect. (*Figure adapted from Miller, 1944.*) (*Dollard and Miller, 1950, p. 356.*)

In short, then, we see that Dollard and Miller regard anxiety as an important, learned drive which usually leads to, and is consequently reinforced by, escape or avoidance behaviors (of a physical or mental nature)—a position consistent with their tension-reduction viewpoint (cf. Dollard and Miller's phobia example presented earlier).

Robert White has not written extensively about anxiety in relation to effectance motivation though he has discussed other emotions, like shame and guilt, in considerable detail. On the other hand, force-for-growth theorists regard anxiety as a significant though often negative force in personality functioning. Rogers, for example, suggests that anxiety often results when there is inconsistency between the self-concept and experience, and that defenses develop to protect the person from the anxiety. Let us look at this position more closely.

As the self-concept begins to emerge (see chapters 4 and 7), the child becomes extremely vulnerable to the wishes and demands of significant others (particularly the parents). Rogers believes this vulnerability is due in large part to the child's strong need for positive regard and to the fact that this approval and love from important others unfortunately seldom comes without reservations (e.g., I will only love you *if* you are smart, or obedient, etc.). These reservations (or *conditions of worth*) rather than the child's own natural standards, tell the child in effect which aspects of his or her experience are "good" and which are "bad." The self-concept becomes a product of social forces, geared largely to securing the acceptance of others.

What happens when the person later experiences things which are not in accord with the self-concept? Can the inconsistencies be tolerated or must they be distorted in some fashion? For example, an individual who views herself to be devoid of sexual feelings because of her strict upbringing may find later that she actually enjoys sexual activity. Rogers argues that because this experience is at odds with her self-concept, she may become threatened and anxious. Why? Because most of our behaviors are aimed at maintaining consistency within the self-concept and between the self-concept and experience. Thus, Rogers sees anxiety as a significant emotional state which warns us that something is not right, that major alterations in our self-concept may be imminent. Incidentally, Rogers believes that incongruencies between the self-concept and experience need not be recognized at a conscious level in order to elicit anxiety—the trouble may be "subceived," that is, recognized without awareness.

To deal with unpleasant anxiety and to maintain integrity of the self-concept, the individual responds with defense mechanisms. Rogers does not elaborate upon defense mechanisms to the extent that Freud or others have done. Nevertheless, he notes that these devices are aimed at reducing the incongruity between the self-concept and experience by either *distorting* or *denying* the experience. Thus, the woman we mentioned earlier might psychologically twist her pleasant sexual experiences into "awful" or "sinful" events in her mind or possibly even deny that she felt anything at all. Notice that defenses cause one to lose contact with genuine thoughts, feelings, and actions and consequently significant aspects of the true self are blocked from awareness—an undesirable state of affairs, according to Rogers, as it prevents self-actualization (see Table 5 showing characteristics of the fully functioning" individual). Nevertheless, the defenses are helpful, even necessary, to the maintenance of personality integration if discrepancies occasionally exist between the self-concept and experience. Once the discrepancies become too large or frequent, however, anxiety may become too intense for the defenses to handle adequately, and personality disorganization (e.g., neuroses) may begin. In extreme cases, the defenses may fail altogether:

> ...if there is a significant degree of incongruence between the individual's self-concept and his evaluation of experience, then his defenses may become inoperable. In his "defenseless" state, with the incongruent experience accurately symbolized in awareness, the self-concept becomes shattered. Thus, personality disorganization and psy-

chopathology occur when the self is unable to defend itself against threatening experiences. Persons undergoing such disorganization are commonly tagged "psychotic." (Hjelle & Ziegler, 1976, p. 304)

In summary, in many theories of personality dynamics, anxiety is regarded as a central and vital component of human motivation. Some theorists (e.g., Skinner) regard emotions such as anxiety to be "private" events, which are most difficult to study and which possess, anyway, little or no motivational significance (at least when compared to environmental influences). Nevertheless, anxiety is an important force in most theories, and the theoretical and empirical literature on anxiety (and other emotions) continues to proliferate at a rapid pace. Future research should provide additional clarification of the relationship between motivation and emotions.

Self-Control

Our discussions of personality have occasionally referred to relationships between various kinds of "control" and human behavior. For example, we have looked at the impact on behavior of *perceived* locus of control (chapter 4), stimulus or environmental controls (chapter 4), and in this chapter, the desire to control or to affect the environment (effectance motivation). Other important theoretical issues and distinctions in personality dynamics, especially motivation, recently have surfaced in the context of what has come to be called "self-control" (the terms "self-regulation" or "self-management" are sometimes preferred). Self-control generally refers to the processes which enable an individual to influence the variables which determine his or her behavior (Pervin, 1975, p. 432). Before examining the concept of self-control in detail, some background materials must be considered.

The theorists we have discussed in this chapter differ in many of their assumptions about human motivation but they do agree in part that the primary causes of behavior are internally generated. That is, tension-reduction, effectance, and force-for-growth theorists argue that the major causes of behavior are found within the person. Opposing this are theorists, such as extreme or radical behaviorists, who believe that behavior is best viewed as a series of responses to stimuli in the outer environment. Thus, there is a continuum (see Hjelle & Ziegler, 1976) along which personologists might be placed, according to their assumptions about the causes of human behavior. For example, of the theorists we have emphasized in this chapter, Maslow and Rogers are probably the most extreme in their positions on the internal causes of behavior (often called the "proactive" view of dynamics), while Freud, White, and Dollard and Miller probably would be near the middle of the continuum. At the other extreme (often called the "reactive" view of dynamics), we would find theorists such as B.F. Skinner (1971) emphasizing stimulus-response and behavior-environment relationships, while minimizing internal factors such as drives, instincts, or self-concepts.

With this in mind, it is not too surprising to learn that some theorists, such as those advocating the force-for-growth model, have often talked about concepts intimately related to self-control (like freedom, choice, self-determination, and will power) in the context of human motivation and improvement. It is believed by these theorists that human behavior is largely self-motivated, guided internally toward reaching (in the sense of process) goals such as self-actualization, selfhood, wholeness, superiority, and so on. Force-for-growth theorists have even described various exercises and therapeutic techniques which may help facilitate greater personal growth through increased self-awareness and self-control (cf. Fadiman & Frager, 1976).

Because "self-control" requires, in part, the study and regulation of many internal private events (e.g., thoughts, feelings, and images), it is rather confusing to learn that behavioral theorists have also shown an interest in this subject for some time (e.g., Skinner, 1953). But their use of the self-control concept needs some elaboration for it seems, at least superficially, to distort the implied intent of the concept. As Lazarus (1974) has noted:

> When behaviorally oriented psychologists have spoken of self-control, they have done so in what I consider to be a strange and contradictory way. Skinner (1953), for example, speaks of it as manipulating one's own behavior just as one might do in the case of another person or, as the environment does, through its pattern of reward and punishment contingencies. To decrease an undesirable behavior in oneself, for instance, the person makes the undesirable response less probable by altering the variables of reward and punishment on which it depends. Thus, if a person wishes not to overeat, he can place a time-lock device on the door of the refrigerator to eliminate snacks between meals. To prevent shopping sprees, he can leave his credit card or money at home. Thus, in this view, which has become exceedingly popular in behavior modification circles, the key agency of control seems to be the environmental contingencies rather than the person.
>
> Although such environmental contingencies are very important, what is often missed is that an *executive agency within the person* determines which of many competing trends and impulses are to be encouraged or discouraged. Oftentimes it is not the environment that is manipulated, but what the person attends to in that environment, or

how he interprets that environment. This is precisely what is meant by intrapsychic or cognitive control mechanisms. To speak of manipulating environment contingencies seems contradictory to me because it makes the environment the locus of self-control rather than the person, and this emphasis distorts the meaning inherent in the term *self-control*. It is the person who makes a commitment or decision on the basis of cognitive activity, whether he is conscious of it or not. (p. 30)*

Let us examine the behavioral approaches to self-control in some detail in order to clarify some of the specific techniques and also to illustrate how some of the currently more popular techniques suggest a relatively new willingness by many behaviorally oriented theorists to study previously forbidden (or at least frowned upon) events such as cognitions and feelings.

Behavioral theorists have studied self-control in relation to a variety of problem behaviors (e.g., smoking, obesity, alcoholism, shyness, nail biting, procrastination, and low self-esteem, to name but a few) and with a variety of people (e.g., students, professionals, prisoners, children, etc.). It should not be surprising, therefore, to discover the large arsenal of self-control techniques which have developed throughout the years—some of which are shown in Table 8. Thoresen and Mahoney, leading proponents of behavioral control, have synthesized the common features of the procedures and techniques in Table 8 and have offered the following definition of self-control:

> *A person displays self-control when in the relative absence of immediate external constraints, he engages in behavior whose previous probability has been less than that of alternatively available behaviors (involving lesser or delayed reward, greater exertion or aversive properties, and so on).* (1974, p. 12)**

In other words, self-control is manifested when a person responds in a situation in a way which previously was less likely than others (e.g., not smoking, rather than smoking, at a party) and which provides long-term benefits rather than immediate gratification.

In order to understand self-control a little better, let us look at a typical behavioral program used to teach individuals to manage their own responses (based on Reese, 1978). You might recall from chapter 1 that Jay once consulted a psychologist. While in therapy, she was trained to develop self-control of her slight weight problem

---

* Copyright © Academic Press, 1974, from *Cognitive Views of Human Motivation*, edited by B. Weiner.

** From *Behavioral Self-Control* by Carl E. Thoresen and Michael J. Mahoney. Copyright © by Holt, Rinehart and Winston, Inc. Reprinted by permission of Holt, Rinehart and Winston.

Table 8

Forms of Self-control

SKINNER (1953):
1. Physical restraint and physical aid
2. Stimulus manipulation (including self-managed stimulus exposure)
3. Deprivation and satiation
4. Manipulation of emotional conditions (controlling predispositions, rehearsal of previous consequences, self-instruction)
5. Aversive stimulation
6. Drugs (anesthetics, aphrodisiacs)
7. Operant conditioning (self-reinforcement and self-managed extinction)
8. Punishment
9. Incompatible response approach ("doing something else")
10. Private events (cognitive consequation)

BANDURA AND WALTERS (1963):
1. Resistance to deviation
2. Regulation of self-administered rewarding resources
3. Delay of gratification

FERSTER (1965):
1. Alteration of behavior-environment relations to reduce ultimately aversive consequences
2. Performances which increase long-range effectiveness (e.g., music lessons)
3. Alteration of the physical environment (rather than individual's behavior)

GOLDIAMOND (1965):
1. Alteration of specified environmental variables that control one's behavior
2. Application of functional behavior analysis

CAUTELA (1969):
1. Reciprocal inhibition techniques (relaxation, desensitization, thought stopping, covert sensitization, assertive training)
2. Operant procedures

KANFER (1970):
1. Abstention despite ad lib availability of reinforcers
2. Execution of a behavior despite its known aversive consequences

STUART (1970):
1. Aversive procedures
2. Instigation techniques

KANFER (1971):
1. Competing responses approach
2. Manipulation of aversive consequences
3. Manipulation of target behaviors' consequences (includes reduction and delay of positive consequences, negative consequation for antecedent responses, and differential reinforcement of other behaviors)
4. Environment manipulation
5. Self-reward

From Thoresen & Mahoney (1974, p. 13)

(once physiological sources were ruled out). The following procedures were used but keep in mind that they could be adapted easily
to other problems (or behaviors) which one might want to manage
personally.

Jay was encouraged first to analyze the conditions which
seemed to control her eating behavior and second to manage or
modify those conditions. Each of these steps had several components
and required considerable effort. To help her analyze the situation,
she was asked to collect preliminary data. This baseline procedure,
which uncovered many relationships between Jay's overeating and
environmental factors (like being alone, watching television, etc.),
provides important information to be used in the design of the self-
control program and in the evaluation of its effectiveness. During
this first phase, Jay had to note when, what, and with whom she ate,
as well as whatever occurred while eating. A sample of this kind of
preliminary analysis is shown in Table 9. On the basis of the baseline data, Jay then could determine which realistic goals and behaviors to measure. For example, she decided to lose twenty pounds
during her self-control program and felt that daily records of weight,
calories, number of between-meal snacks, and extra exercise would
be most important. Other possible measures could have included
behaviors such as number of times she did something else when she
felt like eating, physical measurements of waist, hips, etc., number of
second helpings accepted and refused, and so on (see Reese, 1978,
pp. 222-23).

Jay was now ready for the second part of her self-control program, managing or modifying the controlling conditions of her overeating. There are two strategies for accomplishing this, reflecting the
belief that behavior is controlled by its antecedents and its consequences. The first strategy, often called *environmental planning* or
stimulus control, attempts to prearrange situational factors in order
to disrupt or establish stimulus control, depending on the problem
behavior. In the case of overeating (called a "behavioral excess"), the
objective would be to disrupt stimulus control and in some cases
(when it occurs in too many situations) to establish stimulus control
to the extent of restricting the stimuli that evoke it. For Jay, the mere
sight of food often led to overeating. So, her self-control program
called for removing all food from her dormitory room (disrupting
stimulus control). She found that she ate in a variety of situations, a
common occurrence with overweight people. As Reese (1978) notes:

> People who eat too much often eat in a great many situations: while
> reading, watching television, studying, thinking; at parties, ball games,
> waiting for a bus, waiting in the check-out line at the supermarket;
> when they are bored, anxious, tired, happy; at 8 A.M., 10 A.M., noon,
> mid-afternoon, before, during, and after dinner, before bed—and when-

Table 9

Example of Daily Record Form Used in Self-management of Weight—Baseline Phase

Day _Th_ Date _10/11_ WEIGHT _138_ GOAL _118_ CALORIES, eaten _3828_

Baseline _X_ Program ____ Maintenance ____ Calories, exercise _100_

Amt. sleep last night _6h._ Weather _cold_ Total meals _7_

Time	Place	Activity	People	Mood	Amount	FOOD	Calories	Sum
7:30	Dorm	Breakfast	People?	bitchy	1 1 1 2	o.j. H.B. egg revolting coffee w/crs toast, butter	120 78 40 210	448
10:30	College Inn	break	Debbie, Neal Dinny, Barb	BORED	1 1	Danish coffee	125 40	—165
Noon	Dorm	lunch	Jill, Pearl, Eva, Stephanie	OK	1 1 2	milk spaghetti ☺ cake ☺	160 couldn't eat 500	660
4:30	Snack bar	after lab	Ed, David Jarrilynn	Ravenous	1 1	cheeseburger Fr. fries (make up for lunch)	470 250	720
6:30	Dorm	dinner	Jerri, Betsy Denise, Chip, Cathy	good	2 1 2 1	meat (lamb??) peas sm potatoes choc. ice cream	470 115 120 100	805
10:30	Snack bar	a well-deserved break	Tim & Marci Cindy, Richard Skye & Talley TOM	tired	2 1	beer sm potato chips	300 230	530
11-12	Room	studying	Rhea for a while; Esther & Madeline came by	zonked	½ box (maybe 10?) choc chip cookies		500?	500

448
165
1380
1835
3828

Total meals _7_ Total Cal. _3828_

EXERCISE

Moderate (200/hr; 33/10 min)		Vigorous (300/hr; 50/10 min)		Strenuous (400/hr; 70/10 min)	
Walking (slow)	_15_	Walking (3 mph)	_10_	Stren. sports	____
Bicycling	____	Horseback riding	____	Dancing (fast)	____
House work	____	Bowling	____	Jogging	____
____		Swimming	____	____	
		____			

Total time _15_ Cal. _50_ Time _10_ Cal. _50_ Time ____ Cal. ____

COMMENTS: _This was not a good day_

From Reese (1978, p. 217)

ever anyone drops by for a visit. It helps to make some of these situations discriminative stimuli for *other* classes of behavior, but the main thing is to restrict their control over eating. (p. 226)

Therefore, Jay tried to take her meals consistently in the same place and at predetermined times (restricting stimulus control).

The second strategy for managing the controlling conditions, often called *behavioral programming*, requires the subject to administer consequences to himself or herself following the occurrence of the pertinent behaviors. For example, Jay felt that if she restricted her calorie intake on a certain day to agreed limits, she deserved a reinforcement of some kind (besides and more immediate than the eventual weight loss). Likewise, if she failed to stay within the bounds of her agreement, an appropriate aversive event would follow. Reinforcers and adverse events obviously will vary from person to person, but some typical ones employed in self-control projects with students are shown in Tables 10 and 11.

Once possible reinforcers and aversive stimuli have been se-

Table 10

Potential Reinforcers for Older Students and Those Involved in Self-control Projects

POTENTIAL REINFORCERS
High-School and College Students; Self-control Projects

Sports equipment	Read for pleasure	Drive family car
Hobby equipment	Listen to radio, records	Stay out late
Kitchen utensils	Play bridge, chess, poker,	Have mother (friend)
Furniture, rugs	frisbee; do a puzzle	clean room or type
Clothes	Paint, draw, model	paper
Jewelry	Knit, sew, cook	Telephone friend
Add to collections: coins,	Write poetry, prose	Write letter to friend
stamps, models, charms	Try out for a part in play	Visit friend
Records, posters	Attend movie, concert,	Go to library, gym,
Books, magazines	sports	music room
Tickets to concerts, sports	Participate in music, dance,	Visit greenhouse, zoo,
events	political rally	museum
Gift certificate	Buy or wear new clothes	Sunbathe
Green stamps	Buy or eat snacks (low calo-	Take a walk
Food	rie for weight control)	Work in garden, shop
Money	Comb hair, brush teeth,	Watch television
Gas for Car	take shower	Go out for dinner
	Buy someone else a present	Go away for weekend
	Give someone else the	Play with pet
	present	Feed or train pet
	Earn points for someone	Water plants; garden
	else	Sleep Late
	Take someone out	Free Time
	Tutor someone	

From Reese (1978, p. 60)

Table 11

Aversive Events Used in Self-management Projects
by Mount Holyoke College Students

PUNISHERS

Do 15 push-ups
Do all the homework problems (even the optional ones)
Clean the room
Wash the dishes
Spend time being nice to someone I dislike
Wear a sign on back saying "I blew it"
Confess to boyfriend
Wear a ski mask indoors
Buy and eat cottage cheese
Get up at 6 A.M. and Study
Take bus, instead of drive, to Amherst
Call friend on pay phone in hall instead of phone in room

RESPONSE COSTS

Can't open mail
Can't receive a phone call from _____
No tea at breakfast
Can't brush teeth (shower, wash hair) in morning
Give _____ (friend) a dollar
Give _____ my blue sweater

From Reese (1978, p. 68)

lected, certain procedures must be chosen to administer them. Table 12 lists a number of overt and covert (i.e., cognitive-symbolic) procedures which have been used successfully with various problem behaviors. Although the overt procedures probably have been the most popular, covert ones also are potentially effective and their use, often in combination with overt techniques, seems to be increasing (more on this later). Jay's self-control program included both procedures. For example, she arranged a point or contingency schedule according to which she received varying amounts of credit for carrying out desired behaviors, like keeping food out of her dormitory room, limiting her snacks, and the like. These credits could be exchanged, when enough had been accumulated, for the reinforcers she had selected for use in her program (e.g., movies or clothes). Covert procedures included imagining, when she adhered to her program, how gorgeous she was going to look and, when she failed to stay on the program, how stupid and gluttonous she was.

174

Table 12

Self-management Procedures

OVERT PROCEDURES	COVERT PROCEDURES

Self-instruction

Writing down the rules in a contingency contract; reading or saying them out loud.	Recalling the rules; telling yourself to relax, count to ten, pay attention.

Modeling and Role Playing

Watching someone performing skillfully or appropriately (speaking with confidence; overcoming a problem; demonstrating a skill), then practicing the behavior that has been modeled.	Imagining yourself or another person performing skillfully or appropriately.

Reinforcement

Rewarding performance of the desired behavior by engaging in a preferred activity or by gaining a token or point that you may exchange for a back-up reinforcer.	Imagining yourself in a pleasant situation or telling yourself that you are noble, brave, virtuous, and in command, contingent on imagining or actually performing the desired behavior.

Escape-Avoidance

Making a deposit of money or goods that will be forfeited if the desired behavior is not emitted. "Storing a bag of ugly fat (representing one's own obesity) in the refrigerator and removing pieces as one loses weight." (From Mahoney & Thoreson, 1974, p. 50)	Imagining yourself escaping from an aversive or anxiety-producing situation when you imagine you are performing the desired behavior, or when you actually perform the behavior.

Extinction

Asking friends not to reinforce behavior (such as complaining, swearing) that you are trying to eliminate.	Imagining that the behavior (eating, drug-taking) is emitted but is not followed by the usual reinforcing consequences.

Satiation

If you are spending too much time reading pornographic literature, you might, in one sitting, go through eight or ten of those with the fewest redeeming features. But it might be better to program this as a reinforcer for competing behavior.	Imagining yourself engaging in the problem behavior until it is no longer enjoyable (eating forbidden food until you feel stuffed, sated.)

Punishment

Doing something you dislike: cleaning the room; exercising; wearing the button of a hated politician (also from Mahoney & Thoresen), contingent on problem behavior.	Thinking an unpleasant thought or imagining an aversive consequence, contingent upon emitting the problem behavior or upon the urge to do so.

Table 12 (Continued)

Punishment (cont.)

Arranging to be embarrassed: confessing to someone important; wearing a sign on your back or a glove on one hand that will make people ask why. (Not recommended for self-esteem projects.)	Telling yourself you're stupid, slovenly, gluttonous.

Response Cost

Subtracting tokens or points from those earned, contingent on the problem behavior.	Imagining the loss of a valuable possession, contingent upon overt or covert problem behavior.

Omission Training and DRL

Reinforcing the failure to emit the problem behavior for a specified period of time. (Behavior may be omitted altogether or in a specified situation.) Reinforcing a specified low rate of the behavior.	Imagining a reinforcing event, contingent upon real or imagined omission of the behavior for a specified period of time.

Reinforcement of Alternative Behavior (Alt R)

Reinforcing behavior that prevents or competes with the problem behavior.	Imagining a reinforcing consequence for overt or covert competing behavior, e.g., imagining a pleasant situation following resisting the urge to eat by leaving the table.

From Reese (1978, p. 234)

Writing all this out in the form of a "contract" is most important, because it clarifies and specifies what is expected and the consequences of not living up to the agreement. A sample contract for weight control is shown in Table 13. A contract should be reviewed periodically, and revisions (like changing reinforcers to avoid boredom) should be made when necessary (Kanfer, 1975; Reese, 1978). Moreover, a contract should be written for what will happen once the self-control program is terminated and the person suffers "setbacks." In other words, what happens if the person eventually goes off the self-control program and gradually regains part or all of the lost weight (or starts drinking again, etc.)? A maintenance agreement would specify the exact consequences of failing to avoid the undesirable behaviors (e.g., counting calories or returning to the original program).

The behavioral approach to "self-control" includes a systematic program of observation and planning. By identifying and then modifying the variables affecting us, we exert influence and in turn are influenced—and thereby have exercised self-control. But as Reese (1978) notes, "It is not really ourselves that we control or manage, of course; it is our behavior" (p. 212).

Table 13

Self-management Contract for Weight Control—Program Phase

Name: _____ General Goal: _20 lb. weight loss_____

Duration of Contract (dates) _oct 4_ to _oct 11_.   Program _✓_ Maintenance _____

<u>Data</u>
   Keep daily _✓_ or _____ records of:

   _weight_____   _extra exercise (time)_
   _calories_____   _____
   # between meal snacks   _____

   Data will be analysed and plotted: _every night_____

<u>Program</u>

   <u>Behavior</u>   Consequences
   Keep records at 5 pts each; 10 pts graph   _30 pts_
   1600 cal. weekdays; 1800 weekends (2 days)   _50_
   only 2 snacks a day: Total 300 cal. (500 weekend) _10_
   Eat at least 2 balanced meals a day   _10_
   Exercise 15 min/day (during week)   _10_

   <u>Stimulus control</u>
   No food in room   _10_
   Eat only with someone, in regular place   _10_

   <u>Alternative behavior</u> (if applicable)
   when feel urge to eat, remember Richard can
   wear my jeans and I can't Resist urge –
   think "gorgeous me."
   <u>Covert</u> (behavior, consequences)

                              If points, possible daily total _130_
   Bonus?
      50 points each pound lost
      200 "free" calories if stay within limit whole week
<u>Exchange</u>
                  Reinforcers   (Aversive Consequences?)

   movies, TV, reading etc – 10 pts/hr   _Point cost: 1 pt each 10 cal._
   Shower – 10 pts   _over limit_
   weekend away – 100 pts   _Also: if 200 cal. over,_
   gas for car – 10 pts   _tell Richard I blew it_
   clothes – 100 pts per $10⁰⁰ worth   _if 300 cal. over, all calls_
                                                  from pay phone for a
                                                  week

Signature _____ Date _____

From Reese (1978, p. 236)

The recent trend among some behaviorally oriented personologists (e.g., social learning theorists such as Bandura, 1969, and Mischel, 1976) advocating the importance of cognitive-symbolic (covert) factors in the study of human behavior has been noted elsewhere (e.g., chapter 4). Table 12 demonstrates how significantly the self-control literature has been affected by this radical shift from an almost exclusive emphasis on overt behaviors to the serious study of cognition by its listing of numerous examples of covert self-management procedures. Although the study of covert behaviors and their overt or covert antecedents and consequences is in its infancy and so far lacks substantial controlled investigation (see Koriat, Melkman, Averill, & Lazarus, 1972, for one of the few systematic studies here), we only can applaud behavioral efforts along these lines. These efforts not only help to integrate the interests and concerns of diverse groups (e.g., behavioral and force-for-growth theorists) but also, and more importantly, they help to pay tribute to the complexity and multifarious aspects of human behavior. As Thoresen and Mahoney (1974) note:

> ... Human behavior is no more the exclusive function of some hypothetical inner entity called willpower or self-actualizing drive than it is the sole consequence of external stimuli in the physical environment. Instead, human behavior is partly determined by internal or covert processes involving imaginal, subvocal, and physiological responses as well as by a variety of external events. Bandura (1969), after an extensive review of the literature, has suggested three major sources of regulation: stimulus control, symbolic covert control, and outcome control. These control mechanisms can function at a covert or internal level as well as externally. Such a conception is based on the homogeneity or continuity assumption that internal actions (viewed as responses) are susceptible to the same principles and hypotheses that have been demonstrated to influence overt behavior. Hence, stimulus control may occur through processes within the organism as well as without. In the same way, outcome control (consequences) may operate both within the person as well as externally. In this way, an *interdependent* perspective of self-control is offered whereby combinations of overt and covert events may function as antecedents, behaviors, and consequences. (p. 130)*

Our treatment of personality dynamics has presented some of the major issues related to human motivation, along with various theoretical positions concerning these issues. Earlier chapters have dealt with the nature, determinants (biological and social), and description of personality. We now will turn to an examination of how the personality unfolds over time. Specifically, we want to see how the various personality structures and processes develop throughout a person's life history.

Personality
Development

6

The developmental approach provides a time-oriented perspective to personality theory, since it is concerned with the universal sequences or stages through which personality evolves from its earliest beginnings in infancy.

Formal theories of development first must be differentiated from the effort to identify the biological and social conditions which influence development by facilitating, retarding, shaping, or distorting the "normal" course. In this book, the latter focus was discussed under the heading of determinants of personality (chapters 2 and 3). Our concerns in this chapter are solely with formal development, that is, with describing and cataloguing the *sequence* of psychological changes through which all persons typically pass in the progression from infancy to adulthood and old age.

The perspective of *formal* developmental theory in psychology is analogous to that of embryology in tracing the stages through which human and infrahuman embryos pass from conception to birth. By investigating babies born prematurely at various intrauterine periods, embryologists have demonstrated that the human fetus proceeds through definite stages in its response to local stimulation of the face by a stiff hair or other object (e.g. Hooker, 1943). At a very early stage the embryo reacts with a diffuse, total-body response to the stimulation. Later, as the embryo grows into a fetus, the response becomes more and more differentiated. Eventually, as the fetus approaches full maturity preparatory to being born, the response becomes highly localized and specific; that is, only the immediate part of the body touched reacts to the stimulation. Fetal development demonstrably includes a progression through certain neuromuscular stages. This progression constitutes a universal biological law—it applies to virtually all cases, and to other species. The task of cataloguing and understanding the stages of psychological development is of course far more complicated than in the above illustration, which deals with a relatively limited neurological form of organization. Nevertheless, the illustration portrays how, in the *formal* analysis of development, attention is directed to the universal stages through which certain structures and processes pass, rather than to the factors which account for development.

Since the structures and processes of personality cannot be observed directly but must be inferred from the observed pattern of reaction in a given situational context, it will not be surprising that the stages of personality development have been variously conceived by different writers. For example, in his analysis of psychological development, Freud emphasized the evolution of drives and emotions, particularly during the first three years of life. Other developmentally oriented writers, such as Piaget, were largely unconcerned with the evolution of drives or emotional patterns and gave their attention almost entirely to cognition or adaptive thought. Still others, such as Erikson, retained the basic outlook entailed in Freud's analysis but made modifications (such as emphasizing the development of social relationships) and extensions of the scheme to later periods of life. Some of the differences among theories of development arise from varying developmental phenomena, and other differences concern the periods of life emphasized.

As in the case of the description and dynamics of personality, our brief treatment cannot cover all the important theoretical variations. Comparison of different approaches will be restricted here mainly to two of the most influential systems of thought, that of Freud (including some of the additions and modifications by Erikson) and that of Piaget. An examination of some current thinking and research on personality development will follow our theoretical discussions.

DRIVES AND EMOTIONS: FREUD'S PSYCHOSEXUAL THEORY

We already have mentioned the developmental aspect of Freud's theory, e.g., in chapter 4 in which reference was made to oral, anal, and phallic personality types. You may recall that Freud (1933b, 1949) believed that personality development proceeded through a series of predetermined, biologically fixed stages, each characterized by a particularly sensitive body or "erotic" zone. The focus of sexual pleasure begins at birth in the mouth (*oral* stage) but gradually shifts to the anus during the second year of life (*anal* stage) and eventually to the genitals around the third or fourth year (*phallic* stage). While this developmental sequence is universal, experience greatly affects the final outcome. For example, as we noted in chapter 5, too much or too little gratification could cause the person to become *fixated* or psychologically stuck, so to speak, at one of these early psychosexual stages. This means that later personality development will be somewhat immature, as much of the person's energies will be devoted to earlier concerns (like stimulating the oral region with food, drink, etc.). If fixation is particularly severe, e.g., due to extreme deprivation or punishment, the person will be susceptible to neurotic or psychotic disorders.

While each Freudian stage poses major conflicts and hurdles for the individual, perhaps nothing is as significant to determining mature personality development as the Oedipus complex. This key psychosexual problem occurs during the phallic stage and affects both sexes, though in different ways. Essentially, the complex refers to the young child's love for the opposite-sexed parent and his or her strong hostility toward the same-sexed parent. As you may recall from chapter 1, we noted that when Jay, our illustrative case study, was young, her relationship with her father was significantly closer and more satisfying than that with her mother—a theoretically frequent behavioral manifestation of the Oedipus complex. Let us look at this complex in more detail, discussing the problem first in the case of the young boy as it is simpler.

The boy's first love object is his mother or someone fulfilling that role, and he seeks total access to her affection. This possession, however, is thwarted by the competing presence of the father. The attachment of the boy to the mother and the competition of the father constitute the family love-triangle or, stated differently, the child's first encounter with what White and Watt (1973) have called the "eternal triangle." Freud (1933b) described the boy's dilemma as follows:

> . . . When a boy (from the age of two or three) has entered the phallic phase of his libidinal development, is feeling pleasurable sensations in his sexual organ and has learnt to procure these at will by manual stimulation, he becomes his mother's lover. He wishes to possess her physically in such ways as he has divined from his observations and intuitions about sexual life, and he tries to seduce her by showing her the male organ which he is proud to own. In a word, his early awakened masculinity seeks to take his father's place with her; his father has hitherto in any case been an envied model to the boy,

> owing to the physical strength he perceives in him and the authority
> with which he finds him clothed. His father now becomes a rival who
> stands in his way and whom he would like to get rid of. (quoted in
> Mischel, 1976, p. 43)

The natural response of the boy to this situation is to develop
feelings of hostility (and jealousy) toward the father. But the boy also
realistically perceives the father as far more powerful than he is, and
likely to retaliate for the boy's hostile wishes by his own hostility. It
is not uncommon, by the way, for the attachment between the boy
and his mother to be viewed by the father with some annoyance,
especially if the father feels insecure about his relationship to his
wife. This, plus frequent warnings by the father to the son about
masturbation, could add reality to the boy's impression of danger
from the father. The retaliation that is feared by the Oedipal boy was
conceived by Freud to be "castration," the destruction, literally or
symbolically, of the offending organ, the penis, which expresses his
maleness. The girl is already missing a penis, a fact which the boy
believes to be her punishment for similar transgressions. In any
event, the boy experiences "castration anxiety" in proportion to the
strength of his sexual urge toward the mother and his attendant
degree of hostility toward the father.

The girl's Oedipal problem, often referred to as the Electra
complex, is somewhat parallel to that of the boy. As with the boy it
begins with attachment to the mother in early infancy, but this
attachment must shift later to the father. How and why this shift
occurs is not at all clear, theoretically (see, for example, Helene
Deutsch, 1944, for one account of this). When the girl "cathects" the
father as a love object, she now faces competition from the mother in
a fashion parallel to the case of the boy and his father. She also
perceives the absence of a penis in herself, envies its possession by
the boy ("penis envy") and blames her mother for its loss. (We shall
expand this explanation in a later section.)

From about six years of age until adolescence, the family love-
triangle or romance tends to go underground. What happens is that
as a solution to the unbearable tension produced by the danger of
castration in the boy, or the consequences of its past occurrence in
the case of the girl, the erotic and hostile urges of the family triangle
are reduced. The child goes into what is often called the *latency*
period, in which he or she *represses* erotic feelings toward the
opposite-sexed parent. In addition, by the mechanism of *"identification* with the aggressor," the child takes on the moral and behavior
values of the same-sexed parent (leading to sex-typing, cf. chapter 3).
For example, in the case of the boy, castration anxiety is reduced by

the repressive defense, since it eliminates his awareness of erotic and hostile feelings; and by making himself like the father through identification he gains the father's approval and thus does not have anything to fear from him. Incidentally, because children take on the values and other standards of their parents in order to resolve partially their conflicts here, Freud felt that the superego was the "heir" of the Oedipus complex—in other words, the superego began to develop as an outgrowth of the Oedipal struggle and the mechanisms of coping with it. A summary of the sequence of events in the Oedipus and Electra complexes is shown in Table 14.

The emotional struggles of the family romance are held in abeyance during the latency period until adolescence, when the upsurge of erotic urges breaks through the defensive armor, and the

Table 14

The Successive Stages of the Oedipus and Electra Complexes Contrasted

OEDIPUS COMPLEX (BOY)			ELECTRA COMPLEX (GIRL)		
Motive	*Consequence*	*Outcome*	*Motive*	*Consequence*	*Outcome*
1. Attachment to mother (feeding, bodily care)	Jealousy of rivals, particularly of father	Feelings of hostility toward father	1. Attachment to mother (feeding, bodily care)	Jealousy of rivals	General feelings of inferiority; discovery of genital difference from males
2. Castration fear (sight of female genitals; possible threats)	Fear of punishment by father for his desires to possess mother	Intensification of rivalry with father; development of need to camouflage hostility	2. Penis envy (sight of male genitals)	Jealousy of male organ and of male privileges	Devaluation of mother and of female role; adoption of male behaviors
3. Need to appease father and prevent imagined attack	Creation of facade of meekness and love for father	Repression of hostility and fear; relinquishment of mother; identification with father	3. Attachment to father as more powerful than mother	Seeking from father penis substitute—a baby	Identification with female behaviors to appeal to father; slow fading of penis envy and mother devaluation

From Beneath the Mask: An Introduction to Theories of Personality *by Christopher F. Monte. Copyright © 1977 by Christopher F. Monte. Reprinted by permission of Holt, Rinehart and Winston and Christopher F. Monte.*

Oedipus complex now reappears in full force. The healthy boy and girl resolve these complexes by giving up the opposite-sexed parent as an erotic love object and by selecting a sex partner outside the immediate family. The boy and girl are now free to establish non-erotic friendships with the opposite-sexed parent and in so doing, they pass into the mature *genital* stage of psychosexual development, which includes the ability to love genuinely and to work in productive and effective ways. Only fixated individuals remain "stuck" at a pregenital level, either oral, anal, or phallic.

Social Relationships: Erikson's Contributions to Freudian Psychosexual Theory

Although Erik Erikson (1959, 1963) adopted some of Freud's fundamental assumptions about personality development (e.g., stages which unfold in an invariant sequence), he has made several noteworthy modifications. Two changes include an emphasis greater than Freud's on the interplay of the social context with the biological stages and an expansion of the stages from five (oral, anal, phallic, latency, and genital) to eight. Let us examine these two contributions briefly:

1. Erikson stressed that each psychosexual stage (or "age") has its characteristic mode of social interaction. For example, the biological impulses connected with the early oral stage are to stimulate the mucous membrane of the mouth with food and other objects taken into the oral cavity. At this period, "taking in" is the basic modality for interpersonal relations. The mother feeds the child, and the child depends on this nurturance and develops certain expectations about its social environment; for example, that the environment can be trusted to provide the necessary sustenance or that it is unresponsive to his or her needs. Similarly, in the anal stage, efforts are made to control and discipline the child's bowels and other activities. There develops an interpersonal struggle related to "letting go" (of feces) versus "holding onto," a struggle important to the psychological development of the personality trait of autonomy as opposed to those of shame and doubt. Erikson writes about this interpenetration of the biological and social as follows:

> Muscular maturation sets the stage for experimentation with two simultaneous sets of social modalities: holding on and letting go. As is the case with all of these modalities, their basic conflicts can lead in the end to either hostile or benign expectations and attitudes. Thus, to hold can become a destructive and cruel retaining or restraining, and it can become a pattern of care: to have and to hold. To let go, too, can

turn into an inimical letting loose, of destructive forces, or it can become a relaxed 'to let pass' and 'to let be' (1963, p. 251).

In short, Erikson draws a parallel between social or interpersonal attitudes and the biological processes required at the different psychosexual stages, pointing to the interdependence of each. The basic mode of response is set by the biological process characteristic of the particular stage, and its physical as well as social expression is influenced further by the interpersonal circumstances in which the child finds itself. In his analysis, Erikson much more than Freud, pointed toward the interpersonal features of each psychosexual stage. (In fact, Erikson refers to the developmental stages as being "psychosocial" in nature, rather than psychosexual, reflecting his belief in the importance of interpersonal features.)

2. In expanding the stages of personality development, Erikson argues for significant psychological growth throughout the life cycle, not just during the first five or six years as Freud had maintained. Each stage leads the person through a new crisis or conflict which has to be resolved satisfactorily if adaptive and successful progress to the next stage is to occur. Each crisis, as shown in Table 15, has a positive and negative aspect (e.g., basic trust vs. mistrust), and ideal development demands greater incorporation of the positive aspects of the conflicts. Table 15 illuminates Erikson's stages and shows how they relate to the development of various components of personality.

Perhaps the best-known addition in Erikson's expansion of the psychosexual theory is expressed by the term "ego-identity," which is the outcome of the struggle at puberty to resolve the Oedipus complex of the Freudian phallic stage. In discussing the crisis between identity and role confusion, Erikson (1968) writes:

> Adolescence is the last stage of childhood. The adolescent process, however, is conclusively complete only when the individual has subordinated his childhood identifications to a new kind of identification, achieved in absorbing sociability and in competitive apprenticeship with and among his age mates. These new identifications are no longer characterized by the playfulness of childhood and the experimental zest for youth: with dire urgency they force the young individual to choices and decisions which will, with increasing immediacy, lead to commitments "for life." The task to be performed here by the young person and by his society is formidable. It necessitates, in different individuals and in different societies, great variations in duration, intensity, and ritualization of adolescence. Societies offer, as individuals require, more or less sanctioned intermediary periods between childhood and adulthood, often characterized by a combination of prolonged immaturity and provoked precocity. (p. 155)

Table 15

Erikson's Eight Ages of Ego Development*

SUCCESS BRINGS	FAILURE BRINGS

1st Age
Early Infancy
(birth to about one year)
(corollary to Freudian oral sensory stage)

BASIC TRUST	vs.	MISTRUST
Result of affection and gratification of needs, mutual recognition.		Result of consistent abuse, neglect, deprivation of love; too early or harsh weaning, autistic isolation.

2nd Age
Later Infancy
(about ages one to three years)
(corollary to Freudian muscular anal stage)

AUTONOMY	vs.	SHAME AND DOUBT
Child views self as person in his own right apart from parents but still dependent.		Feels inadequate, doubts self, curtails learning basic skills like walking, talking, wants to "hide" inadequacies.

3rd Age
Early Childhood
(about ages four to five years)
(corollary to Freudian genital locomotor stage)

INITIATIVE	vs.	GUILT
Lively imagination, vigorous reality testing, imitates adults, anticipates roles.		Lacks spontaneity, infantile jealousy, "castration complex," suspicious, evasive, role inhibition.

4th Age
Middle Childhood
(about ages six to eleven years)
(corollary to Freudian latency stage)

INDUSTRY	vs.	INFERIORITY
Has sense of duty and accomplishment, develops scholastic and social competencies, undertakes real tasks, puts fantasy and play in better perspective, learns world of tools, task identification.		Poor work habits, avoids strong competition, feels doomed to mediocrity; lull before the storms of puberty, may conform as slavish behavior, sense of futility.

5th Age
Puberty and Adolescence
(about ages twelve to twenty years)

EGO IDENTITY	vs.	ROLE CONFUSION
Temporal perspective Self-certain Role experimenter Apprenticeship Sexual polarization Leader-followership Ideological commitment.		Time confusion Self-conscious Role fixation Work paralysis Bisexual confusion Authority confusion Value confusion.

Table 15

Erikson's Eight Ages of Ego Development (Continued)

SUCCESS BRINGS		FAILURE BRINGS
	6th Age *Early Adulthood*	
INTIMACY	*vs.*	ISOLATION
Capacity to commit self to others, "true genitability" now possible, *Lieben und Arbeiten*—"to love and to work"; "mutuality of genital orgasm."		Avoids intimacy, "character problems," promiscuous behavior; repudiates, isolates, destroys seemingly dangerous forces.
	7th Age *Middle Adulthood*	
GENERATIVITY	*vs.*	STAGNATION
Productive and creative for self and others, parental pride and pleasure, mature, enriches life, establishes and guides next generation.		Egocentric, nonproductive, early invalidism, excessive self-love, personal impoverishment, self-indulgence.
	8th Age *Late Adulthood*	
INTEGRITY	*vs.*	DESPAIR
Appreciates continuity of past, present, and future, acceptance of life cycle and life style, has learned to cooperate with inevitabilities of life, "state or quality of being complete, undivided, or unbroken; entirety" (Webster's Dictionary); "death loses its sting."		Time is too short; finds no meaning in human existence, has lost faith in self and others, wants second chance at life cycle with more advantages, no feeling of world order or spiritual sense, "fear of death."

---

*"Erikson's Eight Ages of Man's Ego Development" (pp. 578–580) from Interpreting Personality Theory, 2nd ed. by Ledford J. Bischof. Copyright © 1964, 1970 by Ledford S. Bischof. By permission of Harper & Row Publishers, Inc.

In emphasizing the effort to discover one's place in the world and to find successfully one's unique nature, that is, to achieve ego-identity, Erikson stresses the period of late adolescence and early adulthood more than Freud did. One of the more significant writers about the younger generation of social protestors and much influenced by Erikson, Kenneth Kenniston (1965, 1968), refers to a new stage of "youth" in which the relations between oneself and the world are the primary concern of the young adult struggling with political and social systems which often seem alien. We might note too that much of the current professional and lay interest in adult development, aging, and death (topics we shall turn to shortly) is an outgrowth of Erikson's viewpoints on expanded personality development.

Controversy and the Psychosexual Stages

The psychosexual theory has had enormous influence on psychological thought, particularly on clinical psychology in which many forms of psychopathology have been viewed as based on disturbances of psychosexual development. Anthropological and sociological analyses also have been greatly influenced by this theory. For example, examination of weaning and toilet training practices in different cultures and subcultures has been prompted by an interest in the premises of Freud's psychosexual theory. Variations in these practices are studied to determine their influence on the typical personality found in that culture.

There is no portion of Freudian theory that is more controversial than the conception of psychosexual development and its related notion of infantile sexuality. Although everyone agrees that experiences in early childhood are of vital importance to personality development, many writers (e.g., Horney, 1937) have questioned Freud's almost exclusive emphasis on sexual drives. The stages of psychosexual development were viewed by Freud as reflections of a universal, biological law. He gave little attention to the manner in which the culture might have contributed to each stage. In fact, for these and other reasons, many psychologists and feminists currently are attacking Freudian theory for degrading women and portraying them as the "second sex." Some of these criticisms undoubtedly are justified; others seem based somewhat unfairly on isolated aspects of Freudian theory (e.g., penis envy) without just regard for the entire theoretical system or the social climate of Freud's time (cf. Mitchell, 1974b). Let us examine some of these issues in more detail.

You might recall from our earlier discussion of the phallic stage that once the young female notices the anatomical differences between her genitals and those of little boys, she feels she is missing something of value. This feeling intensifies and manifests itself in jealousy and eventually penis envy. The girl becomes angry at her physical condition and sees the mother as the cause of it. In defiance and in hopes of obtaining a penis or a substitute, the young girl turns to the father. Notice that young girls do not fear castration as boys do, for they believe it has already happened and hence is a fact of life. Although Freud believed the threat of castration brought the male Oedipus complex to an end, he thought that realization of a "genital deficiency" actually initiated or stimulated the female Oedipus complex. As Freud (1974a) stated about the young female:

> . . . She acknowledges the fact of her castration, and with it, too, the superiority of the male and her own inferiority; but she rebels against

this unwelcome state of affairs. From this divided attitude three lines of development open up. The first leads to a general revulsion from sexuality. The little girl, frightened by the comparison with boys, grows dissatisfied with her clitoris, and gives up her phallic activity and with it her sexuality in general as well as a good part of her masculinity in other fields. The second line leads her to cling with defiant self-assertiveness to her threatened masculinity. To an incredibly late age she clings to the hope of getting a penis some time. That hope becomes her life's aim; and the phantasy of being a man in spite of everything often persists as a formative factor over long periods. This 'masculinity complex' in women can also result in a manifest homosexual choice of object. Only if her development follows the third, very circuitous, path does she reach the final normal female attitude, in which she takes her father as her object and so finds her way to the feminine form of the Oedipus complex. Thus in women the Oedipus complex is the end-result of a fairly lengthy development. It is not destroyed, but created, by the influence of castration... (p. 43)

An interesting consequence of this lack of castration fear in females is the development of the superego. You might recall that the superego was regarded by Freud as an outgrowth of the Oedipal conflict. In an attempt to cope with the anxieties associated with the Oedipus complex, the child engages in unconscious mechanisms which help to push the family romance underground or out of awareness. One of these mechanisms, identification, leads to the incorporation of the values and standards of the same-sexed parent (and of society too) and thus contributes to superego development. But what happens to the resolution of the Oedipus complex and the development of the superego when the anxieties and conflicts are not too intense, as in the case of the female (remember, she has no castration anxiety)? An obvious result would be that the Oedipus complex is not completely resolved, i.e., the girl does not bring it to a definite end and, consequently, the superego is not highly developed. Freud states:

> ... In the absence of fear of castration the chief motive is lacking which leads boys to surmount the Oedipus complex. Girls remain in it for an indeterminate length of time; they demolish it late and, even so, incompletely. In these circumstances the formation of the super-ego must suffer; it cannot attain the strength and independence which give it its cultural significance, and feminists are not pleased when we point out to them the effects of this factor upon the average feminine character. (1974b, p. 88)
>
> ... I cannot evade the notion (though I hesitate to give it expression) that for women the level of what is ethically normal is different from what it is in men. Their super-ego is never so inexora-

ble, so impersonal, so independent of its emotional origins as we require it to be in men. Character-traits which critics of every epoch have brought up against women—that they show less sense of justice than men, that they are less ready to submit to the great exigencies of life, that they are more often influenced in their judgements by feelings of affection or hostility—all these would be amply accounted for by the modification in the formation of their super-ego which we have inferred above. (1974c, p. 25)

What evidence, if any, exists to support Freud's characterization of female psychological development? You might recall from chapter 1 that Freud based most of his theoretical viewpoints on his observations of patients in psychoanalysis—an idiographic strategy based upon case studies (e.g., see the papers on Dora, 1905, and Little Hans, 1933a). Obviously, these observations can suffer from many sources of potential bias (Liebert & Spiegler, 1974). For example, Freud's patients were probably not representative of the general population and their behaviors on the couch (associations, memories, etc.) not typical of their overall behaviors. Moreover, the observations may have been biased by Freud's own expectations and hypotheses. In a review of empirical research on the female Oedipus complex and its resolution, Sherman (1971) concludes there is little evidence: a) that penis envy plays a crucial role in normal female development; b) that a female Oedipus complex exists; or c) that females have a weaker superego than males do. For example, Sherman notes:

> Females show more superego in the sense of less lawless behavior, more conformity, stronger moral code, more upset after deviation, and anticipating punishment from an internal rather than an external source. Females also tend to judge social violations more severely. (1971, p. 88)

Margaret Mead (1974) and others also have noted that in some cultures boys display considerable envy for female anatomy and childbirth functions. Even Freud's belief that vaginal and clitoral orgasms are different and that the former are preferred by the psychologically mature female has been challenged by recent sex research. To elaborate, Freud felt that the clitoris was equated with the penis and that the young girl must become more of a woman by renouncing this source of pleasure and by shifting her desires to the more "passive" vagina. In the process, she eventually would find a "penis substitute," that is, having a female or more preferably male child (1974b, p. 87). Masters and Johnson (1966) have found, however, that vaginal and clitoral orgasms are not distinct and that there is no such thing as a vaginal orgasm without a clitoral one. The entire genital area is involved in the female orgasm, regardless of where sexual stimulation occurs initially.

What then are we to make of Freud's views on psychosexual development in general and female psychological development in particular? As we have seen, Freud's writings certainly are not complimentary to the "female personality," may be criticized as being chauvinistic, seem concerned more with biological influences of behavior (e.g., anatomical differences) than with social ones, and are most difficult to validate empirically. If one does not accept his basic theoretical assumptions, such as infantile sexuality and the unconscious, then other concepts (e.g., castration anxiety and penis envy) become ludicrous or "ideologically dangerous" (Mitchell, 1974b).

Despite all their faults, Freud's views on personality development do provide an important conceptual framework for understanding how society shapes and influences our behaviors and sexual identities (see also chapter 3). If we are willing to look at Freud's views in the context of his times and as somewhat symbolic, they offer significant insights into how boys and girls incorporate the standards and values of a patriarchal (father-dominated) society and in turn how they pass them on to their children (cf. Mitchell, 1974a). For example, Freud often referred to "the fact of castration" in little girls (as quoted earlier in this chapter), yet no female is ever literally castrated. What he perhaps was referring to, and this is speculation, was the young girl's realization that she lacked many of the social privileges accorded to males in our society. Janeway (1974) has stated this possibility:

> . . . No woman has been deprived of a penis; she never had one to begin with. But she *has* been deprived of something else that men enjoy: namely, autonomy, freedom, and the power to control her destiny. By insisting, falsely, on female deprivation of the male organ, Freud is pointing to an actual deprivation, and one of which he was clearly aware. In Freud's time the advantages enjoyed by the male sex over the inferior female were, of course, even greater than at present and they were also accepted, to a much larger extent, as being inevitable, inescapable. Women were evident *social* castrates, and the mutilation of their potentiality as achieving human creatures was quite analogous to the physical wound . . . (p. 58)

Debate over Freud's psychosexual theory is likely to continue for some time and most probably so are the accusations of chauvinism. Although our society is still male-dominated (though it seems to be changing, albeit slowly) and although Freud's views of women may have helped in some small way to perpetuate this male supremacy, his controversial stance must be evaluated like all theoretical positions for its scientific usefulness in generating predictions about verifiable events (Hall & Lindzey, 1978).

In concluding this section, it might be noted that Freud often revised his opinions on female psychosexual development and was never fully satisfied with his understanding of the topic. At the end of a lecture on women, he once remarked:

> That is all I had to say to you about femininity. It is certainly incomplete and fragmentary and does not always sound friendly. . . . If you want to know more about femininity, enquire from your own experiences of life, or turn to the poets, or wait until science can give you deeper and more coherent information. (Freud, 1974b, p. 93)

COGNITIVE PROCESSES: PIAGET'S THEORY OF COGNITIVE DEVELOPMENT

As in the case of Freud, Jean Piaget (1952) also has been concerned with the universal stages through which a person passes during the early years of life. His too is a formal theory of development. Unlike Freud who emphasized the development of motivational and emotional processes (e.g., sexual drives and the affects connected with them), Piaget has focused almost exclusively on cognitive development, the intellectual processes marking the progression from infancy to adulthood. By the same token, the observations available to Freud and Piaget also were different as were their conceptions of research. For example, Freud studied childhood development mainly by having adults describe their emotional life during childhood while undergoing psychotherapy. In contrast, Piaget studied cognitive development by giving children problems to solve and examining the ways they did this at different chronological ages. Like Freud's, Piaget's point of view is consistent with the Darwinian approach to adaptation. He conceived of behavior as an adaptive life process through which a person maintains a state of equilibrium between himself or herself and the environment. Changes in the environment continually disturb this equilibrium, and adaptation can occur only through changing oneself ("accommodation" to the environment) or manipulating the environment ("assimilation"). Intelligent thought develops out of this continuing adaptive interchange between the person and the environment.

As is necessary in any formal developmental theory, Piaget sought to identify and describe the states through which intelligent thought evolves. He proposed two main stages, the *sensori-motor* and the *conceptual* (or symbolic operational), within which there are a number of definable subperiods. He also used great ingenuity in setting up intellectual tasks that demonstrated the processes of solution children were capable of using at various chronological ages. Most of Piaget's research observations were made on his own children, and although the sample was very small and of doubtful representation, the overall analysis has proved to be remarkably effective.

The sensori-motor stage extends roughly from birth to the age of two. During this time the child acquires its first knowledge of environmental objects. There are six subperiods within the sensori-motor stage. In the first subperiod, from birth to about one month, the infant engages mainly in "innate reflexes" such as sucking. Next is the subperiod of "primary circular reactions," from one to four months, in which simple acts such as opening and closing the fists or fingering a blanket are repeated for their own sake. During later subperiods, activities are more intentional. For example, in the third subperiod, from four to six months, known as "secondary circular reactions," the child repeats actions that produce interesting changes in the environment. The fourth subperiod, from seven to ten months, is the "coordination of secondary reactions"; the child begins to solve simple problems through the use of previously mastered responses. In subperiod five, consisting of what Piaget called "tertiary circular reactions" and taking place from eleven to eighteen months, the child engages in trial-and-error experimentation on the environment and now may try several alternative methods to attain a goal. The child understands that it can have an effect on the world of objects and now recognizes these objects as separate from himself or herself. Finally, in the sixth sensori-motor subperiod, from eighteen months on, the child uses "mental combinations" and appears to be able to predict the effects it creates. Related to this, an individual now will seek out an object which has been hidden and out of view for some time—something he or she could not do earlier. In other words, objects do not dissolve when they disappear; Piaget says the child has developed the concept of "object permanence." At this point, thought has begun to shift from a purely sensori-motor level to a conceptual one.

The second major stage of cognitive development, the conceptual stage, begins with the emergence of thinking somewhat independently of the explicit presence of objects. Before this, symbols and language had not been used extensively. The conceptual stage is divided into four subperiods. The "preconceptual" subperiod begins at about two years of age and proceeds until about four. Objects begin to take on symbolic meaning in that they can be used to stand for or represent other objects or events. A doll or plastic figure can be seen as though it were a parent or sibling. The concept of class or category is emerging. The subperiod of "intuitive thought," from about four to seven years of age, includes the construction of more complex images. Thought is still intuitive in that it is based heavily on simple sense characteristics, and the concept of the object has not yet become divorced from the concrete perceptual experience. For example, if two low jars of the same shape and size are given to the child and filled with beads, the child understands that they contain an equal number of beads. If the contents of one are poured into a tall thin jar, the four-year-old is likely to report that the tall thin jar now contains more beads, since he or she observes that the beads go higher up than they do in the low jar. The concept of amount is tied rigidly to the perceptual quality of height. The height of the jar is intuitively equated with the quantity it holds. Somewhere between five and seven years of age, the child enters the subperiod of "concrete operations," becoming aware that the amount of beads is the same, although the two jars differ in shape. During this subperiod he or she discovers that width compensates for height and the child develops a sense of constancy about the concepts of amount, size, weight, and height, regardless of the perceptual context. (Piaget says the child has now mastered the principle of "conservation.") Finally, beginning at about age eleven, the last subperiod of the conceptual stage arrives, that of "formal operations," during which thought becomes virtually completely freed of the manipulation of concrete objects. Events can now be imagined, manipulated symbolically, reasoned about, evaluated, and planned for, without direct contact with the physical features of these events. An object can be apprehended without its being seen or touched, resulting in thought which is abstract and highly adaptive.

Piaget made certain assumptions about the stages of cognitive development which have sparked some controversy. He maintained, for example, that the sequence is invariant and that none of the stages may be reversed. Moreover, he thought the speed of progression through the stages to be relatively fixed. Research on these issues, however, suggests that these assumptions may not be valid. For example, several studies have demonstrated that youngsters considerably younger than predicted by Piaget's theory can learn to solve conservation tasks with the help of special techniques like feedback on performance (e.g., Miller, Heldmeyer, & Miller, 1975; Siegler & Liebert, 1972).

Despite these and other critical issues (e.g., its applicability to other cultures, both sexes, etc.), Piaget's theory continues to have considerable impact on psychologists and educators. There is little doubt of the accuracy of many of Piaget's keen insights into cognitive growth, and only future research will enable us to delimit their relevance and application to specific populations.

CONTRASTS AND OVERLAPS
BETWEEN FREUD AND PIAGET

The reader may have wondered about the importance to personality of Piaget's analysis of the development of adaptive thought. Freud was quite explicit about the connections of his psychosexual stages with personality. For example, Freud viewed adult personality as often characterized by "hangovers" from pregenital struggles, as in the cases of the oral, anal, or phallic personality types. Even the "normal" individual was said to have some psychological vestiges of the pregenital stages, as in the pattern of sexual foreplay prior to coitus. Kissing exemplifies such a vestige (of oral sexuality) as does "latrinalia" (see, for example, Dundes, 1966), the phenomenon of writing oral and anal sex jokes on toilet walls. In Freud's emphasis or the psychosexual stages, he also presented a kind of implicit blueprint for childrearing, in which overindulgence or underindulgence at any given stage was conceived of as traumatic and likely to produce abnormal fixations impeding advancement to the next stage.

Piaget, on the other hand, has never made explicit nor expressed any extensive interest in the links between developmental stages and adult personality, although links are there implicitly. There are two lines of reasoning linking cognitive developmental theory to personality. First, one could argue that the truly fundamental features of adaptive behavior and thus of personality, are a person's intellectual capacities and modes of thought. It is reasonable to argue that the motivational, emotional, and social life of the individual are determined by what and how one thinks about himself or herself and the surrounding world. In short, a person's cognitive processes are the warp and woof of everything else in his or her life, including the emotional, motivational, and social experiences of healthy and disturbed people. Nevertheless, Piaget did not make the connections clear or express any real interest in them. This remains mainly to be done by those who follow.

The second line of reasoning linking cognitive developmental theory to personality is based on the idea of individual differences in the stage of cognitive development which the person has attained and in the developmentally determined manner in which the tasks of life are managed. This can be seen in Freud's concepts of fixation and regression, and in his treatment of oral, anal, and phallic types. In effect, some individuals remain at pregenital levels, or under traumatic conditions later in life regress to an immature level of functioning. Schizophrenia, for example, was seen by Freud as a regression to a very early oral level, paranoia to an early anal level, and neuroses to late anal or phallic psychosexual levels. The highest developmental level attained thus determines the motivational and emotional life, and probably the pattern of social relations of the person too.

To this point, very few personality characteristics have been related to variations in cognitive developmental level. It is not difficult though to imagine how a variety of personality traits could be linked to a person's level of cognitive development.

For example, an illustration of research on the links between cognitive development and social functioning can be found in a study by Adelson and O'Neil (1966). These social scientists were interested in the manner in which sociopolitical ideas emerged and expressed themselves in adolescence. They conducted intensive interviews with 120 young people, 30 in each age group studied (ages eleven, thirteen, fifteen, and eighteen) to investigate how, as a function of age, the adolescents felt about community issues. Before thirteen, the social consequences of political actions could not be readily imagined by the youngsters, their analysis of these actions being restricted to the stereotyped, concrete polar opposites found within the community. Before the age of fifteen, they had difficulty conceiving of the community as a whole, and they thought of government mainly in respect to its specific, tangible services. The younger adolescents were particularly insensitive to concepts of individual liberties; they usually opted for authoritarian solutions to political problems but could not grasp legitimate claims of the community on the citizen. It was only the older subjects who had a clear sense of future and took into account the long-range effects of political action. With greater age there was more reference to philosophical principles in the determination of their political attitudes. Adelson's and O'Neil's findings suggest that the contents of attitudes and surely, therefore, motivational, emotional, and social behavior, are governed by some of the same rules of cognitive development that Piaget formulated for the child's progression from the concrete, sensori-motor to the abstract and conceptual. (Also see the work of Werner, 1954, and Witkin and coworkers, 1962.)

Although Freud did not emphasize cognitive processes in his theory of psychosexual development, he did not altogether omit reference to them. Some attention was given to ego development and ego defenses at different psychosexual stages. For example, the mechanism of projection, in which one attributes to another unacceptable urges within oneself, was linked theoretically to the early anal stage and considered to be the prime mode of coping used by the paranoid. Similarly, isolation and undoing, considered characteristic of the obsessive-compulsive neurotic, were thought to arise in the late anal period, while repression was viewed as having its origins in the phallic period as a defense against threatening Oedipal urges. Thus, in Freudian theory a connection is assumed between stage of psychosexual development, type of urge or drive (e.g., oral vs. anal), and the adaptive or defensive mode of thought by which the drive is managed. For Freud the energy for the emergence of adaptive thought came mainly from the sexual drives or instincts. For Piaget, the cognitive structures themselves contained all the necessary energy for their emergence and development. Recent innovations in psychoanalysis, for example, the "ego-psychology" movement (cf. Hartmann, 1964; Rapaport, 1967) have turned renewed attention to the cognitive, adaptive processes of the ego. This suggests the possibility of rapprochement between the two orientations to formal development, those of Piaget and Freud. The bases for such a rapprochement have been examined by P. H. Wolff (1960).

Obviously, exclusive focus on cognitive development leaves out essential elements of the personality which are contained in the rubrics of motivation and emotion, or in social behavior. Similarly, exclusive preoccupation with the development of motivation, emotional, and social processes leaves out what is perhaps an underlying theme of the greatest importance in these processes, that is, cognitive activity. What is needed is a system of thought that preserves the most useful elements of both interdependent themes and unites them into a single system that integrates all of the essential features of personality within a developmental framework.

CURRENT RESEARCH:
ADULT DEVELOPMENT AND DEATH

Influenced by writers such as Freud and Piaget, personologists traditionally have devoted considerable attention to early personality development (infancy through adolescence) and concomitantly have ignored almost totally what happens to personality thereafter. Today this situation seems to be changing and for the first time, investigators of human behavior are seriously turning their attention to personality development throughout the life span—perhaps suggesting that if life does not begin at forty, neither does it end at nineteen. Let us then turn briefly to several consequences of this relatively new interest in the "life cycle," i.e., concern for adult development and also for its conclusion, death.

Adult Development—Early to Middle Adulthood

As we noted earlier, Erikson's modification of Freud's developmental theory attempts to encompass the entire spectrum of personality growth (see Table 15). While Erikson does identify many of the major psychological events of adulthood, some investigators (e.g., Gould, 1972; Levinson, 1978a, 1978b) have suggested that he glosses over or ignores important substages and tasks.

For example, several years ago Levinson (1978b) began an intensive study of forty men between the ages of thirty-five and forty-five. Largely through extensive interviews and projective testing materials (see chapter 8), Levinson and his coworkers began to reconstruct the lives of their subjects and eventually were able to identify several age-linked adult (male) developmental periods—see Table 16. Each period is characterized by various tasks which must be performed if successful transition is to be made to the next set of tasks. For example, during the twenties and thirties forming a mentor relationship becomes a crucial element for later personality adjustment. The mentor helps the young man make the transition from his family to the outside adult world. Mentor relationships often evolve from formal work situations but also may develop among friends, relatives, neighbors, and so on. Levinson suggests that:

> The mentor may act as a teacher to enhance the young man's skills and intellectual development. As a sponsor, he may use his influence to promote the young man's entry and advancement. He may be a host and guide, welcoming the initiate into a new occupational and social world and acquainting him with its values, customs, resources, and characters. Through his own virtues, achievements, and way of life, the mentor may be an exemplar that the younger man can admire and emulate. He may provide counsel and moral support in times of stress. (1978a, p. 26)

Once the relationship ends (usually in eight to ten years at the most), the younger man may internalize many of the mentor's qualities. Moreover, he has learned to become a mentor—a step consistent with Erikson's notion of generativity (see Table 15).

---

* D.L. Levinson, *Season's of a Man's Life*, Copyright 1978, Alfred A. Knopf.

Table 16

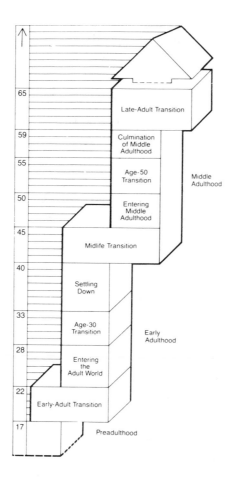

Ages (from top): 65, 59, 55, 50, 45, 40, 33, 28, 22, 17

Late-Adult Transition

Culmination of Middle Adulthood

Age-50 Transition

Entering Middle Adulthood

Midlife Transition

Settling Down

Age-30 Transition

Entering the Adult World

Early-Adult Transition

Preadulthood

Middle Adulthood

Early Adulthood

In an immensely popular study, Sheehy (1974, 1976) also has looked at adult development from the perspective of formal stage theory. She has integrated perhaps somewhat simplistically her own research findings (based on interviews with 115 men and women ranging from 18 to 55 years of age) with those of Freud, Jung, Erikson, Levinson, and others. The widespread enthusiasm for her book, *Passages*, suggests that her conclusions have struck a vital nerve in the American public.

Basically, Sheehy believes that, like the lobster, people too must at times shed a protective shell in order to grow. These periods of exposure, when we are especially vulnerable to psychological hazards such as insecurity, unhappiness, or misery occur during times of transition between the major developmental stages and are called "passages." According to Sheehy, passages occur throughout the life span and are not so much determined by external events as they are by critical internal ones:

> The inner realm is where the crucial shifts in bedrock begin to throw a person off balance, signaling the necessity to change and move on to a new footing in the next stage of development. (1974, 1976, p. 30)

Though change may be difficult, Sheehy feels it is necessary and desirable—in fact, it is the essence of personality development:

> If I've been convinced by one idea in the course of collecting all the life stories that inform the book, it is this: Times of crisis, of disruption or constructive change, are not only predictable but desirable. They mean growth. (1974, 1976, p. 31)

If one does not do the required soul-searching at each transitional period, stagnation and perhaps more suffering later on will take place. The only way to achieve what Sheehy calls "authentic identity" (one based on personal values rather than on those of parents or society) is to appraise our lives at the various passages by, among other things, realistically assessing our strengths and weaknesses as well as our future goals. The soul-searching may be painful but it will eventually lead to new sources of energy and self-acceptance. As Sheehy notes:

> This is not to suggest that people who suffer the most severe crisis always come through with the most inspired rebirth. But people who allow themselves to be stopped, seized by the real issues, shaken into a reexamination—these are the people who find their validity and thrive. (1974, 1976, p. 351)

The following "developmental ladder" is outlined by Sheehy (age ranges are approximate guidelines).

Pulling Up Roots (Ages 18 to 22)—An earnest attempt is made here to break away from parents and to establish an independent life of one's own. A number of tasks must be accomplished if the identity crisis is to be worked through:

The tasks of this passage are to locate ourselves in a peer group role, a sex role, an anticipated occupation, an ideology or world view. As a result, we gather the impetus to leave home physically and the identity to begin leaving home emotionally. (Sheehy, 1974, 1976, p. 39)

The Trying Twenties (Ages 22 to 28)—A shift in focus occurs from a preoccupation with internal matters ("Who am I?") to a concern for external ones ("How do I put my aspirations into effect?"). Choices made during this time are not irrevocable, but they do set in motion a particular life style or pattern (e.g., "locked-in," "transient," "wunderkind," "caregiver"). The tasks of this period include:

To shape a Dream, that vision of ourselves which will generate energy, aliveness, and hope. To prepare for a lifework. To find a mentor if possible. And to form the capacity for intimacy, without losing in the process whatever consistency of self we have thus far mustered. The first test structure must be erected around the life we choose to try. (Sheehy, 1974, 1976, p. 39)

Catch-30 (Ages 28 to 32)—This is a time of feeling restricted by personal and career choices made during the twenties. Changes are common and painful, and lead to things such as marriage, divorce, or new careers.

Rooting and Extending (Ages 32 to 35)—This is a period of settling down, e.g., buying a house, taking career choices seriously and wanting to advance, and focusing on raising a family (though satisfaction with marriage may decline).

The Deadline Decade (Ages 35 to 45)—This is a period of great uncertainty and a sense of time urgency. A realization occurs that life is half over and one wonders "Why am I doing all this?" and "What do I really believe in?" A genuine mid-life crisis occurs which Sheehy believes is "as critical as adolescence and in some ways more harrowing" (1974, 1976, p. 360). Several important events take place during this period: death becomes personalized, dreams become disillusioned, perceptions of self and others become altered, and authenticity becomes a major concern. Sheehy writes:

To reach the clearing beyond, we must stay with the weightless journey through uncertainty. Whatever counterfeit safety we hold from overinvestments in people and institutions must be given up. The inner custodian must be unseated from the controls. No foreign power can direct our journey from now on. It is for each of us to find a course that is valid by our own reckoning. And for each of us there is the opportunity to emerge reborn, *authentically* unique, with an enlarged capacity to love ourselves and embrace others. (1974, 1976, p. 364)

Renewal or Resignation (Ages 45 to 60)—Life during this period depends greatly on how the mid-life transition was handled. If it was avoided or bypassed, staleness and resignation will result. The mid-life crisis may appear finally in the fifties in a form more powerful than if it had come earlier. If, on the other hand, this mid-life transition were tackled directly, great feelings of renewal and happiness ensue and may last throughout the remaining years of life:

> If we have confronted ourselves in the middle passage and found a renewal of purpose around which we are eager to build a more authentic life structure, these may well be the best years. Personal happiness takes a sharp turn upward for partners who can now accept the fact: "I cannot expect *anyone* to fully understand me." Parents can be forgiven for the burdens of our childhood. Children can be let go without leaving us in collapsed silence. At 50, there is a new warmth and mellowing. Friends become more important than ever, but so does privacy. Since it is so often proclaimed by people past midlife, the motto of this stage might be "No more bullshit." (Sheehy, 1974, 1976, p. 46)*

Although studies such as those by Levinson and Sheehy have provided much needed information about early and middle adulthood, many questions and problems remain. For example, how representative are the findings? Most of the current studies have been conducted with white middle-class men, though Levinson (1978a) believes women go through the same developmental stages as men. While Sheehy did interview men and women, her sample is never described adequately, making generalizations extremely hazardous. Clearly, many ethnic and socioeconomic groups, as well as individuals in their late fifties and early sixties, have been underrepresented in the majority of developmental studies to date and these omissions must be corrected. Moreover, it is important to ask how "good" the interviews were in these studies and if we can be confident of the accuracy of the subjects' responses. Do all of us proceed through these stages and crises in the same order or at the same speed? How much stability or consistency is there in the way people handle their crises from one developmental era to another? These and other issues suggest a certain tentativeness about our current knowledge in this field, but they should not detract from the excitement and curiosity surrounding the "discovery" that personality continues to develop throughout early and middle adulthood, often by way of apparently predictable stages, tasks, and crises.

Another important approach to personality development should be discussed here. Specifically, studies such as Sheehy's typically involve rather limited contact with subjects, as least from an overall

* Adapted and excerpted from *PASSAGES: Predictable crises of Adult Life* by Gail Sheehy. Copyright © 1974, 1976 by Gail Sheehy.

time perspective. Subjects, for example, are interviewed or tested once or perhaps several times over a fairly brief period (perhaps, one or two months at the most). Individuals representing different age groups are then compared for differences along specified dimensions (e.g., anxiety, locus of control, intelligence)—a technique called the *cross-sectional* method. This allows research to be done quickly and fairly inexpensively, and is relatively free of significant "accidents" of history (e.g., social security, medicare, wars, etc.). On the other hand, one never really is able to see how any single individual develops over time. An alternative to this rather limited contact approach would be the study of the same individuals over an extended length of time (perhaps, five to ten years) with assessments being made periodically (perhaps semiannually or annually). Because this latter approach to development, called the *longitudinal* method, is costly, time-consuming, and fraught with potential problems (e.g., the unknown effects of repeated exposure to psychological tests, subject attrition, significant historical events, etc.), it is seldom used. Yet it has many advantages, including the study of individual trends in development which can help us assess the extent of personality consistency or change (Mussen, 1979; Kalish, 1975).

One of the main longitudinal studies of personality has been reported by Block (1971). He analyzed an extensive and ever-expanding collection of data gathered from the same set of individuals at the University of California's Institute of Human Development. The 171, largely middle-class, San Francisco Bay area residents have been assessed at the Institute (via interviews, psychological tests, etc.) from birth through middle adulthood, providing the basis for one of the largest and longest projects of its kind. The subjects were born between 1929 and 1932 and were in their middle thirties when Block began to look at the data.

As part of his extensive analyses, Block attempted to determine through factor analysis (see chapter 4) various types of personality development by comparing patterns of psychological growth in his subjects—based upon assessments made during Junior High School (JHS), Senior High School (SHS), and adulthood (during their thirties). Keep in mind that Block was not looking for personality types per se (cf. chapter 4) but rather for types of personality *development*. This approach might reveal, for example, that two groups of relatively similar individuals in JHS might be quite different as adults. Likewise, early dissimilarity might lead to later convergence, depending on developmental pathways.

Block uncovered a total of five male and six female types of personality development. Space limitations permit us to summarize only a few of them. Male *Belated Adjusters* (also labeled "Type B") start out with an unpromising adolescence but by adulthood achieve significant growth and competence. In JHS, the Type B boy is a "nasty adolescent," characterized in part by narcissicism, fickleness, sneaky hostility, and aggressiveness when it is safe. He is passive but resents being controlled by others, does not know how to work, and is uninterested in the uses of the mind. By SHS, there are signs, albeit small, of increasing maturity. He gets along better with others and does not hold grudges as intensely. As an adult, there is even greater change:

> As adults, the Type B men show marked change from their teenage years. Their adolescent oats have been sown and they are now what they were not before—contributing members of their society. They are cheerful, parental, and relaxed, and they are steady workers. They no longer explore to see what they can get away with and they are not wilfully contrary. They enjoy and even seek out the guiding beacon role that was once so inimical. They still cannot be judged especially bright, but they have found their place and within it do well. (Block, 1971, p. 158)

Male *Unsettled Under-Controllers* ("Type E") start out in JHS much like the *Belated Adjusters* but end up in adulthood in an entirely different place. In JHS, the Type E boy is among other things, rebellious, impulsive, dominant, and often inconsiderate. In SHS, he is also impulsive but now displays greater despair and increased reflection on the nature of life. In adulthood, there are subtle signs of maturity, but the Type E individuals "are still quick, moody, under-controllers. They are playful, involved, directly hostile when angry, somewhat selfish, highly self-critical, and freely emotional. They drink too much" (Block, 1971, p. 187). In general, the Type E men became downwardly mobile, and all the other types advanced their socioeconomic positions.

Throughout adolescence and adulthood, *Female Prototypes* ("Type U") display in an exemplary way qualities prescribed by our culture for their sex-role. In JHS, the Type U girl is seen as vivacious, pretty, warm, bright, uncompetitive, and peer-oriented (though also concerned with parents). By SHS, the Type U girl is still poised and gregarious (especially with boys) but has become more talkative, histrionic, and negativistic. By adulthood, the Type U woman is a well-established wife and much like her mother—a fine role model for her children. But some changes have occurred:

> The character changes since SHS of the Type U woman have been primarily recoveries from that earlier "letting go" period. She has returned toward responsibility and guidance by conscience, she as an

adult is again an extroverted, friendly, relatively unruffable individual. But to some extent, the Type U woman has over-corrected for her adolescent period of under-control by becoming in adulthood an over-controller and by propagating the virtues of self-control as a way of life. (Block, 1971, p. 202)

Female *Cognitive Copers* ("Type V") approach the world in an intellectual manner throughout their lives and, though they appear unlike the *Female Prototype* in adolescence, the two types are appreciably similar by adulthood.

> The Type V woman has blossomed with the years, going from inadequacy in adolescence to an admirable competence as an adult. She was bright as a youngster but not unusually so, given our sample context, and her socio-economic origin likewise was not exceptional. Yet she has gone on to more education than any other of our types and has accomplished the greatest leap upward in her socio-economic status. Characterologically, she has moved from appreciable maladjustment in high school to a degree of maturity in adulthood unmatched in our sample. (Block, 1971, p. 209)

In JHS, the Type V girl is fearful, submissive, guilt-ridden, over-controlled, concerned with intellectual matters, and has few friends. In SHS, we see similar characteristics, but now she has more self-confidence and an ability to interact with her peers. She is also effective, ambitious, and independent. As an adult, the Type V woman is intellectually effective and interesting and displays unusual personal maturity and social success; people turn to her for help and reassurance.

> When one looks at the available information surrounding the Type V subject, it is no means clear or even compellingly suggestive why she developed into so impressive a woman, given her tense and constricted earlier qualities. In part, it appears she has modelled herself and sought to outdo an accomplished mother who pushed her and somewhat overwhelmed her in adolescence. But also, and not less important, the Type V subject, by virtue of the earnestness of her intellectuality, appears to have been continually open to experience and to the significance of experience. She has reworked herself, assimilating when she could and accommodating otherwise, and now she is a worthy product of her own cognitive efforts. (Block, 1971, pp. 210-11.)

Block uncovered some additional findings of importance on the various types of personality development. For example, there were striking similarities between the personalities of the adult subjects and their parents, particularly for the male types. The parents of the *Be-*

lated Adjusters, for instance, were warm, affectionate, responsible, and unambitious—and so were their sons after a troubled adolescence. Adult personality seemed to be related, moreover, to the kind of family atmosphere in which the person grew up. "Healthy" or positive atmospheres led to adjusted and well liked adult personalities, while negative family environments led to disturbed or unenvied individuals. Examples of positive family atmospheres, according to Block, included a clear separation of sex roles among the parents, a father who was effective in his work, a mother who was competent and satisfied in her maternal role, consistent and fair treatment of the child, and parents who were affectionate and available to their child. Negative family environments were characterized generally by great family discord in which the parents tended to disagree on most issues. They reacted to their child inconsistently, without respect, and regarded the child's growth process with antagonism or indifference.

Several points about the Block study should be mentioned here. First, though the approach is compatible with formal stage theory, it does not emphasize factors such as universal stages, crises, or tasks. Instead, Block prefers to study general types or patterns of personality development. There is more of a concern with when personality is and is not consistent over time rather than, say, with particular hurdles that must be mastered at specific stages or transitional periods. The findings, pointing to consistent developmental patterns, do support the notion of personality stability (cf. chapter 4). As Block notes:

> I view the sets of empirical relationships surrounding the several types over time and across diverse measures as sufficient proof for the principle of personality consistency. The congruences that have emerged can be assailed and denied existence only by a highly "original" oppositionist weaving a convoluted and fragile web of counter-explanation. I suggest that psychologists stop concerning themselves with the issue of personality consistency—yes or no? Our field will profit more by examination of the conditions and the measurement approaches under which such indications of integrality may be observed or do not appear. We should move on to this more productive phase. (Block, 1971, p. 268)

Block believes that although many people do change over time, they do so along consistent and reasonably well defined developmental pathways. Second, though Block, as well as Levinson and Sheehy, have provided excellent descriptive accounts of personality development during early and middle adulthood, one wonders about the predictive value of such schemes. For example, can we now predict that Adolescent X will take this or that developmental route or whether he or she will have difficulties mastering the Age-30 transition? More research clearly is needed along these lines. Third, are the descriptions of personality development we have presented truly universal or are they tied to a specific culture and time? For instance, if Block's study had been conducted during the 1800s, would the same typology have emerged? Is a "positive" family atmosphere today still one in which sex-roles are clearly differentiated? These questions are important for they try to define the appropriate limits of generalization.

Adult Development—Late Adulthood

The study of aging and personality is in its infancy! Yet professional and lay interest is burgeoning, and we should have reliable empirical data in the near future to confirm or refute some of the stereotypes and myths about this time of life (Butler, 1975). What is the "popular" view of the elderly? A poll of *Retirement Living* magazine readers asked them to choose which of twelve words most accurately described the way television portrays Americans over sixty. The top three choices were "ridiculous," "decrepit," and "childish" (*San Francisco Chronicle*, January 5, 1978). Despite reverence by other cultures and by our own many years ago, the elderly person is now often seen as:

> . . . a white-haired, inactive, unemployed person, making no demands on anyone, least of all the family, docile in putting up with loneliness, rip-offs of every kind and boredom, and able to live on a pittance . . . Their main occupations are religion, grumbling, reminiscing and attending the funerals of friends. If sick, they need not, and should not, be actively treated, and are best stored in unsupervised institutions run by racketeers who fleece them and hasten their demise. (Comfort, 1976, pp. 23-24)

About ten percent of the American population is sixty-five or over and this percentage is expected to double by the year 2000 (Comfort, 1976). Together, these "senior citizens" spend about twenty percent of the allotment of this country's money for food consumption in the home. The most prosperous per capita income group (for ten-year brackets) is Americans between the ages from fifty-five to sixty-four. Those over sixty-five are only five percent below the national income norm (*San Francisco Chronicle*, January 5, 1978). About five percent of those sixty-five and over (1970 estimates) are in mental hospitals, homes for the aged and dependent, other institutions, and other "group quarters." Of this five percent, almost half are in long-term care institutions such as nursing homes and convalescent facilities (Kalish, 1975, p. 19).

Although money and health are undoubtedly major problems for the elderly, the picture is not as bleak as many suspect. Unfortunately, most of our stereotypes of the elderly tend to be based on needy individuals rather than on the typical older person (Neugarten, 1971). Recent studies provide evidence that should help destroy many of our misconceptions of the elderly.

> For example, old persons do not become isolated and neglected by their families, although both generations prefer separate households. Old persons are not dumped into mental hospitals by cruel or indifferent children. They are not necessarily lonely or desolate if they live alone. Few of them ever show overt signs of mental deterioration or senility, and only a small proportion ever become mentally ill. For those who do, psychological and psychiatric treatment is by no means futile.
>
> Retirement and widowhood do not lead to mental illness, nor does social isolation. Retirement is not necessarily bad: some men and women want to keep on working, but more and more choose to retire earlier and earlier. Increasing proportions of the population evidently value leisure more than they value work. Nor do retired persons sicken physically from idleness and feelings of worthlessness. Three fourths of the persons questioned in a recent national sample reported that they were satisfied or very satisfied with their lives since retirement. This is in line with earlier surveys. Most persons over 65 think of themselves as being in good health and they act accordingly, no matter what their physicians think.* (Neugarten, 1971, p. 46)

It is often assumed, largely perhaps because of stereotypes such as those mentioned earlier, that all older persons are much the same and consequently that their personalities must be fairly homogeneous. Yet recent studies (e.g., Lowenthal, Thurnher, & Chiriboga, 1975; Maas & Kuypers, 1974) suggest that this is far from the truth. It seems that the personalities of older people are just as diverse as those of people at any other time in the life cycle—in fact, it appears that people may become even more diverse with age. Let us examine briefly some research by Neugarten, who has long been interested in the effects of aging on personality.

As part of a longitudinal study originally involving more than two thousand men and women, Neugarten and her associates (1968, 1971) attempted to examine relationships between personality, social activity, and life-satisfaction in fairly healthy subjects, seventy to seventy-nine years of age. Interviews and psychological test data were gathered repeatedly over a seven-year period, and subjects also were asked to give pertinent details of their lives at age sixty. Scores

---

* Reprinted from *Psychology Today* magazine. Copyright © 1971, Ziff-Davis Publishing Co.

were gathered from the data, based on complex combinations of various factors. For example, both the extent and intensity of activity in each of eleven social roles (e.g., parent, spouse, church member, etc.) were determined and summarized to obtain a role-activity score. Life-satisfaction scores were based on five components, on whether the person enjoyed his or her daily activities, had a positive self-image, maintained optimistic attitudes, and so on.

Using scores from forty-five dimensions of personality (tapping cognitive and emotional characteristics), Neugarten was able to derive by factor analysis four major personality types among her sample: *integrated* (competent egos, mellow and mature), *defended* (armored, ambitious, tight control over impulses), *passive-dependent* (either sought others or showed little interest in them), and *disintegrated* (disorganized, poor psychological functioning and thought processes). In addition, there were eight important patterns of aging among these personality types, based upon differences in activity patterns and life styles. Even though role-activity scores generally had declined from when the subjects were sixty years of age, clearly there was still a wide range of life styles. Table 17 illustrates the various personality types and patterns of aging (which we shall not describe here) along with their scores for role-activity and life-satisfaction. It is interesting to note that, among the *integrated* person-

Table 17

Personality Types and Patterns of Aging in Relation to Activity and Life Satisfaction (Age 70-79)

PERSONALITY TYPES AND PATTERNS OF AGING	ROLE-ACTIVITY	LIFE-SATISFACTION
A. *Integrated Type*		
1. "reorganizers"	high	high
2. "focused"	medium	high
3. "disengaged"	low	high
B. *Defended Type*		
4. "holding-on"	medium-high	high
5. "constricted"	low	medium-high
C. *Passive-Dependent Type*		
6. "succorance-seeking"	medium	medium
7. "apathetic"	low	low-medium
D. *Disintegrated Type*		
8. "disorganized"	low	low-medium

Adapted from Neugarten, Havighurst, and Tobin (1968).

ality types (the most frequent in Neugarten's sample), life-satisfaction remained high despite variations in the extent and intensity of role-activity.

In addition to following various patterns of aging, Neugarten found that the elderly showed considerable personality consistency. Apparently, once a person reaches "old age," he or she does not suddenly undergo radical or dramatic alterations in personality, becoming a totally new person. As Neugarten notes:

> Just as every person changes as he grows up, he will continue to change as he grows old. But aging will not destroy the continuities between what he has been, what he is, and what he will be. (1971, p. 81)*

Death and Dying as Psychosocial Processes

The study of death and dying as psychosocial events is a fairly recent enterprise. Physicians have long tried to prevent or postpone death in their patients, and in the process have acquired considerable, though far from complete, insight into the physiological mechanisms involved in the cessation of life. But physicians traditionally have not been trained to recognize or to understand the many psychological and social factors which often influence death and the dying process. In fact, to many medically-educated professionals, death represents a personal failure rather than the natural and inevitable ending of life, and hence it is a source of great anxiety. As one prominent clinical psychologist has stated:

> I learned how vital it is to remember that we are dealing not with a professional issue, but a human one. As health-care professionals we are trained as healers, and it is clear that death is an unacceptable outcome for many of us. To imagine that trained healers—i.e., doctors, nurses, and other biomedical personnel who experience themselves as adversaries of illness and death—can respond effectively to the dying patient is often an erroneous expectation. It is more often the case that the professional's anxiety and sense of impotence drives him away, leaving the patient emotionally and psychologically isolated and often physically abandoned. (Garfield, 1977, pp. 150-51)

Though death and dying still are regarded as taboo topics by many, efforts in recent years by thanatologists (professionals interested in

*Reprinted from Psychology Today Magazine, Copyright © 1971, Ziff-Davis Publishing Co.

the study of death) have begun to uncover vital bits of information on what people think about their own deaths and how they cope with it. (Due to space limitations, we shall not discuss here the huge amount of grief and bereavement literature dealing with reactions to another's death).

Studies of individuals of varying ages and degrees of health suggest that a fear of death is commonplace. Whether this fear is innate or learned, however, remains a debated issue (cf. Becker, 1973). It is interesting to note that although older people may think of death more frequently than younger ones, they seem to be less afraid of it (see Kalish, 1975). Perhaps many of the elderly have struggled successfully with the "integrity versus despair" crisis of late adulthood (see Table 15) and consequently, death has lost "its sting." Also, many elderly people escape frequently into the past to reminisce and to review their lives. This "life review" often can help the person integrate his or her life and set the stage for a peaceful death (Butler, 1971).

Our "terror" of death need not be always conscious. A study by Feifel, Freilich, and Hermann (1973) illustrates how important it is, especially when working with dying patients, to realize that death fears may be present yet may not be readily admitted or recognized. These investigators found that over seventy percent of a group of heart and cancer patients and a group of healthy "control" subjects (of similar age ranges) reported no conscious fears of death—though the patients, all of whom were aware of the severity of their illnesses, did think of death more frequently than did control subjects. Nevertheless, the dying patients did demonstrate significantly more disturbance than the healthy subjects to stimuli purporting to tap *unconscious* fears of death. Also of interest is that patients did not differ in the extent of their fears according to *type* of illness. In other words, heart and cancer patients could not be differentiated by their fears of personal death; both groups frequently disclaimed such fears but showed great and essentially similar fear on the unconscious level.

If we accept the notion that death can be a frightening event for many, it becomes important to understand how people cope with the news that they are dying. What kinds of psychological processes do they use to master this threat and how might others assist constructively in the final course of events? A mini-revolution of sorts is taking place in our hospitals and other community agencies dealing with dying individuals. More and more health personnel are working seriously with terminally-ill patients, using them as teachers in order to learn more about the nature of the dying process. Dr.

Charles Garfield's (1976) SHANTI Project in Berkeley is an excellent example of this recently popular "hospice" movement. Dr. Elisabeth Kübler-Ross's (1969) studies with dying patients in Chicago are perhaps the pioneering and best-known works in this field, and she developed some interesting notions about how people cope with death.

Based on her countless interviews with terminally-ill patients of all ages, Kübler-Ross (1969) believes that dying people go through a series of emotional stages as they prepare for death. Following initial shock and disbelief over one's plight, a person engages in *denial* and *isolation*. The reality of the situation will be denied ("X-rays must be mixed up"), and the person will isolate himself or herself from all information confirming the imminence of death. The second stage brings forth feelings of *anger*, as well as rage, envy, and resentment, which unfortunately for others, are projected almost randomly to doctors, nurses, family, and so on. The patient is plagued by the question, "Why me?" The third stage, *bargaining*, involves personal attempts to postpone death, usually by promising (to oneself or God) to be "good," to right past wrongs, and the like.

> Another patient was in utmost pain and discomfort, unable to go home because of her dependence on injections for pain relief. She had a son who proceeded with his plans to get married, as the patient had wished. She was very sad to think that she would be unable to attend this big day, for he was her oldest and favorite child. With combined efforts, we were able to teach her self-hypnosis which enabled her to be quite comfortable for several hours. She had made all sorts of promises if she could only live long enough to attend this marriage. The day preceding the wedding she left the hospital as an elegant lady. Nobody would have believed her real condition. She was "the happiest person in the whole world" and looked radiant. I wondered what her reaction would be when the time was up for which she had bargained. (Kübler-Ross, 1969, p. 83)*

The fourth stage, *depression*, occurs once the person can no longer deny illness or death and simply cannot shake off the ordeal any longer. Earlier emotions give way to those of depression and sadness, as well as to a sense of futility and impending loss (particularly of loved ones). If death is not sudden and the person has been given some help in working through the previous stages, the fifth stage, *acceptance*, will be reached. There are few emotions here but the person has found inner peace and acceptance—the struggle with death has been resolved. The desire to communicate with others, at least verbally, may be diminished and interest in the outside world has all but gone.

Kübler-Ross does not believe these stages are mutually exclusive or irreversible. They simply describe a typical sequence and basic coping processes used by people to deal with death and to come to terms with it. Moreover, the way a person copes with death is determined in part by his or her personality before the onset of illness. For example, Kübler-Ross notes that when first informed of their malignancy diagnosis, patients react according to previous behavioral styles:

> People who use denial as a main defense will use denial much more extensively than others. Patients who faced past stressful situations with open confrontation will do similarly in the present situation. (1969, p. 32)*

Even in the face of death's unknown future, there is continuity with one's past. (It should be noted too that others, e.g., Weisman, 1972, have proposed different stages of coping with death and that some researchers believe no one pattern is seen more frequently than others—see Kalish, 1975.)

An important adjunct to our discussion so far is the controversial issue of whether psychological states can hasten or delay death. Most of the evidence affirming this possibility is descriptive and little understood but, nevertheless, quite compelling. For example, Seligman (1975) has reviewed a variety of studies on sudden and unexpected deaths in animals (e.g., rats, dogs, chicks) and humans (from many cultures and of all ages) and believes each of these examples involves a state of helplessness in which the organism feels an important aspect of life is no longer under personal control. Once the individual loses control, he or she acts depressed and begins to lose hope. How these behaviors and feelings affect physiological mechanisms which in turn hasten one's death is not known, but a slowing of the heart is implicated in many cases.

Kübler-Ross emphasizes that her patients maintained some form of hope throughout their illnesses. Furthermore, she believes that physicians must communicate to their dying patients that, despite malignancy, all is not lost—everything that can be done will be done. She notes: "We have learned that for the patient death itself is not the problem, but dying is feared because of the accompanying sense of hopelessness, helplessness, and isolation" (1969, p. 268). Parenthetically, Seligman argues strongly against social measures

* From *On Death and Dying* by Elisabeth Kübler-Ross, Copyright © 1969 by Elisabeth Kübler-Ross, used by permission of Macmillan Publishing Co.

which would remove or restrict personal control, like mandatory retirement or forced dependency. The following advice regarding the treatment of patients is offered:

> Institutionalized patients, whether in terminal cancer wards, leukemic children's wards, or old-age homes, should be given maximum control over all aspects of their daily lives: choice of omelets or scrambled eggs for breakfast, blue or red curtains, going to the movies on Wednesdays or Thursdays, whether they wake up early or sleep late. If the theory of helplessness set forth here has any validity, these people may live longer, may show more spontaneous remissions, and will certainly be much happier. (Seligman, 1975, p. 183)

Once again it seems that feelings of control assume a vital role in personality functioning (cf. chapters 4 and 5). The perceived absence of control may at times prove to be not only frustrating but also life-threatening, particularly for those individuals previously accustomed to manipulating their environment and currently experiencing feelings of severe helplessness and hopelessness.

Approaches to Personality and their Application

Our discussions of personality issues (the "four D's") and illustrative theories have been quite abstract, though many empirical research examples were given to make the conceptual statements more concrete. Because personology is about people and their lives, it is appropriate for the varied and elaborate theoretical statements to be applied directly to case study material. This chapter deals with this important matter and accordingly, we shall apply many of the theoretical concepts discussed earlier to our illustrative case study, Jay. While making these connections, we will demonstrate: (1) how personality theories can help our understanding of people and their everyday behavior, and (2) how different theories lead to noticeably different conclusions about the best ways to alter or change adult personality.

As should be evident by now, the number and diversity of personality theories are indeed remarkable! Corsini (1977) presented a *partial* listing of current theories of personality which contained approximately eighty noted theorists and their viewpoints. To organize them more clearly, some personologists have classified the various theories into a few manageable categories or approaches (cf. Liebert & Spiegler, 1974; Maddi, 1976; Mischel, 1976). In this chapter, we summarize and apply theoretical stances representing three of these influential approaches to personality, the *psychodynamic*, the *humanistic-existential*, and the *behavioral*. Space limitations require us to illustrate each approach with the viewpoints mainly of

215

only one or two representative theorists, but this should help greatly to integrate materials from previous sections of this book and to unify the approaches and theories.

Let us turn first to a further description of Jay and of her family and social life, and then to the theoretical applications.

JAYLENE ELIZABETH SMITH

We described Jay in some detail earlier, and it is important that you now reread this information (see pp. 23-25). To summarize and elaborate our earlier treatment, Jay is an exceptionally competent individual with many abilities, interests, and special skills. She also has had her share of frailties and disappointments. Acquaintances describe her in glowing terms but for whatever reasons Jay's self-assessment is pessimistic and emphasizes her weaknesses and fears, rather than the strengths so obvious to others. The eldest of three children, Jay has remained her father's favorite child. Her mother, a successful though somewhat insecure person, also cared for Jay, but their relationship has never equaled the one between her husband and only daughter. Throughout adolescence and early adulthood, Jay was active and popular, though periodic bouts with insecurity, depression, and confusion were highly disturbing and often led to increased eating activity (remember her self-control program for a slight weight problem, as described in chapter 5). Today, at age thirty, Jay is a promising medical practitioner, respected by her peers and for the most part more content with life than ever before. She has gained self-confidence in her professional skills and also relates somewhat better now to new and old acquaintances. Yet, insecurities and vague guilt feelings, particularly about sexuality, occasionally plague Jay. Another concern is her inability to maintain a stable heterosexual relationship—this despite her many assets and expressed desire for such an intimate association. Moreover, Jay sometimes wonders whether her compulsive professional dedication and drive should be altered to allow more time for leisure activities and personal relationships. But she is incapable of resolving this conflict now.

Let us examine some additional information about Jay and her family. Jay's first brother, born when she was two years old, was for some time a threat and a source of irritation to Jay, though she does not remember too clearly the details of their early relationship. Her parents recall that Jay would become angry and have temper tantrums when the new infant demanded and received much attention (especially from Mrs. Smith), while she received now relatively little—except on those occasions when, to her parents' dismay, she stubbornly refused to cooperate in her bowel training. The temper tantrums intensified when the second brother was born just one year after the first. As time went on, the brothers seemed to form an alliance to undermine Jay's supreme position with their father. Jay, in turn, frequently fought with her brothers, usually verbally though sometimes physically, to keep her status and to protect herself and, in the process, became closer to her father. Besides the mutual feelings of tenderness which bond most siblings, greater than average jealousy and rivalry characterized Jay's relationship with her younger brothers, from early childhood to the present.

Jay's father is a rather quiet and gentle person who married when he was thirty-five years old. Although an excellent diagnostician, he decided to pursue medical research rather than to have a private practice. His work often allowed him to study at home, and he thus had extensive contact with his children, especially when they were young. His ambitions and goals for Jay were extremely high and as she matured, he responded to her every need and demand almost immediately and with full conviction. Mrs. Smith, who was thirty years old when she married, worked long hours away from home as a store manager and consequently saw her children primarily at nights and on an occasionally free weekend. Tired when she was with her family, she had little energy for "nonessential" interactions and devoted what efforts she could to feeding the children (especially the younger ones) and to making certain the house was in order. Because Dr. Smith was home frequently, he helped with these chores, but the major responsibility fell on Mrs. Smith's shoulders. Dr. and Mrs. Smith have had a "comfortable" relationship, though their interactions occasionally have been marred by intense stormy outbursts over seemingly trivial matters. These episodes always are followed by prolonged periods of mutual silence lasting for days at a time.

Two representative incidents regarding Jay and various boyfriends are worth noting. She often has an explosive fit of anger which terminates an important relationship. Her disposition in most other circumstances, though, is tempered and some would say, even inhibited. Interestingly, too, her relationships with other women, although more stable than those with men, usually are casual, noncommital, and of short duration.

When Jay was thirteen, she became good friends with a male classmate, Mark. They had many hours of conversation, though Jay never was able "to be herself" and really express her feelings. The relationship continued to blossom until one fatal day when a low-keyed disagreement about next weekend's activities suddenly erupted into a major altercation. After labeling Mark with a few choice epithets, of the kind usually reserved for locker-room encounters, Jay ran away and tearfully professed that she did not want to see him again. Despite Mark's persistent efforts to talk with her and despite sharing some classes in school, Jay refused ever to have anything to do with her former friend.

Much later, while finishing her undergraduate college education, Jay met Ted, a graduate student some fifteen years older than herself. At twenty-one, Jay felt she was falling in love again, but this time it was the "real" thing. Unfortunately, their relationship had existed for only about two months when disaster struck. Although Jay and Ted were close and trusted one another (but again, Jay was inhibited in the relationship), an innocent conversation between Ted and a female classmate triggered Jay's rage. As Jay was walking across campus, she spotted Ted and his acquaintance having a lively conversation and enjoying a laugh or two. As Ted turned his head, he caught a glimpse of Jay. He immediately called to her and asked her to come over and meet his friend. Jay turned quickly and hurried away. As Ted finally reached her, she screamed angrily in his face that she never wanted to see him again. And she never did.

Now that we have described Jay in more detail, let us discuss the theoretical approaches and how they might clarify her personality. Three approaches, the psychodynamic, the humanistic-existential, and the behavioral, will be illustrated primarily, though not exclusively, by the theoretical stances of Freud, Rogers, and Skinner, respectively. Our presentation of each approach will begin with a synopsis of the theorist's view of personality followed by the application of these views to Jay. The application will revolve around two important issues. The first concerns the developmental question, How did Jay become the person she is today? The second issue explores the nature of personality change and growth. Is change possible now that Jay has reached adulthood and if so, how would it occur? Psychotherapeutic interventions will be emphasized in this section to illustrate what each personality theory has to offer in the facilitation of alterations in personality. In addition to these two issues, we shall comment on how other prominent theorists, within each approach, would view Jay's personality.

PSYCHODYNAMIC APPROACHES

Psychodynamic approaches to personality are characterized by an internal, subjective orientation to understanding the person. Assumptions generally are made about *complex internal energy forces* (e.g., motives, drives) which propel the person to act, often in seemingly irrational ways. Stated differently, psychodynamic approaches maintain that behavior is caused by, or is symbolic of, underlying (and often unconscious) forces. Many of these underlying forces are often at odds with one another or with goals of society such as communal living and universal harmony. Thus, intrapsychic or psychosocial *conflict* is central to most psychodynamic approaches and suggests that life at best is a compromise of opposing forces (cf. Maddi, 1976).

There are many variants of this approach but, because of its historical and contemporary importance, we shall deal mainly with Sigmund Freud's (1943, 1953) psychoanalytic theory. Erik Erikson's (1963, 1968) theory will be highlighted at the end of this section because it is essentially Freudian, yet it significantly modifies and extends Freud's views and has substantially affected current thought.

Synopsis of Freud's Theory

Freud's approach to personality regards all behavior as a manifestation of intrapsychic conflicts or more generally of underlying dynamic interactions. You will recall that inside the person are a number of psychological processes conveniently summarized by three structures or systems, the id, the ego, and the superego (see chapters 4 and 5). The *id* includes biological instincts which press for immediate discharge as their energies accumulate (the *pleasure principle*), and the resulting tensions, if not discharged, become uncomfortable. This accumulation of "dammed-up" instinctual energy leads to the development of a reality-centered *ego* whose main function is to find a suitable and safe means of discharge (the *reality principle*). The third personality structure, the *superego,* evolves as a result of socialization processes and represents the moral standards (concerning right and wrong) of the society, as interpreted to the child by the parents. Because society sees the expression of certain instincts, particularly sex and aggression, as being against the common good, the superego tries to block them altogether, substituting moral goals for selfish ones.

Conflict among the three structures, with their different aims and objects, is frequent and inevitable in life even under the best of circumstances and ultimately leads to anxiety and defense mechanisms. The healthy personality is able to keep relative harmony among the three structures with the ego maintaining its executive leadership but with the id and superego also being represented.

In short, we have a picture of an individual driven by a dynamic interplay between instinctual energies seeking immediate and unrestrained discharge (i.e., direct and uncensored expression in behavior), and environmental and internalized social forces requiring the instincts to be redirected or altered in some way. Normal, or abnormal, behavior thus is a manifestation of the resulting compromise or solution to the intrapsychic conflict managed by the ego.

Whether in the form of dreams, fantasies, defense mechanisms, overt actions, obsessions, and the like, the ego's solutions express symbolically the underlying instincts and the intrapsychic conflicts and are important clues to the person's unconscious mental life. For example, Freud felt a fear of snakes could reflect an underlying sexual conflict regarding the penis, and paranoid suspicions might reflect latent homosexual wishes. Because instinctual drives must be expressed when tensions mount but cannot be expressed directly (due to the demands of reality and the superego), disguised forms of discharge must be conceived by the ego. These new symbolic forms do not discharge instinctual tensions as effectively as more direct forms, but they do provide some important relief. Just as significant is the fact that these symbolic behaviors (*instinct derivatives*) comprise many of the most noble, and also most destructive, aspects of our personal and social lives (e.g., reasoning, learning, creativity, altruism, neuroses, racial prejudice, and war).

As a person proceeds through biologically programmed psychosexual stages (*oral, anal, phallic,* and *genital*), critical experiences mold the personality (see chapter 6). At each stage there is a basic conflict between sexual demands and the amount of gratification available to meet the demands. For example, during the first year of life, sexual demands are satisfied primarily by stimulating the sensitive tissues surrounding the mouth—e.g., the lips, tongue, and so on. Too much or too little gratification can lead to the permanent fixation of a certain amount of sexual energy at this troublesome stage. This in turn may lead to the adoption of rigid character traits, as well as to a later, symbolic acting-out during adulthood of the earlier conflict (e.g., alcoholism, obesity). Although some fixation occurs normally at each stage, strong conflict leads to severe fixation and to considerably less sexual energy for subsequent development. Character traits associated with each stage of development are shown in Table 18. Notice how the ideal personality should contain a proper balance between the opposing trait pairs so that, for example, the "healthy" individual would not have too much optimism nor too much pessimism—a moderate degree of each is preferable. Once extreme fixation occurs, these characteristics, and many of the ways we have learned to handle the difficult psychosexual conflicts (e.g., defense mechanisms), become inflexible and dominant in the personality. Parenthetically, this fixation makes future satisfactory progress

Table 18

Traits of Psychosexual Stages of Development

	ABNORMAL	NORMAL	ABNORMAL ZERO (ABSENCE OF TRAIT)	NORMAL	ABNORMAL
Oral Traits	optimism	(	◄─────────►	)	pessimism
	gullibility	(		)	suspiciousness
	manipulativeness	(		)	passivity
	admiration	(		)	envy
	cockiness	(		)	self-belittlement
Anal Traits	stinginess	(		)	overgenerosity
	constrictedness	(		)	expansiveness
	stubbornness	(		)	acquiescence
	orderliness	(		)	messiness
	rigid punctuality	(		)	tardiness
	meticulousness	(		)	dirtiness
	precision	(		)	vagueness
Phallic Traits	vanity	(		)	self-hate
	pride	(		)	humility
	blind courage	(		)	timidity
	brashness	(		)	bashfulness
	gregariousness	(		)	isolationism
	stylishness	(		)	plainness
	flirtatiousness	(		)	avoidance of heterosexuality
	chastity	(		)	promiscuity
	gaiety	(		)	sadness
Genital Traits	sentimental love	(		)	indiscriminate hate
	compulsive work	(		)	inability to work

The ideal personality should possess each of the above pairs of traits to a moderate degree. There must be a proper balance between opposing traits. Lack of balance among the traits constitutes a less than ideal personality. Abnormality in a personality may be determined in three ways: (1) possession of a trait to an extreme degree, (2) lack of the trait altogether, (3) imbalance between pairs of traits. *From DiCaprio (1974, p. 52)*

through the developmental sequence more difficult and problematical, though not impossible.

In summary, the Freudian approach to personality concentrates primarily on the interplay of forces within the individual rather than on external behaviors. In an effort to discharge instinctual tensions effectively, the ego must learn to negotiate a subtle yet crucial set of regulations and barriers by concocting highly disguised routes of gratification. The pattern, or prototype, for many of these symbolic behaviors is set during the first five or six years of life when basic conflicts over instinctual gratification are initially encountered and battled.

Application of Freud's Theory

Past and Present. How did Jay become the person she is today? Freudian theory has specific and elaborate answers to this question which are based on two important assumptions: (1) that all behavior is determined by powerful unconscious forces and is symbolically related to those forces—behavior does not occur by chance or by free choice (will) and, (2) that adult personality is determined by early childhood experiences.

Let us consider some of Jay's personality characteristics and behaviors and how they might relate to her childhood experiences. To begin, there is sufficient evidence to suggest that Jay's past and current behaviors reflect an inadequate or inconclusive resolution of her Oedipus complex (see chapter 6). This fixation at the phallic stage, perhaps due to an excessive amount of sexual gratification by self-stimulation and concurrent fantasies of incest when she was between three and five years of age, may be inferred from behaviors such as: (a) difficulties with many men, (b) an especially close and warm relationship with her father and a rather uninspiring one with her mother (and with other women), (c) the choice of a traditionally male occupation and one also pursued by her father, and (d) falling in love with a man fifteen years older than herself. Many of Jay's personality traits theoretically linked to the phallic stage (see Table 18), although perhaps not excessively predominant, do appear somewhat out of proportion or balance within the entire personality. For example, she seems to have an "unhealthy" amount of self-hate, humility, timidity, bashfulness, isolationism, avoidance of heterosexuality, chastity, and sadness—though her most recent feelings and behaviors suggest that some changes in these characteristics may be taking place. This, however, is an unlikely possibility according to the Freudian approach, since personality rarely changes during adulthood, at least not without professional intervention of the kind to be described shortly.

Jay's difficulties with the phallic stage and its Oedipus complex may be related partly to earlier difficulties with instinctual gratification, as later failures often are based upon earlier ones. Specifically, some of her characteristics and behaviors also suggest "carry-overs" or vestiges from the anal and even oral stages of development. For example, let us consider Jay's aggressive outbursts with men and some of her personality characteristics (e.g., compulsiveness) which probably have contributed to her academic and professional progress—qualities theoretically associated with fixation at the anal erotic phase.

You might recall that Jay's brothers were born when she was

two to three years of age and that they posed a threat, real or imagined, to her being the center of attention in the Smith family. In some sense, Jay apparently felt dethroned and reacted with outrage to this usurpation of power (e.g., her temper tantrums). This loss of power took place initially during a time when her parents and society were making their first real demands on Jay's sexual instincts. Specifically, she was required during the anal stage to gain control of her bowel movements to the extent that she could go "to the potty" now only at a specific place and time. Many children overreact to this rule of authority, particularly when parents are unduly demanding, with open and sometimes subtle acts of defiance and manipulation (*anal-aggressive behaviors*). It is not unreasonable to assume that, for Jay, the arrival of her brothers and the onset of new instinctual gratification regulations became fused and unconsciously associated with acts of aggression and defiance. This would help explain Jay's volatile temper in the presence of men important to her. Related to this is the possibility that Jay's violent outbursts with men later in her life represented a further fusing of aggression with sexuality, this time in regard to the Oedipus complex. For example, Jay presumably was protected much of the time from the anxiety generated by the Oedipus complex and its incestual and hostile wishes by defense mechanisms including, according to Freud, repression (see Table 7 in chapter 5). Once she became romantically involved with a man, Jay's anxiety may have increased substantially (because of the symbolic association of important men with her father) and her defenses proved to be inadequate. Thus, when panic-stricken or confused by the threat of incest, Jay would react to a male as she learned to do originally during the anal stage, with aggression. In other words, males, threat, regulation by others, and aggressiveness have become associated unconsciously in Jay's mind and often have led to seemingly "irrational" behaviors.

A Freudian also might point to Jay's academic excellence and career choice as further proof of some anal fixation. To elaborate, part of the struggle between the child and the parents during the anal stage is really over being clean, punctual, and orderly. Especially if the parents become overly concerned with the child's defecation and its timing, the child may react by withholding his or her feces for long periods of time—a manipulation which usually gains attention from the parents. In the process of coping with this struggle, an obsessive-compulsive pattern of dealing with (or controlling) the world often is established. In other words, the child develops persistent thoughts and concerns about cleanliness, punctuality, and saving (retaining), and also develops highly repetitive and inflexible coping behaviors to handle this battle of control with the parents and society. As adults, obsessive-compulsive individuals remain overly burdened with "anal" concerns and show a great deal of stubbornness, ambivalence, and orderliness. Stubbornness is believed to originate from those times when the child defied the parents by holding back bowel movements. Ambivalence in the obsessive-compulsive adult makes it difficult for this person to reach decisions because of his or her perpetual uncertainty. This characteristic has its origins during the anal period when the child must struggle with opposing tendencies to yield or resist, to expel or retain the prized feces. In the process, feelings of love and hate (ambivalence) for the parents are generated. Orderliness in the obsessive-compulsive is aimed at preventing anything from going wrong (e.g., expressing unacceptable impulses). The person controls himself or herself and the environment by relying on ritualistic and highly repetitive ways of behaving—actions which help make the person's world safer and more predictable. Basically, excessive orderliness (being methodical, conforming, clean, etc.) is seen as a reaction formation against anal desires to play with the feces and more generally, to be messy, hostile, and destructive. Reaction formation, as you may recall, is a defense mechanism which converts unacceptable or threatening impulses into opposite and more acceptable ones (e.g., messiness to orderliness), thereby usually protecting the person from considerable anxiety (see Table 7 in chapter 5).

Though we are not privy to detailed information on how Dr. and Mrs. Smith handled her toilet training (but we are told of difficulties here), Jay's academic excellence and career choice suggest the presence of many obsessive-compulsive characteristics. For example, we know Jay has devoted enormous energy to her college and medical studies, a feat requiring considerable persistence, orderliness, and concern for detail. Moreover, being precise, punctual, orderly, and meticulous are characteristics of importance to practicing doctors (and many other professionals too), and this may have been an important attraction of the field for Jay. In other words, since medicine requires qualities which she possesses, Jay's professional selection may have been influenced subtly and in part by the match between her personality characteristics and those demanded by medicine. It might be noted also that the ambivalence characteristic of obsessive-compulsive individuals may help to clarify Jay's emotional outbursts with "father-figures." Specifically, not only does she have positive feelings of love for these men, she also harbors a great deal of hostility and hatred (unconsciously retained from the anal period). When her reaction formation mechanisms fail, the hostility manifests itself in full force.

We shall not discuss in detail possible oral fixations in Jay's development, since we have so little information about this time of her life. But her periods of depression coupled with overeating do suggest partial oral fixation. During the oral stage, some infants learn to associate food with love, since the two often are provided simultaneously during this period. As adults, these people may react to depression by seeking love in the form of food.

In short, the Freudian answer to the question, How did Jay become the person she is today? is a highly abstract and circuitous one and requires much knowledge about the person's early childhood (or more specifically, about his or her *memories* of and *associations* with this period). Personality characteristics and patterns of coping with psychosexual conflicts are jelled by the end of the phallic stage (around five or six years of age) and are destined to be relived throughout the person's life. Though the connections between adult behaviors and early instinctual gratification patterns are unconscious and symbolic, they *do* exist, according to Freudian theory, and must be uncovered to understand the personality fully.

Personality Change.   If, indeed, one's basic traits and defenses are fixed essentially by age five or six, then personality change at a later time is understandably difficult to accomplish. Because Freudian theory sees behavior (or "symptoms") as reflections of the underlying personality, simply altering behavior will have little positive impact on the person. In fact, it may even result in negative consequences. For example, it has been argued frequently by Freudians that symptom removal (e.g., as a consequence of behavior modification techniques to be discussed later), without uncovering the underlying conflicts, leads to equally, or possibly even more, disturbing symptom patterns (*symptom substitution*). In Jay's case, this might mean that simply working on her shyness and her troubled interactions with men, without seeking out and resolving their Oedipal roots, could lead to other "problems" such as frigidity, conversion symptoms such as psychologically caused loss of speech or paralysis of her hands, or dysfunctional obsessions or compulsions. Freudian theory postulates that if personality change is to occur, the person first must learn to become aware of (*insight*) and accept the unconscious roots of behavior. In other words, gaining conscious control of things happening unconsciously shoud make matters better because the ego's effectiveness in gratifying the instincts without hurting the individual will improve dramatically. A basic change in personality structure and functioning, it is argued, leads to increased personal integration and psychological maturity and eventually to the elimination of troublesome, self-defeating behaviors.

To ensure this understanding of the hidden meanings and motivations of behavior, the person must probe unconscious desires and conflicts and see their application in everyday behaviors. Without the help of a trained, objective therapist, this is almost impossible to accomplish as threatening material would simply lead to increased anxiety and further defensive operations, so that the person always would be distorting the true nature of his or her unconscious mind. In Freudian therapy, known as *psychoanalysis,* the therapist listens to the patient and eventually offers interpretations of the workings of the underlying drives and defenses. It is up to the patient to think about and emotionally experience the validity of the therapist's feedback.

Insight alone is not sufficient to ensure behavioral change. Toward the end of the long and arduous therapeutic process, which may be after a two- or three-year period with four or five weekly sessions, the patient must learn to apply the emotional reeducation (insights) to everyday, real-life situations and behaviors. Thus, Jay would be encouraged to see how her unresolved Oedipal conflict manifests itself in her day-to-day interactions. She would be urged by her therapist to resolve this childhood fixation by relating to her parents on a more mature, contemporaneous level. Jay would be asked to improve her relationships with male and female friends, colleagues, and the like, so that she would begin to interact with them as individuals and not as mirror images of her parents. These behavioral changes would be possible now because of the personality changes and growth resulting from the insights into the underlying causes of her behavior, which hitherto had been hidden.

Several techniques are used in psychoanalysis to help uncover and resolve the patient's repressed memories, motives, and conflicts; these techniques include free association and the analysis of resistance, dreams, and transference. *Free association* is a difficult technique to master and involves the patient's willingness to report everything that comes to mind, including those things which may be painful or obscene or which may even seem irrelevant or silly. Freud believed that by relaxing censorship, the patient's associations eventually would lead to the deeper levels of the mind. The therapist points out and interprets the connective threads between the patient's verbalizations and the hidden sources of motivation. *Resistance* often is shown by patients as they get in touch with unconscious material and generally consists of efforts against confronting it. In psychoanalysis, resistance by a patient can be seen in many ways, for example, in disruptive joking, quarreling with the therapist, missed appointments, and the sudden inability to associate freely. The therapist interprets these acts of resistance to the patient and tries to get him or her to understand the nature of the threatening repressed material. *Dreams* are an important aid to psychoanalysis too, because they supposedly reveal unconscious material. The dream images (*manifest content*) are not direct representations of the unconscious but rather are indirect symbolic ones (*latent content*). It is up to the therapist to help the patient analyze and interpret the dream symbols. Finally, as the relationship between the patient and therapist becomes more involved, complex emotions between these two develop and are crucial to the eventual success of the therapy. Perhaps most important are the positive and negative feelings which the patient gradually projects or transfers onto the therapist, as this important person comes to represent others significant to the patient's past. In other words, in therapy itself, the patient will react eventually to the therapist in ways reminiscent of childhood interactions with his or her father, mother, brother, sister, and so on. The therapist will point out this *transference* so the patient can see how earlier conflicts and emotions involving these other people still are affecting current attitudes and behaviors. Positive transference in the form of a childlike dependency on and trust in the therapist and the desire to please also help motivate the patient to tolerate the anxiety inherent in insight.

In short, although changes in adult personality are possible, Freudian theory maintains that they are most difficult and unlikely unless the person is willing to work diligently with a trained therapist over a period of many years. In the process of extensively exploring one's unconscious motivations and past experiences, energy devoted previously to repressed material may be freed to help strengthen the ego and enhance its pursuit of more efficient, reality-oriented ways of instinctual gratification.

Other Psychodynamic Theorists

Though influenced significantly by Freud's viewpoints, many other psychodynamic theorists have proposed distinctive, alternative perspectives for understanding personality. To mention two, Carl Jung's approach to Jay might emphasize her struggle to integrate opposing tendencies in her personality, such as introversion and extroversion or her anima (femaleness) and animus (maleness), rather than conflicts over childhood sexuality. He would try to put Jay in touch with unconscious forces representing not only personal past experiences but also those of our ancestral past (*archetypes*). Alfred Adler would emphasize Jay's struggle with feelings of inferiority (perhaps due in part to her congenital hearing defect and to her being a first-born child later dethroned by siblings) and her tendencies to overcompensate for them. Adler would see Jay's behavior and life style in light of her struggle for superiority (*perfection*).

Perhaps the most influential psychodynamic theorist in recent years has been Erik Erikson. A summary of his theory of personality development is presented in Table 15 (see chapter 6). While there are close parallels with Freud's theory, important extensions are worth noting. First, Erikson's expansion of the developmental cycle to include stages beyond physiological maturity (Freud's genital stage) indicates his belief that personality is capable of significant change until death. Perhaps this is a tribute to the strength and flexibility that Erikson, and other "ego" psychologists, see in the executive structure of personality, the ego. Second, Erikson emphasizes more than Freud did the role of global cultural and social forces in molding the personality at each of the critical stages. Interpersonal relationships of all kinds (e.g., with friends, teachers, etc.), not just those with parents, deeply affect one's development. Third, there is a hint in Erikson's writings that the developmental crises are positive challenges which actually provide opportunities for growth, mastery, competence, and love—qualities sometimes referred to as "ego-attainments." Such a positive orientation is clearly lacking in Freud's developmental viewpoint, which more often than not emphasizes both (1) the ways things can go wrong and lead to psychopathology, and (2) the importance of curbing instinctual appetites for the good of society. Freud devotes relatively little importance to, or concern for, the individual's search for personal meaning or self-actualization, except perhaps as these activities derive from instinctual displacements or transformations. For these and other reasons, some would say that Erikson's developmental viewpoints are more optimistic and hopeful than Freud's.

Applied to Jay, Erikson's theory reveals an individual with many strengths and weaknesses, someone who has successfully resolved many of the "psychosocial crises" but who still must struggle with important developmental issues. Bear in mind as we describe Jay in light of Erikson's theory, that the developing ego ideally should not line up completely with the positive or "healthy" pole of each crisis. The positive and negative poles (e.g., basic trust and mistrust) should be viewed as a continuum with normal adjustment being clearly in the direction of the positive but also incorporating aspects of the negative. It would make little sense in today's world, for example, to be completely devoid of mistrust—some is necessary for adequate success and mastery of the environment.

Jay seems to have acquired at the oral stage a greater degree of mistrust than trust in her physical and social environments. This may be found in her reported fears, anxieties, and depressions, and in her interpersonal difficulties. Erikson might suggest that this outcome resulted partly from Mrs. Smith's own insecurities (which were probably reflected in the quality of her maternal care during Jay's first year) and from her pregnancy shortly after Jay's first birthday. The loss of maternal attention due to the pregnancy and eventual birth of her first brother could have provided Jay with sufficient evidence of an unpredictable and somewhat nonnurturant environment.

At the second, anal, crisis, involving the struggle of autonomy versus shame and doubt, Jay seems also to have incorporated more of the negative qualities than of the positive ones, but perhaps not by very much. Certainly, Jay shows self-doubt at times and an unwillingness to reveal herself to others—a possible result of her dethronement and presumably strict parental control when she was two and three years old. At the same time, she progressed successfully through college and medical school and displays a willingness to tackle a challenging and demanding career which requires many independent decisions. There is every indication that Jay is currently working on this crisis and eventually will resolve it in the more positive direction.

The third, phallic, crisis, involving the conflict between initiative and guilt, seems to have been resolved in the positive direction. Jay appears to have considerable purpose in life and initiates many activities related to her career—a result possibly emanating in part from her father's abundant affections and high aspirations for her. The guilt Jay reports over sexuality probably has its roots during this period and involves conflict over her love for and desire to be loved by her father.

The industry versus inferiority crisis also has been resolved apparently in the positive direction, as reflected by Jay's outstanding work in school and her strong professional affiliations. Inferiority feelings, especially in social contexts, do plague her and perhaps undermine her overall effectiveness. Her obvious concern for this weakness is proof that the crisis is still an important one in her life.

Jay's adolescent crisis, involving ego identity versus role confusion, probably was not resolved as successfully as one might hope. While ego identity emerged to some degree, e.g., with respect to pursuing a medical career, Jay displayed (and continues to display) confusion regarding sexual relationships and possibly conflict over traditional male-female roles. Erikson feels that societies often make it difficult for some groups of people to achieve identity—and women certainly fit this category in Western industrial culture. Traditional sexual and occupational norms (barring women from full participation) coexist with newer ones to create severe conflicts for Jay and other women.

The intimacy versus isolation crisis of early adulthood is still occupying a major portion of Jay's attention. Resolution in the negative direction seems to be the dominant force here, but Jay is very much concerned with establishing intimate relationships with others and with avoiding isolation. Whether she can successfully achieve her goal remains to be seen.

Jay's early contact with the generativity versus stagnation crisis appears to offer hope for resolution in the positive direction. Her commitment to becoming an excellent doctor and helping others with their medical needs is a sign of genuine caring for human welfare and the nature of society. Of course, if personal problems assume too great a role in her middle adulthood years, they could undermine the potentially satisfactory resolution of this crisis and perhaps of the final conflict of integrity versus despair, which has not been reached yet by Jay since it is a crisis of aging. But, based on Jay's continuing personality growth and her struggle to resolve successfully conflicts which have been poorly mastered at earlier periods, there is every reason for optimism.

HUMANISTIC-EXISTENTIAL APPROACHES

With some exceptions, humanistic-existential approaches have had a rather modest theoretical impact on personology, though this appears to be changing. One of the difficulties of dealing with the various humanistic-existential theorists is that they tend to write so individualistically that the resulting body of thought seems amorphous. It is difficult to find a clear and strong unifying thread underlying the writings of this diverse group, which includes theorists such as Carl Rogers, Abraham Maslow, Ludwig Binswanger, Medard Boss, Viktor Frankl, Rollo May, and Paul Tillich. If there are some unifying threads, they probably are in the importance of finding satisfactory meaning for one's existence, the potentialities for growth throughout life, and the emphasis on positive human relations and experience as opposed to negative and destructive ones. In our rapidly changing society with its apparent lack or destruction of previously cherished values, much of what these writers have to say is quite appealing and potentially important to personology.

Many may argue legitimately that the writings of humanists and existentialists are sufficiently dissimilar to justify categorizing them as separate approaches. To mention one such difference, humanists often emphasize self-actualization as the major motivating force in personality and existentialists tend to focus on the pursuit of spiritual meaning. But as noted above, there are similarities among the various writings too (cf. Calhoun, 1977). For example, both humanists and existentialists tend to approach personality from a *phenomenological* perspective, which emphasizes the importance of studying and understanding the person from his or her own subjective experiences (see chapter 4). Other similarities among the two groups of writings include an emphasis on human *freedom, choice,* and *responsibility*, a firm conviction in the individual's *inherent* ability to *grow psychologically* and to *fulfill capabilities*, and a genuine belief in the *uniqueness* of each person. These emphases, parenthetically, are quite at odds with those of the psychodynamic approaches which suggest, for example, that our behavior is completely determined, largely by irrational and unconscious instinctual forces.

We have selected the writings of Carl Rogers (1961, 1974) to illustrate the humanistic-existential approach to personality. Rogers has had a steady impact on personology over the years, and he continues to be a major spokesperson for the phenomenological perspective. Toward the end of this section, Viktor Frankl's (1955, 1962) work also will be mentioned to illustrate an increasingly popular psychological viewpoint which is not as optimistic as that portrayed by Rogers.

Synopsis of Rogers' Theory

As we described earlier (see chapter 5), human beings are motivated primarily by one major internal force, the *self-actualizing tendency*. This biologically inherent tendency is the major motive force postulated by Rogers, and it encompasses both physiological and psychological efforts at growth and differentiation. In the infant, the force-for-growth motive ensures survival by providing the impetus to satisfy basic deficiency needs such as hunger and thirst. Moreover, essential maturational and developmental processes are enhanced by this "master" motive. For example, despite great pain and effort, the infant persists in its first attempts to walk, not only because such behavior is genetically programmed but also because of the strong tendency toward growth. As the child gets older and a self-concept begins to emerge, the self-actualizing tendency also operates to fulfill and enhance psychological properties. Rogers believes, in short, that human beings are motivated to develop all their capacities to the highest degree. The self-actualizing tendency ensures (under most conditions) that the person will maintain, enhance, and fulfill his or her being, even if in the process more, rather than less, tension and discomfort are encountered.

With experience, the infant's inner subjective world (*phenomenal field*) gradually becomes more complex and distinctive. One aspect of this ever-expanding awareness includes an important part called the *self* or *self-concept* (see chapter 4). The self consists of all those experiences which tell the person that he or she exists as a separate entity; it is an awareness that "I," "me," and "myself" refer to someone quite distinct from other things and people. As a distinct entity, the person has certain images of what he or she is, ought to be, and might like to be (*ideal self*). It is on the basis of these self-images that the person symbolizes and interprets experiences and ultimately behaves.

Rogers does not view the self-concept as developing through a critical series of innately determined stages. Rather, it is shaped primarily by the evaluations of significant others. As the self-concept emerges, a strong need to be loved (*need for positive regard*) also is manifested (see chapter 5). This makes the actions of others in the child's environment quite important, for these people have the power to give or to withhold this valued love and acceptance. In fact, if they do *not* give their love freely (*conditional positive regard*), the child is forced to behave in ways to please these people (usually the parents) and consequently to ignore his or her own values and needs. An innate guide for living (*organismic valuing process*), which operates so smoothly, spontaneously, and flexibly in letting children know what experiences maintain and enhance their self-actualizing tendency, is actually suppressed or sacrificed in favor of pleasing others. This has tragic consequences for the individual which need to be spelled out in some detail.

In the process of trying to please others, the child eventually strives to attain standards and goals (e.g., doing well in school or avoiding premarital sex) which have been applied first externally and then incorporated. These new internalized values tend to be rigid and unchanging and may be at odds with what the person really wants or wants to be. Nevertheless, they become an essential part of the individual and serve as a basis for judging one's own worth or value. In other words, a person's *self-regard* is determined by how well he or she is living up to the expectations of others, rather than by how well he or she is fulfilling the self-actualizing tendency. When the child (and later the adult) does not act, think, or feel in accordance with the internalized wishes and demands of important others (*conditions of worth*), guilt, anxiety, and low self-regard result—conditions which eventually lead to defensiveness against the unworthy behaviors. Thus, the person loses touch with, or distorts, those significant and genuine experiences inconsistent with the self-concept and consequently is plagued by a rather restrictive existence, no longer being able to function in full freedom (cf. anxiety discussion in chapter 5).

To what extent can people avoid this estrangement from their self-actualizing tendency and its related guide for living, the organismic valuing process? Theoretically, at least, it is possible to develop one's potentialities and to remain in touch with the valuing process, but only to the degree that one is valued and loved without qualifications or restrictions (*unconditional positive regard*). This does not mean that parents, for example, must never disapprove of, or punish, their child's behavior. Discipline and behavioral control obviously are needed on many occasions, especially those with some threat to the child's welfare, e.g., crossing streets unsafely, touching hot objects, hitting other children, and the like. But the child can be disciplined with assurances of understanding and love, and without a devaluation of him or her as a person. In effect, the child's desire for performing certain undesirable acts should be openly acknowledged and communicated, but the acts themselves should be appropriately punished. By receiving unconditional positive regard, the child will not have conditions of worth and therefore can accept all aspects of his or her experience as valid and worthwhile, making defensiveness unnecessary. For example, feelings such as aggressive impulses toward a parent may be accepted as genuine and non-threatening to the self, though, of course, this does not necessarily mean it would be best to act them out. Most importantly, the individual is capable of becoming self-actualizing (on the path to fulfilling potentialities) and of ultimately proceeding to Rogers' ideal personality type, the *fully functioning person*.

The fully functioning person is described in Table 5 (see chapter 5). In general, this ideal individual has received unconditional positive regard from important people and therefore is not defensive or doubtful about self-worth. This leads to an internal state of complete harmony or consistency between the self and total organismic experiencing, as well as between the self and potentialities. The fully functioning person is just that, functioning fully by using his or her talents and moving to higher and higher levels of actualization. Rogers believes these people may be described effectively by five major personality characteristics: (1) *openness to experience* (non-defensive, emotional depth); (2) *existential living* (living fully in every moment of existence, being spontaneous and flexible); (3) *organismic trusting* (intuitive, doing what feels worth doing); (4) *experiential freedom* (inner sense of free choice and power); and (5) *creativity* (able to produce new ideas and things, constructive and creative living).

In short, Rogers presents a fairly optimistic view of human nature and personality. Under optimal conditions, the individual is guided by an innate tendency to grow and to actualize, to become what he or she is capable of becoming. The person is conscious of experience, is directed toward the future, acts rationally, and seeks stimulation. There is no inherent conflict between the person and others and defensiveness is unnecessary. Even when conditions are inadequate and the person experiences a restrictive and threatening existence, the ability and responsibility for change and growth are ever present and with a minimal amount of therapeutic support, the person readily may regain contact with all organismic experiencing.

Application of Rogers' Theory

Past and Present. How did Jay become the person she is today? Rogers can help us to understand the impact of Jay's past on her current personality, but bear in mind that this issue is not of central importance to his contemporaneously based theory. Gaining an accurate picture of Jay as she exists *today* is of major concern to Rogerian theory, for it is on the basis of present perceptions and interpretations that she characteristically acts and reacts. Nevertheless, Rogers does postulate broadly based, early learning conditions which can significantly affect the developing self-concept and consequent adult perceptions and behaviors.

Many of Jay's behaviors suggest a rather restrictive and perhaps brittle self-concept, e.g., her rivalry with her brothers, a rather disparaging self-image despite accolades from others, heterosexual turbulence, and anxieties and guilt. These various sources of information indicate that she probably did not receive unconditional positive regard from significant others as a child, and thus incorporated many conditions of worth based on the wishes of important people.

Jay's rather reserved relationship with her mother, for example, suggests an initial source of difficulty for the development of Jay's self-concept. From the beginning, it seems that Mrs. Smith harbored many insecurities and doubts about her first-born child, as well as about herself. Having a child for the first time is undoubtedly trying for most women, though considerable excitement and joy are usually present too. Nevertheless, since the Smiths married somewhat late in in life, having children seemed unwise. With time, however, it struck them as a potentially worthwhile and fulfilling venture. When Jay was born she appeared healthy enough, but it was noted eventually that minor difficulties in responding to people and to specific environmental events were due to a hearing defect. Though surgical techniques improved the condition, it still affects Jay to some extent today. As a result of this problem, Mrs. Smith withdrew emotionally from Jay when she was quite young. Ironically perhaps, Mrs. Smith blamed herself for Jay's hearing defect and took out her frustrations on her daughter. When Jay's two younger brothers were born, both in excellent health, Mrs. Smith withdrew even more from Jay. Thus Jay's early relationship with her mother strongly indicates that her need for acceptance and love was partly frustrated.

Jay's early relationship with her father sounds ideal until it is examined in more detail. For example, despite the attention and favoritism she received from her father, Jay saw his lofty goals and ambitions as subtle ways of indicating that she had to excel and achieve if she wanted his admiration. In other words, Dr. Smith's values were interpreted by Jay as conditions of worth—which, it might be added, may not have been congruent with her own potentialities. She, nevertheless, incorporated these values into her self-concept in order to obtain her father's love.

In an attempt to secure the approval of her parents, Jay had to adopt certain behavior patterns and values which quite probably did not reflect her own inherent needs. The influence of the father assumed primary importance for Jay since Mrs. Smith withdrew her love and devoted her energies mostly to the younger children. Without Dr. Smith's love, Jay probably would have experienced even more problems as an adult. Even so, since his love was conditional, Jay gradually lost touch with those organismic experiences inconsistent with her emerging self-concept. To illustrate this, let us consider Dr. Smith's values and some of Jay's prominent characteristics in more detail.

Dr. Smith is not much of a "social" person. Most of his life has centered around his home and family; even his job has been conducted primarily at home. As Jay was growing up, he constantly would tell her that she had to do well in school and, later, in a professional career. Although friends were important, he would preach, they could hinder one's studies. Therefore, Jay was warned often of the dangers of acquiring too many acquaintances or of becoming too serious about men, particularly before she was settled into her chosen career. While sexuality was not portrayed exactly in unflattering terms by Dr. Smith, neither was it assigned a very high priority. Thus, Jay's self-concept has been oriented from a very early age around internalized values of competence and achievement and has included the belief that social and sexual needs must be abdicated in favor of desires for success, wealth, and independence.

Viewed in light of Jay's self-concept, many of her behaviors begin to fall into place. For example, her avoidance of intimate heterosexual relationships can be seen as an attempt to behave in accordance with her self-concept. As Jay becomes attracted to a man and their relationship matures, feelings of affection threaten her values of achievement, and therefore she must deny or distort these experiences in order to prevent disrupting anxiety. In Ted's case, for example, his innocent conversation with a coed was distorted to mean that he no longer cared for Jay. Once that became reality for her, she could legitimately break off the relationship and reduce her anxiety and guilt. And the quicker and nastier the dissolution, the slimmer the chance was for a later reconciliation. With other men, Jay's affection sometimes would be denied altogether or even distorted into feelings of hostility. Of course, these transformations took place outside of Jay's awareness or true understanding.

In general, as Jay becomes involved with other people and nonprofessional activities, threat and anxiety ensue. Defense mechanisms help out, but apparently they fail on many occasions. This suggests that experiences incongruent with her self-concept are increasing in intensity or frequency and lead to periods of severe confusion, depression, and insecurity. Social pressures (regarding dating and marriage) undoubtedly are contributing to Jay's difficulties, but many of her innate potentialities also may be pushing for acceptance and fulfillment. In the process of frequently encountering anxiety, Jay's self-esteem has suffered though she has managed so far to function adequately in her professional role and to keep her self-structure partially intact. Her inner discomfort, however, has impelled her to seek professional help in alleviating the anxiety.

Rogers' theory, in short, suggests that although Jay has the innate potential for a rich and fulfilling life, certain environmental obstacles have created a rigid self-concept which is out of touch with her real needs and which prevents her from fully experiencing many genuine, though incongruent, emotions and thoughts. Knowledge of Jay's self-concept, Rogers argues, greatly increases our understanding of her present behavior because people generally act in accordance with their self-concept.

Personality Change.   Rogers has the firm belief that people are innately programmed to move toward growth and actualization if the right conditions are present. Except under restrictive circumstances, personality is ever changing and growing in a healthy direction. When a person is not able to function freely and is threatened constantly by incongruent experiences, therapeutic intervention may help or facilitate the person's temporarily stunted growth tendencies.

Rogers believes the patient (or "client") has the major responsibility for getting in touch with lost experiences and for integrating them into the self-concept. The therapist's role in *client-centered* therapy is mainly to create a nonthreatening "atmosphere" in which the client is not afraid that the therapist will judge or interpret everything he or she says. Specific techniques are not essential to the creation of this critical therapeutic atmosphere and in fact may even be harmful. For example, Rogers believes that techniques like free association or gathering case histories give the therapist an aura of authority and expertise and might tempt the client to expect correct prescriptions from the therapist. Rather than working and struggling with their problems, some clients would simply relinquish their own responsibility for change and rely instead on the therapist for all the necessary decisions—a very unsatisfactory and unproductive state of affairs, according to Rogers.

If techniques are not emphasized in client-centered therapy, how is the proper atmosphere for change created? Rogers maintains that specific conditions must exist between the client and therapist before the client can begin to explore and resolve his or her problems—in other words, the client/therapist *relationship* must be of a particular nature. It is the therapist's responsibility to shape this relationship constructively by being *congruent, accepting,* and *empathic* with the client. To elaborate, if Jay were to enter Rogerian therapy, ideally she would talk with a therapist who is genuine in the relationship and who is functioning without any defensive facades. This means the therapist should be integrated and functioning well, with congruency between experiences and awareness. The therapist should provide unconditional positive regard for Jay, prizing her for what she is and for what she may become. No conditions of worth would be imposed so that Jay would feel valued regardless of any particular thoughts, feelings, or actions. Finally, the therapist would truly understand Jay's subjective world by experiencing as she experiences, perceiving as she perceives, and so on. The therapist, in other words, genuinely should be able to enter Jay's phenomenological frame of reference without becoming enmeshed in her emotions; a clear perspective is essential if the therapist is to communicate empathic understanding and unconditional positive regard effectively to the client. The communication of this crucial therapeutic atmosphere is facilitated by the therapist's efforts to summarize and *reflect* accurately the client's feelings so that he or she is able to understand them better. Reflecting feelings requires the therapist first to sense the client's meaning and then to put it clearly into words with comments or questions that show respect for the client and his or her problems.

Working within the above conditions, Jay would feel understood and accepted as a whole person. She would be encouraged to get in touch with her organismic valuing process once again and to deal with the incongruities that have developed between her self-concept and her experiences. The therapist would help by clarifying and organizing Jay's feelings and thoughts (without symbolic interpretations, however) and by allowing her to explore previously threatening material in a completely supportive environment. By gaining insights into her present subjective perceptions and interpretations, Jay gradually would be able to repair the shattered unity of her self and her experience and to emerge as a fully functioning person, capable of making constructive choices, of being completely open to experience, and of relating more effectively to others.

In summary, Rogerian therapy is aimed at providing an environment or relationship in which the client once again can find innate callings toward actualization. In the safe and accepting therapeutic setting, the client is freed of any necessity for defense mechanisms and hence can openly confront experiences which are inconsistent with the self-concept. Since the therapist is totally accepting and provides no conditions of worth, the client eventually realizes that all experiences are valid and genuine and may be incorporated constructively into the self-concept. Thus, the self is broadened to include all experience, and personality becomes more unified and flexible as the individual's potential for growth is once again free to assert itself. It should be emphasized that client-centered therapy typically lasts for a relatively brief span of time (two to three months, for example) and is terminated usually at the client's request. Topics for discussion are determined by the client, but he or she is encouraged to talk about matters currently of concern (in the "here-and-now"), rather than about past events from early childhood. The key to personality is an understanding of the client's subjective world as it is currently being experienced.

Other Humanistic-Existential Theorists

Unlike Rogers' self-theory, many existentialists prefer to focus less on individual needs and more on the nature of the "human condition," e.g., the responsibility the person has not only to himself or herself but also to others and the anguish over making choices, experiencing anxiety and guilt, and facing death. Though there are many existential writers, some of whom were mentioned in the beginning of this section, we have selected Viktor Frankl's works to summarize here as they are becoming exceedingly popular among both professionals and laypeople.

Viktor Frankl's harrowing experiences in the Nazi concentration camps during World War II greatly influenced his thinking about personality and the most effective ways for changing it. As is true of most existentialists, Frankl's writings often emphasize the inevitable sorrows and frustrations which must be faced by all of us, but which at the same time present the greatest challenges to human dignity and existence. We are not bound by instincts, the past, or environmental conditions—a spiritual life gives us the freedom to transcend these forces. This freedom in turn makes us responsible for our individual lives. Although our control over external events may be limited, the way we choose to handle these events is always left to us. For example, do we become apathetic and despondent in the face of life's demands or do we find meaning in those demands, even when they involve human suffering? Do we regress to the familiar past in the face of difficulty or do we move forward to an unknown future? The choice may be a difficult one, but it is nevertheless ours to make.

The central motive in human personality, according to Frankl, is the *will to meaning*, an effort to find some justification for our finite and less than ideal existence. Frankl is not talking of a universal meaning to life, as much as of an idiosyncratic one that is important to a particular individual in a particular situation. Each person's search for meaning can be tension producing but at the same time, challenging and highly exciting. Yet how does one discover meaning in life? Pursuing important *values* (creative, experiential, and attitudinal) will help and also will allow the person to transcend the ordinary forces in life which attempt to drive and influence all of us (e.g., pleasure, power). *Creative* values are experienced by *giving* the world products (things or ideas), achieved usually through work-related tasks. *Taking* things from the world, like appreciating what is good and beautiful (in nature or in love), facilitates *experiential* values. *Attitudinal* values are experienced by confronting and *suffering* a fate which restricts one's potentialities (e.g., illness or death); the courage and dignity we display here represent the ultimate test of human fulfillment.

When individuals have not found meaning in life, they often experience *existential frustration*, a condition sometimes leading to a host of neurotic or psychotic problems. On the other hand, those people fortunate enough to find such meaning represent Frankl's ideal personality type, the *self-transcendent person*. This kind of person is characterized partly by a sense of freedom and responsibility to choose consciously his or her own life course and by an ability to transcend a focus on the "self." This latter point suggests that Frankl disagrees with many humanists who emphasize self-actualization as the primary motive and goal of human behavior.

Psychological health, Frankl contends, depends on the ability to relate to the outside world and to other people, to find meaning beyond the self. If this can be accomplished, actualization of the self typically will occur spontaneously.

Applied to Jay, Frankl's theory suggests a person who has refused to accept responsibility for her life and who has preferred to rely on routine patterns of coping rather than to turn to new, though unproved ones. Spiritually, Jay has not developed to the extent of adequately pursuing creative, experiential, or attitudinal values, and consequently her life lacks significant spiritual meaning. Jay is too preoccupied with her own personal problems and has yet to nurture effective relationships with the outside world. She desperately needs, for example, to love and to be loved but remains afraid to try new approaches to establishing intimate relationships. Until she is willing to acknowledge her freedom and assume responsibility for living, Jay's existence is going to be unfulfilling and to lack true meaning. In psychotherapy (called *logotherapy*), Frankl would explore Jay's subjective world, and the two of them would attempt to uncover her troublesome attitudes toward life so that she eventually could pursue the necessary values for establishing a meaningful existence. Even on the road to becoming a self-transcendent person, Jay still will experience anxiety and guilt, as they are to some extent inevitable consequences of living. At the same time, she would have the satisfaction of moving toward the realization of important values and significant goals—things which give life meaning and ultimately make it worth living.

BEHAVIORAL APPROACHES

Behavioral approaches originated around the turn of the twentieth century in protest against the thinking characteristic of psychoanalysis. Behaviorally oriented theorists argued then that subjective experiences and hidden unconscious forces were not "public events" open to verification by others and hence could not be admissible data for the scientific study of personality. In general, behavioral theorists view personality as a *collection of habitual responses* influenced by external stimuli rather than by internal subjective forces. The responses which comprise personality must be capable of being observed and measured by *objective* means so that *prediction* and *control* of behavior are possible. It is assumed that behavior is largely a product of experience, or more specifically, that responses are acquired, maintained, changed, or eliminated according to basic *principles of learning*.

In the present section, we shall highlight the work of B.F. Skinner (1953, 1971), known sometimes as a "radical behaviorist" because of his strict adherence to the basic tenets of behavioral approaches noted above. Skinner has enlarged upon the writings of early behaviorists such as Thorndike (1913) and Watson (1924) and continues to be a major force in the study of personality, though his writings are as controversial as those the behaviorists first attacked. More "moderate" behavioral theorists, influenced primarily by the works of Pavlov (1927), Dollard and Miller (1950), Hull (1943), and Spence (1948), have been more tolerant of incorporating subjective experiences and feelings into the study of personality, but still without resorting to conceptions of unconscious dynamics as causes of behavior. The impact of these moderate behavioral theorists is being felt more and more, and accordingly, we shall discuss also the works of two contemporary representatives of this movement, Albert Bandura (1969, 1974) and Walter Mischel (1968, 1976).

Synopsis of Skinner's Theory

Some of Skinner's underlying assumptions about human behavior and personality are worth noting initially as they provide a background for comprehending his special point of view: 1) Though behavior results from both genetic-physiological and environmental influences, Skinner prefers to study the latter exclusively, mainly because environmental factors currently are more readily amenable to change and manipulation. 2) Behavior is determined, lawful, and hence subject to prediction and control. Human freedom or choice is rejected since behavior is molded almost entirely by past and present environmental controls (rewards and punishments). 3) Causes of human behavior are sought in the environment rather than inside the person. That is, not only are genetic-physiological explanations of behavior avoided, but so are mentalistic constructs such as id, ego, superego, or self. Mentalistic concepts, Skinner contends, are impossible to define or to verify objectively and furthermore explain very little; they even may stifle further inquiry into the causes of behavior. For example, to say Jay avoids heterosexual relationships because of an unresolved Oedipus complex or incongruencies between self and experience is vague and discourages additional investigation into the specific reinforcement history which has shaped and continues to maintain Jay's interpersonal responses. (4) Personality is viewed essentially as a collection of acquired behavior patterns and thus is governed by "principles of learning" (which explain how and under what conditions behavior is acquired). (5) Personality is best studied by a functional analysis of behavior. This is the discovery of the unique set of relationships between the person's behavior patterns and their controlling environmental conditions. All variables in this analysis must be observable and quantifiable, and the ultimate goal is to manipulate environmental stimuli and to predict their impact on behavioral responses (and personality); and (6) Skinner has preferred to study animals (e.g., rats and pigeons) rather than normal or abnormal human beings—though he has generalized freely to the latter. He assumes, though animals are far less complex, that their basic processes are similar to those found in humans. And, of course, animal research allows greater control of genetic/physiological and experiential backgrounds. Since the major concern of psychology is the study of overt behavior and not subjective impressions of childhood or present feelings, why not study basic learning processes in a mute animal fully capable of responding to controlled stimuli? As many of Skinner's principles have been generalized successfully to human beings, his preference for initially studying less complex animals would seem to have some justification. Let us turn to a summary of Skinner's views of personality.

Not surprisingly, Skinner proposes little in the way of personality structures or processes. His emphasis on behavioral control implies an interest in modifiable responses, not in relatively enduring characteristics which defy change. Moreover, Skinner prefers to treat the person as an unopened box, meaning that one does not have to peer inside the person to understand how he or she operates. Motives, drives, conflicts, emotions, and the like, as internal (mediating) causes of behavior, should be discarded in favor of a functional analysis of the person's behavior. That is, external environmental forces should be manipulated to study their effects on overt behavior, without resorting to speculation about unobservable possibilities. For example, why does a person go into a restaurant and eat on one occasion but walk past the restaurant on another? An obvious answer would be that the person was hungry on the first occasion but not on the other. Yet Skinner argues that hunger itself is a function of certain environmental variables (e.g., number of hours since last meal). If you can account for the eating behavior by an observable external stimulus situation, then why refer to an unobservable internal state?

Skinner distinguishes between two categories of behavior, respondent and operant. *Respondent* behavior is *elicited* by a specific stimulus, as in unlearned reflexes like the cough, sneeze, eye blink, pupillary contraction, or knee jerk. The environment, in effect, does something to the person, who then reacts spontaneously and involuntarily. Respondent behaviors may be learned too. Pavlov's (1927) famous study conditioning a dog's salivation to the sound of a bell, and Watson's and Raynor's (1920) experiment conditioning "fear" in an eleven-month-old boy named Albert are primary examples of respondent or "classical" conditioning. The point is that a formerly neutral stimulus (e.g., a bell) eventually can elicit a specific behavior (e.g., salivation) by being associated with an event (e.g., food) which already leads to that behavior.

Skinner believes that most human behavior is more complex than unlearned or learned reflexes. People are not just passive reactors to specific stimuli; rather, they actively *emit* responses which in turn produce consequences affecting the subsequent occurrence of those responses. This active response is called *operant* behavior because it operates or has an effect on the environment. Examples of operant behaviors range from the most simple to the most complex of human actions and include behaviors such as talking, reading, taking a bath, driving a car, and writing a book. But what consequences can these diverse behaviors possibly have for the person? In general, the person will learn (through operant or "instrumental" conditioning) that certain favorable or unfavorable consequences are associated with (or follow) specific actions (operants). When the consequences are favorable (reinforcing), the person is likely to repeat the preceding action. Because Skinner's views on reinforcement and their administration are fundamental to learning and more specifically, to personality development, and constitute his major contributions to the personality field, we shall elaborate upon them in some detail.

Personality is acquired and maintained through the individual's unique reinforcement history. Positive and negative reinforcers affect behavior as a result either of innate biological factors (*primary reinforcers*) or of experience and learning (*conditioned* or *secondary reinforcers*). Examples of primary (p) and conditioned (c) *positive reinforcers* include food (p), water (p), sex (p), money (c), attention (c), approval (c), and affection (c). Primary and conditioned *negative reinforcers* include aversive stimuli such as extreme heat or cold (p), electric shock (p), rude people (c), boring classes (c), and speeding tickets (c). Actually, Skinner maintains that whether these stimuli are in fact positive or negative reinforcers must be determined or confirmed by the effect they have on a particular individual's behavior. This is illustrated best by explaining the four basic ways consequences may affect or control behavior.

When a stimulus follows a response and strengthens it (i.e., increases its probability of occurring again), *positive reinforcement* has taken place—e.g., when receiving an *A* for a test you studied hard for increases the likelihood of future studying. *Negative reinforcement* also strengthens a response when the response successfully removes an aversive stimulus—e.g., when turning off a boring television show makes this escape behavior more likely in the presence of future boring shows. Note that although both positive and negative reinforcements *increase* the likelihood of a future response, the former involve the *addition* of something and the latter involve the *removal* of something. Two ways behavioral consequences may *reduce* the likelihood of a future response are through extinction and punishment. *Extinction* is the withholding of reinforcement following a response and it leads to a weakening of the operant behavior. Thus, if we ignore a child's temper tantrums and do not give in to his or her demands, the tantrums eventually should decrease in frequency. *Punishment* is commonly used to suppress an undesirable behavior and involves either the presentation of a negative reinforcer (aversive stimulus) or the removal of a positive one following a response. For example, if a hungry child starts fighting at the table, he or she could be spanked or not allowed to eat.

One of the above behavioral control techniques, punishment, is opposed by Skinner for several reasons. In everyday life, punishment can lead to the extreme forms of escape and avoidance reactions often associated with abnormal personality patterns. For example, the child who is frequently and severely scolded by its parents may learn to avoid people—thus becoming withdrawn and seclusive. Equally important is that punishment often leads to some unfortunate consequences like anger, guilt, or anxiety—feelings which only upset the person and rarely contribute to adaptive behavior. (Yes, Skinner acknowledges the existence of these emotions but not their causal role in behavior; they are merely by-products of environmental events.) And, finally, the suppression of behavior often is only temporary unless the punishment is continuous. In short, Skinner believes aversive controls are unfortunate and largely unnecessary. He instead advocates the use of other forms of behavioral control, especially positive reinforcement. These techniques can effectively teach desirable behaviors and eliminate undesirable ones without the unpleasant consequences accompanying punishment.

Stimulus generalization, stimulus discrimination, and shaping are key concepts in Skinner's views of personality development and help greatly in understanding how operants are effectively molded and incorporated into behavioral repertoires. As noted in chapter 5, *stimulus generalization* refers principally to the fact that responses strengthened (reinforced) in one situation also will tend to occur in other similar situations—e.g., an infant calling all males "daddy" or a female rape victim hating all men. Obviously, an adequate amount of *stimulus discrimination* is necessary too, and it is learned primarily through the reinforcement of behavior in the presence of certain stimuli but not in the presence of others—e.g., reinforcing the infant when it says "daddy" in the presence of the father but not when "daddy" is said to other males. Because many complex behaviors, like ice skating, reading, or playing a musical instrument, do not emerge full-blown, gradual approximations to the final desired responses must be encouraged. This is done through a procedure of selective reinforcement known as *shaping* (or "successive approximation"). For example, in teaching a child to speak, reinforcement at first is provided for almost anything that approximates a word. Gradually, however, reinforcement of distant approximations is withdrawn and only closer approximations are rewarded. Finally, only the correct pronunciation of the word is reinforced.

Many characteristics of particular behaviors, like their rate of occurrence and resistance to extinction, depend not only on reinforcement itself but also on the *schedule of reinforcement*. Our discussions so far have implied that operant behaviors are reinforced *continuously* or regularly, that is, after each occurrence. In everyday life, of course, behavior is seldom reinforced continuously—good deeds are not always acknowledged by others, a baby's cries are not always answered, the bonus does not always arrive, and so on. Ordinarily, behavior is reinforced *intermittently*, or according to a schedule—e.g., reinforcing a response only after, say, a five-minute interval has elapsed or after, on the average, every tenth occurrence. This has many advantages, including the fact that intermittent schedules produce behaviors which are more persistent or resistant to extinction than those acquired with constant reward.

In short, Skinner's views of personality emphasize the development, maintenance, and alteration of the behavior patterns resulting from an individual's unique reinforcement history. Prediction and control of human behavior are Skinner's major goals for the study of personality, and he believes the best way to achieve them is by studying the relationships between observable behaviors and their visible environmental antecedents and consequences.

Application of Skinner's Theory

Past and Present. How did Jay become the person she is today? Skinner's response to this question would acknowledge a combination of genetic-physiological and environmental contributions to Jay's personality, but the emphasis clearly would fall on the latter. Skinner would argue that if he had full knowledge of Jay's past and present reinforcement history, her current behavior would be completely understandable and therefore predictable. The problem, of course, is that we seldom ever know a person's complete reinforcement history. This is not necessarily a critical flaw in Skinner's position, since he emphasizes the plasticity of behavior and the fact that it is maintained largely by its current reinforcement schedules. In other words, although developmental-historical factors shape actions, these factors are not critical to the contemporary dominance of those actions in the individual's behavioral repertoire. Nevertheless, behavioral theorists often infer previous reinforcement histories from contemporary response patterns and circumstances and from similar situations in the person's past. Let us consider some of Jay's current behaviors and suggest how past objective environmental controls might have helped to shape and maintain them.

Jay's interpersonal relationships are characterized generally by overall shyness and occasional outbursts of aggression in the presence of men important to her. Both types of behavior presumably have been reinforced in the past, and our case history suggests several possible situations in which reinforcement may have occurred. For example, Jay's tendency to isolate herself from others possibly has been shaped and maintained by a combination of rewards and punishments received initially from her father. Dr. Smith, with his strong values and beliefs about the incompatibility of friends and work, no doubt strengthened Jay's shyness behaviors by giving her attention and approval (conditioned positive reinforcers) whenever she declined social invitations. Moreover, if there were times when Jay did participate in social activities, particularly to the exclusion of studying, Dr. Smith most likely withdrew his love and even became upset—aversive stimuli for Jay which also helped to suppress (punish) her social responses and, at the same time, to strengthen her shyness. Through stimulus generalization, her shyness transferred to many relationships, even those not directly threatening her studies or later, her career performance.

Jay's aggressive behaviors may be traced to her relationship with her brothers. Their taunts and threats to her position of favor may be seen as aversive stimuli which Jay attempted to remove with verbal and physical aggression. Since she did remain her father's favorite child, Jay's aggressive behaviors presumably not only removed her brothers' aversive stimuli (at least temporarily on each occasion) but also became associated with her father's affection. Thus, Jay's aggressiveness was shaped and maintained by a combination of negative and positive reinforcements. We can assume also that Jay's aggressiveness occurs with important men, particularly when they threaten her in some way, because of stimulus generalization. Notice that her aggressiveness does not tend to occur with all men or other women (at least not to the same degree as with those significant men in her life). This would indicate that her learning of aggression has discriminated too, that is, it is directed only at those men who share certain key characteristics with her brothers.

Many of Jay's other behaviors may be explained by a similar analysis. For example, her good study habits and academic excellence were no doubt reinforced by her father (e.g., with praise), her teachers (e.g., with good grades), and so on. Her choice of a medical career, too, can be viewed as a result of her previous and presumably present reinforcement history in relationship to her father and others. Even her periodic depressions are maintained probably by the extra attention she receives from others when they attempt to console her. It should be noted that in none of the above cases do we know the frequency with which Jay has received or is still receiving her reinforcements. Nevertheless, we can assume safely that they have been administered intermittently—this would account partly for the persistence and consistency of her behavior throughout the years.

Personality Change. Because Skinner regards personality to be a collection of learned behavior patterns rather than a set of underlying structures or processes, the issue of change involves the modification of overt behavior. Behavior is malleable and subject to a person's conditioning history. This is true regardless of the kind of behavior in question, be it normal or abnormal, adaptive or maladaptive; all behavior is learned and capable of alteration. If a person displays maladaptive behaviors, one need not assume automatically that there is an underlying disorder or conflict as in the psychodynamic view. In contrast to the Freudian viewpoint, for example, Skinner argues that the "symptom" *is* the problem and it alone should be changed—no search for and treatment of some inner conflict is necessary. The claim by Freudians that new symptoms will emerge if old ones are removed, without also tackling underlying problems, is a controversial one. Skinner would say that it is largely unsupported by many research studies conducted over the years, though thorny issues continue to make this research impossible to interpret definitively. For example, even when a "new" symptom seems to appear, it is difficult to determine precisely whether it is really a substitution or just an old unnoticed one, or perhaps simply a response to new environmental demands (cf. Calhoun, 1977).

The behavioral approaches to personality change, sometimes collectively known as *behavior therapies* or *behavior modification techniques*, involve the application of learning principles to the alteration or elimination of undesirable behaviors. As a group, these techniques rely little on verbalization and are not concerned with helping patients gain "insight" or self-understanding; therefore, the patient's past and his or her phenomenological experiences are seldom discussed. Rather, a direct attack is made on symptoms, with the therapist actively participating, not as an interpreter of psychological meanings but as an analyzer of the conditions currently maintaining the undesirable behavior and of the best way for changing the behavior into a preferred response. The client too is active and, in fact, the ultimate goal is not just to change behavior but also to bring the new behavior under the control of the patient—so that he or she can provide or arrange for the necessary rewards and punishments.

Skinner's viewpoints have influenced the development of a large arsenal of techniques designed to alter human behavior. Many of these techniques were illustrated in Jay's self-control program for her overweight problem (see chapter 5) and so we shall not dwell on them here. To review briefly, Jay's efforts at environmental planning (stimulus control) and behavioral programming were based on Skinnerian principles reviewed in this chapter (e.g., discrimination and reinforcement). As an example, one of Jay's self-control procedures included contingency contracting, which is an operant conditioning technique designed to strengthen adaptive responses and to suppress maladaptive ones. Essentially, Jay agreed to a contract in which the rewards and punishments were spelled out in detail and made contingent upon specific behaviors and acquired point totals (see Table 13). Further discussions and applications of behavior modification techniques, many of which have been directly or indirectly influenced by Skinner, will be presented toward the end of the next section on social learning theorists.

Other Behavioral Theorists

Some behavioral theorists, known generally as social learning theorists because of their application of learning principles to human social development, have departed from many of Skinner's radical views and are now acknowledging the person's inner world as an important mediator between stimuli and responses. Events such as nonobservable subjective beliefs, thoughts, and expectations are considered by many behavioral theorists as essential to any analysis of behavior. Though there are many important, social learning theorists, we shall discuss only the views of Albert Bandura and Walter Mischel. Both agree with Skinner that all behavior (normal and abnormal) is learned and that reference to internal traits or unconscious motives as causes of behavior is unjustified. The similarities with Skinner begin to fade fast at this point and important differences rapidly become evident. Let us consider Bandura's viewpoints first.

Bandura disagrees with Skinner's belief that reinforcement is necessary for learning to take place. *Observational learning*, which Bandura argues is much more common and important to human behavior than operant conditioning, results from watching another person behave in a particular situation. When the observer is in a similar situation at a later time, he or she may act in the same manner as the observed person (*model*) formerly behaved (see chapter 3 for a related discussion of socialization through identification).

Observational learning is superior to operant conditioning for a number of reasons. For example, many behaviors are too dangerous or costly to trust to trial-and-error learning—e.g., teaching a person to drive a car, to swim, to ski, or to fly a plane. Also, it is often too cumbersome to teach children important socialization processes (e.g., customs and language) through selective reinforcement procedures like shaping. Having people observe competent models perform certain tasks often accelerates the acquisition of new and complex behaviors. Bandura accepts the idea that rewards and punishments are important to human behavior, but they serve mainly as regulators of *performance*, not learning. A person may learn a response through observation without actually performing it (e.g., learning aggression by simply watching it on television). But when the incentives are right, that is, when the person decides the payoff is worth the effort, he or she may act appropriately (e.g., hitting a sibling or robbing a gas station). Reinforcement is thus more than just a mechanical strengthener of behavior; it also is informative and motivating.

As the above discussion suggests, Bandura's position is much more complex than the behaviorism of Skinner. Between the environment (stimulus) and behavior are a host of cognitions which help the person *anticipate* and appreciate presumed consequences, events he or she has not experienced directly but only observed happening to another (*vicarious reinforcement*). This involves the ability to *symbolize* external events and later to use verbal and imaginal representations to anticipate the probable outcomes of behavior. Unlike Skinner, Bandura sees internal cognitive activity as a mediating link between stimulus and response, that is, as an important determinant of a person's reactions to a particular situation. In fact, Bandura goes so far as to suggest that operant conditioning, which traditionally was thought to occur without conscious involvement, is not very effective without the person's awareness of what is being reinforced and moreover depends greatly on the person's willingness to perform.

Several other points clarifying Bandura's theory should be mentioned. First, people are regarded as self-regulators of behavior. This is a chief characteristic of human beings which allows them to manipulate their environments, just as their environments manipulate them. While it is true that behavior is controlled by its consequences, Bandura believes the consequences are selected partly by the person (see the self-control discussion in chapter 5). The study of personal control has been greatly neglected, especially in comparison with research on environmental controls of behavior, and Bandura feels this situation deserves rectification. Second, as should be evident by now, Bandura does not suggest that observational learning is a passive, mechanical copying process in which a person simply watches another and learns. Many objective characteristics of the observer and model may affect observational learning (e.g., the sex of each, competency of the model, rewards and punishments received by the model, etc.) but only through a variety of subjective internal processes (e.g., attention, memory representation, motor reproduction processes, and incentive and motivational processes). A person does not automatically copy or reproduce the behavior he or she sees in another—an active decision or judgment is necessary. Third and finally, Bandura's respect for the complexity of human behavior makes him critical of Skinner's preference for studying lower animals. Bandura and other contemporary social learning theorists assume that human behavior is radically different from that of infrahumans, not just in degree but also in kind.

Mischel, like Skinner, has found himself enmeshed in controversy over the last decade or so, mostly due to his rather strong attacks on personology's traditional emphasis on "static" traits and underlying motivational states to the exclusion, Mischel says, of situational influences on behavior. The details of this controversy and its related debates were discussed in chapter 4 and therefore will not be presented here. However, Mischel's theoretical views of personality seem to have changed considerably in recent years, perhaps partly because of the exchange of ideas resulting from the person versus situation arguments, and there now may be some hope for a reconciliation among several factions currently dividing personology (a possibility we shall elaborate upon toward the end of this chapter).

Like Bandura, Mischel maintains that the person and the environment interact, each influencing the other. Although personality is still regarded as a learned collection of behavior patterns, cognitive structures are viewed as helping the person to adapt his or her behavior to the demands of the current environment. These cognitive structures vary from person to person so that individual differences exist in the ability to construe the world. In effect, Mischel is arguing that personality functioning is best understood by studying the contributions of both person and situation variables—a position sometimes called "interactionist" (chapter 8 has research examples of this approach).

Mischel's incorporation of person variables into the study of behavior raises some interesting points. First, in order to predict reactions accurately, the person's individual meanings of stimuli and reinforcers must be studied, a requirement suggesting that phenomenology is crucial to social learning theory. Bandura and Mischel insist that adequate measurement of inner cognitions is possible through refined oral and written reports. Second, if traditional person variables, like relatively static traits, are an anathema to Mischel, exactly how does he conceptualize his "cognitive social learning person variables"? They are seen as *styles and strategies* which have resulted from a person's previous history in mediating experiences and which currently affect the impact of stimuli. Five person variables are offered, but Mischel states that they are subject to future revision: competencies, encoding strategies and personal constructs, expectancies, subjective values, and self-regulatory systems and plans.

Competencies, which refer to what a person knows and can do, are defined as "the individual's abilities to transform and use information actively and to create thoughts and actions (as in problem solving), rather than to a store of static cognitions and responses that one 'has' in some mechanical storehouse" (Mischel, 1976, p. 501).* These abilities refer to things such as intelligence, competence, ego development, and social-intellectual achievements and skills. Differences between people in these abilities account in part for the wide range of individual differences in cognitive and behavioral patterns they can generate.

Encoding strategies and *personal constructs* refer to the ways in which people represent and symbolize information from the environment. By perceiving and then cognitively transforming the stimulus (e.g., by coding, categorizing, and selectively attending), we give special meaning to it, and so influence the environment's impact on us. "One person's stress is another's challenge" illustrates the importance of individual differences in encoding strategies and personal constructs for determining an individual's behavior and even for determining what one learns.

Expectancies refer to the determinants of actual, rather than potential, performance and guide the person's selection of behavior from among the many that he or she is capable of constructing within a particular context. *Behavior-outcome* expectancies are the perceived outcomes or consequences of selecting a particular action, and *stimulus-outcome* expectancies are hypotheses about possible outcomes that will occur if certain stimuli are evident. These expect-

---

ancies are acquired primarily from idiosyncratic learning histories, but some expectancies are widely shared by members of the same culture (e.g., stimulus-outcome expectancies involving stereotypes about sex or body build). In effect, expectancies help us predict the world and give us a sense that our environment is a somewhat familiar place.

Subjective values help explain that even if two people have identical expectancies in a given situation, they still may not behave in the same way. The reason for this behavioral discrepancy may be that the two people have different subjective values for the same outcomes. A parent, for example, may be able to influence one child's unruly behavior at the dinner table effectively with promises of extra dessert but may be unsuccessful in changing the actions of another—the latter child probably does not value the extra dessert.

Self-regulatory systems and *plans* refer to the ways people regulate their own behavior by self-imposed goals (standards) and self-produced consequences.These latter consequences include reactions like self-criticism or self-praise which we experience depending on how well our behavior matches our expectations and standards. Moreover, people adopt a series of rules and plans for guiding personal behavior in the absence of, or in spite of, immediate external situational pressures. These subjective rules and plans indicate to the person what kinds of behavior are appropriate to a particular situation, the performance standards he or she wants to achieve, and the consequences of reaching or failing to reach those standards. In other words, plans help the person to control a complicated behavior sequence leading to the attainment of desired goals.

In short, Mischel and other contemporary social learning theorists have a distinctive perspective of personality, one which seems to have borrowed heavily from traditional behavioral and phenomenological (humanistic-existential) approaches but which also contains many features of its own. The emphasis on the active use of cognitive processes and the resulting ability to exercise self-control presents a relatively optimistic view of human behavior and destiny. Mischel describes this social learning image of human beings as follows:

> This image is one of the human being as an active, aware problem-solver, capable of profiting from an enormous range of experiences and cognitive capacities, possessed of great potential for good or ill, actively constructing his or her psychological world, interpreting and processing information in potentially creative ways, influencing the world but also being influenced by it lawfully—even if the laws are difficult to discover and hard to generalize. It views the person as so complex and multi-faceted as to defy easy classifications and comparisons on any single or simple common dimensions, as multiply influ-

enced by a host of determinants, as uniquely organized on the basis of prior experiences and future expectations, and yet as studyable by the methods of science, and continuously responsive to stimulus conditions in meaningful ways. It is an image that has moved a long way from the instinctual drive-reduction models, the static global traits, and the automatic stimulus-response bonds of earlier times ... It is an image that highlights the shortcomings of all simplistic theories that view behavior as the exclusive result of any narrow set of determinants, whether these are habits, traits, drives, constructs, instincts, genes, or reinforcers. And yet it is an image that is sure to shift in still unpredictable directions as our understanding and knowledge increase. (Mischel, 1976, p. 506)*

In general, Jay's personality would be seen by social learning theorists as a collection of learned behavior patterns with cognitive components. Her personality, they would argue, is best understood as a product of the particular models she has been exposed to and the reinforcements she has received. Her reactions to these models and reinforcements would depend, however, on the extent to which her cognitive styles and strategies had developed. The more refined her cognitive capabilities became, for example, the greater freedom she would have from external reinforcements, because of the acquired ability to engage in self-control activities which would be able to change those contingencies.

Social learning theorists, like Skinner too, prefer to emphasize the current conditions maintaining behavior. Let us, nevertheless, briefly examine a few of Jay's characteristic behaviors and suggest some important past learning situations. For example, Jay's aggressive reactions to significant men in her life are reminiscent of her parents' interactions on certain occasions. It was noted that Dr. and Mrs. Smith would have periodic arguments ("stormy outbursts") which were followed by prolonged periods of mutual silence. Jay may have learned this pattern of aggressiveness through observational learning at a very early age, without actually having received reinforcement for it, until using it at a later time (with her brothers and much later with boyfriends). Because of her cognitive capabilities, she was able to generalize what she observed and to transform it into something personal. In other words, she may not have used the aggressive behaviors and subsequent sequence of events in the exact same way or for the same purposes as her parents did, but the aggression apparently has served an important purpose (e.g., remaining her father's favorite child). Jay's general shyness with men and women also has its roots in observation learning and reinforcement, largely in connection with her father. Social learning theorists would argue also that Jay's current environment and cognitive styles and strategies are the main determinants of her present aggressive and withdrawn behaviors. To understand Jay fully, requires an assessment of many factors, including her actual observational learning and reinforcement history (past and present) and her internal "person variables" (competencies, encoding strategies, etc.). Since these factors interact in complex ways, the task of understanding Jay's personality is indeed a most difficult and challenging one.

Regarding personality change, the social learning theorists rely on techniques aimed at identifying problem behaviors and focusing on the precise factors producing them. To change the undesirable behavior is in part a matter then of altering the maintaining conditions. Like therapists influenced directly by Skinner's work, the social learning theorists emphasize behavior modification techniques originating in laboratory studies of respondent and operant conditioning. Social learning theorists also favor techniques influenced by observational learning studies and which include the use and usually the manipulation of cognitive variables. Space does not allow a detailed examination of these techniques, but we shall apply a few of them briefly to the modification of Jay's "shyness"—see chapter 5 for a detailed example of the application of cognitive-symbolic (covert) procedures to a self-control program for weight management.

Let us look at the concept of "shyness" before proceeding to its modification. Zimbardo and Ruch define shyness and the shy person as follows:

> ... basically it is an awareness of one's inability to take action when one both wants to and knows how to. Shyness is a fear of negative self-evaluation and/or negative evaluation from others. The shy person is conspicuous by silence when others are talking, by immobility when others are moving, by isolation when others are affiliating. Thus the shy person is characterized more by an absence of overt responding than by the presence of unusual responses. (1975, p. 442)

In a study reported by Zimbardo and Ruch, over forty percent of a sample of high-school and college students labeled themselves as currently "shy," and over eighty percent reported that they were once "shy." Thirty-five percent of their reported sample said shyness was either "undesirable" or "very undesirable." Negative consequences of shyness listed by the students included: creates social problems, has negative emotional consequences, prevents positive evaluations by others, and makes it difficult to be appropriately assertive, to express opinions, or to take advantage of opportunities.

Shyness is often regarded as an undesirable characteristic (at least in this culture) and may be associated with many of Jay's complaints, particularly those regarding her interpersonal difficulties and anxieties. Four behavior therapies, of the many available that might offer Jay some help, include systematic desensitization, assertiveness training, systematic rational restructuring, and modeling.

Systematic desensitization uses a combination of cognitive and respondent conditioning manipulations and has proved useful particularly in the treatment of behaviors reinforced by anxiety reduction. Individuals often learn to withdraw at the first sign of a painful situation and so never get the opportunity to find out how truly innocuous the aversive situation really might be. Systematic desensitization attempts, in effect, to train individuals to remain calm and relaxed in situations which formerly produced anxiety and avoidance reactions. Wolpe (1973) outlines three steps in the procedure: relaxation training, construction of anxiety hierarchies, and desensitization. *Relaxation training* teaches the patient first to contract and then to relax particular muscles while becoming aware of the various sensations accompanying tension and relaxation. This technique, based on Jacobson's (1938) method of progressive muscular relaxation, may be supplemented or replaced by some therapists with hypnosis or drugs to facilitate the relaxation process. During this training (which may take about six sessions), the therapist and patient also devote time to *constructing a hierarchical list* of related, fear-evoking situations. Each is written on a separate sheet of paper, and the patient is asked to rank them from least to most anxiety-producing. For example, in dealing with her shyness, Jay might list as least anxiety-producing meeting a group of old friends at the library. In the middle of the hierarchy might be a discussion with medical colleagues about personal events. The most anxiety-producing situation might be meeting strangers at a cocktail party. During *desensitization*, the patient is instructed to relax and to indicate by raising a finger whenever he or she feels anxious, while the therapist describes a series of scenes, asking the patient to *imagine* being in them. The first scene is a neutral one. If the patient does not display or report anxiety, then the lowest (least anxiety-producing) scene on the hierarchy is presented. If no anxiety is reported here, the therapist moves progressively up the hierarchy until the patient begins to experience anxiety. That scene is then terminated and the patient returns to the preceding one, to which anxiety no longer occurs. Progress proceeds gradually in this fashion until the patient is able to remain relaxed while imagining the most disturbing situation in the hierarchy. One implication of this procedure is that relaxation and anxiety are incompatible or competing responses and that, through the pairing of the scenes with relaxation (*counterconditioning*), anxiety will no longer be experienced in the formerly upsetting situations. In Jay's case, social situations no longer should lead to anxiety but rather to relaxation. This presumably would increase her chances of initiating approach responses to others and of improving her interpersonal effectiveness.

Assertiveness training is aimed at getting the person to express behaviors inhibited by anxiety or "neurotic" fear, e.g., not expressing differences of opinion with friends because of a fear of rejection or being unable to express affection or praise because they cause personal embarrassment (Wolpe, 1973). Assertiveness, it should be noted, is not the same as aggressiveness for it tries only to balance power in interpersonal situations, not to give one the upper hand—assertiveness, in other words, provides a means for negotiation and for developing social skills. If Jay were to undergo assertiveness training, the first step typically would include an assessment of how she behaves inadequately in a number of different situations. For example, the therapist would ask her a series of questions like "Are you shy?," "Does criticism hurt you badly?," and so on. If affirmative answers are given, Jay would describe how she handles these interpersonal situations and the therapist would point out the flaws in her reactions, e.g., how she lets herself be stepped on or possibly, how she steps on others. In role-playing exercises, Jay first would play herself in a typical problem situation and the therapist (or a peer if in group therapy) would play the part of the other person, the one who generally causes Jay anxiety and difficulties (e.g., a stranger or relative). After Jay's response inadequacies are noted, she and the therapist would switch roles, with Jay modeling properly assertive responses. Other exercises may be used too, like script writing and the "broken record" technique (learning to repeat your wishes calmly in the face of resistance by others without getting irritated— see Smith, 1975). Rehearsals in the therapy context would continue until Jay could make assertive statements in real-life situations. Wolpe has his patients try to say statements outside of therapy like "I like you," "Your behavior disgusts me," or "How dare you speak to me like that!" It is important that these real-life applications start out modestly so that they do not have any punishing consequences. The entire process is a gradual one but Jay's interpersonal anxiety and "shyness" should decrease as her social skills increase.

Systematic rational (cognitive) restructuring, based on Ellis's (1973) rational-emotive therapy, maintains that a person's self-defeating behaviors are the result of a set of false assumptions or irrational beliefs (Goldfried & Goldfried, 1975). As Ellis argues, behavior is a function of beliefs and interpretations, not external stimuli—see Lazarus, Averill, and Opton, 1970, for a similar viewpoint regarding cognition and emotion. Consequently, people with irrational beliefs act irrationally. Typical irrational beliefs in our culture include ideas like:

> a. . . . it is a dire necessity for an adult human being to be loved or approved by virtually every significant other person in his community.
>
> b. . . . one should be thoroughly competent, adequate, and achieving in all possible respects, if one is to consider oneself worthwhile.
>
> c. . . . it is awful and catastrophic when things are not the way one would very much like them to be. (Ellis, 1962, quoted in Goldfried & Goldfried, 1975, p. 92)

The task of systematic rational restructuring is to unmask false ideas, help the person understand his or her role in causing and maintaining the problem behaviors, and facilitate change in the faulty assumptions and the adoption of more constructive ones.

In Jay's case, for example, the systematic rational restructuring techniques would attempt to cast her shyness-related behaviors in rational terms and provide the means for her to modify her false belief assumptions. With a therapist, in an individual or group setting, Jay's statements about her feelings in interpersonal settings would be analyzed from two possible sources of irrationality: (1) How likely is it that Jay's interpretations of the situations are in fact realistic?; and (2) What are the implications of Jay's interpretations? In one example, Jay says she gets upset often when she approaches someone for the first time in order to get to know him or her and consequently usually does not follow through on her wishes. When asked why she feels this way, Jay responds that she is afraid the person might not like her. How rational is this, when you consider that Jay is bright, articulate, and a competent physician? Further probing might ask Jay what would happen if this person did reject her? Would this be so terrible? Why should this upset her? These questions should help Jay realize that the way she reacts in these situations stems from an irrational belief, e.g., that everyone important must love her. In other words, assuming she must be loved by those she selects and not realizing that the world will not end if she is rejected by someone, Jay avoids making new acquaintances—a safe, if not terribly satisfying way of avoiding failure. Once Jay realizes the nature of her problem, she consciously and deliberately would have to engage in new behaviors when she felt upset in social settings. A more realistic appraisal of the situation must replace her inadequate one. Jay and her therapist would practice this rational reevaluation process through imagined presentations of difficult situations. For example, the therapist might ask Jay to imagine that she is carrying a lunch tray and sees an unfamiliar though friendly looking person. How does she feel as she approaches the table to join this person? If Jay reports feeling anxious, she then must determine the irrational thoughts that are making her upset. Jay would be encouraged also to pracice her rational reevaluation techniques in real-life situations, often in the form of homework assignments.

Modeling, a technique strongly advocated by Bandura (1969), is an effective and efficient means for teaching complex responses and skills. The patient learns the new behaviors by watching the performance of the therapist or another model (e.g., peers with a problem similar to the patient's, who gradually overcome it). Then the therapist encourages (reinforces) the patient to perform the responses. Bandura has reported studies of modeling successfully reducing many behavioral problems, including phobias of animals like snakes or dogs. More diffuse fears (e.g., social withdrawal) have been reduced too by modeling techniques. For example, Jay might watch a group of socially effective adults of her own age interact for the first time. This observation, combined with instruction and guided participation by the therapist, should prove effective in increasing her skills and confidence in social settings. Modeling, incidentally, is involved probably to some extent in all forms of psychotherapy as the therapist is usually seen by the patient as an exemplary figure, i.e., as one worthy of imitation (cf. Calhoun, 1977).

In conclusion, the behavior therapies take a direct approach to treating problem behaviors. Unlike the more traditional psychotherapies, global aims such as total personality restructuring or change are replaced by the more modest goal of eliminating undesirable "symptoms." Recent behavior therapies have become more complex than earlier ones dealing exclusively with overt behavior, and they now use techniques oriented around cognitive-symbolic variables as well. Despite the continued controversy surrounding the behavior modification techniques (e.g., some argue that they are overly simplistic or unethical and too dehumanizing), it should be noted that they tend to be relatively easy to learn and use, fast and inexpensive (lasting in many cases only about a few weeks or months), and at least equally as effective as traditional "insight-oriented" therapies in treating many personality disorders.

REFLECTIONS: SUMMARY AND FUTURE DIRECTIONS

The application of the three personality approaches to Jay was intended to illustrate some of the major theoretical tenets currently available in personology and to show how they can lead to very different pictures of the same individual. For example, Freud's theory paints a somewhat negative portrait of Jay, for it sees her as being driven by instinctual forces and conflicts beyond her aware-ness and largely beyond her control. As an adult, Jay still is tied to coping styles acquired during early childhood, which entail some-what rigid ways of perceiving and relating to others. Rogers, on the other hand, offers more optimism for Jay in that he sees her as possessing an innate tendency toward self-actualization and the per-sonal responsibility and capacity for choice necessary to ensure posi-tive growth. Though conflict and defense may result from adverse surroundings, they can be eliminated and growth can be facilitated by providing an accepting and nonthreatening atmosphere in which Jay can once again "be herself," i.e., discover and express her own values, feelings, and potentialities. Skinner's proposals, unlike those of Freud and Rogers, emphasize external attributes, rather than inter-nal ones, as prime determinants of Jay's behavior. By effectively altering these environmental forces (patterns of reward and punish-ment), it should be possible, from his point of view, to redirect selected responses in Jay's behavioral repertoire into different and presumably more desired directions.

For an overview of the three major approaches to personality and of the important issues in personality theory discussed throughout this book, we have summarized our presentation in Table 19. The table is organized to provide a general comparison of the psychodynamic, humanistic-existential, and behavioral approaches. But bear in mind that many details obviously are glossed over and, furthermore, that variants within each approach, although repre-sented, are not given equal treatment with the illustrative theories of Freud, Rogers, and Skinner.

Our emphasis on differences between the various theories and applications should not obscure two very important points, namely, that overlaps and similarities also exist among the perspectives and, moreover, that recent trends suggest a possible reconciliation among several of the approaches. Let us look briefly at each of these issues.

Similarities among the approaches to personality can be illus-trated by first comparing psychodynamic and humanistic-existential therapies. Despite the differences noted in Table 19, remarkable con-sistencies also exist. For example, both therapeutic approaches em-phasize verbal interactions between patient and therapist and both argue, furthermore, that insight into basic unconscious processes (such as defense mechanisms against anxiety) must be gained in order to effect changes in personality. As Mischel (1976) has noted in comparing Freudian and Rogerian approaches to psychotherapy:

> Both approaches retain a verbal, interview format for psycho-therapy; both focus on the client-clinician relationship; both are pri-

Table 19

Three Approaches to Personality

	PSYCHODYNAMIC	HUMANISTIC-EXISTENTIAL	BEHAVIORAL
PERSONALITY DETERMINANTS	Behavior is lawful and completely determined. Biological forces (e.g., sexual and aggressive instincts and an inherited, predetermined, developmental sequence) are heavily emphasized, though social forces also are important to shaping personality. Contemporary versions of this approach acknowledge a greater balance in the interplay of both biological and social determinants.	Free will, choice, and purpose actually allow the person to transcend instinctual and environmental forces. Emphasis is on biologically-rooted forces such as self-actualizing tendency and inherited "potentialities" rather than on tissue drives or deficits. But emergent self-concept is shaped mainly by social forces.	Behavior is lawful and completely determined. Environmental/social forces are the prime shapers of personality. Biological drives (e.g., hunger, thirst, sex) are downplayed: their importance, according to some adopting this approach, is that biological drive satisfaction, when associated with social stimuli, establishes influential social motives.
PERSONALITY DESCRIPTION (STRUCTURE)	Id, ego, and superego comprise the structures of personality, along with various levels of the psyche (conscious, preconscious, and unconscious).	The major structure of personality is the self which consists of the individual's private images of what he or she is and would like to be.	Personality structure consists of a collection of habitual responses or learned behavior patterns. Emphasis is on respondent and operant behaviors, though recent approaches also stress "person variables" such as cognitive styles and strategies.
PERSONALITY DYNAMICS (PROCESS)	Tension-reduction ("pleasure-principle") and the interplay between the expression and inhibition of the life and death instincts constitute the main processes of personality.	"Force-for-growth" and tension-production are psychological processes of most importance, along with congruency between the self and experience. When incongruence exists, threat and anxiety result and lead to defensive reactions. A search for meaning and purpose also motivates much human behavior.	Environment/behavior relationships are emphasized, along with "principles of learning" related to respondent and operant conditioning and modeling. Tension-reduction is a major motivational concept for some behavioral theorists, but largely irrelevant for others.

DEVELOPMENT	unfolding of stages or developmental landmarks and crises. Successful resolution of these developmental landmarks leads to a more mature ego, while unsuccessful resolution may lead to character traits or to inadequate personality functioning.	which influences characteristic ways of acting, feeling, thinking, and perceiving is emphasized. Interactions between the person, with his or her need for positive regard, and significant others, who may freely or conditionally give positive regard, greatly affect the emergent self system.	...ited and unfolding developmental stages or crises. Growth is a function of reinforcement and imitation. Schedules of reinforcement, stimulus generalization and discrimination, shaping, and social learning are key concepts which affect the production of habits and therefore create personality.
PSYCHO-PATHOLOGY	Symptoms reflect underlying conflicts and defensive reactions to anxiety. Fixations and regression under stress result in inadequate (too weak or too strong) development of ego and superego.	Pathology reflects great incongruency between the self and experience, and a rigid, defensive support of a restrictive self-image. Anxiety threatens the person and if defenses fail altogether, total personality disorganization ("psychosis") results. A sense of purposelessness or meaninglessness may also lead to pathology.	Pathology is based on faulty learning. Symptoms are viewed as the problem to be treated, rather than as signs of pervasive underlying conflict or "disease."
PERSONALITY CHANGE (PSYCHOTHERAPY)	Adult personality change is difficult but possible with a highly trained and objective therapist. Resolution of unconscious conflict through insight is the prime goal, along with the strengthening of ego functions. Techniques such as free association and the therapist's analysis of patient's resistances, dreams, and transference, help uncover the patient's past difficulties and illuminate their operation in the present.	Change is highly probable given the proper "atmosphere" of congruence, unconditional positive regard, and empathic understanding. Therapy emphasizes the "client's" perceptions of personal experiences, as well as his or her own innate tendencies and responsibility for healing and growth. Client is encouraged to discuss the "here-and-now" and to gain insight into his or her own functioning. Therapist facilitates growth (e.g., expanding awareness) by providing the proper atmosphere noted above and by reflecting and clarifying the client's feelings and meanings.	Behavior is highly malleable and under the control of environmental contingencies, and hence is readily capable of alteration. Behavior modification techniques emphasize the present, rather than the past, and concentrate on overt behaviors, though cognitive and emotional (covert) variables are often manipulated and changed too. Highly specialized techniques rely on numerous procedures such as extinction, positive reinforcement, desensitization, cognitive restructuring, and modeling. Because goal of therapy is to teach patient to unlearn problem behaviors and/or to learn more adaptive ones, insight into possible underlying and unconscious processes is irrelevant.

Note—The above summary of the psychodynamic, humanistic-existential, and behavioral approaches to personality is based primarily on the writings of Freud, Rogers, and Skinner, respectively. The viewpoints of other influential writers within each approach are also represented, though to a lesser degree.

marily concerned with feelings; both emphasize the importance of unconscious processes (defense, repression); both consider increased awareness and acceptance of unconscious feelings to be major goals of psychotherapy. To be sure, the two approaches differ in the specific content that they believe is repressed (e.g., id impulses versus organismic experiences), in the motives they consider most important (e.g., sex and aggression versus self-realization), and in the specific insights they hope will be achieved by the client who has been successful in psychotherapy (the unconscious becomes conscious and conflict is resolved versus organismic experience is accepted and the self becomes congruent with it). But these differences should not obscure the fact that both approaches are forms of relationship treatment that emphasize awareness of hypothesized unconscious feelings and the need for the client to accept those feelings. (p. 276)*

Psychodynamic and behavioral approaches to therapy also overlap, somewhat surprisingly, on many points. For example, in his important book attempting to integrate psychoanalysis and behavior therapy, Wachtel (1977) has argued that much of what the behavior therapist actually *does* in therapy is in fact quite similar to the techniques employed by the psychoanalyst. As one illustration, although the literature often suggests that "talking" in behavior therapy is nonexistent or at best minimal, it seems that many behavior therapists (excluding perhaps the extreme Skinnerians) actually devote considerable time to interviewing. In his observations of behavior therapists working with patients, Wachtel was surprised to find so much time devoted to such verbal exchanges. Moreover, he notes that the interviews typically are not used in a strictly "behavioristic" sense. In other words:

> The patient's verbal reports are rarely treated simply as behaviors per se, where their mere frequency is studied in relation to something else. Rather, they are listened to essentially as speech is listened to by anyone else, as the meaningful report by an intelligent observer of events that the speaker has been privy to and the listener has not. (Wachtel, 1977, p. 108)

To what degree is reconciliation between the various approaches to personality possible? To some extent, certain differences may in fact be irreconcilable—for example, ideas about the origins and functions of neurotic and psychotic symptoms, the goals of therapy, or the appropriate emphasis to afford unconscious processes. But there are clear signs that historical ideological debates and attacks among the psychodynamic, humanistic-existential, and behavioral approaches may be giving way to more thoughtful and fruitful examinations of the many common constructs, procedures, and goals characterizing the different perspectives.

One prominent behavior therapist, Arnold Lazarus (1971), has led the way for bridging, at least partially, the traditional gap between behavior and psychodynamic therapies. Lazarus has argued that the therapeutic approach must be tailored or custom-designed to the patient and that a complaint, such as a compulsion or phobia, often may not be the real problem but actually is a reflection of a much more complex problem of living. Therapists, according to Lazarus, should not rigidly and automatically apply their favorite behavioral technique to the patient. Rather, they need a broad spectrum of approaches at their disposal, and behavior therapists must begin with a careful examination of the patient's problems to decide which approach or technique is most suitable. Thus, Lazarus favors a balanced or eclectic approach to personality change, one which avoids the extremes of both orthodox behaviorism and psychoanalysis.

In a similar vein, Wachtel (1977) has discussed the potential benefits for helping and understanding people which could emerge from an integration of the psychodynamic and behavioral approaches. He states:

> The work of the behavior therapist promises to provide that which has been most lacking in psychoanalysis: a means to actively intervene in the human dilemmas that psychoanalysis has enabled us to understand so keenly. The psychoanalytic point of view, on the other hand, has made its greatest contribution in revolutionizing our understanding of the meanings latent in our thoughts and acts. Its strength lies in discerning hidden strivings and revealing the enormous complexities of our affective life, not in a causal analysis of behavior. (Wachtel, 1977, p. 5)

Much optimism has been expressed also in the potential merging of the humanistic-existential and behavioral approaches (e.g., Maddi, 1976; Mischel, 1976), perhaps spurred by B.F. Skinner's 1972 award from the American Humanist Association as Humanist of the Year. One forum for the reconciliation between these two approaches is the growing interest in the principles of self-control or self-regulation. As noted in chapter 5, many behavioral theorists currently regard cognitive (covert) mechanisms, as well as environmental (overt) contingencies, to be significant aspects of self-regulatory processes—a shift of interest bringing the behavioral theorists much closer to the traditional domain of humanistic-existential (and to some extent, psychodynamic) approaches. This overlap of the approaches is illustrated nicely by the following statement of two prominent social learning theorists:

> The intersection of social learning and humanistic approaches is perhaps best reflected in the recent development of transpersonal psychology—a movement started by Abraham Maslow in the late 1960s (cf. Sutich, 1969). Transpersonal approaches are aimed at expanding the *personal boundaries* of individuals to facilitate what is termed "mind and body self-control." Processes such as Zen, yoga, hypnosis, autogenic training, biofeedback, and meditation are advocated; in fact, any technique that enhances greater personal self-control may be used. The techniques of behavioral self-control are obviously relevant as means for helping the person expand the range of self-mastery; further "transpersonal techniques" are *not* a distinct new approach as contended (Astor, 1972) but share many things in common with the behavioral strategies presented here. The concept of the "transperson" is in many ways isomorphic with the social learning perspective of behavioral self-control. (Thoresen & Mahoney, 1974, pp. 140-141)*

Personality
Assessment

Personality theory, as we have just seen, can help us understand an individual by postulating various structures and processes and by suggesting how these factors unfold and are shaped throughout the person's lifetime. Without techniques for assessing personality, however, the theoretical constructs cannot be evaluated adequately, nor can important empirical research be pursued. For example, to suggest that Jay's self-concept is inflexible and includes an image of a shy, introverted overachiever is only an exercise in armchair speculation. It is crucial at some point to take further steps to develop ways of carefully measuring her self-concept and, at the same time, of assessing the accuracy of our speculation. Moreover, the scientific evaluation of personality change (e.g., as a result of psychotherapy) requires the availability of reliable and valid tools for assessing personality before and after the application or occurrence of the presumed change agent. To determine, for example, whether Jay's personality changes as a result of client-centered therapy, we must be able to assess her self-concept before she starts therapy and after its completion. It should be clear that without a science of assessment, there could be no science of personality, any more than geology, for example, could exist without an empirically based system for differentiating rocks or biochemistry without methods of distinguishing biochemical substances.

The tasks of assessment can be conceived of generally as the measurement of individual attributes or traits which comprise the personality structure and the assessment of the "whole" person with emphasis on the integration of the individual parts. After all, an adequate psychological description is reached not just by mentioning one or two characteristics, but by drawing a broad, complex picture of a person, i.e., covering a wide and representative range of the individual's functioning, and tapping the depths of his or her resources for managing the unusual as well as the routine demands of living. The latter task (assessing the "whole" person) depends on our ability to accomplish the former (assessing individual attributes).

From a somewhat skeptical position, the assessment of the "whole" person might be viewed as a rather vague goal. One might ask, for example, when or whether we ever adequately can describe a person physiologically. At what point does a medical chart succeed in capturing the essence of one's health? Description of multiple dimensions of personality is at least a quantitative increase from the description of a single dimension. Those who argue for the assessment of the "whole" person seem to be saying that this is not merely the addition of dimensions, but a qualitatively different step in which an organized system is somehow better captured. Assuming that it can be done in a fashion distinguishable from merely adding dimensions of description, attempting to capture the "whole" person is certainly far more ambitious than measuring a single quality. Furthermore, it would be an approach particularly compatible with psychologists of an idiographic bent, while assessment of individual traits would seem to be favored by nomothetically oriented psychologists (see chapter 1). Despite this sort of distinction, most personality descriptions are relative, that is, they must be stated in a way that permits comparison with other individuals. Both kinds of approaches are subject also to common, basic principles, the outlining of which is the major task of this chapter. We shall use the term assessment to refer to both the measurement of single traits and the description of the "whole" person, but the reader should keep in mind the presumed distinction.

Assessment or measurement of personality traits depends on gathering samples of a person's behavior, either in a natural life setting or in a contrived laboratory situation. We have seen many examples of this in the research on personality illustrated throughout the earlier chapters of this book. Quite obviously we are not interested just in the particular situation in which the observations are made, but rather in generalizing from that situation to others to which the person is likely to be exposed and which we are not likely to be able to observe directly. Not only must our observations of the behavior as it occurs in the assessment situation be accurate, but it is crucial that generalizations to other contexts also be possible. The field of assessment utilizes some special principles which concern the above goals of *accuracy* and *generalizability*.

PRINCIPLES OF ASSESSMENT

There are three concepts on which the technology of assessment is based, "standardization," "reliability," and "validity." These concepts, and two currently important approaches to assessment, will be reviewed before specific techniques of assessment are considered.

Standardization

When observations are made of how a person behaves, such as in a test of information or of the extent to which blood pressure rises when insulted, these observations must be evaluated. If one wishes to compare an individual with others, data are required about how others act in similar situations. This makes it possible to say whether, for example, the individual in question is more informed or more easily aroused than others, less so, or somewhere in between. Data of this kind are called "norms"; they are *standards* which permit interpretation of the behavioral attribute measured in any given individual.

The normative data may come from the general population or from some particular portion of the population against which one wishes to compare the individual under study (e.g., men, women, people in a given age bracket, those who have a given level of education, people living in cities or suburbs, and so on), depending on what the comparison is that one wishes to make. For example, if we wanted to know whether a man's blood pressure is normal, we would need data on the blood pressure of other men. If the man in question is fifty years of age, and the group from which the norms are obtained averages twenty years of age, we are almost certain to judge the man's blood pressure as deviant because we know that blood pressure increases with age even in perfectly healthy persons. Therefore, a more appropriate normative sample for such an evaluation might be other men of the same age. Thus, there may be many normative samples rather than only one, each used for quite different purposes. An individual's behavior can be understood and interpreted only if there are appropriate norms or standards about other persons for comparison (interindividual standards), or norms for that individual on other occasions (intraindividual standards). Interpretive statements about how fearful, dependent, effective, happy, or whatever, the person is, depend on such standardization data.

Reliability

Reliability basically deals with (1) the representativeness, stability, and generality of the behavior sampled, and (2) the degree of agreement among observers.

Representativeness, stability, and generality of the behavior sampled. Total observation in every situation to which a person is exposed would provide the assessment psychologist with the most complete raw data from which to form a conception of the individual's personality. Obviously this would be an impossibility even for a close relative to accomplish. It took one pair of psychologists 435 pages of a book to record in some detail the activities of a seven-year-old boy during *one day* of his life, and not even completely at that (cf. Barker and Wright, 1951). Considering the multitude of events, imagine the task of documenting through observation the whole life span of an individual, or even important experiences over so limited a time period as one year! The Library of Congress could not store the data, and no individual could hope to absorb even a small portion of it. For this reason, assessment must be based on a very limited sample of a person's behavior, often as limited as one particular test situation, or perhaps a few situations lasting only a few hours.

Since inferences about personality are made from a limited sample of observations, three aspects of *reliability* become especially significant to assessment. One concerns the *representativeness* of the sample. One may ask, for example, whether the reactions observed on a particular day are typical of that person or are vulnerable to fatigue, changes in mood, and so on. If they are vulnerable to such factors, then it will be hazardous to make inferences based on one or two observational samplings. Second, the behavior in question may not be at all *stable* even in the same type of situation, in which case the measurements will change from one occasion of testing to another. A behavior could be essentially stable, yet show marked variation as a function of mood or fatigue, in which case reliability will be low except when such mood or fatigue variables are controlled. Finally, reliability also involves the *generalizability* of a behavior from one type of situation to another. An observed behavior could be representative and stable in one particular type of situation, but disappear or change in a different situational context. If the testing is done over several such contexts, it will appear most unreliable.

An attempt to evaluate a person's intelligence through testing provides an excellent illustration of these three components of reliability. If the test is repeated several times, the score on the test would undoubtedly vary on each occasion, perhaps a great deal (low reliability), perhaps only slightly (high reliability). This variation could be the result of any or all of the several components—lack of representativeness of the score, lack of stability of intellectual functioning, or poor generalizability across different situations. An example of the first would be variations in attentiveness during the testing; second, intelligence might vary with age, and if there were a fundamental lack of stability in intellectual performance, then keeping fatigue or attention constant would still fail to produce a stable score in a child at different times of life. Finally, intelligence measured by verbal tests might be quite different when measured by performance tests. A person who does very well when tested individually (and given support and encouragement), may do poorly in group testing situations. Of course, low reliability could also result from inadequacies of the measuring instrument, errors in scoring, and the like, which represent still a different level of explanation of low reliability.

When reliability is low, each testing will produce its own score, and one must determine which of these scores is the "true" one, that is, the one which most nearly represents that individual's hypothetical ability. The more variable such scores are (that is, the more unreliable the performance on different occasions), the less confidence can be placed in the accuracy of our assessment of the individual's intelligence. We often assume that intelligence is intelligence no matter what the circumstances. This is only so in a very relative sense, and for many personality traits it would be a marked exaggeration. In fact, it is appropriate to say that *any* personality trait is manifested only in a specific range of stimulus situations or in particular contexts. Some may occur over a wider range than others, but no trait would be expected to operate all the time (cf. chapter 4).

Agreement among observers. Reliability with respect to observers is concerned with the *accuracy* of their observations, descriptions, and interpretations of a behavior sample, rather than its representativeness, and is evaluated by the *degree of agreement* among the observers. If the behavior of the subject under study is variously described or interpreted, then one has no way of knowing which, if any, of the descriptions or interpretations is correct. Such inaccuracy could come from many causes. Observers may selectively note or emphasize different aspects of the complex behavioral event, remember it differently, or see it in a different light. For example, in judging hostility from a person's response to some remark, one observer may view an angry statement as an instance of defensiveness in a vulnerable individual who is easily threatened, while another may see the same statement as evidence of warranted hostility.

The use of permanent and objective records of the behavioral event, such as a tape recording, motion picture film, or videotape, tends to reduce errors of memory and to eliminate some of the distortions that stem from the inability to review the same event a second time to confirm an original impression or to check on it in the context of later events. But even a half-hour recording of a complex social event is filled with too much material to keep clearly and objectively in mind. Inevitably, the whole record must be compressed into a limited number of abstractions and interpretive judgments, a process adding to the likelihood of variations in the characterization of the events by different observers.

Two solutions are possible: 1) The types of behavior which serve as the focus of attention may be intentionally limited so that little or none of the observer's judgment is required. An example of this is the "objective" test of personality in which the subject need only answer each item with a simple "yes" or "no" response. Since the response alternatives are very few, there is little or no problem of observer reliability. 2) Observers can be trained so that the criteria used in their observations and interpretations are clear and agreed upon, and the degree of agreement among their judgments then assessed. In this event, the judges are the measuring instruments, and if they cannot agree about the behavior episode in question, then there is little of scientific value in their observations. Such disagreement is similar to a defective bathroom scale which at one time shows a person's weight as 150 pounds and at another time records the same weight as 200 pounds. Clearly this variation is beyond the limits of usefulness. Since inferences about personality often depend on elaborate patterns of social behavior in complex situations, adequate reliability of the observations is one of the most fundamental requirements of personality assessment.

Validity

Whatever observation or measurement technique is employed in assessment, it must be shown to be valid to justify its use, that is, there must be evidence that it measures what it purports to measure. This is surely self-evident. To move from the banal to the significant we must first recognize that there are several kinds of validity, depending on the purposes of the assessment and the kinds of evidence on which the validity is to be judged. Two main varieties can be distinguished, "criterion-related validity" and "construct validity." *Criterion-related validity* is whether one sample of behavior, say that obtained on a test, correlates as claimed with another sample of behavior obtained at the same time (concurrent validity), or obtained later (predictive validity). *Construct validity* deals with a trait that cannot be directly observed but is a theoretical construct that can be conceived or identified only through inference from some behavior. Often it is merely a creative hypothesis about a possible process which connects a series of otherwise unrelated events. Thus, in construct validity, interest centers on a theoretical (hypothetical) quality of the person (the construct), and validity refers to evidence that this quality can justifiably be inferred from some behavior sample or test. The distinction between the two types of validity can be illustrated concretely by examining briefly an example of research on each.

Criterion-related validity. One of the best illustrations of a successful empirical effort by psychologists to predict one form of behavior from another (i.e., *criterion-related validity* of the predictive type) comes from the work of Alfred Binet and Th. Simon in France at the turn of the last century. As there was a practical need to identify students who could not profit from schooling, Binet accepted the task of attempting to find ways of predicting school performance in Parisian children. He joined forces with Simon, who had already been working on the problem, and in collaboration they selected a variety of tests requiring imagery, memory, comprehension, judgment, and reasoning, and gave these to school children. Binet and Simon's experiments, reported in 1905, demonstrated first, that performance on these tests improved with age and second, that it was substantially correlated with independent estimates by teachers of the child's brightness, and with his or her school grades. Later, a modified and standardized version of the Binet-Simon scale was developed by Lewis M. Terman (1916) at Stanford University, and it became the *Stanford-Binet Intelligence Scale,* probably the most highly regarded test ever made for the measurement of intelligence.

Remember that we have been speaking of criterion-related validity which refers to the empirical question of whether one form of behavior can be predicted, or accompanies, another. The background of Binet's and Simon's work also points out that rarely is our interest in such validity *strictly* empirical or practical. More commonly, it starts from a theoretical question, or the theoretical question arises after it has been shown that two important behavioral variables are indeed related, and we wonder about the mechanism of this relationship. In the case of the above research, a practical need generated the effort which in consequence could be readily separated from the more abstruse theoretical issues underlying the empirical relationship itself. Nevertheless, once we begin to use the word "intelligence" to identify the process or trait underlying the surface findings, we enter the area of interpretation or theory. By saying, in effect, that the behavior in question (in this case, performance on certain tests) is indicative of some inner psychological processes which we call intelligence, a theoretical construct is introduced (see chapter 1).

As it turns out, there had been interest in the concept of intelligence even before Binet and Simon did their practical empirical research. For example, a distinguished psychologist in the United States, James McKeen Cattell, had conceived of intelligence (mental ability) as consisting of basic neurological properties (e.g., the speed of nerve conduction) that determined how rapidly a person could respond to a signal (reaction time). Cattell was one of the first to approach systematically the problem of individual differences. It seemed plausible to him that the better adapted the animal, the faster it should be able to respond to the environment. So he created a number of sensori-motor tasks based on this principle to test the "adequacy" of the nervous systems of different individuals. However, the principle was evidently wrong. A student of Cattell's, Clark Wissler (1901), correlated school grades (as one criterion of intelligence) with performance on Cattell's sensori-motor tasks and found they were not related. This left the field entirely to Binet and Simon who had correctly chosen complex mental tasks as their measure of intellectual functioning. Even today the definition and theory of intelligence are by no means settled, and there remains considerable controversy about its nature (see chapter 2).

Although the distinction between criterion-related and construct validity is blurred in the case of Binet's and Simon's work, as it is in most actual validity research, there are times when the most important thing is to determine the empirical question of whether one behavior is predictable from another, regardless of whether the process underlying the relationship is understood or even of great interest. When the focus of the research is on predicting some observable behavior, such as school grades, learning to be a pilot, becoming emotional, smiling, being a successful executive, voting for a given political candidate, purchasing an advertised product, or what have you, we speak of criterion-related validity; if the emphasis is on measuring some theoretically postulated quality of the personality such as intelligence, impulse control, or strength of conscience, then we speak of "construct validity."

Construct validity.   As our main illustration of *construct validity*, we turn to some research aimed at evaluating a measure of the degree of a person's "socialization." A questionnaire scale developed by Gough (1957), called the California Psychological Inventory (CPI), contains one section or subscale dealing with *socialization.* The questions cover a number of common social attitudes and ways of responding. Examples include, "Before I do something I try to consider how my friends will react to it"; "I often think about how I look and what impression I am making upon others"; "I find it easy to 'drop' or 'break with' a friend"; "I have often gone against my parents' wishes"; and, "If the pay was right I would like to travel with a circus or carnival." Gough interpreted these items as tapping in part the ability of a person to sense and interpret social nuances and subtle interpersonal cues. A scale made up of these items could measure the extent to which a person would behave in accordance with social expectations, in effect, the extent to which the person has internalized the values of his or her society and has been socialized. Construct validity requires evidence that the scale does measure the theoretically inferred process implied by the construct. The emphasis here is not on prediction or empirical correlation, but on the theoretical analysis of personality, although of course, empirical correlations must be used as evidence of construct validity.

Certain strategies of research through which the construct validity of the test can be evaluated follow rather clearly. For example, theoretically speaking, differences among individuals in their socialization scores should be associated with the extent to which they transgress social norms and behave in an antisocial fashion. The reasoning is as follows: if degree of socialization refers to the extent of internalization of social values, then the more socialized the person is, the less he or she will show evidence of antisocial behavior. Such a finding would support the interpretation of the test scale as socialization, while failure to obtain such data would throw the construct validity of the scale into doubt. A comparison was made by Gough (1960) of the socialization scale test scores of groups whose members had on the one hand been nominated as "best citizens," and on the other hand were disciplinary problems, county-jail inmates, imprisoned delinquents, and felons. There was a very strong relationship between the test scores and the chances that the individual belonged to a group either behaving deviantly or showing highly visible acceptance of the social norms.

Another research strategy to evaluate construct validity is to attempt to relate the test scores to personality traits which logically ought to be present on the basis of the theoretical interpretation. In one such study, Reed and Cuadra (1957) showed that, as would be anticipated, persons with low socialization scores were less skillful in sensing and interpreting cues of social approval or disapproval.

These researchers had student nurses describe themselves by a series of adjectives and also guess how other nurses with whom they frequently interacted would describe them. Subjects with high socialization scores were more successful at gauging the reactions of others than were those with low socialization scores. This type of construct validity research makes it possible to interpret with some confidence the trait being measured by a personality test according to some theoretical orientation. These efforts are fundamental to the development of tools for measuring individual traits of personality, and ultimately to further technology to assess the "whole" personality.

Although we have been speaking of the construct validity of a test, such as Gough's socialization scale, such an evaluation also relates intimately to the theory on which the construct is based. Construct validity is entirely theory-dependent, that is, the interpretation of the test score depends on whether the theoretical meaning of the construct is well conceived. If a test of socialization is constructed, for example, certain predicted relationships follow from how socialization is interpreted. That is, the anticipated antecedents or sources of socialization, and likewise the expected consequences of socialization, depend on how the concept itself is understood. This theory provides the logical basis for the empirical deductions which can then be tested in empirical studies.

The above point means that if Gough's conception of socialization were different, he would have expected that the trait would have origins and effects different from those actually assumed in his own research (e.g., Gough, 1960), and in that of Reed and Cuadra (1957) cited above. For example, if one conceived of socialization as a process by which an insecure and dependent person sought social approval by conforming to social norms, he might have predicted that imprisoned delinquents would act as they did when the norms were those of people they did not care about. Under threat of disapproval by their peers or other persons with whom they identified, however, they would be expected to show a high degree of conformity. In short, their observed lack of socialization might be based on a set of social norms created by an alien society, rather than on a set based on social groups whose approval they sought. Socialization would be a relative rather than an absolute thing.

The construct validity of a test is inextricably bound to the validity (or at least serviceability) of the theory on which it is based. In effect, when the findings of construct validity research are supportive, they also support the theory on which they are based. When the findings are negative, they suggest either one or both of the following: (1) that the test does not measure the presupposed quality, or (2) that the theory is wrong, since it leads to inaccurate empirical predictions. Failure to obtain positive results often suggests that the theory itself be abandoned or modified. It is not entirely accurate to refer to construct validity research as though it applied only to the validity of a test; it also involves the whole fabric of the theory. For the beginning student, this is a difficult idea to grasp fully. The interested reader is referred to one of the best and most complete discussions of the problem by Cronbach and Meehl (1955).

The Interactional Approach to Assessment: Persons and Situations

The natural bias of the personality psychologist has been to search for enduring personality structures or dispositions leading the individual to act in certain ways regardless of the situation. The focus is thus on internal tendencies which push the person to behave, rather than on the external circumstances which pull the person in one way or another (see chapter 4). It is evident that both forces are involved in any behavioral event. To focus exclusively on the internal structure is to ignore the important other half of the story deriving from the impact of situations. It may be that personality assessment is moving somewhat away from the extreme trait orientation (cf. Mischel, 1968). This is the key point: To the extent that situations do have substantial influence on behavior, then the attempt to forecast behavior on the basis of assessment procedures is bound always to face severe restrictions, since the situations to which the person will be exposed in the future can never be accurately known in advance, and these will to a large degree determine how he or she acts.

On what basis can future behavior be predicted from observed behavior in an assessment situation? One possibility on which assessment psychologists rely is that if enough is known about the person over a variety of situations, then inferences can be made at least about how the individual *usually* responds, assuming he or she shows a more or less typical pattern. Moreover, a concept can be formed about the classes of situations in which the person will act in such and such a fashion. For example, it may be observed that one individual tends to act defensively and apologetically in situations in which he or she is criticized; another individual responds to the same criticism with anger and verbal attack. The prediction can then be made that in other situations of criticism, similar forms of reaction might be expected from the two persons. The accuracy of these predictions depends on the degree of generality of the disposition to react, that is, the range of situations over which such behavior may be expected, and this can only be determined empirically. A behavior forecast based on assessment should not be a wildly over-generalized statement that the person will behave in some fashion in each and every situation but rather a prediction limited to a given class of situations. This class should include situations that are "functionally equivalent" for that individual in generating either anger or apologetic behavior, as the case may be. The more evidence on which this inferential concept is based and the more clear and well-established its theoretical basis, the more accurately can the limits of the predictive generalization from personality assessment be established (cf. Block, 1968; Mischel, 1976).

The keys to prediction are thus twofold: First, the inferences from an assessment should be based on well-established empirical evidence about how the person acts in a variety of situations in the past or present; second, these inferences also should be based on well-established theoretical principles about the situations which are functionally equivalent to those comprising the sample situations used in the assessment sessions. In effect, we need to know for any given type of person what constitutes a threatening criticism, a loss, a sign of a safe social interaction, a rewarding experience, a source of joy, and so on. Only then can we be in a position to expect that a particular situation in the future will call forth a specified reaction. This is no simple problem, and much research is required to provide the knowledge from which the keys can be fashioned. The general point we have made above should be fairly obvious on reflection, but it is frequently overlooked not only by laypeople who tend to think of assessment either in magical terms or as phony crystal-ball gazing, but also by psychologists who should know better.

Some excellent research has been done by Endler and Hunt (1968, 1969) in an effort to emphasize situational factors in assessment and to pinpoint the proportions of variation in behavior resulting from situational as well as from personality variables. The sources of variation due to a number of factors on any test can be separated out and studied. Endler's and Hunt's efforts have centered on two questionnaires measuring anxiety and hostility. The tests were designed so that subjects could indicate one of several forms of response defining both anxiety and hostility. In the case of anxiety, these might include physiological reactions such as sweating or trembling, subjective reactions such as uneasiness or the inability to concentrate, and behavioral reactions such as sleeplessness or irritability. In addition, these responses could be related to a number of eliciting situations, such as being criticized, meeting strangers, or having to speak in public. There were three main sources of variation in the subjects' answers to the questionnaires. Besides the type of response and the eliciting situation, the third, always present in assessment and usually the main focus of interest, was persons, that is, the various individuals making up the sample of subjects tested.

Endler and Hunt found in the statistical evaluation of their data that anxiety was not an all-powerful characteristic of persons uninfluenced by its context, nor was it a function of that context alone. In other words, the best predictor of anxiety was the *interaction* among situations, responses, and individuals. For example, the relative amount of anxiety indicated on the questionnaire to the different situations (e.g., being criticized vs. meeting strangers) varied considerably among the subjects, and also the type of response (e.g., trembling vs. feeling uneasy) differed from one person to another and from one situation to another.

Endler's and Hunt's research begins systematically to recognize that the assessment of any behavioral reaction depends not only on dispositions of persons to react in some way, but also on the modality of the response and the situation in which the behavior occurs—both person and situation variables must be studied. Until the rules concerning these and other determinants of behavior are understood better, the assessment of such traits as hostility and anxiety will inevitably be less accurate than required for the effective forecasting of behavior.

The Transactional Approach: Emphasis on Relationship and Process

Stirrings of a different approach to assessment are beginning to be noticed, an approach which attempts to measure the *processes* involved in specific instances of commerce between persons and the environment. Sometimes this approach has been called dialectical, because it focuses on conflicting forces and on flux and change rather than on stability (Gergen, 1977; Riegel, 1975). Elsewhere, Lazarus and Launier (in press) have referred to this outlook as *transactional*. Transaction (see also Krauskopf, 1978) refers to description of the changing adaptational *relationship* between a given person and the environment taking place across encounters and over time. For example, if we say that a person is challenged rather than threatened in some encounter, such a statement describes a special kind of relationship or transaction between the person and a specific environment.

This is a different way of thinking about person and environment. When we speak, for instance, of threat or challenge, the two separate factors of person and environment are combined, and we are dealing with a new level of description. The explanation for the relationship is still to be found in characteristics of the person and of the environment and in their interaction. However, personality trait measures or measures designed independently to describe the environment do not give us a picture of the adaptational relationship or transaction. For this we must find new ways of measurement which currently do not exist.

Consider research by Cohen and Lazarus (1973) on how people cope with the threat of surgery scheduled for the next morning. This coping process consisted of a dimension varying from extreme vigilance to extreme avoidance. Vigilance is paying close attention to what is happening, to cues of danger, presumably in an effort to have psychological or actual control over a threatening and unpredictable environment. Avoidance is exactly the opposite, mentally and physically turning away from any information about bad things that might be happening or that are going to happen. Both vigilance and avoidance are ways of dealing with danger.

Cohen and Lazarus used some standard trait measures of this dimension as well as an interview the evening before the surgery designed to get at the coping process being used then and there. The interview permitted assessment of how much the person actually knew about the illness and the surgery. The researchers found that although subjects varied from one end of the vigilance-avoidance coping dimension to the other on both trait and process measures, the trait and process measures did not correlate as they should have if the former indeed were a measure of general (trait) vigilance and avoidance tendencies. As it turned out, the process measure of what was actually on the subjects' minds the night before surgery predicted postsurgical recovery while the trait measures did not. That is, those who avoided thinking about the surgery left the hospital faster, had fewer minor complications, and in general seemed to have a smoother recovery than those who dealt vigilantly with the threat of surgery.

Perhaps it is more adaptive in the hospital context to be avoidant, when knowing what is going on cannot possibly lead to useful behavior and when the only thing one can do is relax as much as possible. On the other hand, there are probably many other contexts in which an avoidant coping process would be maladaptive, for example, when a person must take some charge of a situation. Illustrations of this might include the necessity of seeking medical help for a heart attack, of diagnosing a lump in the breast for malignancy, or of doing one's own hemodialysis at home (a procedure necessary after kidney failure to facilitate survival). In any case the Cohen and Lazarus study is important because it suggests that in some situations process measures of coping often do not coincide with trait measures.

The problems posed for process measurement in personality assessment can be illustrated by another important and common adaptational crisis, bereavement or loss of a loved one. The reactions of the bereaved person and the psychological activities underlying them change greatly as the grief process unfolds, from the first moment of loss to ultimate resolution. At first the person may be stunned, dazed, unable to acknowledge fully that the loved one is dead. There is often an initial period of overactivity, even confusion, and much to do. Friends and relatives cluster around giving sympathy and perhaps tackling necessary tasks such as arranging for the funeral, caring for the children, cooking, and managing the household or financial matters. The bereaved person at first is kept from being alone too much. Later, when the initial furor has subsided, the person often becomes very depressed, turning inward, losing interest in the things that used to be important, and perhaps alternately feeling angry, abused, or guilty. The urgent psychological problem is for the person to acknowledge the loss, then to accept it, and finally to renew commitment to other persons and activities. Grieving is ended when the person has fully accepted what has happened and has reinvested in a new or changed pattern of living.

During the long process of grieving, which may last months and even years, many different things are going on psychologically, that is, many processes are taking place. The person's relationship with the environment is constantly changing as the mental state and the nature of the adaptation problem change. In other words, how thinks and acts, the ways of coping used, the reactions of other people in the environment, and the problems posed by the loss all shift from occasion to occasion and over time. These changes, and what the person is thinking, feeling and doing about them, need to be assessed if we are to understand the nature of the grief process.

The problem is that the standard instruments of personality measurement, geared as they are to what is stable in the person and not to transactions or relationships with the environment, fail to provide measurement approaches to such processes. The newer trends in personality are beginning to recognize the principle that understanding a person requires the ability to describe these processes systematically, though the technology of assessment has not kept up with this shift in emphasis from general traits to ongoing processes. There is clearly a growing need for measurement tools that permit description of what happens when a person confronts the environment and transacts some form of psychological commerce with it.

TECHNIQUES OF ASSESSMENT

We shall turn now from the basic principles of assessment to a discussion of the specific sources of information which assessment psychologists use, that is, the techniques through which sample behavior is obtained for observation and interpretation. Four techniques shall be reviewed, the life history, the interview, the psychological test, and a variety of procedures for obtaining and coding direct observations of behavior.

The Life History

A *life history* is a chronological story about the main facts of a person's life and development. Its use is based on the assumption that the present personality is the product of a continuous process of development, with the events of the past linked to it functionally. Past events provide information about the influences and demands to which the person has been exposed and the manner in which they have consistently been managed. The emphasis is thus on the continuities between the past and present.

The process of obtaining a life history, either from an informant such as another member of the family, from objective records, or directly from the individual, raises the issue of the accuracy of the information which is provided. Even if such a history were obtained while the person is living it, so to speak, questions would arise about the objectivity and representativeness of the observations, questions we have discussed in the preceding section. However, since most life histories are obtained retrospectively, that is, they are based on the memory of the person or other informant about events long past, we should expect that there will be many inaccuracies. People forget details (sometimes even dates of birth or marriage) and embroider them (without necessarily realizing they are doing so) in order to present themselves or their loved ones in a particular light. More objective records, such as birth documents, baby books, school histories, and police or military records, sometimes provide useful checks on the factual data given by the informant.

There are two ways of viewing what the person reports either about himself or herself or about significant others (e.g., parents, sibling, spouse): 1) The emphasis can be on the facts, on the grounds that we can best understand psychological development if we know the actual events which have shaped it. From this point of view, errors in reporting should be regarded as fatal to a correct understanding of the person. 2) One may argue, in contrast, that it is not as important to know what actually happened, but rather how the

280

person perceives the event. The reader will recall the distinction from chapter 4 between personality theories such as that of Dollard and Miller (association-learning through reinforcement), which stressed the objective stimulus as the cause of behavior and development, and those of Rogers, Maslow, and Lewin (phenomenological), which stressed the role of the stimulus as it was subjectively apprehended by the person. Both points of view are important since discrepancies between the objective and subjective facts tell us much that is significant about the individual, for example, the adequacy of his or her reality-testing, or the reliance on reality-distorting defenses which guide decisions.

Since the life history can be at most no more than a limited digest of the person's life, informed judgment of what is important in it is required. Different theoretical systems tend to emphasize somewhat different things and see the life events in different ways. It is no surprise, for example, when a Freudian is particularly interested in the events relevant to pregenital psychosexual stages, or when an Eriksonian seeks information about how the "identity crisis" of late adolescence has been experienced and handled (see chapter 6). Personality theory provides an implicit roadmap for exploring the terrain of the life history.

The Life History as a Personal Document

The life history is not always a story about a person's life; often it is also a personal document which has a special significance to assessment. A personal document, as defined by Gordon Allport, is "any self-revealing record that intentionally or unintentionally yields information regarding the structure, dynamics, and functioning of the author's mental life" (1965, p. xii). If a life history is obtained, as it so often is, by interviewing the person or by examining his or her writings or personal letters, it is also a personal document and subject to the principles applying to such documents.

Allport has enthusiastically supported the use of personal documents in psychological science in spite of the dangers of nonobjectivity and unrepresentativeness inherent in them. He argues that, "Since there are no facts in psychology that are divorced from personal lives, the human document is the most obvious place to find these facts in their raw state" (1942, pp. 143-44). Through these documents one can often observe longitudinal changes in the person which could almost never be observed directly. Moreover, the personal document, particularly when it is obtained without solicitation, as in a person's personal letters or perhaps an autobiography, permits seeing the person in the context of his or her natural, whole life, rather than in an artificial laboratory setting. Although Allport recognizes the special problems inherent in the use of such documents in personality assessment, he considers the personal document to be a source of naturalistic information not usually available in any other way. Shortly before he died, Allport (1965) published an interesting book based on a series of letters written over a period of many years by a woman with the pseudonym of Jenny (see chapter 1 for an excerpt), in which he attempted to reconstruct Jenny's personality by examining these letters from the point of view of several different theoretical perspectives in personality theory (cf. our chapter 7).

Like any other method of assessment, the life history provides an observational base for constructing a picture of the individual's personality: for making inferences about motives, the things which threaten or enhance the person, and the ways in which one characteristically goes about coping, relating, and perceiving. Through descriptions of past life events, that is, the ways in which the person has lived, we gain some sense of the individual's traits which comprise personality, and the continuities between such traits in the past, the present, and presumably the future.

The Interview

The interview can be used in a number of different but overlapping ways. For example, it can be used for assessment exclusively. It can function as psychotherapy. It can be used to establish a working relationship with someone who is to be taught something or to set the stage for providing the person information. Sometimes all of these functions may be combined in the same interview. It is notable, too, that the data of the life history are most often obtained through the interview technique, thus making the former somewhat dependent on the latter.

There is no technique of personality assessment more widely used than the interview, largely because it is the most flexible and revealing of human confrontations when performed skillfully and under appropriate conditions. On the other hand, this very flexibility creates a host of problems, all revolving mainly around the issues of reliability and the validity of the inferences drawn from the interview.

There are three key methodological problems.

1.   Although the interviewer must get the person to *reveal himself or herself candidly*, the interviewee is seldom prepared or willing to do this fully. Motivations for undergoing an interview vary considerably with the individual and with

the circumstances. The motivation to expose oneself is perhaps greatest in the case of the person seeking therapy. But even here, as Freud discovered, the patient comes with a prepared story that ironically is designed to present a false light—the person appears to resist exposing vulnerabilities and defenses even though he or she has come for help. Perhaps the truth is not even known to the individual but has to be discovered in therapy. If revelation of one's own inner nature is so difficult even in the highly motivated situation of voluntary therapy, imagine the problem in the colder context of personality assessment!

There have been two solutions to this critical problem of motivating self-revelation. On the one hand, when feasible, efforts may be made to create an *atmosphere of acceptance,* in contrast to that of evaluation, so that the individual need not feel so threatened by revealing himself or herself. Under these conditions, there should be less desire to conceal information about oneself, although the problem of lack of self-insight is not resolved by this solution. This has been the traditional approach of insight therapies, encouraged since the appearance of psychoanalysis, whose premises have been particularly well articulated by Carl Rogers (1942; cf. Jourard, 1974). The other solution is the *stress interview,* used when evaluation cannot be eliminated as the premise of the interview, for example, in the job interview or in interrogation of criminals or prisoners of war. The person is directly confronted with damaging material, either that he or she has offered, or something based on externally available evidence. The person is deliberately thrown off guard, caught in contradictions or insulted, and his or her reactions to this are carefully observed for strengths and weaknesses. Used skillfully (the problem of ethics aside), the stress interview can be a powerful source of assessment data in appropriate circumstances. It is another way of getting the person to reveal that which he or she might otherwise wish to remain hidden.

2. A critical problem of the interview is the *representativeness* of the elicited sample of the person's behavior or thought. When interviewed, the person may be fatigued, apprehensive about something temporary in his or her life, happy, or unhappy, states which are likely to change greatly from moment to moment. These moods and immediate preoccupations will influence the things a person talks about and the manner of doing so. Unless several interviews are conducted with that person, the interviewer has no way of knowing whether the interview's contents are representative or typical of that person. Interviews based on psychotherapy conducted over a long time provide one answer to this problem, but even here the special relationship of treatment tends to shape the interaction in ways not necessarily typical of other social relationships.

3. Finally, the interview is a *two-way interaction,* with the interviewer having an effect on the interviewee, as well as vice versa. These influences are likely to differ from one case to another, partly because of the different skills and styles of the interviewer but also because the interviewer is a person likely to respond differently to different people. For example, one interviewer will stimulate talkativeness while another will inhibit it or stimulate defensiveness or openness, liking or disliking, a threatening feeling or ease. Interviewees will produce similar variations in the reactions of interviewers, reactions that feed back to the interviewee and influence the contents of the interaction. If the same interviewer is assessing a number of persons and making comparisons among them, it is difficult to separate out of the mix the influence of particular personal qualities brought to

the situation by the two individuals who are party to the interaction. The solution in assessment research using the interview is very costly, since it entails using more than one interviewer with the same subject so as to determine the stimulus influence of the interviewer.

One of the unique features of the interview is that it permits two very diverse approaches to exploring personality structure and dynamics, each utilized simultaneously with one supplementing the other. On the one hand, the person is asked to *introspect,* to look within and to report his or her life experiences and inner thoughts. On the other hand, the person's words and acts serve as behavior to be *observed* and evaluated by the interviewer. In the first approach, the subject is the central and active party to the self-examination process, the one who participates in life and who also stands back and critically looks at himself or herself. Existential psychologist Rollo May (1967) has suggested that this twofold and seemingly contradictory capability is the most fundamental "dilemma" facing human beings, making them unique among the animal species.

Exclusive dependence on introspection in the search for knowledge about mental life poses some serious methodological problems, which were mentioned in chapter 1. As stated, foremost among these is the possibility that a person will be unwilling or unable to reveal the nature of the important psychological processes taking place. A psychological approach which is entirely dependent on what the person says is unable to differentiate between valid and confabulated constructions. This limitation led to the emphasis by modern psychology on the second approach to interview statements, i.e., on the observation of behavior (what the person says is a form of behavior) from which the mediating psychological structures and processes can be inferred. The behaviorally oriented psychologist does not take the contents of introspection to be literally true but treats them as behavior to be interpreted. It is the psychologist who observes, rather than the person being studied.

Using both perspectives, the introspective and behavioral, the interviewer has access to what the individual says about personal experience and what he or she does behaviorally. One can be used as a check against the other. Thus, slips of the tongue, evidence of emotion, gestures, facial expressions, emphasis, and characteristic styles of thinking, all can serve as additional information to be evaluated when the interviewer makes his or her inferences. The interviewer is right on the scene to detect these behavioral events, as well as to record the person's introspections about subjective states and processes.

In summary, used to its fullest advantage, the interview has qualities that set it apart from any other source of information. It can yield profound therapeutic consequences as well as information for assessment purposes. It provides a dynamic, two-person interaction in which the interviewer is both participant and observer. It has the tremendous advantage of enabling the interviewee to indulge in penetrating introspection, while at the same time, because of its face-to-face nature, of permitting the interviewer to observe the subject's behavior as he or she introspects. These important qualities make the interview what is probably the most widely employed technique in personality assessment. More detailed general discussions of the interview may be found in Kahn and Cannell (1957) and Richardson, Dohrenwend, and Klein (1965).

The Psychological Test

Tests are ways of eliciting behaviors and introspections under standardized conditions. Much like a laboratory experiment, testing attempts to control or exclude most of the irrelevant variables so as to focus on a limited number of conditions affecting the behavior in question. As much as possible, subjects are presented with the same stimulus and similar background testing conditions.

There are many kinds of tests, but we shall consider only two main types here, *structured tests* and *unstructured* or *projective tests*. A more complete discussion of the topic of testing may be found in Anastasi (1976), Cronbach (1970) and Tyler and Walsh (1979).

Structured Tests. Structured tests usually take the form of questionnaires. They are called "structured" by some assessment psychologists because they have limited and clearly designed alternative responses. For example, the person must choose among a series of multiple choices or answer each item as "yes," "no," or "cannot say." The task for the subject is relatively limited and unambiguous, and the reliability of the observer does not pose a significant problem.

Personality questionnaires began to appear during World War I. The need to select emotionally stable men for military service led to the creation of a *Personal Data Sheet* by R. S. Woodworth (1919). Its two hundred items dealt with the symptoms of neurosis, and this test later became the father and the grandfather of a host of similar tests. Examples of the items making up the Woodworth Personal Data Sheet are given in Table 20.

During the late 1940s, there was a wave of disillusionment about the usefulness of personality questionnaires, prompted by critical reviews raising doubts about the validity of these tests and the principles underly-

Table 20

SOME SAMPLE ITEMS FROM THE WOODWORTH PERSONAL DATA SHEET
Personal Data Sheet

Have you failed to get a square deal in life?
Is your speech free from stutter or stammer?
Does the sight of blood make you sick or dizzy?
Do people seem to overlook you, that is, fail to notice that you are about?
Do you sometimes wish that you had never been born?
Are you happy most of the time?
Do you find that people understand you and sympathize with you?
Would you rather be with those of your own age than with older people?
Do you nearly always feel that you have strength or energy enough for your work?
Do you feel that you are a little different from other people?
Do people find fault with you much?
Have your thoughts and dreams been free from bad sex stories which you have heard?
Do you feel tired and irritable after a day or evening of visiting and pleasure?
Do you suffer from headaches or dizziness?
Do you ever imagine stories to yourself so that you forget where you are?

From Woodworth (1919)

ing them. Another factor contributing to this negative aura was the increasing impact on psychology (especially clinical psychology) of the Freudian and neo-Freudian concepts of dynamics. During this period projective techniques, seemingly more consistent with the "depth psychologies," became all the rage. Questionnaires, on the other hand, seemed superficial, easily "seen through," and incapable of tapping deeper layers of the personality. Not long after, a similar disillusionment spread to the projective techniques as well, as the claims about what they could do in assessment proved much overextended, and as clinical interest shifted from diagnosis to treatment.

Aside from a growing realism among professional workers about the uses and limitations of structured tests and indeed about assessment in general, the most important developments over recent years have been the increased sophistication of underlying principles and the greater complexity of test design. Whereas Woodworth's questionnaire (and most others) had been constructed simply, designed to measure a single trait such as neuroticism, newer scales were designed to measure a number of traits at the same time and to provide a complex profile of the person. For example, in 1943 one of the most important of this newer breed of personality questionnaires was introduced, the *Minnesota Multiphasic Personality Inventory* (MMPI) (Hathaway & McKinley, 1943).

In addition to having a number of subscales, the MMPI also used an important technique, first employed by Hartshorne and May (1928), that had a series of subscales designed to detect attitudes tending to lower the validity of the subjects' answers. Efforts were made to measure, for example, the tendency of subjects to lie about socially unacceptable impulses and actions, or to be excessively critical of one's shortcomings. The MMPI was also designed to distinguish between a variety of types of maladjustment, with subscales differentiating persons tending to be hypochondriacal, hysterical, obsessional, paranoid, schizophrenic, psychopathic, depressive, and so on. Examples of items from a few of the subscales are shown in Table 21.

A distinctive feature of the MMPI is how it was constructed. Large numbers of questionnaire items were surveyed and reconstructed without explicit regard to theory on types of psychopathology. These items then were administered to many types of persons, known from their hospital diagnosis as hypochondriacs, obsessive-compulsive neurotics, paranoids, and so on. Only those items were selected for the final scale that empirically differentiated one type of patient from another. For this reason, many of the items do not make

Table 21

SOME SAMPLE ITEMS FROM THE MINNESOTA MULTIPHASIC PERSONALITY INVENTORY

*Some Items Contributing Toward a Score for Hypochondriasis**

  T There seems to be a fullness in my head or nose most of the time.

  T Parts of my body often have feelings like burning, tingling, crawling, or like "going to sleep."

  F I have no difficulty in starting or holding my bowel movement.

Some Items Contributing Toward a Score of Psychasthenia
(Obsessive-Compulsive Disorders)

  T I usually have to stop and think before I act even in trifling matters.

  T I have a habit of counting things that are not important such as bulbs on electric signs, and so forth.

  F I have no dread of going into a room by myself where other people have already gathered and are talking.

Some Items Contributing Toward a Score for Paranoia

  T I believe I am being followed.

  F Most people inwardly dislike putting themselves out to help other people.

  F I have no enemies who really wish to harm me.

*Items labeled T and F are those which, when answered true or false respectively, contribute to a positive score in a particular diagnostic category. From Hathaway and McKinley (1943) by permission of University of Minnesota Press.

obvious sense as bases for differentiating one form of psychopathology from another, although those shown in Table 21 were chosen as illustrations because they do make rational sense in connection with the three disorders represented there. In contrast, many other tests are designed more in the fashion of construct validity. By starting out with a conception of each type of disorder or whatever property of personality is to be measured, and from this conception or theory, items are designed to tap the distinguishing traits. The MMPI is thus largely an empirically derived, rather than theoretically derived test, and as such represents a notable departure from the usual approach.

Other complex, structured tests have appeared since the MMPI, although the latter continues to be one of the most widely used in assessment research and clinical practice. Some of these newer scales, such as the California Psychological Inventory (Gough, 1957), or the Edwards' Personal Preference Schedule (1954), are designed to reveal personality traits not necessarily associated with psychopathology, as is the case with the MMPI. Each test has its own theoretical background, standardization, and body of validation research.

There are some very new developments in the design theory of the structured test. While current tests such as the MMPI and the CPI attempt to measure broad personality traits, such as paranoid forms of thinking or degree of socialization, some assessment psychologists have argued that tests and test items should focus on narrower, situationally defined traits. One influential thinker in this area, Donald Fiske (1963), has been quite critical of the adequacy of present-day personality tests, noting among other things that they have very limited predictive value or stability over time. He has blamed this in part (cf. Turner and Fiske, 1968) on several problems.

For one, subjects taking tests interpret the meanings of the items quite differently and use different strategies to decide whether or not an item aptly describes them. The subject usually must indicate how "often" something or other is done. Fiske asks, "How often is 'often'?" The process by which the person arrives at an answer is not indicated explicitly. Fiske writes, "For instance, the question might be: do you find it difficult to give a speech before a large group? The subject can go about the process of answering it in several ways. He can compare this statement to his general picture of himself. He can recall one or several pertinent experiences and base his response on his memory of his feelings. He can also decide that an affirmative answer would be true for most people and therefore is true for him. (These are some of the processes discerned in reports from subjects responding to such an item.) Insofar as various subjects go about answering such a question in different ways, the task is not structured" (1966, p. 78). These variations, says Fiske, decrease the adequacy of the test as a measure of some stable quality of personality.

Fiske recommends that the task of answering a questionnaire should be structured much more carefully and precisely, with the item specifying the exact situation in which the behavioral reaction in question is presumed to occur. In effect, Fiske is saying that the so-called "structured tests" are really not structured enough. The reader will recall that Endler and Hunt (1968), cited earlier, were trying to do essentially this in their efforts to determine the contribution of situation, response modality, and person, to the variations in the subjects' questionnaire answers.

Current tests are designed to *ignore* as much as possible the situational context in which behavior occurs in order to tap broad personality dispositions to respond regardless of that context. Based on the line of reasoning advocated by Fiske, future tests would *emphasize* the situational context, their items tending to specify situations and hence to be narrow in scope. Whether or not personality testing will move in the direction of greater specificity and narrowness, or remain oriented to broad traits or dispositions, is not yet evident. There is clearly a growing but unresolved controversy over the best model to use in creating structured tests of personality (cf. Mischel, 1976).

Unstructured or projective tests. Unstructured or projective tests are designed specifically to provide unstructured or ambiguous stimulus situations for the person to interpret. The use of the term "projection" is related to, but has a slightly different meaning from, the projection defense mechanism in which an unacceptable impulse is attributed to someone else (see Table 7 in chapter 5). The ambiguity of the stimulus and of the task set by the projective test decreases the extent to which the stimulus determines or constrains the nature of the response. For example, if a common, everyday object is presented to a person in full illumination, and he or she is asked to say what it is, little about the person's personality will be revealed. It is obviously a pencil, a book, a telephone, an egg, or what have you, and by and large everyone will agree on what it is. But if the illumination is reduced sharply or the outlines of the object are disturbed, individual differences in interpretation will emerge. With the usual cues missing, the stimulus will appear quite different to different individuals, and to give it meaning each individual must draw upon personal experience, preoccupations, and interests. He or she "projects" these things onto the ambiguous stimulus. This is why projective tests use materials such as inkblots, drawings, and photos of people in provocative but not entirely clear situations.

The projective test is particularly attractive to those who see psychopathology as the intrusion into rational life of primitive, unconscious forces. This is analogous to the way Freud (1938, 1953) viewed the dream and the slip of the tongue (see chapter 7). Unconscious material was assumed to slip through the censorship of the ego to create the dream when the person was asleep and thus less vigilant than usual, or to appear as an unintended verbal slip revealing a hidden impulse or thought. The projective technique as it was originally conceived used the same principle. Interest in it was particularly stimulated by the importation from Europe in the late 1930s of the Rorschach Inkblot Test (e.g., Beck, 1930; Klopfer & Kelley, 1942), and the development in the United States of the Thematic Apperception Test by Henry Murray (1943). Three examples of widely used projective techniques will be described here briefly, the Rorschach Test, the Thematic Apperception Test, and the Sentence Completion Test.

Ten inkblots comprise the stimulus materials of the *Rorschach Test*, originally selected out of many experimented with by its creator, a Swiss psychiatrist named Hermann Rorschach (1942). The subject looks at each of these blots, one at a time, and indicates what they look like or might be. The examiner writes down each response and later inquires about its location and its formal determinants, for example, whether the percept is seen as moving or stationary, and the extent to which shape, color, or shading influenced it. Interpretations of personality are made primarily from individual differences in the manner or *style* of going about the task, and the content of what is seen is given less importance. These interpretations are speculative, presumably based on normative data (some of it informal and part of the tradition of the test, and some of it formal) revealing how different kinds of people perform. An illustration of a Rorschach Inkblot is given in Figure 13.

Stylistic variations weigh heavily in the establishment of inferences about personality derived from performance on the Rorschach Test. For example, expressions of emotion in response to objects that are seen, such as "I despise them" or "How beautiful!" suggest repressive defensive modes, while qualifications such as "It is not a very good version of a bat" or "I can only see it if I stretch my imagination" suggest an obsessive-compulsive personality structure, someone who uses the defense mechanism of isolation or intellectualization. Such interpretations require research evidence of their validity, and much research effort has been devoted to this for every type of major interpretation Rorschach workers have suggested (with the consequent development of a very large literature).

The *Thematic Apperception Test* (TAT) is comprised of a series

FIGURE 13. An example of a Rorschach inkblot. The picture that we project into inkblots like this one gives valuable clues to our thoughts and emotions. Hermann Rorschach, a Swiss psychiatrist, discovered that by carefully classifying responses to inkblots, he had a tool that could be used for the systematic study and appraisal of human personality (Rorschach, 1942).

of twenty ambiguous pictures and drawings, many taken from popular magazines, mostly of men and women (sometimes the sex is not clear) in various settings and relationships. The subject is asked to tell a dramatic story, to spin a fantasy, as it were, about some or all of the pictures. He or she is asked to indicate what the people are thinking and feeling, the events that have led up to the situation depicted, and the outcome. Although many of the pictures tend to stimulate particular types of story content (for example, some of the pictures are commonly seen as showing a father and a son, a mother and a son, a married couple, etc.), there is also great diversity in the story themes and details. It is assumed that the stories reflect the process of identification by the subject with the characters depicted, thus revealing some things also about his or her own impulses, conflicts, sources of threat, and so on.

Although the TAT is commonly used in the clinical setting in order to plan a better course of treatment, experimental versions have been created to measure people's specific motivational characteristics. The best-known example is the research of David C. McClelland and his colleagues (1953) to measure *achievement motivation*. In their early studies, a set of pictures likely to elicit achievement-related story themes was created. Subjects were tested after they had been exposed to an experimental situation designed to induce achievement strivings, and after one designed to be neutral. In the achievement-arousing situation, some tests were given in an atmosphere of formality and seriousness, with the instructions that the subjects' performances would reveal their intelligence, capacity for leadership, and administrative ability. Subjects then wrote stories for pictures especially designed around achievement themes. The same procedure was followed after the neutral situation in which the atmosphere was relaxed and unevaluative. The evaluative context produced more achievement-related imagery in the stories than did the relaxed, unevaluative context, and the difference was explained on the basis of the greater arousal of achievement motivation by the former context. A scoring system was developed to reflect this aroused achievement motivation, and later it was used to differentiate persons with high and low dispositions toward achievement motivation, that is, achievement motivation as a personality trait.

This may be illustrated by two stories reported by Atkinson, the first reflecting a subject high in achievement imagery and presumably strong achievement motivation, the second low in achievement imagery. They were given to the specially designed picture displayed in Figure 14.

High Achievement Imagery

This chap is doing some heavy meditating. He is a sophomore and has reached an intellectual crisis. He cannot make up his mind. He is troubled, worried.

He is trying to reconcile the philosophies of Descartes and Thomas Aquinas—and at his tender age of eighteen. He has read several books on philosophy and feels the weight of the world on his shoulders.

He wants to present a clear-cut synthesis of these two conflicting philosophies, to satisfy his ego and to gain academic recognition from his professor.

He will screw himself up royally. Too inexperienced and uninformed, he has tackled too great a problem. He will give up in despair, go down to the G——— and drown his sorrows in a bucket of beer (1958, p. 697).

Low Achievement Imagery

The boy in the checkered shirt whose name is Ed is in a classroom. He is supposed to be listening to the teacher.

Ed has been troubled by his Father's drunkenness and his maltreatment of Ed's mother. He thinks of this often and worries about it.

Ed is thinking of leaving home for a while in the hope that this might shock his parents into getting along.

He will leave home but will only meet further disillusionment away from home (1958, p. 697).

Both these stories contain considerable conflict. The first story is filled with evidence of intense striving against a standard of

FIGURE 14. One of the pictures used to elicit stories which are scored for achievement. *(From Fig: 3. 1. A. in* The Achievement Motive *by McClelland, Atkinson, Clark, and Lowell, 1953. Reproduced by permission of Prentice-Hall, Inc.*

excellence (McClelland's definition of achievement motivation) expressed by the effort to tackle a difficult problem and to gain recognition and ego satisfaction. The second story about the same picture contains no achievement theme; it revolves around a family conflict and a boy's efforts to patch it up. The differences in achievement-related content between these stories illustrate very well the use of the TAT type procedures in the assessment of personality variables.

It must be recognized that motives are not always directly expressed in storytelling as is implied above. Sometimes, especially when such motives are proscribed in the culture or are unacceptable to the individual, they will be absent from the story content, although perhaps represented symbolically or indirectly (cf. Clark, 1952, 1955). The rules by which personality traits are expressed or inhibited from storytelling are themselves the subject of much research and theorizing by psychologists. This problem is particularly important to the psychologist adopting a Freudian approach to psychodynamics, because much of the impulse life which he or she seeks to explore is assumed to be unconscious or even repressed. The psychologist cannot expect a simple, direct expression of such mental content which the person is deeply ashamed of or threatened by, usually unlike the case for socially acceptable motives such as achievement.

In the *sentence completion* projective technique, an incomplete stem of a sentence must be completed by the subject. The stem, for example, "I feel," "I get angry when," or "Males," suggests the basic theme of the sentence. It may be highly ambiguous as in the first example, or it may constrain to a high degree the kinds of responses that are possible, as in the second and third examples above, which could well suggest aggressive or sexual ideation respectively. This variation in the degree of structure or ambiguity is important, since in the more ambiguous items the subject can volunteer themes which presumably are very pressing, and in the more unambiguous items, the subject is confronted with certain themes which may be disturbing and he or she is forced to deal with them.

Sentence completion tests have many forms depending on the interests of the assessment psychologist. They may be illustrated with one particular version used by Michael Goldstein (1959) to differentiate forms of coping with threatening impulses. Goldstein has been concerned with two styles of coping which he refers to as avoidance and sensitization (or approach). *Avoidance* is reflected in sentence completions that consistently evade the content implied by the stem, while *sensitization* is reflected in an acceptance of the stem content and its further elaboration. An illustration of four items in the sentence completion test used by Goldstein, and the scoring of the items for avoidance and sensitization may be seen in Table 22.

In Table 22, low scores for each of the sentence completion stems are given for avoidance, and high scores are used for sensitization. Consider, for example, item 4, "A girl's figure." An obvious connotation is sexual attraction. The response, "Hard to keep your eyes off," accepts the sexual theme and elaborates it. The subject is saying in effect that he is attracted to a girl's body, so much so that effort is required to look away. This answer is given a high sensitization or approach score. Consider, however, the answer, "Is not her personality," or "I don't know." Here the sexual connotation is completely evaded, and this completion is given a low score implying an avoidance response. Research by Goldstein and his students on the two types of personalities, avoiders and sensitizers, has suggested that they behave in other ways consistent with his interpretation of these coping styles (construct validity). For example, avoiders dealt with threatening propaganda about dental decay by failing to remember the information given afterwards and by failing to change their dental practices, while sensitizers behaved in the opposite fashion.

Table 22

Sample Items and Responses (with their scoring) from Goldstein's
Sentence-completion Test

1. IF I WERE STRUCK:
   (2) I would hit back
       I would get mad
   (1) I'd quit
       I would call for help
   (0) by lightning, I would die
       I don't know

3. I HATE:
   (2) my parents
       Mr. Jones
       my sister
   (1) some people
       Democrats
       being called names
   (0) snakes and wiggly worms
       pickles
       nothing

2. THE WORST THING A GIRL CAN DO:
   (2) sell herself or go willingly
       think about a male's sex
       have a baby before she is married
   (1) lie
       slap a boy
       be stuck up
   (0) go to a beauty parlor
       eat too much
       not be ladylike

4. A GIRL'S FIGURE:
   (2) is very important to me
       is to have fun with
       hard to keep your eyes off
   (1) has a lot to do with friends
       should be feminine
       is pretty good
   (0) is slim
       is not her personality
       I don't know

From Goldstein (1959). Copyright © 1959 by the American Psychological Association. Reprinted by permission.

We should mention the current viewpoint of assessment psychologists toward projective techniques. In the early days of enthusiasm for this approach, projective tests, like the dream, were thought to be, in Freud's words, the "royal road to the unconscious." Although conceivably influenced by unconscious, "primary process" mental activity (see chapter 5), it has become more and more evident that projective test content, such as stories told to TAT cards, is mainly determined by "secondary process" thinking characteristic of mature and adaptive ego activity. In the TAT, for example, the subject is given stimulus pictures and asked to tell stories about them. For the normal individual, the response is likely to be adaptive to the stimuli and to the social context—in general, the stories match the stimulus objects to a high degree, the subject follows the instructions, and he or she is sensitive to the social limitations of the testing relationship. Thus the analogy between primary process (primitive fantasy) and TAT storytelling is rather forced.

It is possible, of course, to score projective test content for primary process and secondary process activity, as Holt and Havel (1960) have done. However, it is no longer regarded as appropriate to

295

regard the general productions of subjects to projective test stimuli as equivalent to primitive ideation or primary process thought as was once assumed. There has been a shift in viewpoint that coincides with a change in emphasis in psychoanalytic thinking, too, from concern mainly with the motivational forces of the "id" to concern with the adaptive processes of the "ego." Just as the views about structured tests have moved sharply from the oversimplified conceptions characteristic of their early beginnings, so have conceptions of projective techniques gradually evolved from naïve and oversanguine early formulations, to a more realistic and modest set of notions about their value in assessment. As we shall see shortly, the chief criticism that can be leveled at such tests and at all assessment devices is that of extremely limited evidence of their validity.

Techniques for Obtaining and Coding Direct Observations of Behavior

In discussing the life history and the interview it was pointed out that the assessment psychologist not only used the subjective contents reported by the subject or other informants, but that simultaneously he or she observed the behavior of the person in order to make sounder inferences about psychological structures and processes. The same point should be made about the psychological test, particularly the projective test. Observations are sometimes made in the natural setting, as when we want to know how children act in school or with their families, or how people respond to captivity, or handle natural disasters such as floods, tornadoes, and bombings. Other observations are derived by creating analogous life situations, that is, laboratory test situations such as the use of simulated airplane or automobile controls which the person can operate to provide data on learning the basic skills of flying or driving.

In the usual laboratory testing situation or in the naturalistic life setting, techniques are needed that will increase the reliability of our observations, and that permit the coding of complex behavior into manageable and theoretically useful analytic categories. Not all of the behavior can be interpreted or is equally important, so such techniques are necessary to aid the assessment psychologist in his or her observational and interpretive task.

Two procedures have become especially important in this regard, the rating scale and the Q-sort. The *rating scale* formalizes the interpretive judgments of observers, whether the behavior is obtained in an interview, a psychological test, or a naturalistic or simulated life setting. It permits observers to translate their impressions of the subject's personality or behavior into roughly similar quantitative terms. In this way, one person can be compared with another on a common scale, and the judgment of two different observers on the same subject also can be compared on the same scale.

Most commonly, rating scales consist of lists of traits or characteristics which observers must evaluate on the basis of the behavior they observe. These scales are as variable as the kinds of behaviors and traits in which assessment psychologists are interested. Sometimes the subject does the rating, as for example when asked to describe the different feelings he or she experiences while watching a movie. An illustrative self-rating scale is shown in Table 23. Note that although these scales have been designed for the subject to rate his or her own feelings, they could be used equally well to enable several observers to estimate another's sociability, tranquility, impulsiveness, or energy.

The *Q-sort* (Stephenson, 1953) is designed to make certain statistical treatments possible, which are difficult to perform properly with most rating scales because the psychological distance between each of the numerical ratings is unknown. For example, in the scale illustrated in Table 23 it is impossible to say whether a rating of 5 on the subscale dealing with "energy versus fatigue" means that a person is half as energetic as one with a rating of 10. The numbers are not like those we use for weights and heights which can be added, subtracted, multiplied, and divided without distortion of their meaning.

In the Q-sort, a person is given a set of descriptive statements to sort into consecutive piles, each pile varying (as in all rating scales) in the degree to which the statement is characteristic of the person, or perhaps of someone else. Unlike the usual, simpler rating scales, the person is not free to place the statements anywhere he or she wishes. They must be sorted into a limited number of piles, say nine, and in such a way that the frequency of the statements in each pile creates a "normal" distribution, that is, a bell-shaped curve with very few items in the extreme categories and most in the middle categories. By doing so and for reasons that we need not go into here, it is possible to do statistical operations on the rating data which ordinarily would not be justified, for example, to correlate one set of Q-sort ratings with another. Thus, the Q-sort method is really a fancy way of arranging rating scale data so that they are amenable to more precise quantification and statistical manipulation than is possible with the more casual type of rating scale. One way in which it has been used extensively is in the evaluation of the changes in

Table 23

Four Personal Feeling Scales Used by Wessman and Ricks

VI. OWN SOCIABILITY VS. WITHDRAWAL
(how socially outgoing or withdrawn you felt today)

10. Immensely sociable and outgoing.
9. Highly outgoing, congenial, and friendly.
8. Very sociable and involved in things.
7. Companionable. Ready to mix with others.
6. Fairly sociable. More or less accessible.
5. Not particularly outgoing. Feel a little bit unsociable.
4. Retiring, would like to avoid people.
3. Feel detached and withdrawn. A great distance between myself and others.
2. Self-contained and solitary.
1. Completely withdrawn. Want no human contact.

XI. TRANQUILITY VS. ANXIETY
(how calm or troubled you felt)

10. Perfect and complete tranquility. Unshakably secure.
9. Exceptional calm, wonderfully secure and carefree.
8. Great sense of well-being. Essentially secure, and very much at ease.
7. Pretty generally secure and free from care.
6. Nothing particularly troubling me. More or less at ease.
5. Somewhat concerned with minor worries or problems. Slightly ill at ease, a bit troubled.
4. Experiencing some worry, fear, trouble, or uncertainty. Nervous, jittery, on edge.
3. Considerable insecurity. Very troubled by significant worries, fears, uncertainties.
2. Tremendous anxiety and concern. Harassed by major worries and fears.
1. Completely beside myself with dread, worry, fear. Overwhelmingly distraught and apprehensive. Obsessed or terrified by insoluble problems and fears.

XII. IMPULSE EXPRESSION VS. SELF-RESTRAINT
(how expressive and impulsive, or internally restrained and controlled, you felt)

10. Wild and complete abandon. No impulse denied.
9. Exhilarating sense of release. Say whatever I feel, and do just as I want.
8. Quick to act on every immediate desire.
7. Allowing my impulses and desires a pretty free rein.
6. Moderate acceptance and expression of my own needs and desires.
5. Keep a check on most whims and impulses.
4. On the straight and narrow path. Keeping myself within strong bounds.
3. Obeying rigorous standards. Strict with myself.
2. Refuse to permit the slightest self-indulgence or impulsive action.
1. Complete renunciation of all desires. Needs and impulses totally conquered.

Table 23 (con't.)

XV. ENERGY VS. FATIGUE
(how energetic, or tired and weary, you felt)

10. Limitless zeal. Surging with energy. Vitality spilling over.
9. Exuberant vitality, tremendous energy, great zest for activity.
8. Great energy and drive.
7. Very fresh, considerable energy.
6. Fairly fresh. Adequate energy.
5. Slightly tired, indolent. Somewhat lacking in energy.
4. Rather tired. Lethargic. Not much energy.
3. Great fatigue. Sluggish. Can hardly keep going. Meager resources.
2. Tremendously weary. Nearly worn out and practically at a standstill. Almost no resources.
1. Utterly exhausted. Entirely worn out. Completely incapable of even the slightest effort.

Mood and Personality by Alden E. Wessman and David F. Ricks. Copyright © 1966 by Holt, Rinehart and Winston, Inc. Reprinted by permission of Holt, Rinehart and Winston.

persons undergoing psychotherapy in which, for example, Q-sorts of persons describing themselves are compared before and after the treatment process (cf. Rogers & Dymond, 1954).*

PERSONALITY ASSESSMENT—AN OVERVIEW

We began this chapter by noting that assessment might be directed at the measurement of a single trait, say intelligence or impulse control, or the description and evaluation of the "whole" person. It is the latter to which the word assessment is technically most appropriate, but much more of the assessment activity in personality research consists of the former. The task of specifying a single trait is far simpler than that of evaluating the "whole" individual, in which a multiplicity of individual traits are integrated into the organized system we call personality.

There are both applied and research contexts in which the assessment psychologist employs not one, but a battery of techniques

---

* Block (1961) has studied the Q-sort extensively and actually used it in his study of personality development (1971; see chapter 6 in this book) to permit comparisons of individuals who had been assessed during different periods of time with different assessment tools. In other words, by having raters Q-sort diverse and relatively unorganized kinds of data, Block was able to generate a set of comparable and normally distributed observations which could then be analyzed constructively via factor analysis.

and observational aids, and tries to draw an integrated psychological picture of the "whole" individual. One such context is the psychological or psychiatric clinic in which the professional worker is concerned with planning a treatment program for a person suffering from an adjustive failure. Personality assessment in the clinical setting often is referred to as "psychodiagnosis," and its emphasis is on the conflicts which trouble the individual, the manner in which he or she copes with them, and the relations between these dynamics and the symptoms of adjustive failure. Such a psychodiagnosis does not consist of compiling a list of individual traits but rather is a psychological portrait of a "whole" person.

One approach that has been gaining stature is the examination of patterns or profiles of traits in individuals. For example, on the MMPI questionnaire, which has been described earlier, one can select all persons who share a profile, such as high scores in hypochondriasis, hysteria, and depression, and low scores in paranoia, schizophrenia, and psychopathic deviate. These can be compared as a group with other types displaying a different profile. This kind of reasoning could be much more complicated than the above example, thus approaching more closely a picture of a complex, organized personality system.

It also might be noted in this connection that when psychologists speak of the "whole" person, as distinguished from a collection of individual traits, they often mean something a bit different from a mere pattern or profile. The "whole" person can be conceived in terms of a set of organizing principles rather than a description of many diverse elements which go together. Such a principle, or set of principles, is an abstraction attempting to express the rule or rules by which the parts or structures of the system are organized, just as the term "internal combustion engine" also connotes a set of general rules for transforming energy in a particular way. Other ways also exist. Presumably the organizing principles characterizing one person will be different from those characterizing another, and the touchstone of personality description would be to specify them in each case. This is not to say, as we have been at pains to make clear in earlier chapters, that the search for common organizing principles applying to all persons is not also an integral part of the science of personality.

Complex assessment programs for research purposes represent another context in which personality assessment of the "whole" person is undertaken. These programs are rare because they are so costly in terms of human and economic resources. Examples include the attempt during World War II by the Office of Strategic Services to assess the fitness of men for the role of undercover agents (OSS Assessment Staff, 1948), studies of clinical psychologists at Michigan (Kelly and Fiske, 1951; Kelly and Goldberg, 1959), a study of psychiatrists at the Menninger Foundation in Topeka, Kansas (Holt and Luborsky, 1958), and a continuing assessment program at the Institute of Personality Assessment and Research (IPAR) at the University of California, Berkeley (MacKinnon, 1966). This latter effort has included personality assessments of the American team that climbed Mt. Everest, creative architects, a group of world-famous writers, and several other groups of distinguished persons.

In an IPAR assessment program, ten subjects typically are studied at one time by fifteen to twenty staff psychologists. The subjects usally live together and are studied intensively over a period of three days. Large numbers of observations, ratings, and descriptions are gathered for each subject. Some staff members interview, others use certain tests, and so on, and finally each staff member must integrate his or her impressions by drawing portraits of each subject using personality-relevant adjectives, Q-sorts, and character sketches. The results of each assessment psychologist's efforts are compared for agreement and averaged to produce a composite account of each individual. This account then can be used in predicting other things about the person, this prediction being the test of the validity and usefulness of the assessment.

In both the limited assessment of single traits and the complex assessment of the "whole" person, the key problem, as might be anticipated, is the validity of the assessments. The knowledge and technology that would permit highly valid assessments is still quite limited but is advancing rapidly (e.g., see McReynolds, 1968, 1971, 1975, 1977). Personality assessment also is handicapped by limitations in personality theory and by problems related to the strong influence of situational factors on a person's behavior. These situational influences, as we have seen, make the task of predicting behavior from assessment statements exceedingly difficult. Assessment as a field, like many other aspects of psychological science, is still in its infancy, a fact which is very discouraging to those who are impatient to resolve practical problems whose solutions depend on accurate assessment.

The task of personality assessment is of the utmost importance to the practical management of many human problems. There are two areas to which assessment is particularly applicable, personnel selection and the clinical treatment of adjustive failure. In personnel selection, it is often important to screen individuals who can function effectively in certain settings, for example, in military service, industry, school, special educational programs, or various trades. Surely it would be better for most individuals to be able to have the work tasks of their lives matched to their particular abilities and interests, and assessment is a means by which this might be done. Human satisfaction, efficiency, and justice all depend on such rational selection, as opposed, for example, to selection by family background, race, socioeconomic criteria, or ethnic origin.

In clinical treatment, programs must be based on a knowledge of the nature of the disturbance, its etiology, and of the most effective ways of dealing with each. The answers depend in part on personality assessment (or in this case, clinical diagnosis). If we are to evaluate treatment programs, we must be able to determine the ways in which the person has changed (or not changed) as a consequence of some given treatment approach. In short, effective assessment is a prerequisite for the evaluation of psychotherapy.

The need for valid personality assessment is equally important if personality theory is to advance. Unless the individual constructs of personality theory can be assessed, empirical verification, rejection, or modification of theoretical principles about personality will be, in the main, impossible. Thus assessment is truly a fundamental aspect of the total field of personality. When the science of personality has finally evolved into a well-established and integrated body of knowledge, it will be in large measure through the creation of a technology of assessment superior to what it is today and on which the necessary research into the determinants, description, dynamics, and development of personality depends.

Suggested Readings

Chapter 1. The Nature of Personality

ALLPORT, G.W. 1937. *Personality.* New York: Holt, Rinehart and Winston.

———. 1961. *Pattern and growth in personality.* New York: Holt, Rinehart and Winston.

CARLSON, R. 1971. Where is the person in personality research? *Psychological Bulletin* 75:203–19.

CATTELL, R.B. 1965. *The scientific analysis of personality.* Baltimore: Penguin Books.

DICAPRIO, N.S. 1974. *Personality theories: Guides to living.* Philadelphia: W.B. Saunders.

HALL, C.S., and LINDZEY, G. 1978. *Theories of personality.* New York: Wiley.

HOGAN, R. 1976. *Personality theory: The personological tradition.* Englewood Cliffs, N.J.: Prentice-Hall.

MADDI, S.R. 1976. *Personality theories: A comparative analysis.* Homewood, Ill.: Dorsey Press.

MONTE, C.F., 1977. *Beneath the mask: An introduction to theories of personality.* New York: Praeger.

MURPHY, G. 1947. *Personality.* New York: Harper & Row.

WIGGINS, J.S.; RENNER, K.E.; CLORE, G.L.; and ROSE, R.J. 1976. *Principles of personality.* Reading, Mass.: Addison-Wesley.

Chapter 2. Personality Determinants— Biological Factors

EYSENCK, H.J. 1977. *The biological basis of personality.* Springfield, Ill.: Charles C. Thomas.

KAMIN, L.J. 1974. *The science and politics of I. Q.* Hillsdale, N.J.: Erlbaum.

LERNER, I.M., and LIBBY, W.J. 1976. *Heredity, evolution, and society.* San Francisco: W.H. Freeman.

MCGAUGH, J.L.; WINBERGER, N.M.; and WHALEN, R.E., eds. 1967. *Psychobiology.* San Francisco: W.H. Freeman.

MEDNICK, S.A., and CHRISTIANSEN, K.O., eds. 1977. *Biosocial bases of criminal behavior.* New York: Gardner.

ORNSTEIN, R.E. 1972. *The psychology of consciousness.* San Francisco: W.H. Freeman.

ROSENZWEIG, M.R.; BENNETT, E.L.; and DIAMOND, M.C. 1972. Brain changes in response to experience. *Scientific American* 226:22–29.

SCHACHTER, S., and SINGER, J.E. 1962. Cognitive, social, and physiological determinants of emotional state. *Psychological Review* 69:379–99.

THOMAS, A.; CHESS, S.; and BIRCH, H.G. 1970. The origin of personality. *Scientific American* 223:102–109.

Chapter 3. Personality Determinants— Social Factors

BANDURA, A. 1969. *Principles of behavior modification.* New York: Holt, Rinehart and Winston.

BERKOWITZ, L. 1969. Simple views of aggression: Review of five recent books on aggression. *American Scientist* 57:372–83.

BLOCK, J.H. 1976. Issues, problems, and pitfalls in assessing sex differences. *Merrill-Palmer Quarterly* 22: 283-308.

BROWN, R. 1965. *Social psychology.* New York: Free Press of Glencoe.

HSU, F.L.K. 1961. *Psychological anthropology: Approaches to culture and personality.* Homewood, Ill.: Dorsey Press.

MACCOBY, E.E., and JACKLIN, C.N. 1974. *The psychology of sex differences.* Stanford, Calif.: Stanford University Press.

NORBECK, E.; PRICE-WILLIAMS, D.; and MCCORD, W.M., eds. 1968. *The study of personality: An interdisciplinary appraisal.* New York: Holt, Rinehart and Winston.

ROSENTHAL, R., and JACOBSON, L. 1968. *Pygmalion in the classroom.* New York: Holt, Rinehart and Winston.

SHERIF, C.W. 1976. *Orientation in social psychology.* New York: Harper & Row.

Chapter 4. Personality Description

ALLPORT, G.W., and ODBERT, H.S. 1936. Trait-names: A psycho-lexical study. *Psychological Monographs* 47:1–171.

CATTELL, R.B. 1965. *The scientific analysis of personality.* Baltimore: Penguin.

EYSENCK, H.J. 1952. *The scientific study of personality.* London: Routledge & Kegan Paul.

FRIEDMAN, M., and ROSENMAN, R.H. 1974. *Type A behavior and your heart.* New York: Knopf.

JONES, E.E., and NISBETT, R.E. 1971. The actor and the observer: Divergent perceptions of the causes of behavior. In *Attribution: Perceiving the causes of behavior,* ed. E.E. Jones, D. Kanouse, H.H. Kelley, R.E. Nisbett, S. Valins, and B. Weiner. Morristown, N.J.: General Learning Press.

JUNG, C.G. 1933. *Psychological types.* New York: Harcourt, Brace & World.

MAGNUSSON, D., and ENDLER, N.S., eds. 1977. *Personality at the crossroads: Current issues in interactional psychology.* Hillsdale, N.J.: Lawrence Erlbaum.

PHARES, E.J. 1976. *Locus of control in personality.* Morristown, N.J.: General Learning Press.

Chapter 5. Personality Dynamics

ABRAMSON, E.E. 1978. *Behavioral approaches to weight control.* New York: Springer.

DOLLARD, J., and MILLER, N.E. 1950. *Personality and psychotherapy: An analysis in terms of learning, thinking and culture.* New York: McGraw-Hill.

FREUD, S. 1943. *A general introduction to psychoanalysis.* Garden City, N.Y.: Garden City Books (First German edition, 1917).

FROMM, E. 1955. *The sane society.* New York: Holt, Rinehart and Winston.

MAHONEY, M.J., and THORESEN, C.E. 1974. *Self-control: Power to the person.* Monterey, Calif.: Brooks/Cole.

MASLOW, A.H. 1970. *Motivation and personality.* New York: Harper & Row.

MONAT, A., and LAZARUS, R.S., eds. 1977. *Stress and coping: An anthology.* New York: Columbia University Press.

RANK, O. 1952. *The trauma of birth.* New York: Robert Brunner.

ROGERS, C.R. 1951. *Client-centered therapy.* Boston: Houghton Mifflin.

WHITE, R.W. 1959. Motivation reconsidered: The concept of competence. *Psychological Review* 66:297–333.

Chapter 6. Personality Development

BLOCK, J. 1971. *Lives through time.* Berkeley, Calif.: Bancroft Books.

BREGER, L. 1974. *From instinct to identity: The development of personality.* Englewood Cliffs, N.J.: Prentice-Hall.

ERIKSON, E.H. 1963. *Childhood and society.* New York: Norton.

FLAVELL, J.H. 1963. *The developmental psychology of Jean Piaget.* New York: Van Nostrand.

FREUD, S. 1943. *A general introduction to psychoanalysis.* Garden City, N.Y.: Garden City Books (First German edition, 1917).

KALISH, R.A. 1975. *Late adulthood: Perspectives on human development.* Monterey, Calif.: Brooks/Cole.

KÜBLER-ROSS, E., ed. 1975. *Death: The final stage of growth.* Englewood Cliffs, N.J.: Prentice-Hall.

LANGER, J. 1969. *Theories of development.* New York: Holt, Rinehart and Winston.

LEVINSON, D.L. 1978. *The seasons of a man's life.* New York: Knopf.

SIEGEL, L.S., and BRAINERD, C.J., eds. 1977. *Alternatives to Piaget: Critical essays on the theory.* New York: Academic Press.

VAILLANT, G.E. 1977. *Adaptation to life.* Boston: Little, Brown.

Chapter 7. Approaches to Personality and their Application

ALLPORT, G.W. 1965. *Letters from Jenny.* New York: Harcourt, Brace & World.

BANDURA, A. 1978. The self system in reciprocal determinism. *American Psychologist* 33:344–58.

BARTON, A. 1974. *Three worlds of therapy.* Palo Alto, Calif.: National Press.

ELLIS, A., and GRIEGER, R. 1977. *Handbook of rational-emotive therapy.* New York: Springer.

ERIKSON, E.H. 1963. *Childhood and society.* New York: Norton.

FRANKL, V.E. 1962. *Man's search for meaning.* Boston: Beacon.

FREUD, S. 1949. *An outline of psychoanalysis.* New York: Norton (First German edition, 1940).

LAZARUS, A.A. 1976. *Multimodal behavior therapy.* New York: Springer.

LAZARUS, R.S. 1976. *Patterns of adjustment.* New York: McGraw-Hill.

NYE, R.D. 1975. *Three views of man.* Monterey, Calif.: Brooks/Cole.

ROGERS, C.R. 1961. *On becoming a person: A therapist's view of psychotherapy.* Boston: Houghton Mifflin.

SKINNER, B.F. 1974. *About behaviorism.* New York: Knopf.

WACHTEL, P.L. 1977. *Psychoanalysis and behavior therapy: Toward an integration.* New York: Basic Books.

ZIMBARDO, P.G. 1977. *Shyness.* Reading, Mass.: Addison-Wesley.

Chapter 8. Personality Assessment

ANASTASI, A. 1976. *Psychological testing.* New York: Macmillan.

BLOCK, J. 1965. *The challenge of response sets.* New York: Appleton.

CRONBACH, L.J. 1970. *Essentials of psychological testing.* New York: Harper & Row.

LAZARUS, R.S., and LAUNIER, R. In press. Stress-related transactions between person and environment. In *Perspectives in interactional psychology,* ed. L.A. Pervin and M. Lewis. New York: Plenum.

MISCHEL, W. 1968. *Personality and assessment.* New York: Wiley.

MURRAY, H.A. 1938. *Explorations in personality.* New York: Oxford University Press.

TYLER, L.E., and WALSH, W. BRUCE. 1979. *Tests and measurements.* Englewood Cliffs, N.J.: Prentice-Hall.

WIGGINS, J.S. 1973. *Personality and prediction: Principles of personality assessment.* Reading, Mass.: Addison-Wesley.

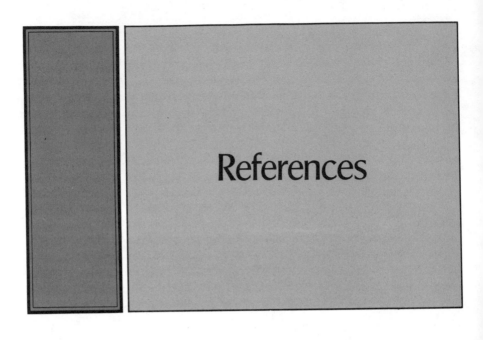

References

Adelson, J. 1969. Personality. In *Annual review of psychology*, ed. P.H. Mussen and M.R. Rosenzweig. Palo Alto, Calif.: Annual Reviews.

―――― **and O'Neil, R.P.** 1966. Growth of political ideas in adolescence: The sense of community. *Journal of Personality and Social Psychology* 4:295–306.

Allport, G.W. 1937a. *Personality*. New York: Holt, Rinehart and Winston.

――――. 1937b. The functional autonomy of motives. *American Journal of Psychology* 50:141–56.

――――. 1942. The use of personal documents in psychological science. *Social Science Research Council Bulletin* 49.

――――. 1955. *Becoming: Basic considerations for a psychology of personality*. New Haven, Conn.: Yale University Press.

――――. 1961. *Pattern and growth in personality*. New York: Holt, Rinehart and Winston.

――――. 1962. The general and the unique in psychological science. *Journal of personality* 30:405–22.

――――, ed. 1965. *Letters from Jenny*. New York: Harcourt, Brace & World.

―――― **and Odbert, H.S.** 1936. Trait-names: A psycho-lexical study. *Psychological Monographs* 47:1–171.

―――― **and Vernon, P.E.** 1933. *Studies in expressive movement*. New York: Macmillan.

Anastasi, A. 1976. *Psychological testing*. New York: Macmillan.

Ansbacher, H.L., and Ansbacher, R.R., eds. 1956. *The individual psychology of Alfred Adler.* New York: Basic Books.

Argyris, C. 1968. Some unintended consequences of rigorous research. *Psychological Bulletin* 70:185–97.

Arkes, H., and Garske, J.P. 1977. *Psychological theories of motivation.* Monterey, Calif.: Brooks/Cole.

Aronfreed, J. 1968. *Conduct and conscience.* New York: Academic Press.

Asch, S.E. 1952. Effects of group pressure upon the modification and distortion of judgments. In *Readings in social psychology,* ed. G.E. Swanson, J.M. Newcomb, and E.L. Hartley, pp. 2–11. New York: Holt, Rinehart and Winston.

———. 1956. Studies of independence and conformity: A minority of one against a unanimous majority. *Psychological Monographs* 70(9):Whole No. 416.

Astor, M.H. 1972. Transpersonal approaches to counseling. *Personnel and Guidance Journal* 50:801–808.

Atkinson, J.W., ed. 1958. *Motives in fantasy, action and society.* Princeton, N.J.: D. Van Nostrand.

Babladelis, G. 1977. The psychology of women. Invited address, 3 May 1977, at University of Hawaii, Department of Psychology, Honolulu, Hawaii.

Bandura, A. 1969. *Principles of behavior modification.* New York: Holt, Rinehart and Winston.

———. 1973. *Aggression: A social learning analysis.* Englewood Cliffs, N.J.: Prentice-Hall.

———. 1974. Behavior theory and the models of man. *American Psychologist* 29:859–69.

———; **Ross, D.; and Ross, S.A.** 1963. A comparative test of the status envy, social power, and the secondary reinforcement theories of identification learning. *Journal of Abnormal and Social Psychology* 67:527–34.

——— **and Walters, R.H.** 1963. *Social learning and personality development.* New York: Holt, Rinehart and Winston.

Bardwick, J.M. 1971. *Psychology of women: A study of biocultural conflicts.* New York: Harper & Row.

Barker, R.G., and Wright, H.F. 1951. *One boy's day.* New York: Harper & Row.

Battle, E.S., and Rotter, J.B. 1963. Children's feelings of personal control as related to social class and ethnic group. *Journal of Personality* 31:482–90.

Baumrind, D., and Black, A.E. 1967. Socialization practices associated with dimensions of competence in preschool boys and girls. *Child Development* 38:291–327.

Beach, F.A. 1955. The descent of instinct. *Psychological Review* 62:401–10.

Beck, S.J. 1930. Personality diagnosis by means of the Rorschach Test. *American Journal of Orthopsychiatry* 1:81–88.

Becker, E. 1973. *The denial of death.* New York: The Free Press.

Becker, W.C. 1964. Consequences of different kinds of parental discipline. In *Review of Child Development Research,* ed. M.L. Hoffman and L.W. Hoffman, pp. 169–208. New York: Russell Sage Foundation.

Bem, D.J., and Allen, A. 1974. On predicting some of the people some of the time: The search for cross-situational consistencies in behavior. *Psychological Review* 81:506–20.

Bem, S.L. 1975. Sex role adaptability: One consequence of psychological androgyny. *Journal of Personality and Social Psychology* 31:634–43.

———— **and Bem, D.J.** 1970. Case study of a non-conscious ideology: Training the woman to know her place. In *Beliefs, attitudes, and human affairs,* ed. D.J. Bem, pp. 80–99. Monterey, Calif.: Brooks/Cole.

Bettelheim, B. 1960. *The informed heart.* New York: Free Press of Glencoe.

Binet, A., and Simon, T.L. 1905. Application des methodes nouvelles au diagnostic du niveau intellectual chez des enfants normaux et anormaux d'hospice et d'école primaire. *Année Psychologique* 11:245–366.

Bischof, L.J. 1970. *Interpreting personality theories.* New York: Harper & Row.

Block, J. 1961. *The Q-sort method in personality assessment and psychiatric research.* Springfield, Ill.: Charles C. Thomas.

————. 1968. Some reasons for the apparent inconsistency of personality. *Psychological Bulletin* 70:210–12.

————, **in collaboration with Haan, N.** 1971. *Lives through time.* Berkeley, Calif.: Bancroft Books.

Boring, E.G. 1950. *A history of experimental psychology.* New York: Appleton-Century-Crofts.

Bowers, K. 1973. Situationism in psychology: An analysis and a critique. *Psychological Review* 80:307–36.

Bowlby, J. 1969. *Attachment and loss: Attachment.* Vol. 1. New York: Basic Books.

Bronfenbrenner, U. 1958. Socialization and social class through time and space. In *Readings in social psychology,* ed. E.E. Maccoby, T.M. Newcomb, and E.L. Hartley. New York: Holt, Rinehart and Winston.

Broverman, I.K.; Broverman, D.M.; Clarkson, F.E.; Rosenkrantz, P.; and Vogel, S.R. 1970. Sex-role stereotypes and clinical judgments of mental health. *Journal of Consulting Psychology* 34:1–7.

Brown, R. 1965. *Social psychology.* New York: Free Press of Glencoe.

Butler, R.N. 1971. Age: The life review. *Psychology Today* (December):51.

————. 1975. *Why survive?: Being old in America.* New York: Harper & Row.

Calhoun, J.F. 1977. *Abnormal psychology: Current perspectives.* New York: CRM/Random House.

Carlson, R. 1971. Where is the person in personality research? *Psychological Bulletin* 75:203–19.

Cattell, R.B. 1950. *Personality: A systematic, theoretical and factual study.* New York: McGraw-Hill.

————. 1965. *The scientific analysis of personality.* Baltimore: Penguin Books.

————; **Eber, H.W.; and Tatsuoka, M.M.** 1970. *Handbook for the Sixteen Personality Factor Questionnaire.* Champaign, Ill.: Institute for Personality and Ability Testing.

Caudill, W. 1959. Observations on the cultural context of Japanese psychiatry. In *Culture and mental health,* ed. M.K. Opler, pp. 213–42. New York: Macmillan.

Cautela, J.R. 1969. Behavior therapy and self-control: Techniques and implications. In *Behavior therapy: Appraisal and status,* ed. C. Franks, pp. 323–40. New York: McGraw-Hill.

Cavalli-Sforza, L.L., and Bodmer, F. 1971. *Genetics of human populations.* San Francisco: W.H. Freeman.

Chesler, P. 1972. *Women and madness.* New York: Doubleday.

Christian, J.J., and Davis, D.E. 1964. Endocrines, behavior, and population. *Science* 146:1550–60.

Clark, G., and Birch, H.B. 1945. Hormonal modifications of social behavior. I. *Psychosomatic Medicine* 7:321–29.

————. 1946. Hormonal modifications of social behavior. II. *Psychosomatic Medicine* 8:320–31.

Clark, R.A. 1952. The projective measurement of experimentally induced levels of sexual motivation. *Journal of Experimental Psychology* 44:391–99.

————. 1955. The effects of sexual motivation on phantasy. In *Studies in motivation,* ed. D.C. McClelland, pp. 132–38. New York: Appleton-Century-Crofts.

Coan, R.W. 1977. *Hero, artist, sage, or saint?* New York: Columbia University Press.

Cohen, F., and Lazarus, R.S. 1973. Active coping processes, coping dispositions, and recovery from surgery. *Psychosomatic Medicine* 35:375–89.

Coleman, J.C. 1976. *Abnormal psychology and modern life.* Glenview, Ill.: Scott, Foresman.

Comfort, A. 1976. *A good age.* New York: Crown.

Corsini, R.J., ed. 1977. *Current personality theories.* Itasca, Ill.: F.E. Peacock.

Court-Brown, W.M. 1967. *Human population cytogenetics.* New York: Wiley.

Cronbach, L.J. 1970. *Essentials of psychological testing.* New York: Harper & Row.

—— **and Meehl, P.E.** 1955. Construct validity in psychological tests. *Psychological Bulletin* 52:281–302.

Crowne, D.P., and Liverant, S. 1963. Conformity under varying conditions of personal commitment. *Journal of Abnormal and Social Psychology* 66:547–55.

Darwin, C. 1859. *The origin of species.* London: John Murray.

Davis, A., and Havighurst, R.J. 1946. Social class and colour differences in childrearing. *American Sociological Review* 11:698–710.

Dember, W.N. 1960. *Psychology of perception.* New York: Holt, Rinehart and Winston.

Deutsch, H. 1944–1945. *The psychology of women.* 2 vols. New York: Grune & Stratton.

DiCaprio, N.S. 1974. *Personality theories: Guides to living.* Philadelphia: W.B. Saunders.

Dobzhansky, T. 1967a. Changing man. *Science* 155:409–15.

——. 1967b. Of flies and men. *American Psychologist* 22:41–48.

Dollard, J., and Miller, N.E. 1950. *Personality and psychotherapy: An analysis in terms of learning, thinking and culture.* New York: McGraw-Hill.

Donelson, E. 1973. *Personality: A scientific approach.* New York: Appleton-Century-Crofts.

Dugdale, R.W. 1877. *The Jukes.* New York: Putnam.

Dukes, W.F. 1965. N=1. *Psychological Bulletin* 64:74–79.

Dundes, A. 1966. Here I sit—a study of American latrinalia. *Kroeber Anthropological Society Papers.* No. 34:91–105.

Edwards, A.L. 1954. *Edwards Personal Preference Schedule.* Manual. New York: Psychological Corporation.

Ekman, P., and Friesen, W.V. 1967. Nonverbal behavior in psychotherapy research. In *Research on psychotherapy,* vol. 3, ed. J. Shlien. Washington, D.C.: American Psychological Association.

Elkins, S. 1961. Slavery and personality. In *Studying personality cross-culturally,* ed. B. Kaplan, pp. 243–70. New York: Harper & Row.

Ellenberger, H.F. 1970. *The discovery of the unconscious.* New York: Basic Books.

Ellis, A. 1962. *Reason and emotion in psychotherapy.* New York: Lyle Stuart.

——. 1973. *Humanistic psychotherapy: The rational-emotive approach.* New York: Julian Press.

Endler, N.S., and Hunt, J. McV. 1968. S-R inventories of hostility and comparisons of the proportions of variance from persons, responses, and situations for hostility and anxiousness. *Journal of Personality and Social Psychology* 9:309–15.

———. 1969. Generalizability of contributions from sources of variance in the S-R inventories of anxiousness. *Journal of Personality* 37:1–24.

Erikson, E.H. 1959. Growth and crises of the healthy personality. *Psychological Issues* 1:5–100.

———. 1963. *Childhood and society.* New York: Norton.

———. 1968. *Identity: Youth and crisis.* New York: Norton.

Eysenck, H.J. 1952. *The scientific study of personality.* London: Routledge & Kegan Paul.

Fadiman, J., and Frager, R. 1976. *Personality and personal growth.* New York: Harper & Row.

Feifel, H.; Freilich, J.; and Hermann, L.J. 1973. Death fear in dying heart and cancer patients. *Journal of Psychosomatic Research* 17:161–66.

Ferster, C.B. 1965. Classification of behavior pathology. In *Research in behavior modification,* ed. L. Krasner and L.P. Ullmann, pp. 6–26. New York: Holt, Rinehart and Winston.

Feshbach, S. 1970. Aggression. In *Carmichael's manual of child psychology,* vol. 2, ed. P.H. Mussen, pp. 159–259. New York: Wiley.

Fiske, D. 1963. Homogeneity and variation in measuring personality. *American Psychologist* 18:643–52.

———. 1966. Some hypotheses concerning test adequacy. *Educational and Psychological Measurement* 26:69–88.

Frankenhaeuser, M. 1975. Experimental approaches to the study of catecholamines and emotion. In *Emotions: Their parameters and measurement.* ed. L. Levi, pp. 209–34. New York: Raven.

Frankl, V.E. 1955. *The doctor and the soul.* New York: Knopf.

———. 1962. *Man's search for meaning.* Boston: Beacon.

Freud, S. 1905. Fragment of an analysis of a case of hysteria. In *The standard edition of the complete psychological works of Sigmund Freud,* vol. 7. London: Hogarth, 1953.

———. 1925. Instincts and their vicissitudes. In *Collected papers,* vol. 4, pp. 60–83. London: Hogarth. (First German edition, 1918).

———. 1926. Inhibitions, symptoms and anxiety. In *Standard edition,* vol. 20, pp. 87–174. London: Hogarth, 1962.

———. 1933a. Analysis of a phobia in a five-year old boy. In *Collected papers,* vol. 3, pp. 149–296. London: Hogarth. (First German edition, 1909).

———. 1933b. *New introductory lectures on psychoanalysis.* New York: Norton. (First German edition, 1933).

———. 1933c. Psychoanalytic notes upon an autobiographical account of a case of paranoia (dementia paranoides). In *Collected papers,* vol. 3, pp. 390–472. London: Hogarth. (First German edition, 1911).

———. 1938. The psychopathology of everyday life. In *The basic writings of Sigmund Freud,* ed. A.A. Brill. New York: Modern Library.

————. 1943. *A general introduction of psychoanalysis.* New York: Doubleday.

————. 1949. *An outline of psychoanalysis.* New York: Norton. (First German edition, 1940).

————. 1953. The interpretation of dreams. In *Standard edition,* vols. 4 and 5. London: Hogarth. (First German edition, 1900).

————. 1957. *Civilization and its discontents,* trans. J. Riviere. London: Hogarth. (First German edition, 1930).

————. 1961. The ego and the id. In *The complete psychological works of Sigmund Freud,* vol. 21, trans. J. Strachey in collaboration with A. Freud. London: Hogarth.

————. 1974a. Female sexuality. In *Women and analysis,* ed. J. Strouse, pp. 39–56. New York: Grossman.

————. 1974b. Femininity. In *Women and analysis,* ed. J. Strouse, pp. 73–94. New York: Grossman.

————. 1974c. Some psychical consequences of the anatomical distinction between the sexes. In *Women and analysis,* ed. J. Strouse, pp. 17–26. New York: Grossman.

Friedman, M., and Rosenman, R.H. 1974. *Type A behavior and your heart.* New York: Knopf.

Fromm, E. 1941. *Escape from freedom.* New York: Holt, Rinehart and Winston.

————. 1947. *Man for himself.* New York: Holt, Rinehart and Winston.

————. 1955. *The sane society.* New York: Holt, Rinehart and Winston.

Galton, F. 1869. *Hereditary genius.* London: Macmillan.

Garfield, C.A., ed. 1976. *Psychosocial care of the dying patient.* Berkeley, Calif.: University of California Printing.

————. 1977. Impact of death on the health-care professional. In *New meanings of death,* ed. H. Feifel, pp. 143–51. New York: McGraw-Hill.

Gazzaniga, M.S. 1967. The split brain in man. *Scientific American* 217:24–29.

Gergen, K.J. 1977. Stability, change, and chance in understanding human development. In *Life-span developmental psychology: Dialectical perspectives on experimental research,* ed. N. Datan and L. Ginsberg, pp. 135–58. New York: Academic Press.

Gibson, J.J. 1966. *The senses considered as perceptual systems.* Boston: Houghton Mifflin.

Glueck, S., and Glueck, E. 1950. *Unraveling juvenile delinquency.* New York: Commonwealth Fund.

Goddard, H.H. 1912. *The Kallikak family.* New York: Macmillan.

Goldfried, M.R., and Goldfried, A.P. 1975. Cognitive change methods. In *Helping people change,* ed. F.H. Kanfer and A.P. Goldstein, pp. 89–116. New York: Pergamon.

Goldiamond, I. 1965. Self-control procedures in personal behavior problems. *Psychological Reports* 17:851–68.

Goldstein, J.H. 1975. *Aggression and crimes of violence.* New York: Oxford University Press.

Goldstein, K. 1940. *Human nature in the light of psychopathology.* Cambridge, Mass.: Harvard University Press.

Goldstein, M.J. 1959. The relationship between coping and avoiding behavior and response to fear-arousing propaganda. *Journal of Abnormal and Social Psychology* 58:247–52.

Gottesman, I.I. 1966. Genetic variance in adaptive personality traits. *Journal of Child Psychology and Psychiatry* 7:199–208.

―――. 1968. Genetics. In *Biology and behavior,* ed. D.C. Glass, pp. 59–68. New York: Rockefeller University Press and Russell Sage Foundation.

Gough, H.G. 1957. *Manual for the California Psychological Inventory.* Palo Alto, Calif.: Consulting Psychologists Press.

―――. 1960. Theory and measurement of socialization. *Journal of Consulting Psychology* 24:23–30.

Gould, R. 1972. The phases of adult life: A study in developmental psychology. *American Journal of Psychiatry* 129:521–31.

Graves, T.D. 1961. Time perspective and the deferred gratification pattern in a tri-ethnic community. Ph.D. dissertation, University of Pennsylvania.

Grossman, J., ed. 1973. *Manual on terminology and classification in mental retardation.* Baltimore: Garamond/Pridemark.

Hall, C.S., and Lindzey, G. 1978. *Theories of personality.* New York: Wiley.

Hall, K.R.L. 1964. Aggression in monkey and ape societies. In *The natural history of aggression,* ed. J.D. Carthy and F.J. Ebling, pp. 51–64. New York: Academic Press.

Hardin, G. 1949. *Biology: Its human implications.* San Francisco: W.H. Freeman.

Harlow, H.F. 1953. Mice, monkeys, men and motives. *Psychological Review* 60:23–32.

Hartmann, H. 1964. *Essays on ego psychology.* New York: International University Press.

Hartshorne, H., and May, M.A. 1928. *Studies in deceit.* New York: Macmillan.

Hathaway, S.R., and McKinley, J.C. 1943. *The Minnesota Multiphasic Personality Inventory.* Minneapolis: University of Minnesota Press.

Healy, W.; Bronner, A.F.; and Bowers, A.M. 1930. *The structure and meaning of psychoanalysis.* New York: Knopf.

Heber, R.F. 1970. *Epidemiology of mental retardation.* Springfield, Ill.: Charles C. Thomas.

Hetherington, E.M., and Wray, N.P. 1964. Aggression, need for social approval, and humor preferences. *Journal of Abnormal and Social Psychology* 68:685–89.

Hjelle, L.A., and Ziegler, D.J. 1976. *Personality theories: Basic assumptions, research, and applications.* New York: McGraw-Hill.

Hollander, E.P., and Marcia, J.E. 1970. Parental determinants of peer orientation and self orientation among preadolescents. *Developmental Psychology* 2:292–302.

Hollingshead, A.B. 1949. *Elmtown's youth.* New York: Wiley.

Holt, R.R. 1962. Individuality and generality in the psychology of personality. *Journal of Personality* 30:377–404.

—— and Havel, J. 1960. A method for assessing primary and secondary process in the Rorschach. In *Rorschach psychology,* ed. M.A. Rickers-Ovsiankina, pp. 263–315. New York: Wiley.

—— and Luborsky, L. 1958. *Personality patterns of psychiatrists.* New York: Basic Books.

Hooker, D. 1943. The reflex activities in the human fetus. In *Child behavior and development,* ed. R.S. Barker, J.S. Kounin, and H.F. Wright. New York: McGraw-Hill.

Horney, K. 1937. *Neurotic personality of our times.* New York: Norton.

Howard, J.H.; Cunningham, D.A.; and Rechnitzer, P.A. 1976. Health patterns associated with Type A behavior: A managerial population. *Journal of Human Stress* 2:24–31.

Hull, C.L. 1943. *Principles of behavior.* New York: Appleton-Century-Crofts.

Huxley, A. 1965. Human potentialities. In *Science and human affairs,* ed. R.E. Farson. Palo Alto, Calif.: Science and Behavior Books.

Jacobs, P.; Brunton, M.; and Melville, M. 1965. Aggressive behavior, mental sub-normality and the XYY male. *Nature* 208:1351–52.

Jacobson, E. 1938. *Progressive relaxation.* Chicago: University of Chicago Press.

Janeway, E. 1974. On "Female sexuality." In *Women and analysis,* ed. J. Strouse, pp. 57–70. New York: Grossman.

Janis, I.L.; Mahl, G.F.; Kagan, J.; and Holt, R.R. 1969. *Personality: Dynamics, development, and assessment.* New York: Harcourt, Brace and World.

Jarvik, L.F., Klodin, V., and Matsuyama, S.S. 1973. Human aggression and the extra Y chromosome: Fact or fantasy? *American Psychologist* 28:674–82.

Jensen, A.R. 1969. How much can we boost IQ and scholastic achievement? *Harvard Educational Review* 39.

Jervis, G.A. 1937. Introductory study of fifty cases of mental deficiency associated with excretion of phenylpyruvic acid. *Archives of Neurology and Psychiatry* 38:944–63.

———. 1959. The mental deficiencies. In *The American handbook of psychiatry,* vol. 2, ed. S. Arieti, pp. 1289–1314. New York: Basic Books.

Johnson, R.N. 1972. *Aggression in man and animals.* Philadelphia: W.B. Saunders.

Jourard, S.M. 1968. *Disclosing man to himself.* New York: D. Van Nostrand.

———. 1974. *Healthy personality: An approach from the viewpoint of humanistic psychology.* New York: Macmillan.

Jung, C.G. 1916. *Analytical psychology.* New York: Moffat Yard.

———. 1933. *Psychological types.* New York: Harcourt, Brace & World.

———. 1953. Two essays on analytical psychology. In *Collected works,* vol. 7. New York: Pantheon.

Kagan, J., and Moss, H.A. 1962. *Birth to maturity: A study in psychological development.* New York: Wiley.

Kahl, J.A., and Davis, J.A. 1955. A comparison of indexes of socio-economic status. *American Sociological Review* 20:314–25.

Kahn, R.L., and Cannell, C.F. 1957. *The dynamics of interviewing.* New York: Wiley.

Kalish, R.A. 1975. *Late adulthood: Perspectives on human development.* Monterey, Calif.: Brooks/Cole.

Kallmann, F.J. 1953. *Heredity in health and mental disorder.* New York: Norton.

Kanfer, F.H. 1970. Self-monitoring: Methodological limitations and clinical applications. *Journal of Consulting and Clinical Psychology* 35:148–152.

———. 1971. The maintenance of behavior by self-generated stimuli and reinforcement. In *The psychology of private events: Perspectives on covert response systems,* ed. A. Jacobs and L.B. Sachs, pp. 39–59. New York: Academic Press.

———. 1975. Self-management methods. In *Helping people change,* ed. F.H. Kanfer and A.P. Goldstein, pp. 309–56. New York: Pergamon.

Kelly, E.L., and Fiske, D.W. 1951. *The prediction of performance in clinical psychology.* Ann Arbor: University of Michigan Press.

——— **and Goldberg, L.R.** 1959. Correlates of later performance and specialization in psychology. *Psychological Monographs* 73.

Kelly, G.A. 1955. *The psychology of personal constructs,* vols. 1 and 2. New York: Norton.

Kelman, H.C. 1961. Processes of opinion change. *Public Opinion Quarterly* 25:57–58.

Kenniston, K. 1965. *The uncommitted: Alienated youth in American society.* New York: Delta, Dell Publishing.

———. 1968. *The young radicals: Notes on committed youth.* New York: Harcourt, Brace & World.

Keys, A.B.; Brozek, J.; Heuschel, A.; Mickelson, O.; and Taylor, H.L. 1950. *The biology of human starvation.* Minneapolis: University of Minnesota Press.

Kleinmuntz, B. 1974. *Essentials of abnormal psychology.* New York: Harper & Row.

Klineberg, O. 1935. *Negro intelligence and selective migration.* New York: Holt, Rinehart and Winston.

Klopfer, B., and Kelley, D.M. 1942. *The Rorschach technique.* New York: World Publishing.

Kohlberg, L. 1963. The development of children's orientations toward a moral order: 1. Sequence in the development of moral thought. *Vita Humana* 6:11–33.

———. 1966. A cognitive-developmental analysis of children's sex-role concepts and attitudes. In *The development of sex differences,* ed. E.E. Maccoby, pp. 82–173. Stanford, Calif.: Stanford University Press.

Koriat, A.; Melkman, R.; Averill, J.R.; and Lazarus, R.S. 1972. The self-control of emotional reactions to a stressful film. *Journal of Personality* 40:601–19.

Krasner, L., and Ullmann, L.P. 1973. *Behavior influence and personality: The social matrix of human action.* New York: Holt, Rinehart and Winston.

Krauskopf, C.J. 1978. Comment on Endler and Magnusson's attempt to redefine personality. *Psychological Bulletin* 85:280–83.

Krech, D.; Crutchfield, R.S.; and Ballachey, E.L. 1962. *Individual in society.* New York: McGraw-Hill.

Kretschmer, E. 1925. *Physique and character.* New York: Harcourt, Brace & World.

Kübler-Ross, E. 1969. *On death and dying.* New York: Macmillan.

Lazarus, A.A. 1971. *Behavior therapy and beyond.* New York: McGraw-Hill.

Lazarus, R.S. 1974. Cognitive and coping processes in emotion. In *Cognitive views of human motivation,* ed. B. Weiner, pp. 21–32. New York: Academic Press.

———. 1976. *Patterns of adjustment.* New York: McGraw-Hill.

———; Averill, J.R.; and Opton, E.M., Jr. 1970. Towards a cognitive theory of emotion. In *Feelings and emotions,* ed. M.B. Arnold, pp. 207–32. New York: Academic Press.

————, and **Launier, R.** In press. Stress-related transactions between person and environment. In *Perspectives in interactional psychology*, ed. L.A. Pervin and M. Lewis. New York: Plenum.

————; **Opton, E.M., Jr.; Nomikos, M.S.; and Rankin, N.O.** 1965. The principle of short-circuiting of threat: Further evidence. *Journal of Personality* 33:622–35.

Leakey, L.S.B. 1967. Development of aggression as a factor in early human and prehuman evolution. In *Aggression and defense*, ed. C.D. Clemente and D.B. Lindsey. Berkeley and Los Angeles: University of California Press.

Lefcourt, H.M. 1966. Internal versus external control of reinforcement: A review. *Psychological Bulletin* 65:206–20.

————. 1976. *Locus of control*. Hillsdale, N.J.: Lawrence Erlbaum.

Lehrman, D.S. 1964. The reproductive behavior of ring doves. *Scientific American* 211:48–54.

Lerner, I.M., and Libby, W.J. 1976. *Heredity, evolution, and society*. San Francisco: W.H. Freeman.

Levine, S. 1966. Sex differences in the brain. *Scientific American* 214:84–90.

———— and **Mullins, R.F., Jr.** 1966. Hormonal influences on brain organization in infant rats. *Science* 152:1585–92.

Levinson, D.L. 1978a. Growing up with the dream. *Psychology Today:* (January): 20–31, 89.

————. 1978b. *The seasons of a man's life*. New York: Knopf.

Levy, D.M. 1955. Oppositional syndromes and oppositional behavior. In *Psychopathology of childhood*, ed. P.H. Hoch and J. Zubin, pp. 204–26. New York: Grune & Stratton.

Lewin, K. 1935. *A dynamic theory of personality*, trans. K.E. Zener and D.K. Adams. New York: McGraw-Hill.

Liebert, R.M., and Spiegler, M.D. 1974. *Personality: Strategies for the study of man*. Homewood, Ill.: Dorsey Press.

Lorenz, K. 1966. *On aggression*. New York: Harcourt, Brace & World.

Lowenthal, M.F.; Thurnher, M.; and Chiriboga, D. 1975. *Four stages of life*. San Francisco: Jossey-Bass.

Maas, H., and Kuypers, J. 1974. *From thirty to seventy: A forty-year longitudinal study of adult life styles and personality*. San Francisco: Jossey-Bass.

Maccoby, E.E., and Jacklin, C.N. 1974. *The psychology of sex differences*. Stanford, Calif.: Stanford University Press.

Mackinnon, D.W. 1966. Some reflections on the current status of personality assessment. Paper presented at faculty symposium, 15 Nov. 1966, Department of Psychology, University of California, Berkeley.

Maddi, S.R. 1976. *Personality theories: A comparative analysis.* Homewood, Ill.: Dorsey Press.

Magnusson, D., and Endler, N.S., eds. 1977. *Personality at the crossroads: Current issues in interactional psychology.* Hillsdale, N.J.: Lawrence Erlbaum.

Mahoney, M.J., and Thoresen, C.E. 1974. *Self-control: Power to the person.* Monterey, Calif.: Brooks/Cole.

Maslow, A.H. 1964. Synergy in the society and in the individual. *Journal of Individual Psychology* 20:153–64.

———. 1968. *Toward a psychology of being.* New York: D. Van Nostrand.

———. 1970. *Motivation and personality.* New York: Harper & Row.

———. 1971. *The farther reaches of human nature.* New York: Viking.

Masters, W.H., and Johnson, V.E. 1966. *Human sexual response.* Boston; Mass.: Little, Brown.

Matthews, L.H. 1964. Overt fighting in mammals. In *The natural history of aggression,* ed. J.D. Carthy and F.J. Ebling, pp. 7–14. New York: Academic Press.

May, R. 1967. *Psychology and the human dilemma.* Princeton, N.J.: D. Van Nostrand.

McClelland, D.C. 1951. *Personality.* New York: Dryden Press.

———; **Atkinson, J.W.; Clark, R.A.; and Lowell, E.L.** 1953. *The achievement motive.* New York: Appleton-Century-Crofts.

McCord, W., and McCord, J. 1956. *Psychopathy and delinquency.* New York: Grune & Stratton.

———. 1958. The effects of parental role model on criminality. *Journal of Social Issues* 14:66–75.

McKusick, V.A. 1964. *Human genetics.* Englewood Cliffs, N.J.: Prentice-Hall.

McMahon, F.B. 1976 *Abnormal behavior: Psychology's view.* Englewood Cliffs, N.J.: Prentice-Hall.

McReynolds, P., ed. 1968, 1971. *Advances in psychological assessment,* vols. 1 and 2. Palo Alto, Calif.: Science and Behavior Books.

———. 1975, 1977. *Advances in psychological assessment,* vols. 3 and 4. San Francisco: Jossey-Bass.

Mead, M. 1935. *Sex and temperament in three primitive societies.* New York: Morrow.

———. 1974. On Freud's view of female psychology. In *Women and analysis,* ed. J. Strouse, pp. 95–106. New York: Grossman.

Mechanic, D. 1963. Religion, religiosity, and illness behavior: The special case of the Jews. *Human Organization* 22:202–8.

———. 1968. *Medical sociology.* New York: Free Press of Glencoe.

Milgram, S. 1963. Behavioral study of obedience. *Journal of Abnormal and Social Psychology* 67:371–78.

————. 1965. Some conditions of obedience and disobedience to authority. In *Current studies in social psychology*, ed. I.D. Steiner and M. Fishbein. New York: Holt, Rinehart & Winston.

————. 1974. *Studies on obedience*. New York: Harper & Row.

Miller, N.E. 1944. Experimental studies of conflict. In *Personality and the behavior disorders*, vol. 1, ed. J. McV. Hunt, pp. 431–65. New York: Ronald Press.

———— **and Dollard, J.** 1941. *Social learning and imitation*. New Haven, Conn.: Yale University Press.

Miller, P.H.; Heldmeyer, K.H.; and Miller, S.A. 1975. Facilitation of conservation of number in young children. *Developmental Psychology* 11:253.

Mischel, W. 1968. *Personality and assessment*. New York: Wiley.

————. 1969. Continuity and change in personality. *American Psychologist* 24:1012–18.

————. 1970. Sex-typing and socialization. In *Carmichael's manual of child psychology*, vol. 2, ed. P.H. Mussen, pp. 3–72. New York: Wiley.

————. 1973. Toward a cognitive social learning reconceptualization of personality. *Psychological Review* 80:252–83.

————. 1976. *Introduction to personality*. New York: Holt, Rinehart, and Winston.

Mitchell, J. 1974a. On Freud and the distinction between the sexes. In *Women and analysis*, ed. J. Strouse, pp. 27–36. New York: Grossman.

————. 1974b. *Psychoanalysis and feminism*. New York: Pantheon.

Money, J. 1974. Prenatal hormones and postnatal socialization in gender identity differentiation. In *Nebraska symposium on motivation*, ed. J.K. Cole and R. Dienstbier. Lincoln: University of Nebraska Press.

Monte, C.F. 1977. *Beneath the mask: An introduction to theories of personality*. New York: Praeger.

Moyer, K.E. 1967. *Kinds of aggression and their physiological basis*. Carnegie-Mellon University Report No. 67–12.

Murphy, G. 1947. *Personality*. New York: Harper & Row.

Murray, H.A. 1938. *Explorations in personality*. New York: Oxford University Press.

————. 1943. *Manual for the Thematic Apperception Test*. Cambridge, Mass.: Harvard University Press.

Mussen, P.H. 1979. *The psychological development of the child*. Englewood Cliffs, N.J.: Prentice-Hall.

Nathan, P.E., and Harris, S.L. 1975. *Psychopathology and society*. New York: McGraw-Hill.

Neugarten, B.L. 1968. Adult personality: Toward a psychology of the life cycle. In *Middle age and aging*, ed. B.L. Neugarten. Chicago: University of Chicago Press.

————. 1971. Grow old along with me! The best is yet to be. *Psychology Today* (December):45–48, 79, 81.

————; Havighurst, R.J.; and Tobin, S.S. 1968. Personality and patterns of aging. In *Middle age and aging*, ed. B.L. Neugarten, pp. 173–77. Chicago: University of Chicago Press. Reprinted from *Gawein* Jrg. 13, Afl. (May 1965):249–56.

O'Leary, V.E. 1977. *Toward understanding women*. Monterey, Calif.: Brooks/ Cole.

Opler, M.K., ed. 1959. *Culture and mental health*. New York: Macmillan.

Ornstein, R.E. 1973. Right and left thinking. *Psychology Today* 6:86–93.

OSS Assessment Staff. 1948. *Assessment of men*. New York: Holt, Rinehart and Winston.

Page, J.D. 1975. *Psychopathology: The science of understanding deviance*. Chicago: Aldine.

Pavlov, I.P. 1927. *Conditioned reflexes*. London: Oxford University Press.

Pearson, K., and Moul, M. 1925. The problem of alien immigration into Great Britain, illustrated by an examination of Russian and Polish Jewish children. *Annals of Eugenics* 1:5–127.

Pervin, L.A. 1975. *Personality: Theory, assessment, and research*. New York: Wiley.

———— and Lewis, M., eds. In press. *Internal and external determinants of behavior*. New York: Plenum.

Petersen, W., and Matza, D. 1963. *Social controversy*. Belmont, Calif.: Wadsworth.

Piaget, J. 1948. *The moral judgment of the child*. New York: Free Press of Glencoe.

————. 1952. *The origins of intelligence in children*. New York: International University Press.

Prince, M. 1920. Miss Beauchamp—The theory of the psychogenesis of multiple personality. *Journal of Abnormal and Social Psychology* 15:82–85, 87–91, 96–98, 102–4, 135.

Rank, O. 1952. *The trauma of birth*. New York: Robert Brunner.

Rapaport, D. 1967. *Collected papers*, ed. M.M. Gill. New York: Basic Books.

Reed, C.F., and Cuadra, C.A. 1957. The role-taking hypothesis in delinquency. *Journal of Consulting Psychology* 21:386–90.

Reese, E.P. 1978. *Human behavior: Analysis and application*. Dubuque, Iowa: Wm. C. Brown.

Richardson, S.A.; Dohrenwend, B.S.; and Klein, D. 1965. *Interviewing: Its forms and functions*. New York: Basic Books.

Riegel, K.F. 1975. From traits and equilibrium toward developmental dialectics. In *Nebraska symposium on motivation*, ed. W. Arnold, pp. 349–407. Lincoln: University of Nebraska Press.

Rimm., D.C., and Somervill, J.W. 1977. *Abnormal psychology.* New York: Academic Press.

Rogers, C.R. 1942. *Counseling and psychotherapy.* Boston: Houghton Mifflin.

———. 1947. Some observations on the organization of personality. *American Psychologist* 2:358–68.

———. 1951. *Client-centered therapy.* Boston: Houghton Mifflin.

———. 1961. *On becoming a person: A therapist's view of psychotherapy.* Boston: Houghton Mifflin.

———. 1972. *Becoming partners: Marriage and its alternatives.* New York: Delacorte.

———. 1974. In retrospect: Forty-six years. *American Psychologist* 29:115–23.

——— and Dymond, R.F., eds. 1954. *Psychotherapy and personality change.* Chicago: University of Chicago Press.

——— and Roethlisberger, F.J. 1952. Barriers and gateways to communication. *Harvard Business Review* 30 (July-August):46–52.

Rorschach, H. 1942. *Psychodiagnostics,* trans. P. Lemkau and B. Kronenberg. New York: Grune & Stratton. (First German edition, 1932).

Rosenfeld, H.M. 1966. Instrumental affiliation functions of facial and gestural expressions. *Journal of Personality and Social Psychology* 4:65–72.

Rosenman, R.H., and Friedman, M. 1971a. Observations on the pathogenesis of coronary heart disease. *Nutritional News* 34:9–14.

———. 1971b. The central nervous system and coronary heart disease. *Hospital Practice* 6:87–97.

Rothballer, A.G. 1967. Aggression, defense, and neurohumors. In *Aggression and defense: Neural mechanisms and social patterns,* ed. C.D. Clemente and D.B. Lindsley, pp. 135–70. Los Angeles: University of California Press.

Rotter, J.B. 1966. Generalized expectancies for internal versus external control of reinforcement. *Psychological Monographs* 80: Whole No. 609.

———. 1971. External control and internal control. *Psychology Today* 5:37–42, 58–59.

———; Chance, J.E., and Phares, E.J. 1972. *Applications of a social learning theory of personality.* New York: Holt, Rinehart and Winston.

Rowland, K.F., and Sokol, B. 1977. A review of research examining the coronary-prone behavior pattern. *Journal of Human Stress* 3:26–33.

San Francisco Chronicle. 1978. The elderly on television—our last stereotype? 5 January 1978.

Scaramella, T.J., and Brown, W.A. 1978. Serum testosterone and aggressiveness in hockey players. *Psychosomatic Medicine* 40:262–65.

Schachter, S. 1951. Deviation, rejection, and communication. *Journal of Abnormal and Social Psychology* 46:190–207.

Schreiber, F.R. 1973. *Sybil.* New York: Warner Books.

Schultz, D.P. 1969. The human subject in psychological research. *Psychological Bulletin* 72:214–28.

Sears, R.R.; Maccoby, E.E.; and Levin, H. 1957. *Patterns of child rearing.* New York: Harper & Row.

Seeman, M., and Evans, J.W. 1962. Alienation and learning in a hospital setting. *American Sociological Review* 27:772–83.

Seligman, M.E.P. 1975. *Helplessness: On depression, development, and death.* San Francisco: W.H. Freeman.

Selye, H. 1956, 1976. *The stress of life.* New York: McGraw-Hill.

Serbin, L.A.; O'Leary, K.D.; Kent, R.N.; and Tonick, I.S. 1973. A comparison of teacher response to the pre-academic and problem behavior of boys and girls. *Child Development* 44:796–804.

Shah, S.A. 1970a. Recent developments in human genetics and their implication for problems of social deviance. Paper presented at the American Association for the Advancement of Science, Chicago, 28 December 1970.

———. 1970b. *Report on the XYY chromosomal abnormality.* National Institutes of Mental Health conference report (Public Health Service Publication No. 2103)

Sheehy, G. 1974, 1976. *Passages: Predictable crises of adult life.* New York: E.P. Dutton.

Sheldon, W.H. (with S.S. Stevens and W.B. Tucker). 1940. *The varieties of human physique: An introduction to constitutional psychology.* New York: Harper & Row.

——— **(with S.S. Stevens).** 1942. *The varieties of temperament: A psychology of constitutional differences.* New York: Harper & Row.

Sherif, M. 1935. A study of some social factors in perception. *Archives of Psychology,* no. 187.

Sherman, J.A. 1971. *On the psychology of women: A survey of empirical studies.* Springfield, Ill.: Charles C. Thomas.

Shockley, W. 1972. Dysgenics, geneticity, raceology: A challenge to the intellectual responsibility of educators. *Phi Delta Kappan* (January):297–307.

Siegler, R.S., and Liebert, R.M. 1972. Effects of presenting relevant rules and complete feedback on the conservation of liquid quantity task. *Developmental Psychology* 7:133–38.

Sims, J.H., and Baumann, D.D. 1972. The tornado threat: Coping styles of the north and south. *Science* 176:1386–91.

Singer, J.L., and Opler, M.K. 1956. Contrasting patterns of fantasy and motility in Irish and Italian schizophrenics. *Journal of Abnormal and Social Psychology* 53:42–47.

Skeels, H.M. 1940. Some Iowa studies of the mental growth of children in relation to differentials in the environment: A summary. In *Intelligence: Its nature and nurture*, pp. 281–308. Thirty-ninth Yearbook, Part II. National Society for the Study of Education.

————. 1942. A study of the effects of differential stimulation on mentally retarded children: A follow up report. *American Journal of Mental Deficiency* 46:340–50.

————. 1966. Adult status of children with contrasting early life experiences. *Monographs of the Society for Research in Child Development* 31 (Serial no. 105).

Skinner, B.F. 1953. *Science and human behavior.* New York: Macmillan.

————. 1971. *Beyond freedom and dignity.* New York: Knopf.

Smelser, N.J., and Smelser, W.T. 1963. Introduction: Analyzing personality and social systems. In *Personality and social systems*, ed. N.J. Smelser and W.T. Smelser, pp. 1–18. New York: Wiley.

Smith, M.J. 1975. *When I say no, I feel guilty.* New York: Dial Press.

Spence, K.W. 1948. The postulates and methods of "behaviorism." *Psychological Review* 55:67–78.

Sperry, R.W. 1964. The great cerebral commissure. *Scientific American* 210:42–52.

Spielberger, C.D., ed. 1972. *Anxiety: Current trends in theory and research*, vols. 1 and 2. New York: Academic Press.

Spock, B. 1957. *Baby and child care.* New York: Pocket Books.

Stephenson, W. 1953. *The study of behavior: Q-technique and its methodology.* Chicago: University of Chicago Press.

Stone, A.A., and Stone, S.S., eds. 1966. *The abnormal personality through literature.* Englewood Cliffs, N.J.: Prentice-Hall.

Strouse, J., ed. 1974. *Women and analysis.* New York: Grossman.

Stuart, R.B. 1970. *Trick or treatment: How and when psychotherapy fails.* Champaign, Ill.: Research Press.

Sutich, A.J. 1969. Some considerations regarding transpersonal psychology. *Journal of Transpersonal Psychology* 1:11–20.

Teillard, A. 1948. *L'âme et l'écriture*, pp. 89–94. Paris: Stock.

Terman, L.M. 1916. *The measurement of intelligence.* Boston: Houghton Mifflin.

Thigpen, C.H., and Cleckley, H.M. 1957. *The three faces of Eve.* New York: McGraw-Hill.

Thompson, W.R. 1965. Behavior genetics. In *McGraw-Hill Yearbook of Science and Technology*, pp. 27–35. New York: McGraw-Hill.

Thoresen, C.E., and Mahoney, M.J. 1974. *Behavioral self-control.* New York: Holt, Rinehart and Winston.

Thorndike, E.L. 1913. *The psychology of learning.* New York: Teachers College.

Tinbergen, N. 1951. *The study of instincts.* London: Oxford University Press.

Toffler, A. 1970. *Future shock.* New York: Bantam.

Tryon, R.C. 1940. Genetic differences in maze-learning ability in rats. *Yearbook of the National Society for the Study of Education* 39 (part 1):111–19.

—————. 1955a. Identification of social areas by cluster analysis: A general method with an application to the San Francisco Bay Area. *University of California Publications in Psychology* 8: (no. 1).

—————. 1955b. Biosocial constancy of urban social areas. Paper read at American Psychological Association.

—————. 1959. The social dimensions of metropolitan man (revised title). Paper read at American Psychological Association.

Turner, C.B., and Fiske, D.W. 1968. Item quality and appropriateness of response processes. *Educational and Psychological Measurement* 28:297–315.

Tyler, L.E., and Walsh, W. Bruce. 1979. *Tests and measurements.* Englewood Cliffs, N.J.: Prentice-Hall.

Ullmann, L.P., and Krasner, L. 1969. *A psychological approach to abnormal behavior.* Englewood Cliffs, N.J.: Prentice-Hall.

Wachtel, P.L. 1977. *Psychoanalysis and behavior therapy: Toward an integration.* New York: Basic Books.

Wallach, M.A.; Green, L.R.; Lipsitt, P.D.; and Minehart, J.B. 1962. Contradiction between overt and projective personality indicators as a function of defensiveness. *Psychological Monographs* 76: Whole No. 1.

Warner, W.L., and Lunt, P.S. 1941. *The social life of a modern community.* New Haven, Conn.: Yale University Press.

Washburn, S.L. 1963. Presidential address to the American Anthropological Association. *American Anthropologist* 65:521–31.

Watson, J.B. 1924. *Behaviorism.* New York: Norton.

————— and Rayner, R. 1920. Conditioning emotional responses. *Journal of Experimental Psychology* 3:1–14.

Weinstein, J.; Averill, J.R.; Opton, E.M., Jr.; and Lazarus, R.S. 1968. Defensive style and discrepancy between self-report and physiological indexes of stress. *Journal of Personality and Social Psychology* 10:406–13.

Weisman, A.D. 1972. Psychosocial death. *Psychology Today* (November): 77–78, 83–84, 86.

Werner, H. 1954. Developmental approaches to general and clinical psychology. Paper read as part of a symposium, "Developmental Approach to Problems of General and Clinical Psychology," at a meeting of the Massachusetts Psychological Association, March 1954.

Wessman, A.E., and Ricks, D.F. 1966. *Mood and personality.* New York: Holt, Rinehart and Winston.

White, R.W. 1960. Competence and the psychosexual stages of development. In *Nebraska symposium on motivation,* ed. M.R. Jones, pp. 97–141. Lincoln: University of Nebraska Press.

———. 1963. Ego and reality in psychoanalytic theory. *Psychological Issues* 3:1–210.

———. 1966. *Lives in progress.* New York: Holt, Rinehart and Winston.

———; **Riggs, M.M.; and Gilbert, D.C.** 1976. *Case workbook in personality.* New York: Holt, Rinehart and Winston.

——— **and Watt, N.F.** 1973. *The abnormal personality.* New York: Ronald Press.

Wiggins, J.S.; Renner, K.E.; Clore, G.L.; and Rose, R.J. 1976. *Principles of personality.* Reading, Mass.: Addison-Wesley.

Williams, J.H. 1977. *Psychology of women: Behavior in a biosocial context.* New York: Norton.

Wissler, C. 1901. The correlation of mental and physical tests. *Psychological Review* 3 (no. 6). Monograph Supplement.

Witkin, H.A.; Dyk, R.B.; Faterson, H.F.; Goodenough, D.R.; and Karp, S.A. 1962. *Psychological differentiation.* New York: Wiley.

———; **Mednick, S.A.; Schulsinger, F.; Bakkestrom, E.; Christiansen, K.O.; Goodenough, D.R.; Hirschhorn, K.; Lundsteen, C.; Owen, D.R.; Philip, J.; Rubin, D.B.; and Stocking, M.** 1976. Criminality in XYY and XXY men. *Science* 193:547–55.

Wolfenstein, M. 1953. Trends in infant care. *American Journal of Orthopsychiatry* 23:120–30.

Wolff, H., ed. 1950. Life stress and bodily disease. *Proceedings of the Association for Research in Nervous and Mental Diseases.* Baltimore: Williams & Wilkins.

Wolff, P.H. 1960. The developmental psychologies of Jean Piaget and psychoanalysis. *Psychological Issues* 2: No. 5.

Wolpe, J. 1973. *The practice of behavior therapy.* New York: Pergamon.

Woodworth, R.S. 1919. *Personal data sheet.* Chicago: Stoelting.

Zborowski, M. 1958. Cultural components in response to pain. In *Patients, physicians, and illness,* ed. E.G. Jaco, pp. 256–68. New York: Free Press of Glencoe.

———. 1969. *People in pain.* San Francisco: Jossey-Bass.

Zigler, E. 1967. Familial mental retardation: A continuing dilemma. *Science* 155:292–98.

Zimbardo, P.G., and Ruch, F.L. 1975. *Psychology and life.* Glenview, Ill.: Scott, Foresman.

Zola, I.K. 1966. Culture and symptoms—An analysis of patients' presenting complaints. *American Sociological Review* 31:615–30.

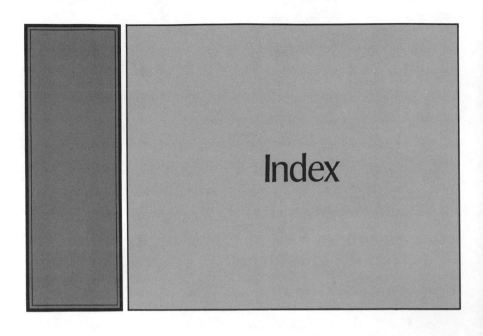

Index

328